Baseball Barnstorming
and Exhibition Games,
1901–1962

ALSO BY THOMAS BARTHEL

Pepper Martin: A Baseball Biography
(McFarland, 2003)

Baseball Barnstorming and Exhibition Games, 1901–1962

A History of Off-Season Major League Play

THOMAS BARTHEL

McFarland & Company, Inc., Publishers
Jefferson, North Carolina, and London

LIBRARY OF CONGRESS CATALOGUING-IN-PUBLICATION DATA

Barthel, Thomas, 1941–
    Baseball barnstorming and exhibition games, 1901–1962 : a
history of off-season major league play / Thomas Barthel.
        p.   cm.
    Includes bibliographical references and index.

    ISBN-13: 978-0-7864-2811-3
    (softcover : 50# alkaline paper) ∞

    1. Baseball — United States— History — 20th century.   I. Title.
    GV863.A1B3745   2007
    796.3570973 — dc22   2006100321

British Library cataloguing data are available

On the cover: Manager Birdie Tebbetts *(front row, far right)* with
one of his barnstorming teams *(year unknown)*

Manufactured in the United States of America

McFarland & Company, Inc., Publishers
  Box 611, Jefferson, North Carolina 28640
    www.mcfarlandpub.com

This book goes out to my son,
Michael Lewis Barthel,
who barnstorms inside New York City,
and to my wife, Judy Barthel,
who barnstorms inside my heart.

Acknowledgments

My thanks to all these generous people:

Librarian Ruth Cosgrove in Clinton, New York, and librarian Mary Mueller.

SABR fellows and others: Bob Timmermann, Andy McCue, Charlie Bevis, Lyle Spatz, Doug Pappas, Kerry Keene, Elvis Cobb, R. J. Lesch, Robert Wilson, Ted Kubiak, Steve Steinberg, David McDonald, Larry E. Johnson, Billy Mills, David J. Piwinski, Mike Welsh, David Ball, Tom Shieber, John Freyer, David Black, Steve Gietschier, Craig W. Gill, Russ Wolinsky, Tim Wiles, Kevin Saldana, Carlos Bauer, Jim Tootle, Richard Smiley, Patrick Rock, Jerry Wachs, Darren Viola, Clifford Otto, Cecilia Tan, Dennis Van Langen, Rod Nelson, Jonathan Daly, Dean R. Thilgen, T. Kent Morgan, Kevin Johnson, Denis Dillon, Bob Schaefer, Crash Parr, and Rick Huhn.

Table of Contents

Preface

THIS BOOK IS THE PRODUCT of searching through 134 newspapers. Many were read at the Library of Congress. But often there were no Sunday editions of those papers so there was no report of a Saturday game. Frequently, too, the games, though mentioned beforehand, were ignored or given little space. *The Sporting News* began extensive coverage of barnstorming only in 1948, and in that paper, though these postseason games were played by hundreds of mostly white major leaguers, and by scores of Hall of Fame caliber players, reports were mostly limited to the publication of itineraries.

As for books, barnstorming has been ignored in all but a few biographies, even the most recent. This absence could be partially explained by the fact that teams were not always what was advertised. Sometimes players were not, for example, New York Giants players, but retired players from years before.

This book covers major leaguers who were still playing at the time of their barnstorming tours.

It is my hope that someday all these games might be more fully explored, one by one, as copies of local newspapers become more accessible. It was simply impossible for me to read about all 1,494 games without traveling to each town's library or historical society in the 39 states where games were played.

Mainly, I relied on whatever newspapers the Library of Congress had in its collection and the search engine ProQuest, available to me through membership in the Society for American Baseball Research (SABR). Many other avenues — state libraries, historical societies, SABR members willing to share their knowledge and information — were explored as well.

My travel to the Library of Congress was made possible by support from Herkimer County Community College in Herkimer, New York.

Introduction: The 200 Days

Barnstorming is a phenomenon peculiar to baseball and to American sports. By my count a minimum of 1,494 games were scheduled from 1901 to 1962. Exhibition games added even more liveliness to the postseason hubbub.

The phenomenon has never been explored in any detail and, in fact, there are only really two essays of scholarship about barnstorming, both by Robert C. Cole. *The Cultural Encyclopedia of Baseball* gives barnstorming one column (half of a page). It is important to understand, I think, that this is baseball at its best: baseball played in small towns and cities mostly for fun. This book will restrict itself to coverage of white major leaguers, for the most part, but it does cover black or Latino players who came along after Jackie Robinson made his mark.

Until 1953, the major leagues had ballparks in cities from Boston to St. Louis—1,200 miles. From Minneapolis to Houston and from St. Louis to Los Angeles—1,800 by 1,200 miles—there were no major league teams. For the majority of the years up to 1953, those teams in existence were mostly composed of white players. Moreover, of the continental United States, only the District of Columbia and seven states had teams, with New York and Pennsylvania home to six of the sixteen teams in both leagues.

How else before 1950 could most fans actually see Christy Mathewson, Honus Wagner, Rogers Hornsby, Babe Ruth, Dizzy Dean, and Bob Feller? After 1950 fans could see Stan Musial, Willie Mays, Mickey Mantle, Roy Campanella, and Henry Aaron, but on a black-and-white television. Those baseball heroes had shrunk to fuzzy figures eight inches high. But a barnstorming team allowed a fan to see all the great stars, as well as many of the lesser ones (but major league players nonetheless), and to see them in his hometown at the field where he had played against friends and neighbors. Even after television, barnstorming let fans see, and talk to, Whitey Ford and Mickey Mantle and Willie Mays. Fans could see how big they were in real life — how tall and how muscular, how lithe and how quick, how each sounded — and get an idea of what kind of person each player was. There they were, on the fields of their fans' hometowns.

I mean these towns: Atkins and Odell and Olney and Sabine and Osgood and Ponca City.

And baseball there is gone now and so is barnstorming. But the tours are not forgotten because the major leaguers who played there are remembered with pleasure.

What Is Barnstorming?

The word "barnstorming" needs to be understood properly. Sometimes the term was used to mean the movement north (or east) from spring training in Florida and Texas and California, with stops for games at a number of small towns and cities. So the "barn" part of the word was used to emphasize the rural aspect of the games. The "storm" part was used to describe the speed of the movement from city to city. For the players, the trip north simply meant more games played without pay, more work requirements — not barnstorming at all.

The Negro leagues team barnstormed all the time; the majority of those games were played *during* the regular season, though some were played afterwards.

From Brad Snyder's *Beyond the Shadow of the Senators*:

> According to Negro League historian John Holway, black professional teams won eighty-nine games, lost sixty-seven and tied one against white major leaguers. "We won the majority of those games — not because we were better. The major league ballplayers couldn't afford to twist an ankle," Buck O'Neil explained. "We wanted to prove that major leaguers were not superior, and that Negro Leaguers were not inferior. So we'd stretch that single into a double" [116].

By the end of the 1800s baseball fanciers were reading about the "barnstorming" Nebraska Indians and the "barnstorming" Canadian star Nellie McClung.

> During the 1890s, scores of women's baseball teams sprang up across the country calling themselves Bloomer Girls ... because the majority of the players were women.... Belonging to no league, all bloomer teams were barnstormers.... Fired by competitive drive and thrilled to play baseball, the bloomers endured the hardships and earned the victories. The earliest of these sexually integrated teams carried at least one male player: the catcher ... Hall of Famers Smoky Joe Wood and Rogers Hornsby played on bloomer girl teams in their youth [Gregorich, 12].

Neither of these examples is barnstorming properly understood; they have more to do with not playing any games in a home park.

A more accurate description of barnstorming, but in amateur baseball, is provided by Nebraskan Sam Crawford in Larry Ritter's *The Glory of Their Times*:

> Every town had its own team in those days.... A bunch of us from Wahoo ... made a trip overland in a wagon drawn by a team of horses.... It had room to seat all of us. I think that there were 11 or 12 of us and we just started out and went from town to town, playing their teams.... Every little town out there on the prairie had its own ball team and ball grounds, and we challenged them all. We didn't have any uniforms or anything. Just baseball shoes maybe but we had a manager.... We were gone three or four weeks.

As described, this game meets part of the definition: the pleasure part.

But true barnstorming, post-season and post-contract barnstorming and exhibition games, like all of major league baseball, is that difficult amalgam of pleasure and money.

Why Barnstorm?

Put simply, until 1947, players did not receive any money from the day the season closed until the day season opened. The club paid for the player's trip south to spring training in late winter, paid his hotel and food bills while he was there, and let the player take care of the rest. So a trip to the movies, the cost of laundry, and so on, was money pulled from the player's wallet without any money going into that wallet. Only after the season started, and only after the season's first two weeks had passed, for a period of about 165 days did a team member have money put in his hand.

How to live the other 200 days? Let's look at one typical player, Pepper Martin. Martin lived in McAlester, Oklahoma, with his wife, Ruby. With a rookie salary of $2,500, family man Martin was making about $1,100 more than the average American's yearly salary of about $1,400. If Martin used his money wisely, he could save much of the money he was paid in that 165 day period of the regular season.

Or could he?

He needed to support his family back in Oklahoma, and maybe his mother too, while he maintained a residence in St. Louis during the season. For road games, the club would pick up his room and meals. But for half the season, he was responsible for those expenditures and all the others. Certainly the costs of living in McAlester, Oklahoma, were far less than the money needed to survive in St. Louis. For example, the rent on an apartment or small house in Oklahoma would not even be close to the money paid for a hotel room or apartment in St. Louis. In addition to room, board and transportation, Martin paid for everything his work required except his uniform and cap. (It may have been the reason he did not wear a jock.) So his income was reduced because he had, in effect, twice the expenses of someone living in one place. The club also demanded that he dress well on road trips. Expenses for clothing that, say, a carpenter in Oklahoma didn't have to pay for and to maintain. When he took trains to away games, his shaves, his shoe shines, his hat blocking came out of his pocket.

This is all to say that though his salary may have appeared to be high, his expenses were also high, very high.

Important to remember, too, was that for most employees of the time, there was no health insurance, there was no unemployment money, there were no savings. A player had no pension and if he got hurt playing baseball, he was on his own. His pay stopped until he was ready to take the field again. Other weapons in the arsenal of the owners included suspending or fining a player, creating fees for washing uniforms, or charging for Cokes in the locker room. And, of course, determining a player's salary.

And there was the reserve clause. Leo Durocher, a man of strong opinions, was being paid $6,500 in 1934 by the Cardinals after being in the professional ranks for ten years. During that Gas House Gang year should Durocher have displeased his employers he could have been traded to the notorious Phillies who often paid their wealthiest employee what other teams were paying their lowest-paid man. Or he could be sent to the minors where his pay might easily decrease from $1,180 per month to the money that Elbie Fletcher made that year — $250 per month. Durocher's only other choices, under the reserve clause, were to accept the owner's decision to trade him or send him down, or to quit baseball and go back to Springfield, Massachusetts, and find himself a job at the firearms factory. He would be blackballed from playing sanctioned baseball — declared an outlaw — if he chose not to obey his owner's wishes.

A player could be declared ineligible for almost any reason: even if only accused of car theft, the ineligible label might be applied. Owners had declared some leagues outlaw because they refused to abide by the reserve clause, or because they raided other teams and lured away players with the offer of higher pay. So playing in an outlaw league or playing against a player who had played in an outlaw league or playing against a team from an outlaw league like the Players or the Federal League might end one's professional baseball paydays.

Most players, of course, planned ahead to the off-season since they had to have jobs waiting for them for the winter. Jobs were at times difficult to find because the employer knew he had the employee on hand to work only between October 1 and March 1. Some players owned farms or worked at family-run concerns. Harold Seymour registered "a sampling of winter occupations" of many of the players which

> would include streetcar conductor, glassblower, interpreter, newspaper writer, undertaker, snow remover, policeman and printer. One spent a winter in jail-working as turnkey for his father-in-law the jailer. Others engaged in more long-term enterprises in which they sometimes invested their own capital as well as their services. For example, Johnny Evers put his money into a shoe store in Chicago, and Miller Huggins invested in a roller-skating rink. Joe McGinnity was associated with his father in the management of the family ironworks in Indiana. A good many players qualified as farmers: Fred Clarke had a wheat ranch in Kansas, Chance owned an orchard, Snodgrass had a California farm, and Lobert raised chickens. Louis Drucke was in the cotton business in Texas. Many other well-known players were also listed as farmers. "It was observed that more players than ever were preparing for the professions, among them Richard Hoblitzel, a dentist, Ray Fisher who taught school, and Dummy Taylor, a deaf-mute who taught others" [Seymour, 32].

Having a job waiting for you would be a guarantee of income for the 200 days you weren't playing baseball. Only the very highest paid players could afford to not have money coming in for the 200 days.

Players looked for ways to use their profession, their skills, their celebrity. Since professional baseball was not permitted on Sundays under the Blue Laws from 1901 to 1920 in most of baseball's eastern cities— New York (which had three teams), Boston (two teams), Philadelphia (two teams) and Pittsburgh (one team)— many players had the chance to pick up some Sunday money with semipro teams when they were in those four cities during the regular season.

Barnstorming for himself, not for his team, could take place after a player's contract ended at the close of the season or even after a sanctioned series. These owner-approved games, called a city series because they pitted two teams from the same city or state against each other, began in 1882 and were a chance for both owners and players to make some extra money after the season. So those first games matching Cleveland and Cincinnati in 1882 were considered to be a championship for the league each belonged to as well as the championship of the state of Ohio. Not all teams played in these series and not in all years. Those who did not barnstormed as a team or joined a team that went out after the season.

As you will see in this book many major leaguers sought chances to barnstorm and play exhibitions: Walter Johnson, Honus Wagner, Tris Speaker, George Sisler, Zach Wheat, Jimmie Foxx, Lefty Grove, Yogi Berra, and Whitey Ford all led or were involved with teams who barnstormed to accumulate money to take them through the 200 days and to have some fun too. Stan Musial claimed in 1946 that he made more money barnstorming than he did playing in the World Series that year.

Early in the century, a player who could take home an extra $100 or

$200 (or more) for a week or two of barnstorming was taking home ten to twenty weeks of average pay. So barnstorming money alone might get him through the 200 days of autumn and winter before his pay began again with his team. *Might.* A player could sign on to barnstorm and bad weather or low attendance might mean he would make only a little money or no money at all.

Barnstorming and the Owners

What about the men who owned the contracts?

Were they happy to see their employees enjoying a pleasant winter? Though some were tolerant, most owners hated barnstorming and tried repeatedly to have the touring delayed, or banned, or restricted. Battles between commissioner and player would go on and on over the matter of barnstorming. One famous fight described in this book is between Babe Ruth and Kenesaw Mountain Landis in 1921.

As far as the team owners were concerned, the players were taking the chance of being hurt while barnstorming. To the owners, this meant a danger of having their investment, their rolling stock, become less efficient or even useless. The owners often understood their employees to be not unlike machines they might own in a factory. Who would keep a machine running after the factory had closed for the day?

A standard player contract for years had a clause that read

> The player shall not without the consent of his Club engage during the term of this contract or any renewal thereof in any game or exhibition of baseball, football, basket ball or other athletic sport except for the Club or any assignee of this contract.

And part "C" of the reserve clause in each contract had similar language: "The promise of the Players not to play during said year otherwise than with the Club or assignee hereof...."

Early Tours

This book begins with the year 1901 when both of the two current major leagues began operating. Many baseball historians are willing to say that barnstorming began as early as 1860. Many 19th century trips were for the purpose of selling baseball to others, or proselytizing, going out on a kind of missionary trip. But this book concentrates on when both major leagues and the minors had their structures in place.

True Barnstorming 1901–1962

The barnstorming story, then, properly understood, begins when there are two major leagues, each with eight teams, and an organization to oversee all the sanctioned minor leagues. Barnstorming effectively ends in a futile attempt by Willie Mays and others to lead a tour in 1962, when there are still the two leagues but now with 20 teams.

What did it take to get a barnstorming trip started? As the history of the phenomenon reveals itself, it is clear that often the trip was in the hands of one man, that man often being the traveling secretary or business manager of a major league team. In this instance, the entire team, or most of it, went on tour. This format was particularly true in the early years of the century. So we see that both Pittsburgh and Cincinnati went on many trips. A team of players from many teams — Babe Ruth was one — would get together to tour. And after World War II, there was an explosion in barnstorming that lasted only a very few years. In some years, however, as many as twelve all-star teams were touring at once and *The Sporting News* found it necessary to create its own column called "Barnstorming Notes."

Some players, many of them not what are now called superstars, but great stars in their time, including 1950s World Series opponents Carl Furillo of the Dodgers and Gene Woodling of the Yankees, eagerly signed up for tours of small towns. Future great players of the fifties — Whitey Ford, Duke Snider, Eddie Mathews, and Red Schoendienst — signed on for barnstorming tours. Joe DiMaggio played exhibitions with his brothers. And the fifties saw not only barnstorming through a rigorous schedule of major cities, but also the first of the great black major leaguers began their tours. Jackie Robinson, as was so typical of the man, led the first integrated team though the country, including the Deep South, in 1953.

While money was the more tangible result of barnstorming, there were other pleasures as well. Many men used these tours as sort of paid vacations, even honeymoons, with their wives. Some used the trips to rural areas as paid hunting and fishing trips at season's end. Some used it as the only vacation they would have all year.

Black professional players were frequent opponents of white major leaguers on tours and most of that material has been mined. To put it bluntly, white major league players wanted to make money, and playing black teams in black ballparks would draw both whites and blacks who would pay to see the game. The Cubs played the black Chicago team owned by Rube Foster, the Leland Giants, in late October 1907. Foster had played in Cuba the previous winter as a kind of extended winter barnstorming. Bob Feller's 1946 black-against-white barnstorming teams included Ralph Kiner, Jackie Robinson, Buck O'Neil, and Stan Musial as well as the leaders, Feller and Satchel Paige. For that tour, the teams flew to games in two DC-3s.

Tours covered Nebraska and rural Oklahoma. Barnstormers traveled though Pennsylvania by automobile and Babe Ruth had to ferry across the Hudson River to get to a game in Kingston, New York, on October 18, 1926. Pirates and Reds players early in the century went by trolley to towns within reach of their home cities for their post-season money.

So it is safe to say that barnstorming is a very complicated topic since it covers so many aspects of baseball. Barnstorming could not escape controversies— many of which have confronted baseball over the years:

- Owners/player arguments
- Racial integration
- Salary and contract disputes
- The reserve clause

Problems in the coverage of barnstorming and exhibitions come from brief reports of the games. Truly, to absolutely complete this work, each town where a game was played would have to have its newspaper read and its historical society contacted. For example, *The Sporting News* began organized coverage of barnstorming only in 1948.

So, for the purposes of this book, barnstorming, not exhibition, games will be considered to have the following characteristics:

1. played in October and early November
2. by a team of current major league players touring full time
3. played mainly in non-major league parks
4. not in a league of any sort, such as the California Winter League
5. played in the continental United States
6. not by a team organized to play in a tournament
7. not for a charity
8. not simply a traveling team for mostly entertainment purposes

The reasons for these strictures should be noted. For example, a fine book on winter leagues starring both white and black major leaguers is *The California Winter League: America's First Integrated Professional Baseball League* by William McNeil but these teams did not tour. The Indianapolis Clowns toured (see *Some Are Called Clowns* by Bill Heward) but were not major leaguers.

There has been other scholarship about postseason games but they fall mostly in three categories. Black versus white games are covered extensively by John Holway in his book *The Complete Book of Baseball's Negro Leagues: The Other Half of Baseball History*, so those games need not be recapitulated here except for emphasis, or for particular historical influences. Games played postseason in Cuba, Canada, Hawaii, Japan and the Near East have also been studied. The James E. Elfers book, for example, titled *The Tour to End All Tours*, covers games in 1913-14 both in the United States and overseas. Many of those trips were under the direct aegis of the baseball cartel, as were some of the early tours, such as those to Australia, Egypt, London and Paris. Other postseason games, now called city series games, as described previously, did not give the team full pay for their efforts and so are not true barnstorming. The work done by Frederick Ivor-Campbell in *Total Baseball* covers those city games which were contested from 1882 to 1942.

Beyond those, games played in the continental United States for charity, or by teams made up specially for just a game or two, or featuring just one or two major league level players, will be covered in this book's exhibition sections.

Appendices A and B list all of these barnstorming tours. These lists are my attempt to be as thorough as possible about post-season major league baseball, and I list them for future writers and for local historians. These exhibition games often featured players who did not barnstorm.

Significant barnstorming tours will be dealt with in some detail. The book is organized around a chronological framework.

Likewise, another section of the book, also chronological, will deal with exhibition games, those games that do fit into these three categories, for the most part:

1. teams put together for just a few games, generally made up of players either from the area or players who had not yet left for their homes

2. benefit games

3. civic duty games, in which players pitched for their home town, for instance, against a neighboring town.

Prologue

What did it matter if the contest was only an exhibition or if it was interrupted or even terminated by eager droves of fans mobbing some particularly renowned star for his autograph? Such scenes were a measure of the depth and spread of baseball's roots, and over the years a rich store of baseball lore accumulated around these barnstorming experiences [Seymour, 79–80].

Barnstorming: applied deprecatively to a strolling player [*Oxford English Dictionary Compact Edition*].

THE FIRST BASEBALL TEAM to travel any long distance to play a game was the Excelsior club of Brooklyn and it was "The Excelsiors' tour of the East in 1860 ... [that] helped popularize the sport" (Selzer, 43). Covering many miles for most of July, the team played eight games, from July 2 to July 11, 1860, in upstate New York, and then from July 22–24 in Baltimore and Philadelphia. There is evidence that this trip vastly helped popularize a sport that soon was to be recognized as "the National Pastime."

Seven years later, a Midwestern journey was attempted by the "powerful Washington Nationals" in Columbus and Cincinnati, Ohio; Louisville, Kentucky; Indianapolis; St. Louis; and Chicago from July 12–26, 1867.

This tour (covered in more detail in "The Nine of the Nationals—Champions of the South Going West" in *Wilkes' Spirit of the Times*, July 13, 1867, vol. 16, no. 3, p. 367) may or may not have been the first undertaken for money reasons. But if it was not, the *Spalding Guide*, reflecting back from 1903, wrote of another club's trip that was designed for dominance and cash.

After beating all the prominent clubs of Illinois, Indiana, and Ohio, [the Cincinnati Red Stockings] went East and defeated every club in the Atlantic cities, viz., in Troy, Albany, Boston, New York, Philadelphia, Baltimore, and Washington. Then they went west to St. Louis and also to San Francisco, and ended the season of 1869 without a loss, thereby becoming the legitimate champions of the base ball world of the period.... In fact, the Cincinnatis' season of 1869 was a season of tours. This continental touring pattern was true for 1870 as well [Spalding, 17–19].

By 1871 the National Association of Professionals was formed, meaning that a complete schedule was drawn up. Yet in 1874, Harry Wright's Boston Red Stockings of that association, along with the Philadelphia Athletics, toured Britain for a month and a half "in hopes of persuading English sportsmen to adopt America's 'national game'" (Voigt). With the formation of the first minor league, the International Association, there remained the problem of adhering to the schedule, a problem often encountered in the early days of new leagues. It was true that Frank Bancroft, called Banny, the business and field manager of the New Bedford, Massachusetts, team of the International Association, pulled his team from the league in 1878 and barnstormed for 130 games for the cash it would bring in. Bancroft needed to be able to rely on teams showing up so that paying customers would be assured of a game when they made the effort to go to the park. If he arranged his own games and made his own guarantees, then he and his team could make money on a more regular basis. This touring went so well that he and his team continued to travel by sailing to Cuba and playing there in the winter of 1878-1879. The Cuban trip proved so salutary that he took his Rochester, New York, Hop Bitters to Cuba in 1879.

This trip is often credited as the first trip of American professionals to the island. The *Los Angeles Times* wrote, "In Cuba, [Bancroft] is known as 'the father of baseball'" (February 11, 1921). The *Spalding Guide* also took note when Banny died:

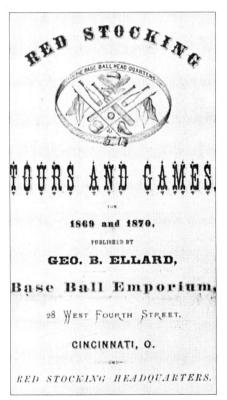

A list of Cincinnati Red Stockings games in 1869 and 1870. (National Baseball Hall of Fame Library, Cooperstown, New York.)

Frank C. Bancroft One of the men in Base Ball who had done something for Base

The Brooklyn Atlantics, who defeated the touring Red Stockings. (National Baseball Hall of Fame Library, Cooperstown, New York.)

Ball.... His executive ability and knowledge of Base Ball, combined with the fact that he was for sport first and the show element of Base Ball secondarily, rendered him one of the most competent of men to handle the affairs of a professional team.

Eight years later, the paper *Sporting Life*, on October 26, 1887, printed a story concerning a barnstorming trip by the New York Giants, who finished fourth but would win in 1888. The New Yorkers trekked to San Francisco under Walter Appleton's direction with most of the regulars on board, including future Hall of Fame players John Montgomery Ward, Buck Ewing and Tim Keefe.

After stops for games in Cincinnati and New Orleans, by November 24 the Giants contended in San Francisco and remained there until February, exclusively at the Haight Street Grounds. There, Carlos Bauer explained, they played the Haverlies on Thanksgiving Day and the Oakland G & M later.

As for the Philadelphia Athletics who finished second, Arthur Irwin — in his eighth year as a shortstop and two years away from managing — was in charge, and when they finished their season in Cincinnati they moved quickly west, arriving in Los Angeles on November 5.

The St. Louis Browns, champions of the American Association, traveled with Chicago going south, so these two teams, it appeared, met each other from

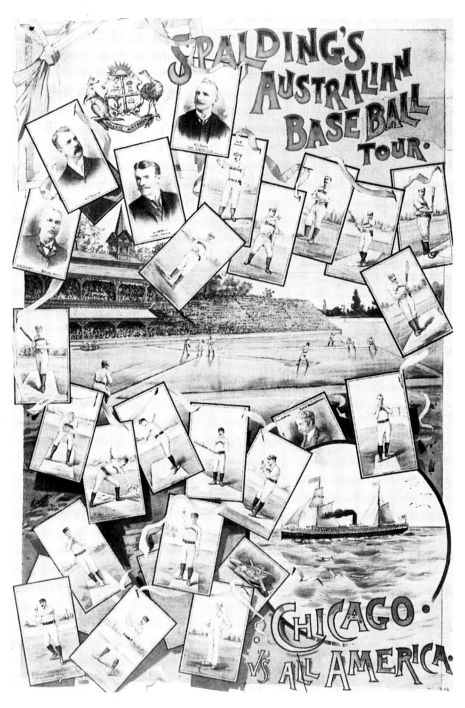

Cover of a brochure for an 1888-1889 international tour. (National Baseball Hall of Fame Library, Cooperstown, New York.)

Illustration for an 1888-1889 tour in Italy. (National Baseball Hall of Fame Library, Cooperstown, New York.)

St. Louis to New Orleans and then moved on to San Francisco. Chicago, the National League pennant winners in 1886, was managed by Cap Anson, with Ned Hanlon of Detroit along for the tour also heading for California. The Browns, for example, played in Los Angeles on December 11, 1887, and won 8–3 before 800 fans.

These California games would attract enough attention for the games to be listed in the *Spalding Guide*: "In all twenty first-class matches were played by the visiting teams with the three club teams of the California League during November, December and January, the home teams at times being aided by visiting players. There were eight games played on the Central Park grounds, and twelve on the California League grounds" (87).

At the Central Park site, games between the Philadelphia, Chicago and St. Louis teams were contested from November 19 until December 31, while at the league ballpark, New York played two games on the 19th, then met the Haverlies, G & M, and the Pioneers until Christmas Day. Thereafter, the games were matches between St. Louis and New York, four games until January 15. Almost all of these games were played on Saturday and Sunday.

These four teams were combining the best aspects of barnstorming. A leisurely tour in the warm climes in late autumn took care of a lot of their needs and wants. The need for off-season money might be looked to by the paid admissions to their games. The vacation time, perhaps with wives, was also an aspect of these tours. They continued to play the game that gave them the most professional pleasure and gave them the opportunity to see the country while showing off their skills. There was no particular pressure to win games, although they most certainly would. Fans would turn out simply to see the sport — "base-ball" — now called the National Game by *Harper's Weekly* in its November 26, 1887, issue.

Like the Bloomer Girls, in 1897, a semipro team, the Nebraska Indians, also toured extensively. They were known to schedule games under that name as late as 1921. Canadian barnstorming star Nellie McClung appeared throughout the 1880s.

Ballplayers at the Sphinx in Egypt in 1889. (National Baseball Hall of Fame Library, Cooperstown, New York.)

In 1888-89, another world tour was tried during December and January, going this time to Australia and India "in hopes of spreading the American game to other lands" (Voigt). Peter Levine, writing about this tour, quotes a newspaper: "'The Chicagos,' the *Chicago Tribune* said, '[were] bedecked in light grey shirts, knee britches and black stockings,'" while the All-Americas "'[were] dazzling in while flannel with a silk American flag draped over their shoulders.'" The touring teams demonstrated their only game in Paris, the All-Americas winning 6–2 at Parc Aristotique. But Chicago shortstop Ned Williamson was injured there, effectively ending his days as a top player, as *Baseball Library* writes on its Web site.

Frank Bancroft (Banny) was hired by the Cincinnati team in 1890, as business manager, later managing the team in 1902 for 17 games. Banny had grown an affinity for touring back in 1878 and had developed contacts in Cuba. Cap Anson remembered "the fall of 1890, [when] Al Lawson collected an assortment of players from the Iron and Oil League [i.e., the Pennsylvania and New York League] who, along with one or two colts from his Wellsville team, congregated in New York City, where they were joined by a few outcasts from the big leagues. (*Sporting Life*, in the November 2, 1907, issue, reported that Al W. Lawson, born in London, took a team of American ballplayers to England in 1892, two years after his brief career with Boston and Pittsburgh of the National League, playing in three games. He repeated the trip in 1895. There is evidence that most of the team was not at major league level.)

CHAPTER ONE

Barnstorming Tours and Exhibition Games, 1901–1909

THE FIRST DECADE OF BARNSTORMING was dominated by three teams: the Reds of Cincinnati, the Pirates of Pittsburgh and the Giants of New York. Two of these three teams, from 1901–1910, won three of the seven World Series during this time. That the Reds did not win any did not make a difference to them. Employing the organizational skills of Frank Bancroft, the Cincinnati teams traveled extensively, and to good profit. The Pirates and the Giants, being champions, would naturally attract crowds in the postseason. Using the words "world champions" in the advertising for the games would always help barnstormers.

With the names of John McGraw and Christy Mathewson being featured in the ads for the Giants, and Honus Wagner for the Pirates, fans would be sure to turn out. As for the Reds, who finished as high as third in the National League just once in the decade, their appearance in towns like Wapakonete and Catlettsburg would be eagerly awaited simply because they were a big-league ball club in baseball-mad America.

In addition, players did go out on their own. For example, catcher Roger Bresnahan and pitcher Christy Mathewson traveled one year with each other.

But, from the very beginning owners were objecting to postseason play, though the contract of a player ran from opening day to closing day. Disingenuous from the start, the owners and their representative National Commission objected to players making money even as the magnates worked hard to maximize their own profits. The objections, often citing the National Agreement, were invented objections, such as saying in print that barnstorming cheapens the game of baseball, when it was quite clear that the games were exhibitions, not championship contests. There was strong opposition particularly to games in which white major leaguers were beaten by black teams. The owners, sometimes through their cartel's spokesman, seized every opportunity to attach blame to a player's misfortune in the off-season to the barnstorming games. What the owners really wanted was control over their employees and control over their assigned territory.

The owners certainly had no objections when they were getting their slice of the pie from postseason play. That may have been one of the attractions for beginning the World Series contests in 1903.

Barnstorming Tours

> Barnstorming baseball was baseball in its purest sense. There wasn't any pennant race or World Series involved, no pressure, no heated rivalries producing charges and counter-charges, no tension-filled controversies. It was just baseball for the fun of it, played in the heartland of America in Rockwell-like scenes where the folks wanted to see what major league players looked like and watch us play and talk to us and have fun around us.... Barnstorming was baseball at its best—innocent and fun, in towns big and small [Feller, Gilbert, 136].

In 1900, the country was 60 percent rural and could claim only 150 miles of paved roads. But, in addition to a vast railroad system, first horse-drawn and then electrified rail transports were able to move people around for shorter distances via trolleys and then longer trips by the use of faster trolleys called interurbans.

Still, the country was getting more urban each year and companies had been growing to monstrous sizes. In this atmosphere of business being encouraged, praised, and rewarded, the business of professional baseball came fully of age.

When the contract between professional baseball outfits—called the National Agreement—lapsed in 1900, the successful American League asserted itself a major league and declared war on the National League. Taking prisoners in the form of stars in this battle, the American League under Ban Johnson was able to offer higher salaries to players than the National League and more than a hundred jumped leagues, with the new league brazenly moving into cities occupied by the old (since 1876) league.

The leagues did seem to agree on two things even before a peace treaty was ratified: that there would be fourteen men on each team and that the Reserve Clause would stay in place. Sean Lahman writes about some of the background:

In 1882, the American Association started to compete with reduced ticket prices and teams in large cities. Rather than fight each other, the two leagues reached an accord, ratifying a National Agreement. It called for teams in both major leagues and all of the minor leagues to honor each other's player contracts. In addition, the agreement allowed each team to bind a certain number of players with the Reserve Clause. This clause granted teams the rights to unilaterally renew a player's contract, preventing him from entertaining other offers [http://baseball1.com/bb-data/e-hist-2.html].

The players hated the clause and over the years had made attempts to organize to redress this grievance, their latest attempt being the creation of the Players' Protective Association in 1900. Nevertheless, this clause would be a long time with professional baseball.

So, the year 1901 was an unsettled year in baseball. There was not a strong organization of minor leagues until September of 1901 and then the two major leagues battled for supremacy, or, at least, co-existence, including higher pay going to men who stayed with the National League.

In the first years of the twentieth century, at least five teams went out on the road after the season. It was not the postseason play that bothered the organized baseball cartel. So long as it was paid its share, these postseason affairs were perfectly acceptable. They were dignified and even artistic whenever the cartel took its slice.

That year's postseason (teams in both leagues contended in fewer than 142 games that year) looked no more tranquil. The *New York Tribune* reported a game on October 1, 1901, in Worcester, Massachusetts, between the Chicago Americans and the All Americans. But were there two groups called All-Americans? For some papers there was no difference. But there was a latter aggregation better known as the All Nationals that planned travels southward. The confusion lies in the fact that the newspaper was reporting just batteries, just pitcher and catcher.

For the game in Worcester, the All American batteries were Joe Sugden and John Katoll from the Chicago White Sox and on the other side were Hall of Famer Roger Bresnahan and Bill Bernhard. Four days later in Cincinnati on October 5, 1901, the Cincinnati team met the All Americans. Now the batteries were, from the Reds, Noodles Hahn and Bill Bergen, and from the White Sox, players Billy Sullivan and Bill Bernhard. Next reported was a game watched by 3,700 in Chicago, and the next day in Pittsburgh against "the champion Pittsburghs" before 2,200. One of the pitchers was Strawberry Bill Bernhard, with the umpires named as Hank O'Day and Silk O'Loughlin.

The next day there was also a game in Pittsburgh before 4,500 with the batteries being Deacon Phillippe and Chief Zimmer for the home team and Addie Joss and Billy Sullivan for the barnstormers. Additional games were planned for October 11 and October 12 in Cleveland, probably between the champions and the All Americans for the "third and fourth games in the series."

But the newspapers often neglected to cover barnstorming games at all, though the *Chicago Daily Tribune* was critical when it did take notice, covering the October 12 game in that city with the headline "Crowd Objects To Hippodrome." Much of the cause for the disappointment was the failure to appear by Nap Lajoie, Bill Bradley and Bill Dahlen, and Adie Joss's simple refusal to throw.

First scheduled for October 13, 1901, at Vincennes, Indiana, was another grouping of games between teams first called the All Nationals and the remainders of those All Americans. The Reds chieftain, Frank Bancroft, busied himself arranging a tour by the All-Nationals. This team, which featured Roger Bresnahan, did include minor leaguers and they were supposed to meet the All-Americans, a team that now shone with the presence of Turkey Donlin and Nap Lajoie. These two groups planned to go to smaller cities such as Olney, Illinois (4,300); Evansville, Indiana; Cairo, Illinois (13,000); and Memphis. By themselves, the Americans planned to go on until January 1 by playing first in Greenville, Mississippi, on October 21; Vicksburg, Mississippi, on October 22 and October 23; then to New Orleans on Saturday, October 26. Following that Saturday game they were to move on to Texas and Louisiana until they crossed the country to open in San Francisco on Thanksgiving Day. A few Nationals were to stay on the tour only until New Orleans.

These fine plans were disrupted as *Sporting Life* on October 19, 1901, reported:

> The All-National team disbanded at Memphis on October 22, 1902. This breakup occurred after the following players refused to join the club: Daly, Dahlen, Donovan, Sheckard, McGuire and Keeler of the Brooklyns. Jake Beckely quit at Vincennes, and Hahn planned to leave the team in New Orleans. The All-American team will open in San Francisco on Thanksgiving Day and play on until January 1.

This team now starred Roger Bresnahan of the New York Giants and Nap Lajoie of Cleveland. "Each man deposited $150 with William (Win) Mercer, who will act as treasurer, as a guarantee that they will stick together."

Other reports remain confusing. The Boston Americans, the Somersets, were said to have made $50 barnstorming, with big leaguers Tommy Dowd, Chick Stahl, Jimmy Collins, and pitcher Fred Mitchell. October began with a contest at Lynn, Massachusetts, with Cy Young in right field before 1,000. Games were also arranged in Manchester (an October 2 game at Varick Park with 600 watching), Nashua, Greenville, and Marlboro. Likewise, also out in the towns were the Boston Nationals, the Beaneaters, with Jedediah Kitteridge, Billy Hamilton, and Kid Nichols playing at Torrington, home to 9,000 in Connecticut. Then they moved to Leominster on October 11 and its trotting park grounds where they met the Has-Beens in a game marked by 11 errors. They next were in action at Webster on October 10 (where the nose of Kid

Nichols was broken) and then later in Chester, Pennsylvania, ending, it seems, on Columbus Day in Trenton, New Jersey. Another incomplete-sounding report was the one on October 19, 1901, of the October 13 game the White Sox played against "Napoleon Lajoie's all-star gang" before 9,000 people; this gang was still competing in New Orleans on October 27. Also mentioned were the Phillies at Chester, Pennsylvania, and Brooklyn at the Hobokens on October 10, 1901, where the visitors won 6–4.

Additionally, there was a report in the *New York Times* of October 30, 1901, that the independent Kansas City Blues had been barnstorming in Texas "with a team of National and American leaguers."

In Pittsburgh, the postseason's extra paydays began. The *Sporting Life*, on October 12, 1901, wrote about a field day for the Pirates on October 4, with a parade featuring fifty amateur teams in costumes, three brass bands, and rooters parading in carriages before 4,556 people. The field events starred Hans Wagner, who came in third in the accurate throwing contest, first in the long distance throwing, third in running all the bases, tied for first in Blue Rock (clay pigeon) shooting championship with ten kills, first in the 100 yard dash. He also won the greased pig chase. The other men on the roster, not so skilled in the contests, would pocket about $200 each.

The money did not end there as they started their tour of Pennsylvania towns on October 7, 1901. Arranged by Colonel Harry Pullman, the longest trip of the expedition was to be 85 miles, Deacon Phillippe and Sam Leever serving as two advance men tasked to talk to the papers and put up posters.

This was a full team affair with 14 men on the barnstorming roster, including Ginger Beaumont, and showcased three future Hall of Fame players: pitcher Jack Chesbro, shortstop Honus Wagner, and manager–left fielder Fred Clarke. The team took a five-trolley ride to Homestead, a borough of 13,000, eight miles away from the team hotel in downtown Pittsburgh, for the first game on October 7, 1901, winning 3–2. At Charleroi the next day, a borough of 6,000 souls, the *Pittsburgh Daily Dispatch* took note that "Before the game there will be a street parade. Hans Wagner and a local shooter, George Snyder, will be pitted against each other in a pigeon shoot, followed by a 100 yard foot race between Clarence Beaumont and John Stanley, the latter of Vesta." Big wins followed at Johnstown, Altoona and Dubois, a borough of 9,400. After a win on Columbus Day in Warren, Pennsylvania, before 1,500, the team ventured north into New York State, to Jamestown, on October 13, winning there 11–2 before moving south into Meadsville, one of the more populous stops, being a city of 11,000, achieving a 4–0 win for their last game. The 14 tourists divided $1,400 for their trip.

The Cincinnati Reds were efficiently organized for their touring. The team's last championship season game was October 2, 1901, and the Reds entrained on the Louisville and Nashville Railroad for three games in Nashville.

Born in that Tennessee city, pitcher Noodles Hahn was to be honored by his home town. The *Sporting Life* for October 12, 1901, told its readers that the "Red Barnstormers" were to tour Ohio. Players under Lou Wolfson were not as glittering a team as Pittsburgh, but a major league team nevertheless. On October 8, 1901, a game had been arranged in Zanesville, Ohio, an industrial city of almost 24,000. But the promoter there felt cheated. An argument soon developed over the $100 guaranteed the team because Zanesville disliked the absence of Noodles Hahn and Beckley, who was with All-Americans, and there was some doubt that the two games might even be played. The agreement worked out seemed to be that the $100 would be paid if the Reds would split the gate 50-50 for game two. Ten players divided the money. With each man making, say $5 for the game (the business manager of the team and the promoter had their cuts), in today's purchasing power that $5 becomes about $110, according to the Web site http://eh.net/hmit/ppowerusd/.

For the rest of the games, all we know is that the Reds moved, probably by trolley or interurban, to Hamilton, Ohio (24,000 people living 22 miles from Cincinnati), and won 6–1, and then they played their last game in a small city of 5,000, Greensburg, Indiana (62 miles from Cincinnati), on October 14, 1901.

These two teams, Cincinnati and Pittsburgh, would take many of the barnstorming trips as teams in the postseason and geography had much to do with that fact. Only St. Louis and Washington were farther south than Cincinnati of the major league teams and that Ohio city was almost on an east-west line with Washington, D.C. Pittsburgh, slightly farther north, had easy access to warmer climates in the first month of postseason traveling, just as Cincinnati did.

1902

Though the first city series games were contended in 1882, there were no city series played in 1902, and little news of barnstorming. It is true that the *Washington Post* reported that "The Phillies are doing one-day stunts through New Jersey and Eastern Pennsylvania," and "The champion Athletics are picking up a dollar or two on a barnstorming tour among the crack Pennsylvania amateur clubs." Players named for this expedition were Rube Waddell, Pop Foster, Buck Freeman, and Louis Castro. After reporting planned games in Pittsburgh, *Sporting Times* in October quoted veteran catcher Charles Zimmer, in charge of the soon-to-be-touring Pittsburgh team, as he tried to line up games with "all clubs within 300 miles" advertising that "the Pittsburgh club wants to meet them between the 12th and 20th of October. There will be no skylarking about it — genuine ball games." After October 20

Beaumont, Clarke and Ritchey, those men who were apparently very well salaried, intended to return home for the year, while the rest of the team was looking for games.

In addition, the Reds had plans for games in Louisville and Indianapolis and the *Louisville Courier-Journal* reported on the big league team's loss to Louisville on September 30, 1902.

The paper also took note of an All-American team with its star Napoleon Lajoie. This second attempt, after 1901's debacle, was organized and operated by three men. First, serving as promoter, was Joe Cantillon who would have a full career in baseball. He served as an umpire in both leagues, a manager at both Milwaukee and Minneapolis in the minors, and, for three years, field boss of the Washington American League team. Next was Tip O'Neill, a ten year player of the deadball era, and last was Detroit pitcher Win Mercer, elected as the treasurer of the team. Beginning in 1894, Mercer went on to pitch for three teams in his nine-year career. The team secured the help of Barney Dreyfuss, Pittsburgh president, to line up five games against his barnstorming aggregation. In addition to Lajoie, Wahoo Sam Crawford was recruited as was Jake Beckley and Addie Joss, the third and fourth of the future Hall of Fame honorees on the tour. Mentioned as well were Dick Harley (not yet a major leaguer from Georgetown University) and Bill Coughlin (then an infielder with Washington).

Drawing 18,000 fans from October 5 through October 11 in big league cities, both Lajoie and Cy Young opted out before the tour moved farther across the country, a tour now made up of 23 players, some from the National League (Jack Chesbro for one) and some from the original tourists from the American. In order to guarantee the appearance of the rest of the two squads, all twenty-three men were obliged to pay $175 each. *Sporting Life* summed up by saying:

> The American will tog out in red, white, and blue and the Nationals in black and yellow.... Two weeks will be spent touring the southern part of California, and November 30 the teams open in San Francisco. After playing two or three weeks there arrangements will be perfected, if considered for the best, for a trip to Honolulu.

This venture would, in fact, turn out to be a 76-game tour, with the games billed as the All-Americans vs. the All-Nationals. The contests began in Chicago on October 12 and soon moved across the country — meeting, for example, in Louisville, Denver, Albuquerque, and Las Vegas — before arriving on the West Coast, the last known game date recorded on November 2.

And besides, each player took home almost $600.

However, two months after the tour ended, Win Mercer was found dead of gas inhalation in San Francisco. The *Washington Post*, January 18, 1903,

understood his death to be an opportunity to rail against the kind of baseball excursion he had taken:

> The calamity which befell the roving ball players in the death of Winnie Mercer
> ... should be a lesson to all barnstorming clubs. Temptations were thrown in the
> way of Mercer that only such a trip as this would suggest. There was no master
> hand to guide these men, and discipline, if there ever was such a thing, was lax.
> Suicide or the careless handling of others' funds would have been the least of
> Mercer's thoughts or intentions had not the way been paved by a frolic, at least,
> and maybe a tour of riotous living. The tragedy that overtook the young player
> was the last of a series of misfortunes that met the wandering ball players, and
> the harvest they have reaped is death and demoralization. The fortune of one's
> baseball career cannot be served by skipping from town to town and giving exhi-
> bitions of the national game that are, at best, unsatisfactory to the spectator and
> the players themselves.
>
> A ball player needs rest the same as any other athlete, and when a season of
> hard work is ended he owes it to himself and to his employer to recuperate the
> forces spent in the arduous campaign of the summer and not engage in an all-
> winter tour that has no value and tends to stale the athlete, to say nothing of the
> demoralization that so often follows such enterprises. Several members of the
> two clubs that have spent the winter on the coast have been injured, and Willie
> Keeler, who is a valuable baseball asset, was nearly canceled from the field of
> usefulness by an accident that has laid him up with broken bones and many
> bruises. When these players agree to do service for their employers they owe it to
> these magnates to keep themselves in physical condition during the idle season.
> Barnstorming destroys morals and discipline and stales one's playing energies.
> There is so much baseball all the year that when the spring campaign opens few
> of these men are fitted to do justice to the game. Their enthusiasm has degener-
> ated and their energies have been badly invested.

The reports of Mercer's death indicated that he died from both mount-
ing gambling debts and an overpowering fear of contracting the deadly tuber-
culosis that had ravaged his brother.

The source of this backbiting was the column "Gossip of the Diamond."
One reason for the column's strident tone may have been the alarm at some
of the apparent damage to some of the players. Willie Keeler was injured and
after the tour ended Lajoie contracted pleurisy. In the science of the time,
fatigue might be blamed for causing the lung inflammation, though the per-
formances of Keeler and Lajoie on the diamond in 1903 were not affected.
The only connection between barnstorming and Mercer's death was the fact
that Mercer visited his tubercular brother in Las Vegas as part of the tour.

But the attack on barnstorming was one which would be repeated over
and over again. League presidents, sporting newspapers and some writers
would assail barnstorming, though no real evidence about its ill effects was
ever presented except in the most vague language, as this: "Barnstorming
destroys morals and discipline and stales one's playing energies." There was
no evidence for these guesses and players would fight against the attacks on
a regular basis and go on making the winter's extra money.

Even worse in this regard was the betrayal, as Joe McGinnity character-ized it, of the players by the team's front office management. Said Iron Man in the *Chicago Daily Tribune,*

> John T. Brush and other officials of the club promised us that if we would finish in first, second, or third position he would make us all a present. Besides that he promised us the entire receipts of the exhibition games played after the league season ended. He has not kept his word. We got no presents and for the exhibition games we played each of us got the insignificant sum of $56.35. We appreciate the fact that Brush and the others interested financially in the club are under heavy expense, but at that we figured they cleared over $200,000.

1903

In late 1901, with hostilities between the American League (AL) and National League (NL) at their peak, minor leagues which recognized the reserve system formed the National Association of Professional Baseball Leagues. The AL–NL war ended in January 1903 with the signing of the AL–NL Peace Agreement, which reaffirmed the reserve system and resolved all conflicting claims to players. Paragraph 8 of the AL–NL Peace Agreement appointed AL president Ban Johnson and NL president Harry Pulliam to draft the National Agreement in consultation with National Association president P.T. Powers.

There were 37 city series games in 1903 for the championships in Chicago, Ohio, and St. Louis, and, during the city series at Ohio, the first moving picture of a baseball game was made.

First to tour that year were the Brooklyn Nationals (called the Superbas from 1899 until 1910) who had finished 19 games behind the Pirates in 1903. This team went out with most of its stars, featuring shortstop Bill

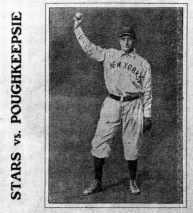

An advertisement featuring pitcher Joe "Iron Man" McGinnity in an exhibition game in New Jersey. (Hudson *Observer.*)

Dahlen, now 33, and, to begin with, pitcher Ned Garvin, who had thrown 298 innings that year. On the fifth day after the season ended, the team gathered at Trenton, New Jersey, on October 2, a two-hour trip from New York. There they met Jersey City, winners of the Eastern League pennant, and the minor leaguers beat Brooklyn 5–2. After a day off, they met the Bayside A.C. at Bayonne, New Jersey, and Brooklyn lost again, this time by 1–0 with rookie Jack Doscher joining them to pitch. Here we see the shifting nature of early barnstorming. Players might drop out for a while and rejoin the team; they might be on hand for a game or two as wanted or needed. Next, the team jumped to Pennsylvania's capital city, Harrisburg, where two games were played. Briefly detailed games followed in Wilmington, Delaware, and Buffalo, New York, were capped by a Columbus Day meeting at a city of 42,000, Lancaster, Pennsylvania, where another pitcher, Ulysses Grant Thatcher, helped the team to a 12–3 win. Thatcher's home was just 15 miles from the ballpark in Lancaster.

The tour of the New York Giants was led by John McGraw and three pitchers. With Iron Man McGinnity opting out of the tour, the Giants relied on Jack Cronin, Dummy Taylor and Christy Mathewson, who was a very big star. And he knew how to use that celebrity to his advantage.

The *New York Daily Tribune* reported on the first of the Giants' barnstorming games beginning with a September 30 appearance at Elmira, New York (population 35,672), where the New Yorkers with Mathewson beat the Father Matthew aggregation 8–2. The Detroit Tigers had arrived the next day, 23 miles south, in Williamsport, Pennsylvania, with 29,000 people living in the city, winning over the home team 5–0, though Pittsburgh, touring earlier, had lost to that city ball team.

For the game at Athletic Park against the Giants, the *Williamsport Sun* covered its third barnstorming game, the October 2 game which ended tied at 5–5. Gloated the *Sun*,

> The game was a virtual victory and regarded so by New York.... In spite of their determined efforts, they could not win, much to the chagrin of Christy Mathewson who sat on the bench and chewed gum while the swelling in his head was undergoing the process of reduction.

Mathewson did not pitch, but John Cronin, the team's number four starter did, opposed by Rube Bressler, who may have been the father of the major leaguer Rube Bressler whose career was still 11 years away. The 100-minute game was partly described by the scornful words, "Two hits [by the Giants] good for only singles, bounded badly just as the fielders were going after them, got over the bank and got lost in the hay in that part of the field, making home runs."

That embarrassing game being done, the team boarded a train for the five hour trip to Trenton, New Jersey, to face the Trenton Y.M.C.A. club.

Mathewson was supposed to pitch that October 3 game, the local paper, the *Daily True American*, wrote, but though he "took quarters with them in this city at the Hotel Windsor ... about noon he received a telegram from the management of a team in Ohio with whom he has been dickering" and that management gave him a deal that was too lucrative to turn down. So while his team was playing the Y.M.C.A. in Trenton, Mattie was pitching in Ohio for 40 percent of the gross gate, which the Trenton paper guessed would amount to $200. "In face of these terms, he could not be expected to remain here."

Also, while the Giants were going through warm-ups in Trenton, they were told that the members of the Christian Association would not have to pay admission, since it was part of their membership dues. But McGraw, seeing the crowd of about 3,000, and estimating his share of it, demanded that *everyone* be charged 25¢ or the team would not take the field. Trenton acceded. According to the *Daily True American*:

> Just before the first man stepped to the plate, a tally-ho drawn by four stylish horses pulled upon the field. Hanging from the side of the vehicle was a large banner bearing the inscription "Third Ward Friends of Billy." The tally-ho halted in front of the scoreboard and cornetist Mart Myer, who was in the party, sang the chorus of the song, substituting the word "Gilbert" for "Bailey."

The following days saw more barnstorming games at grounds called Olympia Field but was probably Olympic Field at 135th Street in Manhattan where a strong semipro team, the Murray Hills, the team run by Nat Strong, met the major leaguers.

Back in Trenton, where they would stay for six more games, the Giants faced another match with the Trenton Y.M.C.A., bringing in 5,000 fans. The money was good in Trenton and so after a few more days a game was set up as a benefit game for the Y.M.C.A. players. Admission was set at 25¢ with an additional fee of 10¢ for a spot in the grandstand. In exactly one and a half hours, the New Yorkers won 4–2 at the Trenton Association Field. It was at Roebling Field that the October 10 game was played against those Roeblings and after taking Sunday off, again the Giants met the Y.M.C.A. on Columbus Day with Matty and Jack Cronin pitching a win.

Meeting the Trenton Wiremakers at Roebling Athletic Grounds on October 13, 1903, the New Yorkers let the Trenton fans see Matty pitch a complete game, 9–0 win. The sojourn in Jersey ended on October 16 with the Y.M.C.A. again being the opposition. It was still a gate attraction, even for a Friday in October, and 3,000 paid to see the 4–1 Giants win in one hour, 39 minutes.

In the games with published attendance, the Giants drew 11,000 for three games. That means a gross of $2,750 just for those games. If Matty made 40 percent just for his appearance, there is a good chance that the team took 70 percent or 80 percent of the gross, or $2,200. So there may have been a very minimum of $100 being paid to each team member and for some much more just for those three games. With most of the people in the stands taking home less than $10 a week for their winters, this barnstorming bonus would certainly help the team members to make it through the coldest time of the year.

1904

Though there was a city series arranged between the two St. Louis teams in 1904, there was no World Series at all. When the Giants refused to play the Boston Americans (called the Pilgrims then), McGraw, the team manager, and John Brush, team owner, encouraged the team to barnstorm once more to make up the lost revue from the World Series. The series of 1903, for example, paid about $1,200 to the winners.

And so, two days after the National League season ended on October 10, the team gathered for games intended to last until October 23, with Jack Dunn, in his last year as a player, serving as the manager. Hooks Wiltse, a first line pitcher, came along on the trip but Bill Dahlen, the team's shortstop, did not. Christy Mathewson elected to barnstorm with his club. Pennsylvania games started the postseason activity, with a stop in Easton first with Reading next. The game there was covered in great detail by the *Reading Daily Times and Dispatch*, Naming the opposition as the All-Readings, "a team composed of professionals who make Reading their home during the winter months," the 1,500 spectators were happy to see

> Mathewson, the pitching wonder of the day. He was in the box for the Giants and for two innings he shot the ball across the plate with the speed of a projectile fired from a cannon. Then, when the champions had all the runs necessary to put them beyond the danger line, the big pitcher merely lobbed and at that the home men bent their backs to get at it. The ease with which the big men fielded the ball was a revelation to the lovers of the game and who have not the privilege of seeing many contests between teams composed of the artists of the diamond. All Reading's men appeared nervous and fidgety at times.

However, in York the next day the *Daily* found no such nervousness. "The Penn Park boys" or the Ponies, outhit McGraw's men 7–6 and with the help of Stoney McGlynn who struck on nine and set down in order the big leaguers from inning five through inning nine (he would pitch later for the Cardinals), the York team pushed the Giants hard. But McGraw's third baseman Art Devlin was struck by a pitch in the 10th, moved to second on a wild pitch, and came home on a single with the run that won the game.

After Harrisburg, with Hooks Wiltse and Warner as the battery, the team moved into Plainfield, New Jersey, where the crowd was surprised to see an odd setup. Apparently to make the game more interesting, McGraw now gave the home team Wiltse to pitch against Mathewson.

Afterwards it was back into the Keystone State for two games in Hazleton and Scranton. The last game for the barnstormers was in Hoboken, New Jersey, a ferry ride across the Hudson from Manhattan. After that game, Matty then went to the California Winter League where, according to *Sporting Life*, he would be teamed in Los Angeles with Honus Wagner and Frank Chance.

Briefly covered in the press, the Reds again barnstormed in 1904 for seven games in three states, their most noticeable player the second baseman Miller Huggins (who would go on to be manager of the great Yankees teams of the 1920s).

Other jaunts were not so specific. In *The Glory of their Times*, Rube Marquard said he barnstormed with Bill Bradley (Cleveland third baseman) and his Boo Gang in 1904 when Rube was fifteen. The *Sporting Life* noted that Detroit barnstormers had to stop after two games due to the cold. The Athletics were at Trenton with Eddie Plank and Rube Waddell on October 15 or 22, 1904, around the same time the Brooklyn Superbas took a ferry to Hoboken (where their third baseman Dude McCormick had played) as its *Observer* took note of and then moved to St. George's Cricket Grounds in Staten Island on Sunday, October 16, 1904, charging 25¢ to the 3,000 fans. After the Brooklyns won there by 3–1, the team then traveled to a small city of 28,000, Atlantic City, and there met the Negro team the Cuban X Giants, and traveled again in New Jersey to Marquette Field for an October 16 game.

The *Washington Post* reported that touring as well were manager Ned Hanlon's team, while a team that called itself the All Nationals had a contest at Elizabethport, New Jersey, on October 23, 1904. The name may have little currency as a big league team, but no box score exists of the game.

1905

By 1905, shouts were again being heard about the practice of earning extra money by the players. Those men felt that any opportunity to earn extra money ought to be seized. The owners, however, did not agree to these extracurricular contests, beginning with objections to players who found games to play where the law forbade Sunday baseball where admission was collected.

To give an idea of the extent of the influence of that ban, in 1906 the Brooklyn Nationals played a Sunday game against the Boston Nationals, as James Charlton records (*The Baseball Chronology*), charging no admission but asking fans to contribute as they entered the park.

Blue laws, championed by groups known as Sabbatarians, prevented games that charged admission on Sunday for the major leagues as well as for semi-pros. On Sundays, because no admission could be charged, semipro baseball winked at the law and fans got in for free but had to buy a candy bar or a scorecard for a half dollar. Sometimes the New York state Sunday Blue Law was strictly observed, as when police refused to let start the game between the Washington team and the semipro Cedars at Bronx Oval in New York City.

Sunday games *were* being played. At the time, it was the only day of the week when workers did not have to be on the job. The *New York Times* reported an October 9 match of a big league team against the potent semi-pro Ridgewoods at the Wallace Grounds. (Known by many names, including Meyerrose's Union League Park and The Horse Market, the field was situated at Onderdunk and Elm in Ridgewood not far from Manhattan.) Two items of note here: first that a baseball team called the Ridgewoods was known as far back at least as 1885. In the *New York Times* of October 9, 1905, was a report of a game that drew 12,000 to the Wallace Grounds, one of the best attended fields in the city. (The park was situated in a section of Queens, the farthest east of the New York City boroughs.) Because the team and the diamond were well known for quality baseball contests, the Greater New York team of the American League, that is, the Yankees, played there at least twice in the postseason. In the 1905 game, 12,000 paid to see, on a Sunday, the major league team with six regulars starting, including Willie Keeler and pitcher-manager Clark Griffith. In fact, in two games against the Ridgewoods in the first decade of the twentieth century, the average attendance was 10,500. No matter how the money was divided, these were fine paydays for the men on the field.

This pattern — barnstormers opposing a nearby team with a strong reputation, often a semipro outfit who played on a first-rate field, in the area — would be repeated over and over throughout the seven decades of barnstorming.

It was these Sabbath games that were the worry of another New York City team owner, Brooklyn president Charles Ebbets, and led to an article in *The Sporting News* of September 30, 1905. Remember that although the strictly observed major leagues did not play Sunday games, the semipros got fat on them. "AGAIN ON WARPATH. EBBETS AFTER PLAYERS WHO MAKE EXTRA MONEY. ASSERTS THAT STARS ON SUNDAY TAKE SHINE OFF SUPERBAS WEEKDAY EXHIBITIONS," the headline read. "His crusade is against major league players who invade his territory to play Sunday games with semiprofessional teams." In mid–September Iron Man McGinnity pitched for the All-Nationals against the Visitations on Brooklyn's Visitation Field, a day's work that paid $100.

> Ebbets grew hot, naturally, as the aspect of the most talked about twirler in this vicinity [his contract was owned by the Giants] pitching semiprofessional ball on a local ground could not help but hurt the business.... He does not object to

the players making a little extra money, but it must be done legitimately in exhibitions sanctioned by himself ... Ebbets asserts that one of the Brooklyn pitchers after working Saturday, pitched a semiprofessional game on Sunday and was all in when called upon to pitch on Tuesday.... Next year he threatens to have detectives on every semiprofessional ball field in Greater New York for the purpose of not only watching his own players but other New York clubs as well [*Sporting News*].

Clearly Ebbets *was* agitated, particularly so since he saw himself and his fellow owners as the only source of legitimate baseball. The contracts he had made with the team members extended from opening day to closing day and he meant to enforce that contract's stipulations. That year rookie Al Bridwell said that he was paid $2,100. For the contract span of 165 days, that means that the rookie was being paid $32 a day. (To live on the money for a full year means that he was being paid $5.75 per day.) Given the chance to more than triple that daily amount as McGinnity had done, it would be hard to refuse the offer.

Still the owners insisted on gathering all the power they could. For example, an injury clause in the standard player contract allowed clubs to suspend any player after laying out 15 days pay. The power of the owners went even further. Even though the National League Board of Directors exonerated St. Louis Cardinal right-hander Jack Taylor on the charge of throwing games, Taylor was still fined $300 for using poor judgment and practicing bad conduct.

John Brush and John McGraw, owner and manager of the World Series champion New York Giants, did not seem to agree with Ebbets and on two successive Mondays the Giants gathered at Trenton, New Jersey, for postseason games.

Attended by 3,500, the game on October 16 saw the stands so packed that "the crowd overflowed to the left and right field lines." The New Yorkers fielded a championship team that lacked only Bresnahan behind the plate, featuring the fearsome submarine baller Joe McGinnity on the mound. Certainly McGinnity would prefer throwing a baseball to his usual off-season job of being a smelter. Billy Gilbert, called "the little magnet" at second base, lived in Trenton for some time and his "many friends and admirers here started a subscription Saturday," the *Trenton Times* noted, "and raised $300 with which a beautiful diamond stud was purchased" and then presented the stud to Gilbert at home plate when he came to bat in the third inning.

After a game at Wilkes-Barre, Pennsylvania (October 20), the Giants came back to Trenton for a "game for the benefit of the local players." The game was won again by the Giants, that day by 6–2, followed by a banquet at the Hotel Sterling after the game, hosted by state Excise Commissioner Gallagher. The *Trenton Daily True American* reported

That year the Giants had each already been paid $1,142 in World Series shares. Concerning money, especially the payday for the 1905 World Series, the Paterson, NJ, *Daily Press* newspaper noted that baseball was clearly a business for all concerned when it wrote that yesterday was the last day on which there was anything in it for the players. The winners will receive about $1,500 and the losers $500 each. It is safe to predict that the players will see to it that today ends the series, as they are not inclined to make money for other people. Today, and in the remaining games, if any, the receipts go to the respective club owners. With no more money in sight, the Athletics were not like to put forth too strenuous an effort to keep the series going.

The A's were behind at that point three games to one and the series ended the next day, October 14, when the American Leaguers lost 2–0.

"Lon Wolfson will go on the road with the Red Troopers," *Sporting Life* said in its October 7 issue; the team made six published stops, including towns with populations of 5,132 and 3,915. Pittsburgh traveled too with Honus Wagner and Fred Clarke going along on four dates in Ohio.

There in Ohio, within a space of four days in mid–October, fans in the city of Zanesville, with a population just over 24,000, could go out to Gant Park to watch two very good teams be matched with the hometown Moguls. (Zanesville had a team in the minor leagues, the Ohio-Pennsylvania League, for the first time in 1905. For entertainment, the people of Zanesville, for the price of a ticket to the ballgame, could see *The Triumph of Betty*, a "complete scenic production and accessories"; the Metropolitan company acting in a four-act drama, *The Clay Baker*; the musical *Uncle Josh Spruceby* with "20 People! the Hayseed Band! Grand Operatic Orchestra! Car Load Special Scenery! Novel Mechanical Effects! and "The Great Saw-Mill Scene.")

And yet, 2,000 "lovers of the sport," as the *Zanesville Daily Courier* labeled them, turned out on a cloudy afternoon to see the fine performance of Hans Wagner and Tommy Leach remain unavailing in the 6–2 win by the local team. That same winning Zanesville club traveled over 200 miles to face the Cincinnati Reds in a town of 3,100 — Catlettsburg, Kentucky — on Friday, the 16th, losing to the big leaguers in the last inning. Traveling north to Zanesville, probably on the Baltimore and Ohio, the Reds too met defeat at Gant Park, watched by 1,500; this of course means paid admissions, as "no count could be made of the large number who came in over the back fence." Though on the roster of the Pirates in 1905, Heiney Peitz, the catcher, did not travel with his team since the team manager for the Pirates while barnstorming was the catcher as well. So the Reds signed Peitz for the postseason work and in Zanesville the thirty-five-year-old made three misjudgments which cost his team the win, as once again the hometown locals beat the visiting major leaguers.

Toward the end of October *Sporting Life* told of how from the Detroit organization, George Mullin, Herman Schaefer, Charlie O'Leary and Sam

Crawford would all go barnstorming with Joe Cantillon (from Milwaukee) to the Pacific Coast, starting in Chicago on October 20, 1905. But the next week, an editorial called "Timely Topics" had bad news:

> The proposed trip to the Pacific Coast of an All-National and an All-American team has been called off by the promoters, Messers Cantillon and O'Neil.... Just as well, as such jaunts are of no particular benefit to players at best; and are very often the cause of sickness, injury and other subsequent disabilities. Summer play and winter rest is the course best suited to the average base ball player's mental, physical and moral welfare.

Chiming in on the dangers of barnstorming was the *Milwaukee Sentinel*:

> Do barnstorming tours about the country by base ball clubs pay? That is a question that many ball players have been asking themselves since the nearly fatal stabbing affray at Des Moines, Iowa, in which pitcher Quate Bateman was the victim. In most cases the player's club gets together at the end of the championship season and tours around some state in the hope of picking up enough extra coin to buy their winter clothing. As a rule, they come back no richer than when they started and many times much poorer. It seems to be the usual thing for most of them to start on what they call a good old time and to pay little attention to conditions, etc. That was the trouble at Des Moines. The boys were having a good time and many of them were drinking. The trouble all arose over a trivial matter and had they been in their proper senses it would not have happened. When a man faces a charge that may send him up for life, he stops to consider whether such methods pay. The Milwaukee players who were on that trip came back just $1 richer for their trouble. That is the amount of money they made, but most of them spent much more money while on the trip, so that they were out money.

1906

In September of 1906, young Joe Wood — later called "Smokey" — was on the roster of his town's team, Ness City in Kansas. The opposition that day was a Bloomer Girls team, who were in their last three weeks of their traveling season and after the game Wood was offered $20, he recalled in *The Glory of Their Times*, to play the infield with the travelers for those three weeks. So Wood, not yet seventeen years old, became the fourth male on the team. In two more years he would be on the mound for the Red Sox.

Sporting Life of October 6, 1906, called Frank Bancroft "The Pioneer Barnstormer." This year Bancroft planned on a trip to the Philippines. His Reds planned on touring, too.

In its third year of activity, the governing body of professional baseball, the National Commission, was beginning to flex its muscles. "Basically, the Commission's responsibility was interpretation and enforcement of the National Agreement, and punishment of violations by fines and suspensions" (Suehsdorf).

Since the disingenuous attempt to stop barnstorming by claiming it hurt or did not help players was apparently unavailing, *The Sporting News* on October 17, 1906, felt it important to remind players:

> The National Agreement of the National Association forbids players under contract or reserve to engage in games with ineligible players. The National Commission has ruled that the player is under the control of the club between seasons.

This fear of infection was codified under rule 47 of the National Agreement in 1909:

> No National Agreement player will be permitted at any time ... to participate in any game, or games with or against clubs harboring ineligible players or whose owners or managers are ineligible players. Every National Agreement player who hereafter violates this rule will be fined not less that $200.00 for the first offense.

Threats worked on players oftentimes and since the very first year of the National League players have been "declared ineligible"—an official-sounding phrase meaning kicked out of organized baseball. That phrase included the two major leagues and the teams allied with the single minor league association. In other words, if you were put on the somewhat nebulous ineligible list, you could play ball but not for the kind of money or prestige that came from signing with the controlling cartel. The cartel had been known, for example, to allow the Cardinals in 1900 to withhold the final month's pay (20 percent) "on all but 5 players, including John McGraw and Wilbert Robinson, citing late hours, dissipation and gambling as reasons for the poor showing of the team, which finished tied for fifth" (Charlton, 127). Rube Marquard was fined $25 for pitching in a semipro game on his day off. At about the same time, the president of the American League paid himself $10,000.

Nevertheless the New York Americans arranged their first 1906 postseason game the day after their season ended at Elizabeth, New Jersey, and seemingly played the last of a series of games at Hoboken eleven days later.

The first of the Philadelphia barnstorming groups set out on Sunday, October 7, at Hoboken, New Jersey, with future Hall of Fame pitcher Eddie Plank on the mound. His Athletics managed a 3–1 win. This was a team that included two more Hall of Famers, Chief Bender and Connie Mack, as well as Socks Seybold among others. Then it was north to Hartford, Connecticut, facing the Washington Americans for the benefit of Workingman's Free Bed Fund in the Cedar Mountain Hospital. For this game, probably contested on the diamond used by the Hartford Senators of the Connecticut League, Mack sent Rube Waddell out to pitch and his win netted $2,344, with $1,250 going to the hospital. "After the game, the 30 players, now splitting $1,094 ($36 each), were banqueted by prominent citizens."

In Chester, Pennsylvania, on October 12 they met another team, the Negro

Philadelphia Giants with Pop Lloyd and Rube Foster, a team that had won 108 games with a winning percentage of .734 who were recognized to be the black champions of the East, their third such crown in a row. *Sporting Times*, in the accepted diction of the time, took note that the white team "just manag[ed] to beat the 'duskies'" by 5 to 4. Played at Seaboard Park, Rube Waddell umpired the game. "The attendance was quite large," wrote the *Chester Times*, over 1,000 paid admissions being in the park. This concluded a series of five games against black opponents. Waddell, Jack Coombs and Plank all pitched in the games. Holway reports that there were six games but lists five games. The missing game may be an October 20th game at Wilkes-Barre.

The Phillies of the National League, once their closing day had arrived, featured Kid Gleason at second as it began its touring by meeting the Athletics on the 10th at Reading, Pennsylvania, a game matching Jack Coombs and Tully Sparks. As described by the *Reading Times*, the field was soft and soggy from rain, "the air was chilly and a stiff wind blew" but "a crowd ... completely filled the bleachers and three fourths of the grandstands at the Reading grounds." There was unexpected action:

> A party of boys looking at the game back of the outfield fence stirred up a rabbit. In a moment the bunnie streaked across the field. The fielders of two clubs saw it coming and almost instantly gave chase to it. Bunnie made its escape after a hard run.

In a well-pitched game the Athletics came out on top by a score of 2–1. In a moment not unlike the times spent by the Excelsior club of Brooklyn in 1860, a time when much of the pleasure of barnstorming came from the time after the game, here in Reading, 46 years after the Excelsiors' journey through New York state, players enjoyed socializing:

> A number of the members of both clubs have been intimate friends for years of Manager Hill, of the Orpheum, this city, and both organizations were his guests at the theater last evening.

For the next game, the Phillies moved to Williamsport, Pennsylvania, and the *Gazette & Bulletin* named the members of the Elks lodge who would oppose the big leaguers while it reminded its readers that "Box seats were on sale at Walton's Drug store." The Phillies would bring with them to Athletic Park Lew Ritchie to pitch and Red Dooin to catch him. In the outfield were Sherry Magee, John Titus, and manager Hugh Duffy, a future Hall of Fame selection. But only "a handful of faithful fans shivered and shook through nine innings.... The pitchers did not think it safe to take chances with their salary arms and did not exert themselves to any great extent" right up to the time when a long foul ball hit by first baseman Sebring "broke up the game because there were no more balls on the ground with which to put out the last man" in the one hour and fifty minute contest. But "after the game," the *Grit* reported, the Elks and their guests returned to the Elks' hall and spent a social evening.... The Elks band was present at the game and the banquet."

After the 9–4 win in Williamsport, the next stop for the Phillies was at Lock Haven, a tie, and then to Frankford, Pennsylvania, losing there 4–3. Returning to Lock Haven, the Phillies match against the Lock Haven All-Professionals at Normal Park drew about 1,300 people, many of whom were behind ropes and this play happened, as written in the pages of the Clinton, Pennsylvania, *Republican*:

> Neuer hit one into the crowd on the right field foul line and was given second base, as the ball was blocked. Blair threw the ball to second base to hold him there but there was no one on the base to receive the ball and it rolled into the crowd on the other side of the field and Neuer waltzed home.

Then "the game was called as it was getting too cold and too dark to play" with the score tied at 5–5. It was the last game that brought the Phillies the greatest success for at Pottsville, Pennsylvania, not only did they make a 7–2 win but they also drew 5,000 fans, in a city that was counted as having 15,000 people.

Sporting Life of October 27, 1906, mentioned the White Sox, the "hitless wonders" who became champion, and after cashing their World Series checks of $1,874.63, played three days after the Series including stops at Joliet, Illinois, and Kenosha, Wisconsin.

Success, or the lack of it, and money had something to do with another article from *Sporting Life*, October 13, 1906, with the dateline Pittsburgh, October 8:

> Because the Pirates were beaten out for second place in the pennant race, [President] Dreyfuss recently said that some of his men had too much money to play ball, and that he would compel them to play exhibition games until October 15, when their contracts expired for the season. [Manager Fred] Clarke objected to this from the start.

But players began to drift away from the team: Fred Clarke left the team before season's end; Hans Wagner left for Hot Springs; Nealon left the team in Cincinnati. "Some friends of the players," the *Boston Globe* wrote, "say that Dreyfuss weakened all the way and paid the team off by allowing players to do as they pleased and that the barnstormers who start tomorrow [October 9] will pocket all the proceeds."

The *Globe*'s continuing story had Dreyfuss worried about his captain-manager and the owner left for Chicago to seek him out, and "those who know Clarke best say that he will not agree to manage the Pittsburgh team another year unless Dreyfuss promises to keep his hands off the team all the time." So, the players had some influence with the owners.

Three days after the season ended, with the *Pittsburgh Sun* following the team carefully, Tommy Leach's team scheduled its first game at West Liverpool, Ohio, and lost 1–0 with Ohioan Tom Needham of the Boston Nationals catching for West Liverpool. The Beaver Falls, Pennsylvania, *Daily Tribune* covered the next game, a win by their hometown Athletics though only five innings were played as a snowstorm arrived "and they hastened the contest to keep warm."

Games awaited the Pirates in towns who most times had populations of under 6,000 and often under 2,000. Town teams from Fairmount, a town of 5,700, Mannington (1,700) and Wheeling being beaten, the team traveled to Natrona, and then Dillonvale, Ohio.

After four more contests, one game remained at Witherup, Pennsylvania (really Emlenton, a town of 1,200), second baseman Claude Ritchey's home town.

Finally, the *Pittsburgh Sun* of October 25, 1906, took note of the game at Etna, Pennsylvania (6,000 residents in Allegheny County), a 4–1 victory before 3,000 people, opposed by hometown hero infielder Whitey Alperman of the Brooklyn National Superbas.

> The eleven games of the tour being over, *The Sporting News* wrote, The Pirate barnstormers hung together until last Wednesday night when the team disbanded [one day after the Etna game].... This barnstorming trip was probably the most successful ever indulged in by the Pirates.... The boys went home several hundred dollars richer.

This quote proves both that the owner's ire had disappeared and that the players had added about 40 percent of an average worker's pay to their yearly wages.

One way of comparing money in the first decade of 1900 and today's money is to use the statistical device called "purchasing power," a number available on a Web site called EH.net. If we say the Pirates took home $200 dollars each, that would be worth about $4,100 today.

This possible postseason money would keep players on the Pumpkin Circuit for some time though the cartel and some individual owners spoke against it. Factors working against teams playing were logistical problems: who would arrange for the tour and then conduct it; that is, who would stand at the box office and collect the money after the last admission had been paid? Who would take on the job of front man, advertising each game? If a team had someone to do those jobs, they might go on tour. Then, too, there would have to be enough team members willing to risk bad weather and small crowds in the midst of the football season while each man might be home working his 200-day job in the off-season.

1907

Many sports fans were now accustomed to close attention being paid to each game, but the *Sporting Life* of October 12, 1907, was aware of the common practice of newspapers, who, if nothing else were an advertising business. "EXTREME LACK OF INTEREST IN FINAL GAMES," the headline read. "New York papers would not pay for messengers to carry copy from park in order that the telegraph companies could send the matter East."

Another problem was the active belief of Sabbatarians as is in this story in the Wilkes-Barre paper with a headline "MINISTERS STOP BASEBALL GAME." The story told of a game that was supposed to be played with the Phillies at Driving Park against the local Wilkes-Barre All-Professionals.

> A number of ministers of the Wyoming Valley prevented a baseball game at Hanover Park near here to-day between the New York league team and a nine composed of professionals from this city. The park is owned by the Delaware, Lackawanna, and Western Coal Company, and the ministers prevailed upon the officials of the company to refuse to allow the teams to play. Tomorrow the New York Nationals and Philadelphia Nationals will play an exhibition game here.

The next day the Phillies *did* play, but the opposition was the Giants at Driving Park, and partly thanks to the 2,000 fans that day the Giants' trip "netted each man $100." The Athletics toured too but scant information is available, as is true of the Cincinnati group's work which at least drew this observation from *Sporting Life* on October 26, 1907: "Once in a while these barnstorming after-the-season expeditions result in a good pick-up. [Pitcher] Bob Ewing's work in one of these Ham and Eggs League contests attracted the attention of the Cincinnati club to the tall sycamore of old Anglaize." In modern American, so a SABR member reports, "tall sycamore" refers to his height (his nickname was Long Bob) and where Ewing was from (Anglaize County in Ohio). Another SABR man, Darren Viola, suggested that Ham and Eggs means a lower lowly skilled league.

The St. Louis Browns barnstormed for a while, so did the White Sox, and rookie Nap Rucker went off on his own, perhaps near his native Crabapple, Georgia, until November 4. The Tigers went out too and the Cubs were in line to play an "all-star" team led by Jake Stahl who, being independently wealthy, had taken that year off from big league ball.

As the owners and their commission continued successfully to oppose most clubs from touring, the players were looking ahead to their lives after baseball, since most of them were aware of a number of pitfalls in their profession. And few of them had the bank account of Jake Stahl.

> Few ball players made enough money to save for old age, and many of them were reduced in their declining years to dependence on handouts from old friends in baseball or on small jobs as gatekeepers or watchmen at ball parks. When Ezra

Sutton, a veteran of eighteen years in the major leagues, died destitute in 1907, a sportswriter suggested that some kind of pension be set up for players. Ban Johnson more than once recommended that a relief fund for indigent players be established out of World Series receipts. Several other baseball men proposed a home for aged players. But these ideas went unfulfilled until a later day. Players also resented the inconsiderate treatment sometimes given veterans. After years of service they could be shunted unceremoniously to the minors, like rookies without any say-so in the matter, as was [14 year veteran] Three-Finger Brown [Seymour, *The Early Years*, 191].

A pension would have to wait, in fact, another forty years.

As for the Pirates, who had finished a very distant second, they were on the road once more, and they brought Honus Wagner along, though his hand was broken, to umpire the games. As a champion batsman, his presence alone would be a major attraction. And, in fact on October 16, it was to Carnegie, Pennsylvania, Wagner's home town of 7,400, that the team traveled, probably by trolley since the town was but a few miles from Pittsburgh. There at the Heidelberg grounds during a "traditional game against the Fosters of Carnegie, he was presented with a solid-gold medal decorated with a finely cut diamond in recognition of the 1907 batting title" [Hageman, 169].

By excursion's end, according to *Sporting Life*:

Veterans of the Pittsburgh team ... [were] proud of the fact that they set a high mark for excellence in the matter of barnstorming. No cheap plays, jew-down of hotel rates, or other points were essayed. First-class stopping places, best of everything in train lines, etc. was the motto.

Harold Seymour, in the first of his first pioneering volumes, *Baseball: The Early Years*, was aware of sweetheart deals for both teams and players. As an inducement, railroads offered special or professional

rates to ball clubs.... Streetcar lines had a very close connection with professional baseball. Owners of transportation facilities were among the first sports promoters. To increase traffic, streetcar lines established amusement parks and went into the entertainment business. The *Street Railway Journal* of May 1896 estimated that in the previous ten years at least a hundred companies had trolley parks of their own. Traction magnates also recognized that ball games were well patronized, and found it profitable to co-operate with the ball clubs. As one of them said, it was in their interests "to keep in with the baseball people" [32].

The close tie-up between car lines and professional baseball is revealed in several ways. Baseball magnates like Al Johnson, Frank Robison, and Henry V. Lucas were also active in the traction business. Regular "baseball trains ran from town to grounds in some cities, and, whenever possible, ball parks were located near the trolley car lines" (203). Trolley car lines often paid ball clubs for the privilege of stopping at the park.

This sweetheart deal meant, of course, that barnstorming players could travel from the city to outlying districts where there were ball fields, say from the Monongahela Hotel in Pittsburgh which offered special rates to ball teams (a $3 double in those days was not uncommon). The trip to Carnegie, for example, was a mere three miles by trolley. "Some trolley lines would help to support the ballclub by picking up some of the expenses like grounds keeping."

Hotels, too, advertised for baseball business and contracted to house them and would offer to pick up teams at the train depot and carry them to the hotel and then back to the depot.

Sporting Life continued its coverage of Pittsburgh, writing, "Secretary Locke, running the team, was pleased that business men with fine ratings [were] identified and you can take their check for the visiting club's share and have no worry as to its validity."

1908

Some teams took postseason trips out of the country in 1907. The Reach All-Americans went to Japan, Hawaii, China and the Philippines and the Leland Giants of Chicago played a series against the Detroit Tigers in Cuba.

As yet another aspect of the life of the professional, Harry Hooper signed for $85 per month, for five months, to play in the outlaw California State League, probably on weekends; he was paid $75 per month to be a surveyor on the weekdays during the off-season.

Sometimes players could add to the earnings just by showing up after the season. The *New York Times* on October 19, 1908, covered a "benefit performance for the Giants" on 14th Street and Irving Place at the Academy of Music and that night fans collected $3,500 for the players. The fans wanted to say, like manager John McGraw, that the team finished one game behind the Cubs that year because they had been cheated out of the flag. (Really, though, they lost partly because of a blunder by young Fred Merkle and partly because pitcher Harry Coveleski shut them out twice during the stretch run.)

Harry Coveleski's brother Stan pitched in the off-season back in Pennsylvania against the touring Athletics and Eddie Plank. The Giants planned to go to Cuba, but after some games in the states they decided not to. The Reds did go to Cuba, led by their inveterate tour guide, Frank Bancroft, and played a few games in Florida before (in Tampa they played the Negro team the Brooklyn Royal Giants) and after the trip. Before they even left the states, "The Cincinnati players in twelve games of the Cornfield Circuit each got $200 over expenses" at a time when the average weekly salary was $9.70. If the players had chosen to work in the 200 days of the off-season, $9.70 was what they would have been paid as well.

The Pirates, like the Giants also one game back of the Cubs, were offered a "benefit and testimonial" from area businessmen "in recognition of their efforts to win the pennant." At Exposition Park, arranged was a game of ball between the Pirates and star players of the county league and a field day program, including track events, circling the bases, fungo hitting, accurate and long distance throw and other similar contests [Philadelphia *Evening Bulletin*, October 7, 1908].

With the World Series completed after five games, the victorious Chicago Cubs each were paid $1,400. Still, more money might be made. The Chicagoans entered into negotiations to barnstorm against some Pacific Coast League teams; in fact, they were offered $10,000 with expenses guaranteed. But the Cubs wanted $1,000 per player for the series so the league declined. This chasing after money might have been due to the marked decrease in a World Series share for the winner.

Other games did become available for the Cubs. "With the world's championship tucked safely away ... Chicago could well afford to be generous" in their two post–World Series games with Detroit. ("In this game the players will appear as individuals and not as clubs," one paper took care to write.) The *Philadelphia Evening Bulletin* reported that the Tigers won both games, one in Chicago (fans numbered 6,864) and lastly in Terre Haute, Indiana. The Cubs made $105 each on that last game on October 20, 1908, in Mordecai Brown's hometown.

In one of the games there were pre-game contests. The winners were recognized in the October 20, 1908, *Philadelphia Evening Bulletin*:

The 100 yard dash: Cobb (10.4) and Davy Jones; Circling bases: Durbin and Evers; Cobb (won at 13 4/5 seconds) and Davy Jones; Bunting and Running: Schulte, Chance and Evers, Cobb and Davy Jones; Long Distance Throwing: Durbin and Evers; Sam Crawford, Schaefer, McIntyre and Cobb; Fungo Hitting: Tinker, Hoffman, Schulte, Zimmerman, Marshall and Evers; Overall: Killian, Summers and Mullin; Brown, and Marshall; Accurate throwing by catcher: Thomas, Kling and Moran.

In another part of Chicago, the American League team, as well as Washington, met the Logan Squares (owned by Rube Foster) of the Chicago City League. The aftermath of these games was that, in the language of the Chicago *Tribune*,

Eighteen or more players may be barred from baseball.... The Washington players subjected themselves to investigation by playing games after the season closed in violation of one of the rules of the commission and particularly by playing the Logan Squares which are not in good standing with the commission having harbored ineligible players.

On October 20, the *Tribune* declared that "under this ruling, the Washington American League club is directed not to enter into any contracts for 1909" with eight members of the team as well with as team players from Milwaukee and Minneapolis. The prohibition did not hold for most major league players though.

What did hold? On April 19, 1908, the National Commission reinstated Jake Stahl and Mike Donlin after fining them $100 each for playing with teams outside organized ball (the Logan Squares) in 1907.

1909

The conflicts continued. On March 31, 1909, the National Commission let it be known that players who jumped contracts would be suspended for five years. Players joining outlaw organizations would be suspended for three years as punishment for going outside organized baseball. As for Red Sox outfielder Harry Hooper, he claimed in *The Glory of Their Times*, he was paid $2,800 by the cartel for the year, a salary close to $60,000 today.

A large tour run by Frank Bancroft called the All Nationals featured pitchers Walter Johnson of Washington and from the Giants Rube Marquard and Chief Meyers. Starting in Chicago on October 19, the All Nationals opposed the Cubs, after which Bancroft had set up 27 days of contests.

When both leagues had finished the season on October 7, there were still many postseason games to make money from. A vague notice in *Sporting Life* on October 2, 1909, said that substitute infielder Charlie Starr of the Phillies was working on arranging a barnstorming

Advertisement for an overseas tour of 1908–1909. (National Baseball Hall of Fame Library, Cooperstown, New York.)

tour with National League players, including Otto Knabe and Johnny Bates, but that tour seemingly did not take place. The Tigers, the World Series over, played at Chattanooga, Tennessee, on October 24–25 and at Jacksonville, Florida, on October 26 and 27 before moving on to Tampa on October 28, and from Tampa to Havana, Cuba.

The Pirates decided not to barnstorm in 1909. The *Louisville Courier-Journal* reported that two games were played in that Kentucky city, both starring Nap Lajoie and his "All-Americans, before 500 on September 30 and with 2,000 in attendance the next day."

Labeled an inter-league series, the New York Giants met the Boston Red Sox, and the first game two days after the season ended drew 4,573 paid. Five games were contested, with Boston winning four, bringing in a total of $12,862.50. A total of $4,008.73 went to the Boston players (about $265 each) and $2,671.16 (about $180 each) for New York. In these city series games, everybody had a share. The National Commission got its 10 percent ($1,286.25), the team owners 38 percent ($4,887.75), and the players 52 percent or $6,679.89. And the National Commission was empowered to hold onto the cash prior to disbursement, including initially, without any thought of paying the players interest on the money held.

Given this revenue system, it is easy to understand why the owners and National Commission might approve of *these* games and work hard against games with semipro teams who functioned outside of the National Agreement.

In the Chicago City Series, the first game matching the Cubs against the White Sox at South Side Grounds recorded 16,762 paid. The National League squad pocketed its winnings, about $900, and then arranged more games with four teams, the best known of which were the champions of the City League, the renowned Leland Giants. Their leader, on the mound, in the dugout and in the front office, was Andrew "Rube" Foster. By the time the six games were done on October 24, it is quite possible that the Cubs could have matched money taken home by the World Series winning team, the Pirates share being $1,825.22 that year.

But in 1909 it was the Philadelphia Athletics, finishing second that year as did the Cubs, who first drew the barnstorming attention. First, the *Philadelphia Evening Bulletin* of October 5 reported that the Athletics split into teams called the regulars who would barnstorm for about a month, and the other team called the left-overs or stay behinds.

Four pitchers appeared in these games for the Athletics but some of them were absent from the team for a time, a team that included five future Hall of Fame honorees: Connie Mack, Eddie Collins, Frank Baker, Eddie Plank, and Chief Bender.

This is the team that arranged games from October 5 through October

17 after which they left for Chicago. In between those two dates, there were articles, for example, that said the team played at Tri-State Field in Trenton on October 6 with 1,350 in attendance, a sizeable crowd for a Wednesday. *Sporting Life* on October 16 reported that the Athletics played in Hartford, Connecticut, on October 5, 1909, against the New York Highlanders (who would not be called the Yankees until 1913), the games netting $1,200 for the Athletics.

To sum up, *The Sporting News* on October 14, 1909, wrote,

> The Athletics went on a barnstorming trip last Monday [October 11], played every day since and have made a nice sum of extra money. They will keep at it for another week and then start on October 18 [after three weeks of barnstorming] for their long trip to California. From present indications the 12 White Elephants who are on the barnstorming trip play about 12 games and make nearly as much money out of it as the losers of the World Series will get out of their four games. Up to last night [game nine of fourteen] each player's share of their trip was over $700.

Before entraining for Chicago, the Athletics found a game at Shamokin, Pennsylvania, on October 17, where Eddie Plank and Jack Coombs pitched against the hometown Coveleski brothers, Stan, the future Hall of Famer, then being in the Class "B" Tri-State League, and Harry, a twenty-three-year-old with the Phillies.

Then, for the next two months, Mack's team was to play the All-Nationals during a 50-game schedule. After a 5–3 win by the Athletics on October 27, the teams parted company and some men continued to play in California, Walter Johnson being the most prominent example. This play led directly to the startup of that season's California Winter League.

The battle between Pirates president Dreyfuss and his players was outlined in *Sporting Life* on November 6, 1909:

> The president of the Pirates, Barney Dreyfuss, went to manager Fred Clarke and asked him to cancel the proposed barnstorming tour and the trip was called off. The reasons for President Dreyfuss' request are sound and sensible and it would be well if other club owners of the big leagues followed his lead and put a permanent end to the practice of prolonging the base ball season with a series of more less "Joke" exhibition games. To be sure, ball players want to make the money they can, and no one can blame them for it. But the fact that they are so manifestly "out for the coin" hurts the game directly and themselves indirectly. In other words, the practice cheapens the national pastime and does more toward making it look entirely commercial than any other one thing. Furthermore, the big leagues are often made to look cheap artistically in these post-season exhibitions.

Worse, wrote the *Chicago Tribune* on October 24, 1909,

> Suppose the Cubs had lost their three games to the Leland Giants.... Does anyone think there would not be a number of persons who would have been convinced firmly that the Lelands would be right up there fighting for the National League

pennant if they were asked into that organization? It is all right to make money but let us make it without losing our dignity.

The Leland Giants were a black team.

Exhibition Games

> The smaller the town was the more important the ball team was [Smoky Joe Wood in Seymour's *The People's Game*].

EXHIBITION GAMES NOTE: These games, unlike barnstorming, are postseason games that fall into three categories.

1. games contested by teams put together for just a few games, generally made up of players either from the area, or players who had not yet left for their homes
2. benefit games
3. civic duty games, when a player took the field for his home town, for instance, against a neighboring town

1901

When the season ended on September 30, 1901, for Rube Waddell, the Pirates' pitcher was about to return home to Pennsylvania. A minor league pitcher who had returned home to Wisconsin, Addie Joss, had just completed his season with the Toledo Mud Hens (and had played some exhibitions already). As the *Milwaukee Journal Sentinel* online tells the story, "On three successive Sundays in early fall, Racine and Appleton [Wisconsin] played each other to supposedly determine a state champion." After losing game one, the city of Racine hired Joss to pitch the remaining games. When that tactic worked, their Kenosha opponents brought in Waddell to pitch the deciding game against Joss on October 20. This game was won by Racine, which "more than 5,000 fans attended, including 1,500 who traveled from Kenosha to Racine on a special train."

Both teams had hired superior talent. Joss, born in Woodland, Wisconsin, joined the Cleveland Bronchos in 1902 and won 17 games for them; Waddell went 24–7 for the Athletics. Both men have plaques in the Hall of Fame.

Then, typically, there were reports that turned out to be incomplete. While being told that the White Sox met the Red Sox in Boston on September 30, 1901, before 2,803, an article was headlined "White Sox Begin Junketing Trip." But nothing further about that proposed trip was reported. Likewise though the *Brooklyn Daily Eagle* wrote about a game on October 1,

1901, in which the Brooklyn National Leaguers played the Johnstown, Pennsylvania, club, beyond the mention of lineups little information was forthcoming. Tom Daly, "once king of the backstops," had signed up with Johnstown. Doc Newton and Wright piched for Brooklyn with Duke Farrell on first, Bill Dahlen on second, John Gochnaur at shortstop, Wille Keeler on third with the outfield being Joe Kelley, Cozy Dolan, and pitcher Bill Donovan for Brooklyn. Brooklyn was scheduled to play at Columbia, Pennsylvania, "the home of Jimmy Sheckard and a big reception is anticipated. It has not been decided whether the New Yorks and Brooklyns will play on Thursday, Friday and Saturday." Once again the names of some of the players are not known or even if they did play, or, for that matter where the other games might be played.

There was also a report that Bill Dahlen and Willie Keeler would go to Cuba, under Frank Leonard, former manager of Worchester.

No games are listed for the next year but *The Sporting News* of October 17, 1903, reported that an all-star team was wanted to play in Cuba beginning at the end of the Cuban National League season. The promise was that team would stay in Cuba for six weeks and play two games a week, the players to split about $300 per game.

At the end of the next season, *Sporting Life* on October 29, 1904, wrote that a Los Angeles team had signed Christy Mathewson, Honus Wagner, and Frank Chance to play in the California Winter League. *The Sporting News* on October 16, 1904, told of a post-season series "between the two tail-enders— Washington and Philadelphia Nationals." The paper also underscored the importance of these games by writing that the contests "would have established beyond the shadow of a doubt the superiority of one or the other league."

Postseason coverage of teams included a story of a benefit for the Giants at the Majestic Theater on October 8 before they left for game one of the second World Series in Philadelphia. While that celebration took place, seven of the Athletics, fresh from a doubleheader in Philadelphia, took part in a benefit game in Brooklyn's Washington Park the day before the World Series was about to begin. The game clearly demonstrates the mysterious aspect of some of thse postseason games. It may also show the fear that players felt in playing a forbidden game. The *Brooklyn Daily Eagle* reported on October 9, 1904:

> In addition to their recent pitching recruit, [Jimmy] Dygert and [Sam] Mertes, who played under the name of Gallagher, and [Eddie?] Grant, a South Brooklyn man, played a picked team under the auspices of St. John's Catholic Club of Brooklyn, and as a testimonial to Tom Daly, the old second baseman of the Brooklyn Club and last year's manager of the Providence team of the Eastern League, at Washington Park yesterday. No initiation fee was charged, but every person upon entering the park was reminded of the presence of a contribution

box. The attraction served to bring out a crowd of about 3,500 persons, and as only a few failed to contribute, a snug sum must have been realized for the veteran player. Of the picked team the best known were "Sammy" Strang of the New York Nationals, who played under the name of Green; Sheckard and Pitcher Mcintyre of the Brooklyns, and Tom Daly himself. Tom Burns officiated as umpire. Few of the players seemed to overexert themselves, particularly Waddell who was very careful about handling and throwing balls at right field. The Crosses and Harry Davis played well and so did Daly, while Dygert during the latter part of the game simply tossed the balls to batsmen.

A benefit game often meant for the benefit of the players, who picked up more money by the series' end on October 14 and though the A's were $382 each for the series, "the club owners donated their share of the gate, raising the players' checks to $832.22." But the very next day the Athletics lost on the road to the Paterson, New Jersey, team of the Hudson River League at Ryle Park. A crowd of 2,000 showed up, mostly to see Rube Waddell but he did not play. Eddie Plank and a Hudson River League player did the pitching for Mack. That same day the World Series champion Giants lost to the semiprofessional Ridgewoods 5–2.

They played the next day too, at Trenton, opposing the local YMCA team with Iron Man McGinnity and Boileryard Clarke the battery. They also were on the field there on October 21. Money to divide from these exhibition games added to their winning World Series shares of $1,142 each.

Earlier, the Tigers also arranged games in New Jersey at Newark, with rookie pitcher Eddie Cicotte and Tom Doran as the battery on October 1, 1905, a date which also saw Boston of the American League playing a team from Providence, Rhode Island.

But these games were on an off day during the season for both teams: the Tigers, for instance, were on their way from Boston to New York for game 148 on their schedule on that date, and Boston having an off day in between visits from Detroit and Cleveland. Both of these off day games were played on a Sunday and the influence of the Sabbatarians, the Blue Law people, was still strong.

Like Joss and Waddell before them, catcher Roger Bresnahan and pitcher Christy Mathewson planned to barnstorm through Ohio and Indiana "visiting Columbus, Akron, Canton, Dayton, Youngstown, Toledo, Cleveland, Cincinnati and other cities in Indiana, doing battery work for any clubs that may desire their services," according to *The Sporting News*. Two other future Hall of Fame players, Tris Speaker and Harry Hooper, plus Eddie Cicotte, were on the field in Portland, Maine, on October 5, 1906, against the All Maine team.

The New York Americans were busy after the 1907 season meeting the Philadelphia Athletics on October 7 for a hospital benefit game at Hartford, Connecticut. The *New York Times* mentioned that "after the teams had received their $1,000 guarantee, a nice balance was left for the Tuberculosis Hospital." The Athletics also visited Reading, Pennsylvania, on October 16. Three days prior to that, another New York team, the Giants, had visited that city where Christy Mathewson pitched a complete game shutout with 14 strikeouts.

Additionally, in Pennsylvania, before an all–Pirates intrasquad game on October 7, at least five contests were arranged at Exhibition Park: running out a fair bunt, throwing accuracy for catchers, circling the bases, throwing accuracy for outfielders, and circling the bases with slides at second and third.

Chicago presented postseason activity too. The day after their World Series victory, the Cubs met the crosstown White Sox before 3,500 fans in "a fast burlesque game." An accounting was featured in the *Chicago Daily Tribune* which told its readers that the Cubs players divided $45,000 in 19 full shares with $500 excepted, amounting to a check for $2,342.10 each, accumulated this way:

World Series player pool money of $32,960.04
Exhibition game of October 13, 1907 — $1,000
Exhibition games during the season — $2,000
Bonus by Cubs president Murphy — $8,639.96

Yet with that the players wanted more. And so on October 17, 1907, the Cubs — or at least Tinker, Evers and Kling — played against Jimmy Callahan's semipros at West Side Park attracting 3,000 inside and another 1,000 outside. A banquet followed. Their counterparts, the White Sox, met the Gunthers at their park, with Nick Altrock starting, relieved by Lou Fiene.

Mentioned too was that three major league teams — the Cubs, White Sox and Tigers — were going to play from October 19 through October 28 in the Chicago area.

All these contests drew the attention of *The Sporting News* on October 24, 1907, and of the ruling cartel. Independence was not a virtue to this American organization. "It is not likely that members of the Chicago National and American League teams, who ... took part in exhibitions with Chicago's independent organizations, harboring rebellious players, will escape punishment [for a] violation of Section 1, Article 26 of the National Agreement."

Sporting Life of October 26, 1907, took notice that on October 14 the three-member National Commission acted "relative to the *California State League*." The Pacific Coast League complained that the California State League was "operating outside of the National Agreement in employing Reserved and Contracted players of National Agreement clubs, and occupying prohibited territory.... The California State League is therefore declared to be an Outlaw Organization." If the players on those teams don't "signify their intention" of returning to the team which has "title to them, and upon failure to do so, they shall be declared forever ineligible, to participate in any games with National Agreement Clubs." In addition, National Agreement Clubs were forbidden to play against any team in the California State League. If a National Agreement player took part in a game with one of the outlawed teams, the first punishment meted out was a fine of $100, the second penalty being suspension.

But there were, apparently, at least two groups that did exist with the permission of the National Commission, one being the California Winter League, organized around the fact that "It is probable that more than 50 professionals from the Coast and the east will winter in and about Los Angeles" (*Los Angeles Times*, August 4, 1907). In fact, *The Glory of Their Times* tells us that Walter Johnson pitched for Santa Ana in the league in 1907 on Sundays. And "in a time when major league pay was in the range of $135–$175 per month, the California Winter League paid $50 a month plus expenses (Burk, 33). If the games were scheduled only on weekends—meaning that players could work most weekday jobs around Los Angeles—then the pay and the scheduling made the league even more attractive.

Another winter league — the East Coast Winter League in Florida — was made up of hotel teams at Ormond, Miami, and Palm Beach. "Whether Ty Cobb and Matty McIntyre will play in it is unknown" but an article dated October 10 called the organization an "outlaw league" (*Sporting Life*).

Talk of the California Winter League continued in 1908. In a letter to *Sporting Life*, Ed Crolie from Santa Ana, California, wrote that "we have just formed the California Winter League.... There will be scheduled about 28 games to be played from October 11 to March 15; most all will be played on Sundays and holidays."

Those not in the winter leagues had changed their lives in the 200 days of the off-season, according to *The Sporting News* of October 29:

> In times of old, when professional base ball was largely a joy jaunt and the players dissipated freely, ball players used to spend their winters behind bars.... Of late years however ... if he works during the winter at all, enters some of the more aesthetic walks of life. If he is married, he invests his proceeds in some profitable little business and leaves it in the charge of a brother to manage during his absence in the summer.

Meanwhile the cartel hung on to its authority. The National Commission tried very hard, through heavier fines of $200, to prevent eligible players from competing with or against ineligible players during the off-season. And the *Philadelphia Evening Bulletin* of October 20, 1908, reported that almost all of of Joe Cantillon's Washington players were suspended by the National League Commission because they had

> defied the mandates of base ball law and order by playing an exhibition game with the Logan Squares, Jimmy Callahan's Chicago "independent outlaws."...

Every player is blacklisted for the present. Washington is warned to consider no 1909 contracts with the offenders.

Players on the Milwaukee and Minneapolis teams of the American Association "who sinned in playing other Chicago outlaw clubs, have drawn the ban" as well. "The action taken ... was based on a clause prohibiting any National Agreement player from at any time participating in games with clubs harboring ineligible players ... rule 47." Players included Walter Johnson.

1909

Perhaps because of the stridency of the cartel, there were fewer exhibition games in 1909. True, winter ball was of great interest in New Orleans, and true, "Big Chief Bender of the Athletics let the Cubs down with two hits, Philadelphia winning by the score of 2 to 0," *Sporting Life* stated on November 6. *Sporting Life* on November 13 detailed a game that pitcher Jim Scott of the White Sox pitched for the Douglas, Arizona, team at the El Paso Fair tournament and the team won $1,000. Up north, the Boston Americans played in Portland, Maine, on October 5 before 5,000 against the All-Maine team.

On October 6, 1909, in New York City a game was arranged for the benefit of Sam Crane between the Highlanders and Tigers. Crane was accounted as "dean of the baseball writers and former National League star." The contest raised over $7,000, partly by an auction. A ball autographed by Christy Mathewson went for $275. Mathewson and Joe McGinnity were the opposing pitchers, with Willie Keeler, Hughie Jennings, and Hal Chase in the field.

CHAPTER TWO

Barnstorming Tours and Exhibition Games, 1910–1919

THE SECOND DECADE OF BARNSTORMING was marked by a decline in the effectiveness of the National Commission, with more authority being grabbed by the individual owners. These owners were to share in approved tours in the decade, plus in the receipts of City Series games and the World Series.

The Pirates continued to tour as did the Reds and others joined in too in the 1910–1919 period. The last mega-tour was completed after the 1915 season. With the Giants and Athletics controlling the first half of the decade, the Red Sox and White Sox were the powers in the second half. But exhibition games, including the first by Babe Ruth of those powerful Red Sox teams, were becoming more and more prevalent. The star-laden team that faced the Athletics in some warm-up games for the World Series in both 1910 and 1911 demonstrated the clout that such a team might have.

The postseason play during this second decade was shortened after 1916, by fiat of the National Commission. The dual effects of World War I and the Spanish Influenza epidemic took their toll as well.

Barnstorming Tours

1910

Games beyond the cartel's control were becoming increasingly troublesome. What to do? Since organized baseball was a loose confederation of independent owners, regulation of the barnstorming problem would have to come from the magnates.

In January 1910, the first action taken by the clubs through the National Commission was to try to extend the player contract for a full year, rather than from the 165 days of opening day to closing day. At the same time, the owners saw to it that no ballparks, under the control of the National Agreement, would be leased to barnstormers.

There were those who agreed with the commission. The *New York Times* on January 19, 1910, took the point of view that

> "It doesn't look good for a professional baseball player to be beaten by an amateur or semi-professional. It discredits the league players, and if they are defeated causes remarks to be made about their inability to beat a town nine." This is the way President Johnson answered the criticisms recently made about the barnstorming clause in the new baseball contract. "Now an owner is not going to stop the players from earning a little extra money in a legitimate way after the season is over, but the owner has a right to protect the good name of his club," he continued. "Barnstorming doesn't help baseball."

These battles for control over games would continue. In March, the commission ruled that only World Series contestants would be "awarded pennants and emblems by the National Baseball Commission" the *New York Times* noted. This was a relatively meaningless way for the commission to extend its authority, by ruling out the authority of awards, for example, to the champions of the various city and state series sanctioned by the commission. More meaningful, though, because it concerned "the division of receipts," was the decision that money made from city series games must now "be made up on the same basis as the World Series, instead of allowing the interested clubs to divide the money as they see fit."

After all, the National Commission in 1909 was able to insist sometimes that it got its 10 percent, the team owners made their 38 percent, leaving the players with 52 percent of the receipts. Now sometimes would have to be all of the time.

Insist they might try to do but yet the independence of the owners (Harold Seymour labels it "pressure from dissident owners") frequently went contrary to the desires of the commission. The commission would not survive the decade.

Nevertheless, Frank Bancroft went on the road in 1910 and as *Sporting Life* noted, as soon as the Ohio state series (Cleveland against the Reds) was over, the Cincinnati schedule of barnstorming games would extend from October 19 with a game in Athens, Ohio, to October 31, with the last of the 12 games scheduled in Madison, Indiana, population 7,000. The Cincinnati paper did not report on these games, as happened so often, since the reporter might have to travel to do so and travel costs money.

Or one reason for the lack of coverage by the home town paper may have had something to do with the game as described by the Trenton, New Jersey, *True American*, a game played on October 5 in Trenton against the Dicksmiths. "It did not look as if the big leaguers were extending themselves at all times," the paper wrote. Still, the big leaguers won 2–1.

One of the pleasures of barnstorming for the players was the lack of pressure in these games since nothing was really at stake. Whatever money they would earn from this game would have been collected at the gate, watched over by someone from the team. So Eddie Plank and Chief Bender, who pitched this game, could know from the outset that it was truly unlikely that anyone on a team called the Dicksmiths could hit them to much purpose.

Scant coverage also included the Cubs. The *New York Times* of October 24 merely said that Thomas Needham and eleven other Cubs will barnstorm "with the permission of manager F. L. Chance."

Though there were games in New York City in the postseason of 1910, the teams either were contestants in a few games, or it is simply impossible to say who was on what team. There seemed to be a team made up of New York Giants, or not; or Boston Red Sox, or not. There were teams called all-stars, all-leaguers, an all-star aggregation, and John J. McGrath's all-stars. A reliable source did have a team mostly from the Red Sox and Senators in New York at the time.

Lastly for the year was some brief mention of a barnstorming event in a baseball book, this one the extensive *Cultural Encyclopedia of Baseball*, which gave one column to the subject. Light wrote,

> In 1910, promoter Daniel A. Fletcher offered $500–$1000 to Major League players to appear in postseason exhibition games. The National Commission objected on the ground that it diminished the glamour and importance of the World Series. It probably did neither, but the governing National Commission was looking for ways to control the activity and collect the revenue.

Control would have been achieved if the National Commission had gone through with its threat: those who signed with Fletcher would not be permitted to play in the World Series that year.

Reporting on the tour, the *Philadelphia Evening Bulletin* of October 11, 1910, said that 42 NL and AL players "voted yesterday to play in the postseason series arranged by D. A. Fletcher. Ten games will be played. This is in open defy [*sic*] of the National Commission." *Sporting Life* on October 11, 1910, continued: "According to reports from Detroit, Johnson, Street Milan and Gray have signed contracts to play in the all-star tour promoted by D. A. Fletcher of Cincinnati. President Noyes will not give his consent to the trip and if the mentioned players make it they will be subject to fines" (11).

Not only that, but as Seymour relates, "All ballparks in organized baseball were closed to Fletcher's troupe, and those ballplayers that had succumbed to Fletcher's blandishment were persuaded to return his checks."

The *Chicago Daily Tribune* on October 25, 1910, wrote that the series was off. *Sporting Life*, on October 29, 1910, published a letter from A. G. Spalding about Fletcher's scheme:

> I have read something in the California papers about some western promoter who tried to organize some sort of barnstorming tour after the close of the season with a collection of National and American League players, but the National Commission had very properly ruled against such an undertaking. Such tours invariably result in financial loss to the promoters, are demoralizing to the players and tend to disgust the base ball public with the game.

In fact, the *Chicago Daily Tribune* that same day wrote that "the Commission held a lengthy session in which it placed a ban on the contemplated series [of Fletcher's].... No specific reasons for the ban were given except that it would interfere greatly with the World Series."

The *New York Times* of September 2, 1910, saw that "The outlook for a series of games [between the Yankees and the Giants] now looks favorable and more so since the decision of the National Commission in tabooing of the barnstorming trip of the all-star teams of the two leagues." This ban led to the first New York City series since 1886.

Major tours covered that year also included the Pittsburgh Pirates, who traveled from October 12 through 21, as spokesman Tommy Leach informed *Sporting Life*. It was that paper that had the most to say about what it sometimes called "The Pumpkin League" on October 22, 1910: "The Pittsburgh Pirates spent the past week barnstorming in West Virginia with profitable results." On October 29, 1910, *Sporting Life* had a longer piece:

> The barnstorming jaunt indulged in by nine of the boys was a veritable joy ride. It was the best and most profitable trip ever taken by the Pittsburgh band. No wonder John B. Miller was sore he didn't go along. The boys just burned up the towns they visited. After one week's tripping, the boys reached old Pittsburgh for an overnight stop. Walter Smith, boss, canvasman, ticket taker, treasurer, et al., chased to the newspaper offices to hand over the itinerary for the next week. "Great trip, great time," remarked Walter, his face wreathed in smiles. "Over $1,700 clear in five games, with a bunch of dandy dates ahead. That's going some." Then Smith told of the demand to see the Pirates. After they had played before one burg to a handsome gate, the management of the home nine came along with a proposition to return for five games at a guaranteed $1,500. Smith assured the writer that the Pittsburgh men who had the temerity to risk a whirl around the Tri-State towns would split up a neat piece of money.
> One year the boys got a divy of $104 each. This sum is going to be beaten to a frazzle for 1910. The Pirates visited towns where they had not been seen for two and three seasons, last Fall no barnstorming tour being undertaken. Their schedule was well-arranged; no long jumps, no sleepers, no big hotel bills. The boys started out to make Christmas coin. They certainly succeeded.

Finally, for the November 5 issue: "The Pirate barnstormers stayed out two weeks, quitting Friday, October 21. Football was too strong to buck against on Saturday."

But there was no football in Cuba and three teams went to that island for baseball in the sun: the Tigers, plus the opponents in the 1910 World Series, the Cubs and the Athletics.

> Back in 1910, the Athletics, after winning the World Series with the Chicago Cubs, went on a barnstorming trip to Havana, Cuba. They had forgot the rules of discipline, had a good, old-fashioned junket, and were badly beaten on numerous occasions. To the dismay of Connie Mack and other American League men, the Cubans proclaimed themselves "champions of the world whereupon the magnates passed the "barnstorming rule [on January 5, 1911] which has been in effect ever since [*Washington Post*, November 2, 1921].

Numbered 691 and dated January 7, 1911, the decision of the National Commission stated that the "victorious team [was required to disband immediately after the World] Series has been completed." This decision was codified in 1912 as rule 9, forbidding any of the winners from participating "as individuals or a team in exhibition games during the year in which such World Series was decided."

Harold Seymour thinks that Ban Johnson's reaction is a lot stronger than the "dismay" of Connie Mack:

> We want no makeshift Club calling themselves the Athletics to go to Cuba to be beaten by colored teams." Johnson doubtless sensed that ... if dark-skinned Cuban clubs, many of them sprinkled with players from American Negro teams, could beat the vaunted white major-leaguers ... people might have second thoughts about Organized Baseball's segregation policy.... Was it not enough that Jack Johnson was the heavyweight boxing champion of the world?" [Seymour *Early Years*, 191]

1911

In 1911, the average player salary was $2,400, worth about $47,000 today.

The effect of the Cuban trip of 1910 by the Athletics turned out to be a longer explanation of the prohibitions put into place by the National Commission:

> The question of Major League clubs playing exhibition games either before or after the commencement of the playing season will be left in the hands of the various Major League Club owners ... provided, however, that the teams securing permission to play exhibition games ... shall be required to be represented in such games by the actual members of the respective teams ... in order that there be no imposition upon the public who may witness games of this character.

This rule waited ten years to be powerfully invoked, and it cost Babe Ruth, who was about to turn sixteen in Baltimore.

This rule was supposed to cover only the winning World Series team. But the commission did not again ignore Sunday games that it felt were outside of the player's contract:

Decision #797 of the National Commission:

Player Cobb of the Detroit Club participated in an exhibition game at Lenox Oval, New York City, on Sunday, September 17 as a member of the All Star Team.... Players will not be permitted to violate with impunity regulations for the protection of territorial rights of clubs and a fine of $100 is imposed on Player Cobb.

Cobb paid. On October 5, 1911, the National Commission sold motion picture rights to the World Series for $3,500. When the players demanded a share of the money, the commission canceled the deal.

Having gone out on the road so often, the 1911 Reds were now being labeled Banny's Barnstormers. There were not many stars on the sixth place National League team but some had done well that year: Bob Bescher led the league with 70 steals and was fifth in runs; Doc Hoblitzel finished third in hits; Mike Mitchell led his league in triples with 18 and was second in RBI.

After games in small towns in Ohio and West Virginia (the village of Athens having 575 residents and the city of Charleston, West Virginia, being the exceptions) a game in Ironton, Ohio, on October 29 received some attention. The 1,500 paid that day saw St. Louis Cardinals player Joe Willis pitching for the home team. As was not unusual for the time, Ironton was picked for personal reasons, because Mrs. Bancroft's relatives lived in that small town, and this game was a way for her to visit.

In its November 11 issue, *Sporting Life* wrote that "Frank Bancroft and the Red Wanderers are back from their swing around the Pumpkin Circuit" and after the last game of twelve, all wins, "the players added over $200 apiece to their season's salary by these games." They also divided about $1,680 (about $100 each) from the Ohio series, a 60 percent cut for winning. That $300 may have been sufficient to carry some players through the rest of the 200 days of the off-season.

1912

It does seem like the tighter the National Commission wished to exercise control, the more players tried to barnstorm. The barnstormers had to go off on their own, since the latest attempt at unionization, the Fraternity of Professional Baseball Players of America, did not appear to have much authority.

The Reds barnstormers were out on the road once again and now the papers had new names for barnstorming. After some games in Indiana, the sports weekly *Sporting Life* (October 26, 1912) focused again on

Frank Bancroft [who] has taken the Redbirds under his care and they are uncaged in the Sunflower Circuit. The barnstormers will keep on the go as long as they find dates waiting and no frost. They will be back in Cincinnati just before Halloween.

Two weeks later, *Sporting Life* was calling the barnstorming games the "Whippoorwill Circuit" when the Reds traveled not only in West Virginia, but moved into Virginia as well at Gloucester, Racine, Caldwell, and Mariette, where they drew 1,600 fans, and in Portsmouth, where only 117 paid. At that point it was being reported that players made $210.40 "over and above all expenses." Later in *Sporting Life*, on November 9, 1912, it was reported that in 14 games, the Reds made $275 each.

Out on the road too, said *Sporting Life*, were the Athletics, who split up their squad. The Connie Macks played at Shenandoah, Pennsylvania, while brother Earle Mack's team stopped in Renovo, Pennsylvania, where Rube Bressler was discovered. Bressler at the time was employed by the Pennsylvania Railroad at its shop at Renovo (population 4,700) when Earle Mack's team came through. He pitched so well that day that he was sent to the ball club in Harrisburg, Pennsylvania, for 1913 and graduated to the Athletics in 1914, as *The Glory of Their Times* relates. Bressler's career, starting from that barnstorming game in 1912, lasted in the big leagues until 1932. Earle Mack's career as the leader of a barnstorming team would go on for a quarter century.

Howard, called Heimie, Camnitz, briefly a Pirates player in 1911 but now out of the big leagues, along with assistant Pirates team secretary Walter Smith, handled the Pittsburgh team that visited Kentucky, Ohio, West Virginia, and Pennsylvania. Camnitz, educated at Centre College in Danville, Kentucky, was able to convince Concordia College graduate (and future Hall of Fame outfielder) Max Carey to go on the trip but not Hans Wagner and catcher George Gibson. With the exception of those two, the barnstormers were the first string players. Leaving the night the season ended, they boarded a train for a six-hour ride to Lexington, Kentucky, home of the minor league Colts of the Blue Grass League.

At the end of the first week, road secretary Smith had to return to Pittsburgh to see what would be arranged for the rest of the tour, while it seemed that W. H. Locke (who was near to being named president of the Phillies) was in charge of writing to the nearby newspapers. Four games of note were contested throughout the junket and in those towns the fans had a yardstick to compare ticket prices, for they knew that in the Giants and Red Sox World Series, a bleacher seat could be bought for $1. In Clarksburg, West Virginia, in addition to many minor leaguers, the home team had enlisted the play of Bull Smith, former Pirate; Guy Zinn of the Yankees; and Del Gainer of the Tigers. But the Pirates still won 8–2. Just west of Clarksburg is Ironton, Ohio, and there on Thursday, October 10, the Pirates met a local team of minor league players, two from the American Association, with all admissions to Beechwood Park set at 50¢. When Max Carey banged out three hits and the opposing pitcher walked five, the major leaguers eased to a 6–3 win.

Next to be visited, on October 18, 1912, was Scottdale, a small town in southwestern Pennsylvania where 1,800 paid to see the Pirates win by 7–0. That night the team was the guest of the local lodge of the B. P. O. Elks. The final game took place on October 20, 1912, in Steubenville, Ohio, a city which had had a team in the Ohio-Pennsylvania League. The *Sporting Life* of October 19, 1912, wrote a summary of the tour:

> The Corsairs coin tour is a record Breaker ... Cammy as spokesman for the boys, called on Colonel Dreyfuss and asked the necessary permission, the team still being under contract. Dreyfuss sanctioned the move.... Next day at Chicago Secretary Locke got busy. Dates were sought by wire and mail. Inside of four hours the nucleus of a handsome trip was arranged, with not only rain but game guarantees in every burg except the first played.... Manger Camnitz is watching the business end. Superintendent of Forbes Field Walter Smith is the custodian of the gates. Smith has spent a lifetime in this line. No one will ring up phonies on him. Starting this week the second-place holders will play ball within a radius of 50 miles of the Steel City.

When the traveling ended, Walter Smith handed out the checks in room 904 of the Farmers Bank Building.

There were shortened reports on the White Sox going out on the road under trainer Semmens and games had been arranged at Dixon, Illinois, and at South Bend and Whiting, Indiana. The Cardinals, under Stub Hauser, the team's shortstop, planned to barnstorm. The Cubs apparently went out as well.

In 1912, as Charles C. Alexander tells it in his biography of Rogers Hornsby, a Bloomer Girls team promoter did not have enough players for a game in Dallas, Texas, and so he

> advertised in local newspapers for two players under the age of eighteen–sex unspecified ... Hornsby and a friend caught the interurban electric train over to Dallas ... only to learn that they were expected to wear wigs and bloomers and pretend to be female. Apparently any chance to play ball and make a little extra money was worth taking so the two lads acted their parts as Bloomer girls while the team met its Dallas dates, then appeared in towns along the rail line north. When the team reached the Red River, their collected their pay — seventy-eight cents apiece after expenses — and headed home [15].

1913

The country was changing. For example, 1913 was the first year that the country registered one million motor vehicles.

In the minors Edd Roush was paid $120 per month in 1913 ($2,300 now) in the Western League, as Roush related in *The Glory of Their Times*.

The postseason games that were given the most national press were those of the world tour which prepared to begin in mid–October with players taken mostly from the Giants and White Sox. At the same time, the Brooklyn Superbas barnstorming team with Casey Stengel, as *Sporting Life* of October 4, 1913, reported, were not going to have on this year's roster the two great stars Zach Wheat and Nap Rucker, as well as most of the pitchers. The *New York Times* reported on September 28, 1913, that the team "will make an exhibition tour of Pennsylvania and the South and will then proceed for Cuba ... in an announcement made to-night by president Charles H. Ebbets of the Brooklyn Club."

One of their earliest games was a short ride away, at the Bushwicks' home field, Dexter Park, on the border of Brooklyn and Queens in New York City on October 19, 1913.

> To end the season at Dexter Park, Brooklyn played Max Rosner's Cypress Hills team. The major league players drawing attention were first baseman Gentleman Jake Daubert, 1913 winner of the Most Valuable player award and recipient for the award of a new Chalmers motor car; manning second base was George Cutshaw. At shorstop, was Tom Fisher and Catcher Otto Miller pinch hit during the game and both Pat Ragan (15–18) and Earl Yingling (8–8) pitched [Barthel, *Those Peerless Semipros*].

Shortly thereafter the Brooklyns headed south, stopping on October 21, at Charlottesville, Virginia, to meet Joe Jackson's All-Stars and then stopping again at Jackson's hometown of Greenville, South Carolina, the next day.

On October 15, 1913, Earle Mack's team decided to face the Black Lincoln Giants, the fine pitcher being Joe Williams. Some talk was heard of the Pirates going out on the road again after their intercity series. There was some truth too apparently that the Cubs stayed out until October 21.

In yet more New York City games, *Sporting Life* reported on November 8, 1913, that after Chief Bender pitched for a semipro team in Brooklyn, and when his teammates, the $100,000 infield of McInnis, Baker, Collins and Barry signed on with a semipro team in the Bronx, New York, the National Commission reacted by saying

> that it detracts from the dignity of the game to have such great players mingling on the sandlot with any pick-up team willing to give them a little money.... The commission takes the stand that when a World's Series star plays with a makeshift team on a lot where an admission of only 15 or 25 cents is charged, he cheapens himself and the National game.

The *New York Times* added that "the Commission believes that a player should not lose all his dignity for a few extra dollars" and that "the club owners [ought] to prohibit their players from mixing in with the semipros."

But for those teams that provided the National Commission with a part of the receipts, there remained highly approved games, highly dignified games. The Elfers book, *The Tour to End All Tours*, deals in detail with a four month trip which included games both in the States and overseas. A few stops on the tour in the States can be revealing. It was a journey with Christy Mathewson, Tris Speaker, Sam Crawford, Jim Thorpe, Germany Schaefer, and John McGraw among other stellar lights of the game,

> while accompanying the ball players were a number of personal friends who were taking advantage of the opportunity to make the tour and Harry P. Burchell of the *New York Times*, Gus Axelson of the Chicago *Record-Herald*, and other newspaper writers.
> The world tourists left Chicago on a special train of five steel cars. This consisted of three sleepers, an observation car, and combination baggage and buffet car. This train was to be their home until they sailed for Japan from Vancouver.... The umpires selected to go with the players were William J. Klem for the National League and John J. Sheridan for the American. They "wore uniforms decorated with gold braid and the American emblems" [Elfers, 43].

Games in Cincinnati and Chicago drew a total of over 10,000 fans and in Springfield, Illinois, on October 20, the tourists played at the local Three I League park. Though snow fell until 1:30, the skies cleared and the game went on. Before 500 fans the Giants came out on top by 6–4. After the game the players were guests at a local theater, and left for Peoria at 11:30. There, 2,000 fans sat in a wintry wind to see the 6–4 victory by the Americans. The fans in the bleachers ripped boards from the wooden structure and built small fires to keep warm.

For the stop in Ottumwa, Iowa, the two teams arrived at 5 a.m. on the Rock Island special for the game at the Myrtle Street grounds in South Ottumwa. While the players rested in their railroad cars until game time, local officials of the city of 22,000, once notified that veteran umpires Jack Sheridan and Bill Klem would work the game, wanted everyone to know that anyone "who attends the game can feel assured that here will be no rowdyism either by the players or boisterous fans as these two officials will not stand for anything like that." Those fans who had come north by train and connecting interurban (and were ready to pay the $1 admission) were guaranteed by the *Ottumwa Daily Courier* that their Milwaukee Railroad southbound train would be held for an extra half hour.

It was the Chicago team that seemed to be the local favorite that day. They were given a warm welcome as they rode through the streets in carriages.

The game began with umpire Klem announcing the lineups to the 1,400 attendees who sat in cool weather for the 100-minute game. After the game, a disappointed *Daily Courier's* narrative which began with the description "a poor exhibition of the great national game," continued with a story that stressed the nine errors made by both outfits. The local writer took note, too, of the continuing absence of Tris Speaker and of the appearance of Christy Mathewson, only coaching at first. At game's end the players were invited to be guests at the Grand Theater to watch the movie *Officer 666.*

With the temperature at 70 degrees, the game in Sioux City on October 24 drew a much bigger crowd — 5,000 — who watched a game with but one error in the 6–3 win for the Giants. Featuring three doubles by Doyle and two by Merkle, the double plays turned by the Giants combined to overcome the home run by Sam Crawford.

On October 28, 1913, the *Tulsa World* said on its front page that, "The two teams played yesterday in Joplin, Missouri. They left on their elegantly appointed special train last night and will arrive in Tulsa before daylight this morning." The teams stayed at the Hotel Tulsa, filled with guests who were attending the International Dry-Farming Congress, featuring the International Soil Product Exposition, during that time. The players then dressed for the game at South Main Street Park and paraded to the ballpark accompanied by the Fifth Regiment Artillery Band. The paper noted that "Adequate street car service will be provided by the Tulsa Street Railway Company" or fans could walk since "there is pavement all the way" from the center of the city. Children had been released from school and it was said that "six special trainloads" were heading for Tulsa to see that 2 o'clock game.

The headline the next day, however, screamed, "ONE KILLED, 52 INJURED" with 700 people buried in the wreckage of a span of thirty feet of bleacher which collapsed. Nevertheless, with 4,780 in attendance at the time, most fans stayed in the stands to watch the game start, 45 minutes after it was due to begin. The *Tulsa World* said:

> Sorrowed by the terrible accident that preceded the game, and chilled by a north wind that threatened to break into snow at any minute, the crowd still greeted each new player as he came to bat, his appearance announced by umpire Klem. Walter Johnson ... came down to Tulsa from his home in Coffeyville, Kansas, and offered his services gratis to the Chicago White Sox just to get a chance to pitch against the master twirler of the National League, Christy Mathewson.

Buck Weaver had five hits and both Sam Crawford and Tris Speaker made three each. The Nationals could produce only "eight nicely scattered hits" against Johnson and so the White Sox team won 6–0.

For the October 29 stop, the *Muskogee Phoenix* reported that Sam Crawford drove a ball 492 feet, a grand slam that drove in Weaver, Morrie Rath and Speaker, and the place where the ball stopped was measured from home plate by the superintendent of the grounds at the new fairground park in Muskogee. (The claim was that Ed Walsh on September 30, 1911, hit a home run 419 feet.) Walter Johnson appeared as the first base coach. Speaker had two of the nine hits for his team and Magee, playing left field, had two of his team's six hits in its 7–1 loss in 1:45.

Today! Today!

South Main Street Base Ball Park

New York Giants

vs.

Chicago White Sox

Christy Matthewson

vs.

Walter Johnson

Game starts promptly at 2:00 o'clock—Gates open at 12:30 p. m.

United States Infantry, artillery band, Gov. Cruce and others will attend the game.

A promotion for a game in Tulsa, Oklahoma, part of the world tour of the Giants and White Sox in 1913. (National Baseball Hall of Fame Library, Cooperstown, N.Y.)

Hans Lobert from *The Glory of Their Times*:

When we were almost finished with the American part of the tour we played a game in Oxnard, California.... It was one of the most bizarre incidents I ever took part in. The mayor of the town ... asked me if I would race a horse around the bases that afternoon.

"Lord," I said, "I'm not here to run horses around the bases. I'm here to play baseball." But he wouldn't take no for an answer, and McGraw finally talked me into agreeing to it. See, I was very fast in those days.

The idea was that first we'd play the game, and then after the game I'd race the horse.... The cowboys kept creeping in closer and closer, till we hardly had any room left to play. So along about the seventh inning McGraw came to me and said, "John, we can't finish this game. You might as well get ready to run the horse around the bases."

Then, from this mass of cowboys encircling the outfield, out steps the most beautiful black animal you ever saw....

Finally, everything was all set.... A pistol started us, and off we went. I led at first base by at least five feet, and by second base I had picked up and was at least ten feet ahead. I was in perfect stride, hitting each bag with my right foot and going faster all the time. But ... the horse ... crowded me between second and third and I had to dodge to avoid being knocked down. I broke stride, and that was the end. I still think I would have won if I hadn't been practically bowled over at shortstop [Ritter, 195–196].

Ending the American part of the trip in Tacoma and Seattle on November 19, "the American tour gave a total of $97,240 for the thirty-one games played or an average of more than $3,000 per game," which The *New York Times* recorded the next day. Frank McGlynn in *Baseball Magazine* wrote, "Each player on leaving America received a check for $550, being his deposit of $300 as a guarantee of good faith, and a present of an additional $250 with the compliments of Messrs. Comiskey and McGraw." Eleven men chose not to got overseas, yet sailing from Vancouver were sixty-seven persons.

The tour ended in England on February 26, 1914.

1914

In an attempt to get a share of the money being made in major league baseball, the new Federal League organized on March 8 and opened May 6, the teams playing 154 games each. Edd Roush said he jumped to the Federal League to raise his salary to $225 per month, or about $1,200 per season ($22,000 now); Walter Johnson was offered $20,000. Intended to be the third major league, these eight new teams were able to attract eighty-one former and current major league players and one-hundred forty former and current minor league players.

The Pirates, apparently with permission from owner Barney Dreyfuss, hit the road again in 1914, without Fred Clarke and Honus Wagner, but pitcher Babe Adams and the great outfielder Max Carey did choose to go. Wagner was paid close to $20,000 that year ($366,773.33 in purchasing power today) and could easily afford to forgo any more travel for the 200 days.

Departing after their last championship season games against the Reds, by Tuesday, October 6, 1914, the Pirates were ready to play their first contest in Huntington, West Virginia.

Sporting Life of October 10, 1914, communicated news from the business manger of the trip:

> October 2, A Pleasing Trip. Here are the Pirates gallivanting over the Tri-State zone.... They have been going handsomely, scooping in loose change ... Sam McWatters [not a player], boss canvasman [supervisor of tickets?], writing headquarters, says that the initial game in Pomeroy, OH, drew 2,100 people ... each man is liable to get $300.

A pleasing trip indeed, no more so than the game in Sistersville, where the Chamber of Commerce threw them an after-game reception and dance and where four Pirates sang together. At Huntington, West Virginia, on the sixteenth, the game had to be halted for five minutes so the players could all chase a rabbit. Al Mamaux pitched and Coleman caught. Huntington had Jack Scheneberg, who had pitched six innings for the Pirates at the end of the 1913 season. The tour ended on October 18, 1914, at Youngstown where the last game was rained out. Carey had left the day before to join another barnstorming club.

"Though the tour struck bad weather," *Sporting Life* reported on November 7, 1914 "they lived in the best hotels ... McWatters dug up a trolley jump, saving four hours in time and $18 in cold cash."

An earlier *Sporting Life* spoke of the Reds of Cincinnati, who had a chance at the pennant but finished 34 games below .500. The season had started brightly enough with "Cincinnati business men, who promised a gift of $50,000 to the Reds in case they won the pennant." But no extra money would come to them during the regular season so veteran pitcher Red Ames acted "as playing manager of the Red Barnstormers on their annual trip this Fall, with Charlie Starr as business manager."

These two men led the Reds' team through just two states—Ohio and West Virginia—because there was another big tour, with the American League led by Connie Mack and the National League by Frank Bancroft. In the cards for them this year was Hawaii, the first visit by organized baseball in twenty years. Starring Max Carey, Grover Cleveland Alexander, Fred Snodgrass, and Big Ed Walsh, the team's players put up $200 in good faith money for the journey that began on October 17, leaving from Chicago.

One of the interesting stops along the way to the Pacific Coast was on October 26, 1914, in Potlatch, Idaho. The town fathers of Potlatch, with a population 2,100, understood that large out-of-town crowds might attend the game and so special train fares and schedules were arranged from Moscow, Idaho, as well as planning "to have the big Potlatch mills in operation Monday morning so that visitors may have a chance to observe the mill in operation." But, the *Moscow Daily Star-Mirror* wrote, "the big plant will close down during the afternoon to permit the employees to witness the game."

"The all-stars' manager," we can read in the book *Company Town*, "wary of playing in such a small community, required a $1,000 guarantee with an option of taking 80 percent of gate receipts, whichever he felt would bring him the greatest revenue." But early in the morning of the game, once the private railroads cars of the team pulled into Potlatch from Spokane, "the streets were nearly vacant since the lumber mill was closed for the game. Seeing no likely mass of fans, the business manager announced he would be accepting the $1,000, an eventual loss in revenue to the team of almost $1,400." That money however was put to good use in town "for the profits purchased a electric player piano that was used regularly at community dances." (Petersen, 130)

On November 23 the two league teams sailed from San Francisco on the steamship *Manona* and arrived in Honolulu on December 1. They all departed Hawaii on the return trip on December 15 and played more games in California from December 23–27, disbanding at San Diego after 44 games across the states and in Hawaii. According to *The Sporting News* on January 7, 1915, the players got back their $200 in good faith money plus "$1,321.95 of the profits plus expenses." They also received a paid vacation in warm weather and a sea cruise. The National League team won 29 of 50 games completed.

On November 5, 1914, *The Sporting News* took notice of the "Many players now on the Coast. California was getting to be a great winter resort for the majors" players including Chief Meyers, Fred Snodgrass, Gavy Cravath, and Irish Meusel.

1915

Once again, Wagner chose not to travel in the postseason. The fun was still there for the troupers and when they once more played in Sistersville, where the Chamber of Commerce gave them a reception and dance, again four Pirates teammates sang together. At East Liverpool, Ohio, on Sunday, October 17, 500 fans paid their way in and another 2,000 watched from the outside. Since the players made almost $20 each, the outsiders didn't matter.

Scheduled for the Reds on October 16, 1915, was Dayton on Cash Register Day. As reported by the *Cincinnati Enquirer*, there was good news and bad news.

> During two innings the Reds played real ball game this afternoon against the N. C. R. team at the Country Club diamond. During the remainder of the time they merely saw to it that the local players did not score.... The game at Springfield tomorrow has been called off, owing to a dispute between Springfield management and the Barnstormers.

The dispute was probably over a guarantee.

And then when the Reds took the field at Versailles: "Unser Fritz Mollwitz [German-born first baseman] had his collar bone broken in a run to

PAMPRED BALL PLAYERS OBJECT TO CURB ON BARNSTORMING EXHIBITIONS
I E SANBORN
Chicago Daily Tribune (1872-1963); Nov 14, 1915; ProQuest Historical Newspapers Chicago Tribune (1890 - 1958)
pg. B3

PAMPERED BALL PLAYERS OBJECT TO CURB ON BARNSTORMING EXHIBITIONS

Experienced Performers Know Playing Ball Out of Season is Penny Wise and Pound Foolish Policy.

BY I. E. SANBORN.

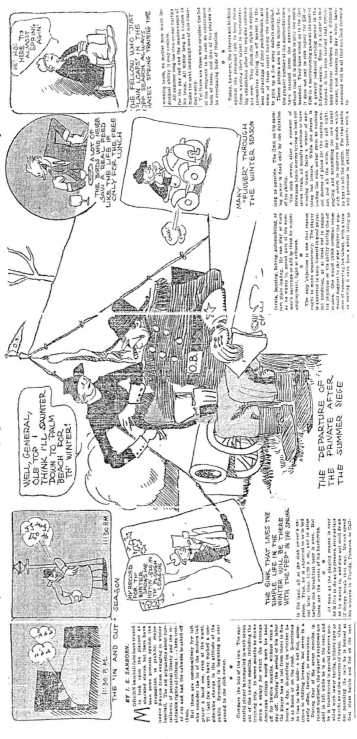

THE "IN AND OUT" SEASON

WELL, GENERAL, OLE TOP! THINK I'LL SAUNTER DOWN TO PALM BEACH FOR TH' WINTER!

MY RECORD FOR TH' WINTER SHOWS ME HITTIN' 310 IN TH' PLOUGH LEAGUE!

THE GINK THAT LIVES THE SIMPLE LIFE IN THE WINTER WILL BE THERE WITH THE "PEP" IN THE SPRING

A LOT OF THE BIRDS WHO NEVER SAW A REAL RED LIKE THE LIFE FED ONLY FOR THE FREE LUNCH

MANY "FLIVVER" THROUGH THE WINTER SEASON

HI! HO! HERE 'TIS ALMOST SPRING AGIN!

THE FELLOW WHO "JUST PLAIN LOAFS" IN THE OFF SEASON ALWAYS HATES SPRING TRAINING TIME

THE DEPARTURE AFTER THE PRIVATE AFTER THE SUMMER SIEGE

MODERN baseball fans have ceased to look upon the players as shackled slaves, but there have been some protests against the proposition to prohibit major league players from engaging in winter baseball. The old constitutional curtailments of personal liberty and the unalienable rights of citizens... been trotted out and had the cobwebs brushed off them.

first." Mollwitz had his most productive year in 1915, his average dropping the year after.

With a far grander tour in mind, the Red Sox were said to play a transcontinental tour against the Philadelphia Nationals. But because of schedule clashes, primarily the Phillies being due at a banquet, the trip was called off even though the two teams were to play at the Panama-Pacific International Exposition, the 1915 World's Fair held in San Francisco, California, as a celebration of the completion of the Panama Canal, and the 400th anniversary of the discovery of the Pacific Ocean by the explorer Balboa.

But Balboa wasn't the reason, nor was the banquet.

President Baker and President Lannin were willing to permit their players to make the trip only with the understanding that they would share equally in the profits. Heretofore, the players state, all barn-storming trips, excepting in the regular season, have been for the players' benefit alone, and the demands of the owners of the Boston and Philadelphia Clubs is something unheard of in baseball.

The *Reach Guide* for 1916 explained further:

The Exposition Directors were, however, unable to meet the demands of the players who desired a guarantee of $15,000 and expenses ... and it was announced that steps would be taken to end all post-season tours, a threat that was carried into effect at the annual meetings of the American League and the National League, at which resolutions against barnstorming trips were passed. The Bancroft Tour Of All-Stars was, however, carried out as projected, as all arrangements had been made long before the Exposition imbroglio came up; and, moreover, the various club presidents had given their consent to the participation of their various players in the tour.

The battle between owners and players, between the demand by barnstormers for a guarantee and the reluctance of promoters continued. The *New York Times* paid attention to the completed tour of the northwest and west by an American League team against the National League matchup, with Max Carey, Jake Daubert, Johnny Evers, Heine Groh, and Grover Cleveland Alexander being the most memorable players. With the expected first game on October 21 in St. Paul,

The two teams thus played a total of 28 games, of which the All-Americans won 11 games, the All-Nationals won 15 games, and two games were drawn. Good ball and good conduct were the rule; and though part of the tour was marred by bad weather, each player netted several hundreds of dollars [*New York Times*].

The reaction to the "unreasonable" demands of the players led to the decision of the directors of the Pacific Coast League, feeling they did not receive respect from the big leaguers, to lock parks to exhibitions.

The moguls, too, were upset and a series of stories appeared voicing

Opposite: "Pampered" barnstormers in a 1915 *Chicago Daily Tribune* cartoon and article.

their distaste. The ownership of the New York Giants, for one, let it be known that "any club playing in the vicinity of New York under the name of the Giants have no connection with the New York National League baseball club."

The objection was at times legitimate, since sometimes these teams would have only two or three men from the big club.

The next was more debatable. In the *Chicago Daily Tribune* of October 27, 1915:

> Tex Russell of the White Sox is a concrete example which comes home to Chicago fans. In the winter following his phenomenal entrance in major league baseball in 1913 [22 wins], Russell spent the winter in California and picked up more or less coin exhibiting his celebrated self to native sons. He was of practically no use to the White Sox in 1914 and has not yet recovered the splendid form he displayed on the slab two seasons ago.... Today, the players are kicking against the proposed rule to keep them from wasting their talent in barnstorming exhibitions after the season is over ... they have [not] wised up to the fact that it does not pay to risk injury for $50 or $100 in a barnstorming game at the cost of a greatly reduced earning power in the following season. Even if a player is not injured, it has been learned that continuous endeavor shortens one's diamond career.

There may have been some truth to the assertion, at first glance. From a rookie season during which he amassed 22 wins, Reb Russell sank to an 8–11 year in 1914 and rose slightly to an 11–10 year in 1915. But his ERA when he went 11–10 was 2.89. So his record may simply reflect his team's support of his pitching.

The *Spalding Guide* for 1916 in its summary of the year 1915 found it necessary to remind players that

> It was voted that any player in any game, participating either in or out of the regular playing season, with an ineligible or disqualified player shall be declared ineligible to play on any associating club and shall be liable to fine, suspension or other penalty at the discretion of the National Board of Arbitration.

The owners were handed a clear victory on December 15, 1915, when the Federal League was effectively co-opted. Any peace present handed to top players like Tris Speaker — in his case an offer for a 1916 contract of $20,000 to keep him with the Red Sox — was quickly withdrawn. The power of the major league moguls was solidified. Organized baseball remained two major leagues and one association of minor leagues.

1916

In December of 1916, there was a breakthrough for players through their fraternity. They were able to pressure the owners, through their National

Commission, to pay injured players the period of their contracts. The injury clause previously let clubs suspend players after 15 days' pay.

Yet, feeling *his* power, one owner wanted money from the Pirates' barnstorming. From the book *Honus*:

> The Pirate president alienated all of his players in October [of 1916] by announcing that, unlike previous years, all of the proceeds of the squad's barnstorming tour would be retained by the club [Hageman, 270].

Some few dollars were earned on the last day of the season, October 1, 1916, according to the *Pittsburgh Dispatch*. In a field day, Max Carey won $40 for winning the base circling contest in 13⅕ seconds and for winning the 100 yard dash in a baseball uniform in ten seconds flat. Jimmy Smith, Wagner's backup, won the long distance throwing contest with 368 feet, while Heinie Groh won the bunt and race to first contest in 3⅕ seconds, so that each man took home $20.

After some successful negotiations with team president Dreyfuss, the barnstorming team moved on October 6, 1916, to Denison, Ohio. "Places of business were closed at noon," the Pittsburgh *Dispatch* reported,

> and the day was known as Wagner Day in honor of Honus Wagner who started his baseball career here with the Twin Cities club of the old Inter-State League.... Honus Wagner received a great ovation when he went to bat in the first inning and showed his respects by hitting for three bases. Cy Young, the grand old man of baseball [49] umpired at the plate.

Playing in Tarentum the next day, perhaps with Wagner, the team won over the Allegheny Steel Works team at Peterson Park by 10–1. Later, as reported in the *Cleveland Plain Dealer*, the Sam McWatters–led troupe traveled by trolley to many places including Tatum-Breckenridge. Other contests were lined up against the Dayton, Ohio, metal products team and the Sandusky Shamrocks.

The same Cleveland paper covered the story that "Elmer Smith and a Boo club recruited Cleveland shortstop Bill Wambsganss, first baseman Chick Gandil and pitcher Bagby" to play the Sandusky Shamrocks at League Park in Sandusky, Ohio. Clarence "Pop-Boy" Smith and Jim Bagby took turns on the mound and in right field. Oddly, neither Bill Wambsganss nor first baseman Gandil's names appeared in the box score, suggesting that they may have been listed under other names.

On October 15, 1916, there was another contest in Sandusky, that day with Elmer Smith and Jack Adams playing for the Shamrocks. Bill Bradley, a Federal League player, reorganized his Boo Gang team now with Nap Lajoie, Jim Delahanty, Jimmy Breen and his brother (both black players), Jack Graney, Bill Wambsganss and Dode Paskert, Jim Bagby and Pop-Boy Smith. In that Shelby, Ohio, third annual baseball tournament among the four teams could be found Sam Crawford and Hal Chase (and maybe Wally Pipp).

Without printing another word about it, *The Sporting News* of October 26, 1916, revealed that Tris Speaker went on a post-season barnstorming tour with Jean Dubuc, a Tigers pitcher, instead of playing a game at Cleveland for which he would have made $500 because he had promised Dubuc.

With a eye on all this postseason play the *Plain Dealer* wrote:

> Scores of big league ball players ... are likely to be fined for having participated in barnstorming contests as the National Commission does not intend to allow players who knowingly violate the rule to escape.... It is said that others have participated in post-season games, two of them under assumed names.

Sporting Life early in November agreed: "John K. Tener, president of the National League ... said that in each contract there is a clause in which the player agrees not to play after the season without consent of the Commission. He says that this clause was inserted to protect territorial rights of the different clubs."

Because they dared to exhibit at New Haven on Sunday, October 14, Ban Johnson said, "the Red Sox will be deprived of the emblems usually presented by the commission to the world's champions." The game apparently was not the sole reason, as Cecilia Tan explained:

> The 1918 Sox were deprived of their championship emblems as punishment for trying to organize a strike during the World Series, when the owners cut the players' share from an expected $3,500 down to about $1,000 per player. This despite sworn promises—sworn in front of the honorable mayor of Boston, no less—from the commissioner and league presidents not to retaliate against the players for the hold out. The emblems were finally awarded to the surviving relatives of the players in 1993, thanks to the efforts of SABR member and historian Glenn Stout [e-mail to author].

In addition, "sixty or seventy other major league players who have engaged in barnstorming without the consent of the commission are to suffer various penalties." In reaction to these declarations, the president, David L. Fultz, of the Baseball Players Fraternity, a 700-member group, argued this way:

> The fraternity cannot recognize the right of organized baseball to fine players for taking part in games after the season is over and after their contracts have expired. The players have, of course, no right to represent any club without the consent of its owner, but as long as they trade upon their own personal reputations they are clearly within their rights. The relation of player to magnate is purely contractual, and gives no basis for the principle of paternalism which the magnates now attempt to inject into it. In addition, for years, representatives of organized baseball have conducted postseason trips in which they shared the receipts, and it is difficult for the players to see the distinction between these trips and the ones the magnates are seeking to abolish.... If the National Commission thinks the alleged offense of such importance and that the act would be a wise and dignified one, they have every right to withhold the world series emblems from the Red Sox, but as far as fining them is concerned, that is an entirely different matter [Chicago *Daily Tribune*, October 24, 1916, 12].

But as the *Los Angeles Times* pointed out, weighing in on the matter, the anti-barnstorming clause in the contracts of players "does not express any fine for violating it."

Another aspect of the barnstorming imbroglio is found on October 4, 1916, in the *Cincinnati Enquirer*: "BANNY VINDICATED. DECLARES TRIPS TO COAST HELP CLUBS WIN PENNANTS."

Brooklyn's success in winning the flag has knocked the foundation out of those opposed to trips to the coast after the season ends. Frank Bancroft points out with pride to Coombs, Pfeffer, McCarthy, Miller and Daubert [of the Brooklyn Nationals who] were on his All-National line-up; Hoblitzell and Cady [of the Red Sox], members of the Americans, and both of these teams winning the pennants this season. Previous to that he took the Athletics to Cuba, they coming back and winning both the American League and world's series pennants the following season. It is hoped the ban on transcontinental trips, under proper management, will be removed next fall.

1917

Brooklyn Dodger owner Charles Ebbets laid down this law to his star pitcher, Rube Marquard, when the hurler went out to tour with one such "All-Star" aggregation after the 1917 season. Marquard ignored the order and pitched against the Lincoln Giants, who drove him from the mound in a lopsided win. An apoplectic Charlie Ebbets then fined Marquard $100. Ebbets explained the reproof in the following: The Brooklyn team is averse to permitting its team, or any of its players, participating in games with Negroes. There are only semi-professional Negro teams, and when there is an outcome like yesterday's game, when Rube was beaten, President Ebbets believes it tends to lower the caliber of ball played by the big leagues in the eyes of the public, and at the same time make the major league team the subject of ridicule at the hands of the more caustic fans [Rogosin, 97].

The *New York Times* of October 16, 1917, reported that neither the National Commission nor the team owners hesitated to be paid their share of the players' labors, no matter what the circumstances. So the payouts for the seven St. Louis city series games (played in five days) showed receipts for the players of $2,361 for the winning Cardinals and just $1,574 for the Browns. For the Browns' 14 players, that's $112 each for the series. The clubs each received $2,876 and the National Commission was paid $756.

The National Commission could use its authority over players to control purses, as the *New York Times* took note:

The National Commission ... passed a rule forbidding the players [of the World's Series opponents] from taking any barnstorming trips at the close of the series.... The commission had decided to retain $1,000 from each player's share of the receipts of the world's series as a bond to prevent them from playing these exhibition games.... The White Sox had been offered $10,000 by John P. Croizier of Upland to play an exhibition game with the Upland Club of the Delaware

County League on October 19.... When the players heard about the ruling at the Polo Grounds after the game yesterday, they were furious.

The Sporting News continued the story in its November 18 issue:

Pittsburgh, Nov. 5, 1917 ... As is generally known, the Commission has made a rule which prohibits ball players from engaging in exhibition games without the consent of their employers. Since the season of 1917 closed, a number of National and American League luminaries have been playing more or less regularly in the vicinity of St. Louis and Kansas City and the chances are that some of them will get themselves into trouble ... Max Carey, Chuck Ward and Bob Steele have played in these games but only Carey was wise enough to secure Barney Dreyfuss' permission.

The National Commission and the owners did not appear to fear the anger of the players, and, in fact, refused to speak to the Players Fraternity. They thought the players had no right to make money in ways the owners did not approve of. The World Series of 1919 was not that far away.

1918

The year 1918 would be the year that World War I had the most impact on baseball. Besides the enlistees from the sport, the game was adjudged to be not essential to the winning of the war. Around this time, as Baseball-Almanac.com reports, "Secretary of War Newton D. Baker ruled that baseball was not considered an essential occupation and that all players of draft age were subject to the 'work-in-essential-industries-or-fight' rule."

The point was not argued, particularly as the number of American soldiers now in France grew after the battles of Belleau Wood and Chateau-Thierry in June of 1918, when American casualties were recorded as more than 10,000, and American deaths as more than 1,500; after the terrible battle of Verdun, American casualties reached 120,000 and deaths 18,000.

For those away from the battlefront, of course, life continued on pretty much the same. People still worried about the same old thing and players still considered their salaries to be important.

The reputed parsimony of at least one owner would have long-lasting effects. A White Sox star, Joe Jackson, was paid $6,000 in both 1918 and 1919, while Eddie Collins and Tris Speaker were making three times the $6,000. Jackson's teammate, pitcher Eddie Cicotte, was sat down with 29 wins with three weeks left in the season because if he won number 30 he would collect a bonus of $10,000 from Sox owner Charles Comiskey.

William H. Dunbar wrote in 1918,

now $4,000 is not a whale of a salary in these days. But the fact remains that there are very many major leaguers now in uniform who never received $4,000 and in all probability never will.... And yet even now $5,000 would be considered a very good salary by most ball players.

That amount — $4,000 — has the purchasing power of about $49,000 today. With an average workingman's salary of about $20 a week in 1918, that comes out to $13,000 today. But, it is important to keep in mind that it is unfair to compare the two. A major league baseball player is at the top of his profession. He is not being paid an average salary because he is not at the bottom nor in the middle of his occupation.

Look at the salary of a class D player: $40 per week for twenty-two weeks, for a total of $900 for the season. This equals about $2,000 for the year, if the sport were played year round. In 1918, even a clerical worker in manufacturing was being paid $2,000 a year and that was someone not in a particularly skilled profession. Public school teachers, for example, were making $377 a year or $4,700 a year in purchasing power now.

At the same time, major league players, men at the top of their profession, were given increased shares of their club's performance in the regular season so that second-, third- and fourth-place teams shared in World Series receipts for the first time in 1918. (From 1919 to 1925, only players on second- and third-place teams shared in receipts, but fourth-place teams were included again in 1926.)

As for the perennial barnstormers, the Cincinnati Reds "will disband immediately after today's game [September 2, 1918] and nearly all of them have secured employment of an essential nature" wrote the *Cincinnati Enquirer*.

But a name now in the sports news, his nickname almost always capitalized as "Babe," was begnning to exert his own influence on the game and on his own pocketbook. *The Sporting News* of October 3, 1918, carried this story on its page 6: "'Babe' Ruth is capitalizing his fame into dollars and cents by pitching Saturday and Sunday games in the East.... He got $350 for pitching one game up in New England." The games included games in Hartford, Connecticut, and in Springfield, Massachusetts.

Rembering the need for "essential" work, Babe traveled on to Lebanon, Pennsylvania, where he joined his old batterymate Sam Agnew on the baseball team of the Bethlehem Steel Company, clearly an essential war-time industry. The only game was played on Saturday, September 28. Later Hornsby was signed by Ruth's team and the last game of the year was played on October 12. According to the *Reading Eagle*, "Hornsby was in the lineup, but Ruth was not [in] the game which was played against Babe's World Champion Red Sox. Wally Schang, Amos Strunk, Joe Bush and Wally Mayer were the only members of the Red Sox."

At the same time, the players, all young men, were made to be aware of the Spanish influenza that was murdering its way around the world. An unusual feature of this deadly virus was the age of its victims; unlike most flu viruses, the Spanish flu was particularly deadly for adults age 20 to 40. By epidemic's end in America, there lay more than 600,000 dead. It was not a good idea then to go barnstorming with that illness decimating the countryside.

Still, the weakened National Commission was unhappy with Ruth and his teammates as reported in the *New York Times* on October 6, 1918:

> The National Baseball Commission has decided to discipline members of the championship Boston Americans, who, after the World Series, engaged in a trip under the name of Red Sox. Bush, Schang, Strunk and Mayer are among the players under investigation.

1919

According to Voigt in *The History of Major League Baseball, Part 1,* when "to their surprise the war ended, and the attenuated 1919 campaign attracted 6.5 million fans," the National Commission found itself "caught short by this unexpected boom, [and so] officials sought to recoup money by upping the World Series schedule to a best-of-nine-games format." Suehsdorf in his *Total Baseball* essay writes:

> As it turned out the expanded 1919 World Series precipitated the final crisis that ended the commissioner system. Embittered over their low salaries, eight Chicago White Sox players accepted bribes from gamblers to throw the World Series to the NL champion Cincinnati Reds.

A few teams continued to go out on the road: "The barnstorming Giants, after a successful tour through upper New York, New England and Canada, returned to this city yesterday and disbanded" (*The Sporting News*, October 27, 1919). Run by Eddie Brannick, they played 14 games including one in Montreal and one in Vermont, though these games attracted little coverage. The ballplayers had each earned a full share of $800 for finishing second that year.

Electing to put George Cutshaw in charge of the team, some Pirates barnstormed though Illinois, Indiana and Ohio and the Cubs were said to have arranged a few postseason games, notably at Beloit, Wisconsin, a city of 21,000, where they were matched with the Fairbanks Morse team, called the Fairies. The Washington Nationals were said to "do some barnstorming this week to pick up a little change out in the provinces," while "The Cincinnati Reds in their late exhibition games in which the players shared 50–50 with the club took in over $10,000 and the players who took part netted over $200 each" (*The Sporting News*, October 19, 1919, 5).

Exhibition Games

1910

The most unusual of exhibition games at the time was called the All-Stars-Athletic Series. It came about because, while the Athletics had finished their season on October 6, the National League's Cubs did not complete their schedule until October 15. The Athletics manager, Connie Mack, wanting to stay ready for the World Series, arranged to have tune-up games through Jimmy McAleer.

McAleer played with three Cleveland teams in three leagues—the National, the Players, and the American Leagues—and was, in turn, a major league outfielder, umpire, manager and team owner. With a career in the big leagues dating back to 1889, McAleer was an outstanding choice to organize a team to meet the Athletics. In that year, McAleer was managing the Washington team and from that club he was able to recruit Clyde Milan to play in left field, George McBride was to handle the shortstop, Kid Elberfeld second base, with the great Walter Johnson on the mound. From the Red Sox, McAleer brought along Jake Stahl to play first and the great Tris Speaker to play center field. The White Sox were represented by two pitchers, Doc White and the great Big Ed Walsh with Billy Sullivan as a catcher. Cleveland sent Bris Lord to man third base. And Ty Cobb agreed to play right field.

With four future Hall of Fame players in the lineup, the all-star team, looking to maximize its profits, played in Newark, New Jersey, on October 8.

Though this lineup of All-Stars was announced on October 9 in Philadelphia, very soon added were both catcher Gabby Street and outfielder Germany Schaefer from McAleer's Washington team. Later a catcher named Cunningham and Red Sox infielder Pat Donahue were added to the roster.

In the other lineup, the Athletics of Connie Mack featured future Hall of Fame players Eddie Collins and Home Run Baker along with pitchers Eddie Plank and Chief Bender. The Athletics were to use both catchers and all three of their strongest starters in each of these games but the position players were used for the whole game most of the time.

Once the Athletics finished their regular season home schedule on October 8, the games could commence. But the first game of the series had to wait until Shibe Park's other tenant, the Phillies of the National League, were out of town. So the first of the all-star game series was played on October 11 at Shibe Park, won by the all-stars 8–3. Manager McAleer told a story about Schaefer a year later in *The Sporting News*:

> When I got up a team to play against the Athletics last fall after the American League season closed, I included "Schaef" in the squad.

In the first game in Philadelphia Cobb did not play. He lost a wheel on his auto coming to Philly, so I had Schaefer in right.

Of course, the crowd wanted to see Cobb above all others, and they continually asked Schaefer, "Where's Cobb?" Finally "Schaef" turned to the mob in the bleachers and yelled: "Cobb? Cobb? Who the hell's Cobb. Ladies and gentlemen, keep you eyes focused on me and you will witness the greatest exhibition ever staged on a ball field. Cobb? Why, say, if that guy would see me play he'd burn his uniform."

When Cobb did arrive in Philadelphia for game two on October 12, the *Boston Globe* headlined "Ty Cobb Runs Bases at Will," and his team won again, this time by a score of 5–1. On October 13 in Philadelphia more of the same, at least at the end, the all-stars taking game three 6–2. Walter Johnson won again, this time in his home park on October 14. With Gabby Street now catching, the all-stars won 4–1.

Back in Philadelphia on October 15 for game five, the all-stars were held to two hits. The Athletics hitters, with the world championship about to begin on October 17, banged out just three runs, but the pitching staff gave up no runs to end this series.

Harry Davis, captain of the Athletics, said after the World Series was completed that

the all-star series of games is one of the wisest moves that Mack ever made and he is all praise for the members of the all-star nine, for he claims that the men comprising the team worked their hardest to give the Athletics the same style of play which they thought the Cubs might use in the series. He says the Athletics did not give a thought whether they won or lost those games.

But the all-stars were not through earning money. The following Sunday, October 16, 1910, a game was reported by the *New York Times*, featuring the all-star team that played the Athletics who had come to New York City's Olympic Field. On that diamond they met John J. McGrath's All-Leaguers, comprised of Larry Doyle and many others of the New York Giants. Doc White pitched that 2–0 loss. Then he, plus Ty Cobb, Hal Chase and Larry Gardner, all appeared in games played in the District of Columbia for which each player earned $275. These all-stars went on to play in Baltimore against an International League team.

They were prepared to play someone not named at Loughlin Oval in Brooklyn at 2:45 for the benefit of St. Cecilia's new school, but it is not known if that game took place. Likewise, the Athletics may have played at Olympic Field against the same team the all-stars played.

Also in New York City, at Meyerrose Park in Ridgewood, while the Giants and Yankees were playing an extended city series, two semipro teams played the opening game and then the Phillies met the powerful semipros, the Ridgewoods, at 3:15. The next day — October 10, 1910 — Mike Donlin's all-stars with Cy Seymour, Hal Chase and Billy Gilbert, met the Yankees with Rube Manning and Ray

Fisher at 3:30. Before game time, the 6,000 attendees were told that the National League's President Lynch had ruled that Donlin couldn't play. The second place New York Giants were scheduled to play at Olympic Field, New York, on October 19 and vs. "an all-star aggregation," but there is no record of those games.

It is known that the so-called New York Giants came to meet the Bronx Athletics on October 20 at the Bronx Oval at 163rd Street and Southern Boulevard. "With the score 12 to 0 in favor of the Giants, the *Boston Daily Globe* wrote, "the umpire was forced to call the game at the end of the first half of the ninth inning because the crowd mobbed Larry Doyle, tearing his baseball paraphernalia from him for souvenirs."

Also wanting that extra money for the winter, the Cubs in 1910 played not one but two forbidden games, one against Fisk's Colts in the morning and then against the Logan Squares in the afternoon. The two games drew 5,500 and the Cubs players got about $55 each. The Red Sox appeared in Burlington, Vermont, where Larry Gardner and Ray Collins had attended college, in a game in which three fine outfielders, Harry Hooper, Tris Speaker and Duffy Lewis, were watched by 4,000.

A 1910 advertisement read, "Olson's Cherokee Indian Base Ball Club supporting Maud Nelson champion lady pitcher of the world. Genuine Redskins from Western Plains and reservations. Maud Nelson will appear in afternoon game only for 2 innings. The above club with Maud Nelson, Famous Female Pitcher, will play a game of Base Ball vs. Your Local Ball Club Admission 25¢."

1911

As they had in 1910, a team was put together by Jimmy McAleer to keep the Athletics at peak prior to the World Series. And once again the stars played a Sunday exhibition in Newark, New Jersey. That 2–0 win on October 8 had this lineup:

> Clyde Milan, left field
> Ty Cobb, center field
> Doc Gessler, right field
> Hal Chase, first base
> Kid Elberfeld, second base
> Larry Gardner, third base
> George McBride, shortstop
> Gabby Street, catcher
> Smoky Joe Wood, pitcher

in a game that drew only 5,000 people. The all-stars could not score on the first pitcher, Iron Man McGinnity, now out of the majors for good and in his third year with the minor league Newark team. Germany Schaefer served as umpire.

On Monday and Tuesday, October 9 and 10, the first two games of the series were played in Washington. Bull Henry caught the October 9 game, and George Mullin pitched; these two were the only lineup changes in their team's 5–2 win over Bender, Plank and Coombs, who again pitched for Mack. The Athletics faced Walter Johnson on the mound the next day in an 85-minute game. The all-stars manged two runs but the Athletics rallied for the wining run in the ninth for a 3–2 victory.

After the teams had drawn a respectable 6,000 in those two games, they moved south to Richmond, Virginia, for game three, there attracting 15,000 fans. Here the all-stars could afford to call on two pitchers, Mullins and Ray Collins, in their 13–8, 15-hit win. Germany Schaefer served as a pinch hitter for Collins in the seventh inning, the contest probably played in Mayo Island Park before 9,000.

Back in Philadelphia the Athletics looked fit in the final, figuring out a way to use their five hits off of Smoky Joe Wood to bring them a 3–2 win. Mack used 16 men in the game, the all-stars ten, employing both Milan and Schaefer in left field. Mack also used four pitchers, Chief Bender as a starter and then Dave Danforth, Doc Martin and Cy Morgan.

The all-stars went on to play in Baltimore on October 13, with Johnson and his catcher, Street, being the only two men mentioned. Two days later at Olympic Field, Johnson made $600 and Gabby Street $300 against a black team, the Lincoln Giants.

The amount of money is interesting. Johnson's all-star team and its like in 1910 were not simply being altruistic and loyal to their league. A *Washington Post* story 18 years later stated flatly that "the money taken in minus expenses was divided among the members of the all-star cast." As for the amount in 1911, "the $275 each player received from the Athletics was considerably less than the year before" (Thomas, 69), though, in appreciation, Connie Mack gave each of men on the 1911 roster a diamond studded gold fob for their watch.

Brooklyn put together a team that played at Morristown, New Jersey, that year and won 8–4. Brooklyn put its regular team in the field and pitched Bill Schardt, Elmer Steele and Elmer Knetzer and used Otto Miller and Tex Erwin to catch. Later, "a squad of Cubs motored down to Indiana" to play a few games beginning around October 21, according to Sam Weller of the *Chicago Daily Tribune.*

After losing to the Athletics in six games, John McGraw and 15 New York Giants had plans to go to Cuba for 12 games starting on November 11. So did the Phillies under Hans Lobert, who left on October 31, 1911, to go to Cuba from November 5–20. Bancroft may have gone along with the Phillies

and they may have played games in Key West, Miami, Daytona and Ormond Beach on the way back from Cuba.

1912

Hal Chase's team led off the exhibition games this year. Some of his Highlander teammates were playing the Giants on October 7 at the Polo Grounds. There a crowd of 15,000 "sailors, marines and schoolboys" watched the 1912 edition of a tune up before the Giants faced the Red Sox in the 1912 World Series. But that exhibition saw only two regulars in the lineup. Meanwhile, the rest of the regulars were engaged in a game in Hartford, Connecticut, against the Senators which attracted 8,000. Knowing how much Hal Chase was attracted to money, it is likely that the payday in Connecticut was better than that back in the city.

Chase's name comes up again for a game at an amusement park in New Brunswick, New Jersey, on October 18, 1912. The Chase-led team, probably the same as the one in Connecticut, featured seven Highlander regulars in the lineup, a game lost by the major leaguers.

The remaining New York City team, the Brooklyns, played against the Eastern League Newark, New Jersey, team; Frank Allen pitched. No games were contested by the Pirates but during a field day $25 in cash was awarded to the winner of each event at Redland Field. *Walter Johnson: Baseball's Big Train* notes that in 1912 Johnson pitched for the Whitinsville, Massachusetts, team in Woonsocket, Rhode Island, and made $250. That same year

> Johnson began a tradition of pitching a charity game for both Coffeyville and Humboldt.... The first of these contests drew 3,000 people to Forest Park in Coffeyville on October 27.... Johnson was relieved by Larry Cheney, winner of 26 games for the Chicago Cubs that year, and playing center field for Coffeyville was Kansas City native Charles "Dutch" Stengel (later known as "Casey").... On November 7, he went up to Humboldt for the first time [Thomas, 106].

Games continued to be played by World Series participants past mid–October. But since nineteen states, in whole or in part, were still under the thumb of blue laws, Larry Doyle, Arlie Latham, George Wiltsie and Tobc Thompson were fined $5 for playing on the Sabbath in an game on October 20, 1912, at Lenox Oval, New York, where admission was charged. Had there been no admission charged, or if, say, all those seated had to buy a candy bar, the fines could have been avoided. On the other hand, certainly Doyle and the others made more than they were fined. A week later, also fined for playing on the Sabbath were Louis Drucke, Hal Chase, Cy Seymour and Josh Devore who were playing with Larry Doyle's All Giants against the black Lincoln Giants at Olympic Park. Also fined $5 were Nick Altrock and Germany Schaefer of Washington plus eight others who played at Lenox Oval at 145th and Lenox.

And while World Series-losing manager John McGraw could be found on the stage of the Colonial Theater, four of the winning Red Sox players barnstormed together around New England. Those men — Buck O'Brien, Hugh Bradley, McHale and "an outsider named Lyons" — toured after the World Series was won by the Red Sox 4–3–1.

Warmer weather attracted California residents from the big leagues who formed a barnstorming team called the Coast All-Stars. Chief Meyers was catching, with Snodgrass at second, Art Shafer at short, Duffy Lewis and Harry Hooper in the outfield with Gary Cravath of the Phillies with pitchers Ray Collins and Charley Hall of the Red Sox. Myers later that winter signed on with San Diego, awarding to *Sporting Life* on November 9, 1912.

The Philadelphia Athletics under infielder Danny Murphy went to Cuba with the first game on November 4, 1912. Twelve games were scheduled on Sunday, Monday and Thursday. Monday because it was a half day in the cigar factories; Sunday because it was a full day off for fans, while Thursday had no particular benefit. All games were at Havana Stadium. Umpire Cy Riegler also took a team to Cuba. Players included Larry Doyle and Jack Tesreau of the Giants; from the Cubs, Jimmy Sheckard and rookie Jimmy Lavender; from the Cardinals, Joe Hauser, Lee Magee and Steve Evans; from the Phillies, Grover Alexander and Bill Killifer; and from Boston, Hub Perdue.

Why travel to Cuba? The island had the advantage of mild temperatures, cheap prices, and a three-games-a-week schedule. It was, in effect, a trip to the tropics that you were paid to go on. Besides, back in 1903, players were offered the chance to divide amongst them $300 per game.

But the owners decided that the "Pearl of the Antilles" was a dangerous place, a den of iniquity. President Dreyfuss of the Pirates warned:

> In Cuba a man is liable to contract malaria or other fevers that one does not know in the temperate zone. When a club picks up a young man, pays him a good salary, carries him along at an expense that amounts to thousands and develops him into a real ballplayer the owner of the club should have something to say about the risks he takes of ruining his health [*Sporting Life*, November 9, 1912].

Earlier Dreyfuss wanted a clause in players' contracts prohibiting the use of intoxicating liquor during the championship season. The players had to ask themselves if this was a desire for control, or a way to protect an investment. Or perhaps both.

1913

The next year the National Commission decided that players could cover the World Series for newspapers but thereafter, the practice would be abol-

ished. In fact, not just the World Series. By 1916, the league agreed to enforce the rule prohibiting baseball players from writing signed stories.

Nevertheless, no matter how much control the cartel wished to exert, the players continued to look for ways to earn money for the 200 off-season days. In New York City alone, three games were arranged on October 5, 1913, establishing the players' wishes. The Red Sox with Harry Hooper beat the Long Island City semipros at Recreation Park. An all-star team starring Max Carey played the Gallaghers at Flatbush Field, and the Brooklyn Superbas beat the Suburbans at Suburban Oval.

Those same Superbas, Jake Daubert and Otto Miller with them, met another semipro team, the Cypress Hills, at Dexter Park.

The Cultural Encyclopedia of Baseball takes note of the formalizing of the no barnstorming rule in 1914 "by adding a clause to the standard players contract that prohibited non-sanctioned exhibition games." *Sporting Life* quickly understood that "players [were] now in winter quarters without any post-season money to help pay coal bills."

This rule would be ignored or obeyed on a whim, until there was a commissioner of baseball.

1914–1915

And yet that year, 1914, and the next year would see no barnstorming and only two interesting exhibition games. *The Babe in Red Stockings* reports that on October 24, 1915, Babe Ruth pitched the entire game for the St. Mary's team in Baltimore against the Albrecht Athletic Club before 8,000. Ruth, in his second year, was throwing a benefit game for his former home.

The other game concerned a team outside of the power of the National Commission because it was a black team. Five days after Ruth pitched in Baltimore, an All-Stars team led by Tigers shortstop Donny "Ownie" Bush (who was born and died in Indianapolis) was playing in Indianapolis' Federal League Park on October 29, 1915. That date marked the third game of the series against the local ABCs.

1916

Late in 1916, November 29, fans were treated to a star-filled game in Kansas City, Missouri. One team featured Walter Johnson and Zach Wheat and the other Grover Cleveland Alexander and Hal Chase, Casey Stengel and Max Carey.

1917

In 1917 Ownie Bush again recruited a team to play a series in Indianapolis. And again the practice of tuneup games before the World Series was observed. The White Stockings played a practice contest in Cleveland. Their opponents in the series, the New York Giants, met the Cubs on October 3 before 2,500, "a nine inning game [played] in such a way as to give the Giants the best possible batting practice," according to I. E. Sanborn of the *Chicago Tribune*.

Since May of 1917, the United States government had been drafting men for the armed forces, and so those same White Sox and Giants met in an exhibition at Camp Mills in Mineola, New York, for 600 soldiers on October 17, 1917, the day after the two finished their final World Series game.

It is also known that on October 21 in Kansas City Walter Johnson's team, labeled the Americans, starring George Sisler and the two Wheat brothers (the more famous Zach and his brother Mack), met the Nationals, with Grover Cleveland Alexander on the mound, and a stellar team including Max Carey, Hal Chase, Casey Stengel and Rogers Hornsby. This added up to seven Hall of Fame level players in the game.

Lastly for the year, *The Sporting News* reported on its front page the big game between Chester and Upland of the Delaware County League championship in which Chief Bender took part. Another game featured "[Ralph?] Young at shortstop, [Amos] Strunk in center field, [Wally] Schang at third base, [George] Burns at first base, [Roy?] Grover at second base, [Chief] Meyers behind the bat and [Joe] Bush and [Bob] Shawkey as the pitchers." In the article the players were reminded that the previous Friday

> the National Commission issued a warning against major league players playing in individual games, either as individuals or as members of a club and also in territory which was claimed by National Agreement clubs.... It had been planned for Eddie Collins to bring about a dozen members of the White Sox to Upland ... and play a team with Bender pitching for the Upland team ... which would have netted each man picked by Eddie Collins about $400 for one game. Then the National Commission stepped in with its threat to withhold $1,000 for each player's share of the World's Series money until January 1.... Later the Commission broadened its order to include all players under contract to the major league clubs.

1918

The year 1918 is remembered for the horror of the deaths of World War I and of the horror of the deaths from the Spanish influenza, a disease that would kill 600,000 in the United States alone.

In baseball the war-shortened season ended on September 2 and the last World Series game, attended by just 15,238, was contested on September 11. The small crowd may have been a realization of the danger of mixing with too many people. In October 1918 alone, 195,000 Americans would die from influenza.

Babe Ruth, after his first year in leading the league in home runs, began his postseason by pitching games in Hartford, Connecticut, and in Springfield, Massachusetts, that game paying him $300.

In the need for national defense, enacted by Congress was a "work or fight" law that demanded that men be productive in the war effort. Even Ruth had to pay attention to the rule. When Babe Ruth moved to Lebanon, Pennsylvania, Rogers Hornsby too would become a part of baseball in the Lebanon and Reading area. The *Reading Eagle* wrote, "Arrangements were made to play the Boston Red Sox, with Ruth pitching for the industrial team." Though a Texas native, and a Cardinals player, Rogers Hornsby "was seen in several Sunday Industrial games," recently played by "the Reading Steel Casting team at Lauer's Park [and] is now a resident of this city," wrote the *Reading Eagle* on October 9, 1918. "Hornsby is securing work at the local plant of the Bethlehem Steel Corporation, has moved his belongings here, and is living at the Berkshire Hotel."

Later Hornsby was signed by Ruth's team. "The last game of the year was played on October 12. Hornsby was in the lineup, but Ruth was not [in] the game which was played against Babe's World Champion Red Sox. Wally Schang, Amos Strunk, Joe Bush and Wally Mayer were the only members of the Red Sox" (Keene, Sinibaldi, Hickey). *The Sporting News* put the news this way: "Babe Ruth, while trying to make up his mind as to what sort of war work he should take up worked overtime for several industrial teams playing ball around Philadelphia," at Reading on Saturday and then against the Cramp ship yard in Lebanon. Joe Bush pitched for Cramp and Ralph Stroud for Lebanon.

Now baseball fans were excited about the prospect of seeing more games at Lauer's Park involving such greats as Babe Ruth, Rogers Hornsby and Shoeless Joe Jackson, as the Web site berksweb.com records.

The *Reading Eagle* looked beyond its city and saw

a series of baseball games between major leaguers now in the service and the teams representing the various units of the American expeditionary forces in France have been completed. The plan is to have the team make the rounds of the front.

At the end of October, *The Sporting News* reported on a game between a team called the All-Nationals and the New York Giants on a Sunday in New Jersey. It is known that Rube Marquard played for the Giants and Al Demaree and rookie Red Causey played as well.

1919

Some notable games in 1919 included one in which Babe Adams pitched a game for Mount Moriah, Missouri, against a Shenandoah team. In the game were Dutch Zwilling, and Joe Kelly of the Braves. There were two games in Ebbets Field: the one on October 5, 1919, promised to be a doubleheader between the Brooklyn players and the International Stars, but when only Caddy Cadore and Ernie Kruger showed up the game was declared to be admission free at Ebbets Field. (Many Brooklyn players were leaving for Cuba that night.) The Columbus Day doubleheader matching Babe Ruth's American League Stars with the International League Stars found major leaguers Al Schacht (Washington rookie), Lew Malone (Brooklyn), Allen Russell (Yankees) pitching and in the field Dick Rudolf (Red Sox), Johnny Enzmann (Cleveland), and Frank Gilhooley (Red Sox). The 1,100 fans, as the *Brooklyn Daily Eagle* wrote, "want to see Ruth do all the batting in a game; that is, to come up three or four times in each inning of a game. If he hits anything less than a home run he will be out." Babe Ruth, just 24 years old, made $200 while playing left field. To understand this payday better, Frankie Frisch in 1919 was paid $18 a day during the regular season. But then, the Babe had been paid in five figures for 1919, at a rate equaling $60 per day.

George Weiss, himself 24, was also on his way. The future New York Yankees executive (and Hall of Fame electee) bought the Eastern League's New Haven team in 1919 and brought a barnstorming team to Yale on October 13. His team was Rube Marquard from the Brooklyn team with Steve O'Neill his catcher from the Indians; Joe Judge, Joe Wood, and Joe Dugan of the Athletics; George Bancroft from the Phillies; Chick Shorten from Detroit; Sam Rice from Washington; and Nick Altrock.

Remaining active were the New York Giants. In Rutland, Vermont, on October 9 were pitcher Jesse Barnes and catchers Lew McCarthy and Pancho Snyder. Position players included Benny Kauff in the outfield. Local big leaguers playing for Rutland were pitcher Frank Woodward of the Cardinals and Larry Gardner of Cleveland. Bill Klem umpired. Not long after the Giants completed a game in St. Johnsbury, Vermont, the next day, the *Boston Daily Globe* mentioned that these Giants "toured the New England States and part of Canada on a barnstorming trip, report[ing] that they made $600 each. This, with the $600 awarded them for finishing second in the National League, made it altogether a profitable season, after all." (From 1919 to 1925, only players on second- and third-place teams shared in receipts, but fourth-place teams were included again in 1926.)

CHAPTER THREE

Barnstorming Tours and Exhibition Games, 1920–1929

THE DECADE OF THE TWENTIES would have a marked effect on salary, with a 60 percent rise in average salary. The decade also saw the disappearance from barnstorming by a team named for one of the sixteen franchises; it was to be all-star teams from here on.

Judge Landis, with his new broom, began to sweep out miscreants, even deciding to enforce a mostly-ignored "rule" from 1914, the anti-barnstorming edict. He employed this most notably against Babe Ruth in 1921. Still, players, as well as owners, reacted in many different ways to the burgeoning power of the commissioner, particularly about postseason play.

By 1920, all-star teams fronted by Casey Stengel and Babe Ruth were beginning to show great profits and become exemplars to other players. That these two men had lined up games against a black team, the Hilldale Daisies, was a precursor to games against the new Negro League teams in this decade. In fact, the St. Louis Cardinals played a series of games with a charter member of Rube Foster's Negro National League, then in its first year of play.

The end of the decade saw the last great barnstorming tour by Babe Ruth and the emergence of Earle Mack as a leader of barnstorming teams, peopled mostly by Athletics players. It was, after all, the Yankees who ruled for most of the decade and the Athletics rising to prominence toward the end. More and more, exhibition games were played against Negro Leaguers and more and more the office of the commissioner feared these games.

Barnstorming Tours

1920

Organized by Buck Weaver, soon to be indicted as one of the Black Sox fixers, a series of Pacific Coast games at the end of 1919 was arranged and Babe Ruth signed on to play with Weaver in San Francisco, Oakland, and Sacramento (Smith, 71).

And it was Weaver and his seven teammates who occupied much of the sporting and non-sporting pages of newspapers all over the country.

When revelations of this "Black Sox Scandal" came to light, it destroyed the National Commission and ended the old National Agreement. Horrified, if not surprised, by this corruption of their enterprise, the owners took dramatic action to restore public confidence in the game. Although splintered by in-house controversy and intrigue, they mustered a majority vote to scrap the National Agreement and create a new three-man commission [Suehsdorf].

In the American League, President Ban Johnson was under attack and legendary manager John McGraw "was called to testify in Chicago hearings investigating gambling and bribery among players" (Charlton, 206). There was even a movement for the Yankees, White Sox, and Red Sox to leave the American League and join a 12-team National League.

These three years to begin the 1920s were to be pivotal in establishing the course of organized baseball for years to come. In addition to the building Black Sox scandal (the grand jury convened on September 22, 1920), Cleveland infielder Ray Chapman was struck in the head by a pitched ball on August 16, 1920, and died the next day. Perhaps flowing from this incident, as Ken Burns' *Baseball* interprets, two aspects of the game were altered: "As soon as a ball got dirty, the umpire had orders to substitute a spotless new one and the ball itself had been made livelier by winding more tightly the yarn within it." (Ward and Burns, 153) The numbers of baseballs put into play, for instance, from 1919 to 1920 increased in the major leagues by 272 percent.

Not only those changes were transpiring but Baseball-Almanac.com also lists 1920 as the year in which two more important changes were made: "The batter was given credit for a home run in the last of the ninth inning if the winning run was on base when the ball was hit out of the field" and "All freak deliveries, including the spitball, were outlawed."

The new lively ball, the whiter ball that made it easier for the batter to pick up on its way to the plate, the tightening of restrictions on the pitchers' options, and the new emphasis on the home run may have all been incorporated in order to help organized baseball survive and flourish in the midst of a shocking scandal.

And, if there was a vacuum in baseball power in 1920, the time between the collapse of the National Commission and Commissioner Landis taking office, there were enough barnstormers to exploit it.

In addition to the white barnstorming teams playing after the season ended, for the first time there was an organized league of black teams whose season also had just ended. Called the Negro National League, the Midwestern-based enterprise, organized on February 13, was the brainchild of Rube Foster.

> Foster's new organization marked the third attempt of the century to meld black teams into a viable league. In 1906, the International League of Independent Baseball Clubs, which had four black and two white teams, struggled through one season characterized by shifting and collapsing franchises. Four years later, Beauregard Moseley, secretary of Chicago's Leland Giants, attempted to form a National Negro Baseball League, but the association folded before a single game had been played. The new Negro National League, which included the top teams from Chicago, St. Louis, Detroit, and other Midwestern cities, fared far better. At Foster's insistence, all clubs, with the exception of the Kansas City Monarchs, whom Foster reluctantly accepted, were controlled by blacks [Tygiel].

If the white leagues would not accept blacks and dark-skinned Latinos, then these players could now play in quality ballparks against strong competition on a regular basis. The opportunity to make major league money, of course, was denied them. Cool Papa Bell claimed to be pleased playing with the St. Louis Stars, once his monthly salary reached two hundred twenty dollars. Joe Jackson was paid $3,600 a month.

White teams had faced black teams for many years in the postseason and, for example, Foster himself had opposed the Athletics in a series of games in 1906. But with the founding of the Negro National League came a certain new legitimacy to the black players, even parity with white major leaguers.

In 1920, the Hilldale, a team with its own park in Darby, Pennsylvania, a suburb of Philadelphia, had recently played against the peerless semipro white team of New York City, the Brooklyn Bushwicks, at Dexter Park, winning 10–2 and 5–1. That year the Bushwicks had signed St. Louis Cardinals' player Specs Toporcer.

At their home park at 9th and Cedar Streets, the Hilldale then faced a black team, the Brooklyn Royal Giants, who boasted of their shortstop, Pop Lloyd, a 1977 inductee into the National Baseball Hall of Fame. Fans found there that a pavillion seat cost 55 cents and the bleachers 30 cents.

During a crowded early October, the first set of these games against strong white major leaguers was played in Philadelphia, from October 4 to October 8, and extended further into smaller cities in Pennsylvania later in the month, the majority of the games being black against white teams.

First in Philadelphia on a day that was a prime day for baseball, on October 3, 1920, a team identified as the American League All-Stars (which was really the Athletics) met the Negro team Hilldale at the major league Phillies Park on Broad and Huntington. The Athletics players notably were Jumping Joe Dugan and Jimmie Dykes, with Pep Young of the Tigers. Slim Harriss was the winning pitcher in a 2–1 game against the Hilldale. With three hits and one of the runs, another pitcher, Roy Moore, playing center, was the game's star. Three Athletics pitchers surrendered just four hits in that next 2–1 win. This team later (on the 24th) took on the Atlantic City Bacharachs in Ebbets Field.

On its way into Philadelphia next was Casey Stengel's Philadelphia Nationals. On October 4, 1920, the Stengel team won at Parkersburg, West Virginia. In addition to the many Phillies on the team, some leftover Athletics' players also had signed on, as did the brothers Irish and Bob Meusel, Jumping Joe Dugan and pitcher Bill Hubbell.

The team Stengel was about to meet was an independent club run by Philadelphia legend Ed Bolden. The best-known of the Hilldale was catcher Louis Santop.

On Tuesday, Stengel's team beat Bolden's team 5–2, though outhit 10–9. On Wednesday, the Stengels won again 4–3, outhit again, this time 6–5. The Hilldale were now 0–4 against major league talent.

The Stengel team went on to play the St. Louis Giants, and next up, as they moved across the country, was a trip to Stengel's birthplace to win two games against the Kansas City Monarchs. The trip westward (and homeward for Casey) ended by losing two games (numbers seven and eight in their tour) in Los Angeles against the White Sox of the California Winter League.

The third group to meet in Philadelphia games, the Babe Ruth and Carl Mays' All-Stars team, lost to the Bacharach Giants in Shibe Park on October 4, 1920. There, Cannonball Dick Redding, one of the 400 greatest players according to *Total Baseball*, allowed ten spaced hits while the Ruth team made six errors in the loss won by manager Redding 9–4. Mays pitched the first six innings of that game, letting Ruth finish. For the Atlantic City team, this was merely a warm-up for the beginning of the "World's Colored Championship" against Rube Foster's Chicago American Giants right there in Shibe Park. The *Philadelphia Inquirer* said only five major leaguers appeared for the all-stars: Ruth, Carl Mays, Wally Schang, Bootnose Hoffman, and Lefty O'Doul.

Those same five big leaguers moved to the Phillies Park on Broad and Huntington to play the Hilldales on Thursday and Friday. The game with the Hilldale, "the colored champions of the east," drew 2,500 fans who saw Ruth's team lose 5–0, making just three hits. Pud Flournoy pitched for the Hilldale, before 2,500 and gave up but three hits, none to Ruth. Santop, on the other hand had three hits and Pelayo Chacon two. The next day Ruth had a three-run homer off of Lefty Stark and the Babe's team won 5–3. This all-star team was on its way to a few more games in the states and then on to Cuba at month's end.

As for the Hilldale, that club went on later that month to play home-and-home pair of games, one on the sixteenth and again on the twenty-third at Hilldale Park in Darby. Played for the benefit of the Hilldale squad, the game could be reached by the city fans via car number 13 on Walnut Street. Their opposition was a team from Upland, Pennsylvania, led by Home Run Baker. The semipro team was able to sign Baker at the end of a sad year from him. Baker opted not to play the 1920 major league season after his wife died, but kept his skills high with Upland in the Delco Baseball League.

The New York Giants, though without Frankie Frisch, could boast of three future Hall of Fame men — John McGraw, Dave Bancroft, and George Kelly. They played in Lancaster, Pennsylvania, on October 7 where they lost to Parkersburg Iron 6–5. Also, a *New York Times* story reported on the Pirates in Pontiac, Michigan. The Reds planned to tour mostly in West Virginia (with the exception of Greasy Neale, who was obligated to coach football at Marrietta, Ohio) though their last game was at Chillicothe, Ohio.

But it was the Cardinals, with the *St. Louis Post-Dispatch* following them closely, who had the most ambitious tour planned. To be on the road for almost three weeks, the team would see a country changing too, if slowly. From 1900–1910, the country counted 8,000 cars and ten miles of paved roads. By 1920, the paved roads now approached 400,000 miles. Almost 4 percent of farms could boast of the use of tractors and 7 percent said they used gas or electric light.

The Cardinals began their excursion with three games at the Columbia County Fair on Wednesday, October 6. The seat of that Wisconsin county was Portage, then with a population of 5,000. Served by two railroads; the Chicago, Milwaukee and St. Paul; and the Minneapolis, St. Paul and Sault Ste. Marie Railway (the Soo Line), it was most likely that the players arrived via one of those roads.

The fairgrounds ball field seated just over 2,700 and plans for 2,100 more seats had been completed. Many stores in town were working with half of their staff so that the others could attend the fair. As for that event, 10,000 people — double the size of the city — jammed the fair and its midway, which included "the real living unmummified Egyptian seeress to peep into the confines of the spirit world" as well as "Kewpies and hot dogs, teddy bears and juicy peaches, snake lineament and stick candy," as the *Portage Register-Democrat* reported. These games were intended after the World Series games between Cleveland and Brooklyn would be over. In Portage, you could track those championship "games ... reproduced on the electric scoreboard at Elks' Hall promptly at one o'clock."

So Portage drew not only the Cardinals, but for the three game set the

Pirates as well, managed in his first year as a field boss by George Gibson. With only their regular third baseman not in Portage, the Pirates could boast of a fine outfield, with left fielder Skeeter Bigbee and two excellent baseball men: Billy Southworth in right, who would go on to manage more than 1,700 major league games with the Cardinals and the Braves, and in center field the great Max Carey. Once Charlie Grimm, the first baseman, was inserted in the lineup, there were three future managers for the Pirates: Grimm, Southworth and Carey.

Pitching for the Cardinals on October 6 (the first day of the fair) was Ferdie Schupp. The right hander who had won sixteen games that year won this exhibition by shutting out the Pirates 6–0 on six hits. With an even larger crowd of fairgoers—15,000—in attendance the next day, the grandstand and bleachers were filled to overflowing and thousands had to stand. The series was evened when Hal Carson threw a six-hitter to take his team to a 5–2 win in a sloppy game (nine errors) by both teams. Pittsburgh took the rubber game by 6–2, Earl Hamilton holding off the St. Louis team 6–2.

Three days later back in St. Louis the Cardinals met the St. Louis Giants—a charter member of Rube Foster's Negro National League, then in its first year. The Cardinals went on to play games in Illinois and Iowa as well until October 22.

There were rumors of minor players calling themselves by the names of big league stars in semipro games, but not actually being those stars, something heard occasionally. In *The Sporting News* of January 20, 1921, Ruth claimed he made "$10,000 for barnstorming around the East after the regular season" and he was in Havana playing 11 games for $1,000 per game.

1921

Later that same year, 1921, when barnstorming games were spoken of as being played "in the jungle" or "out in the timbers," both the first game and the first World Series game were broadcast on radio station KDKA in Pittsburgh.

Though federal judge Kenesaw Landis was named the game's sole commissioner in the fall of 1920, it was not until January 12, 1921, that Landis was installed in office. Landis, as eager for money as any barnstormer, insisted that he continue as a federal judge as well, adding that $7,500 to his baseball salary of $50,000. Why shouldn't Landis make a lot of money, what with the still-pending litigation of the Black Sox scandal and the Baltimore Federal League club.

"When the latter case was at the stage in which organized baseball stood under a $240,000 fine for violation of the anti-trust laws" (Pietrusza, 143), Landis still sat on the federal bench in charge of that trial.

By the end of 1920, the judgment came from the courts that baseball was not subject to antitrust laws nor the rules of interstate commerce and could use the reserve clause as it wished.

The end of that five-year-old case was followed by the death of one of the great early barnstormers on March 31, 1921. Frank Bancroft — "Banny" — died at age 75 in Cincinnati. "He was," the *New York Times* wrote in his obituary, "the pioneer of the barnstorming trips of baseball and took the first American team to Cuba, where he introduced the pastime that has since become so popular there." Bancroft was a baseball man from 1874 to 1921.

Briefly mentioned in the *New York Times* were the return of Brooklyn players from Cuba and of Pep Young of the Tigers who "had been on a barnstorming tour with other major league players," including a stop at Scranton during the World Series. Keep in mind that most of the travel must of necessity have been by railroad since only 8 percent of the country's roads were surfaced in 1921.

An Associated Press story of October 15, 1921, said that "Babe Ruth ... was formally crowned in the clubhouse after the final of the series. Manager Miller Huggins officiated at the coronation ceremony, placing on the regal head $600 worth of silver crown presented by admirers. The crown was inscribed 'King Ruth.'"

A king must exercise his power. Remember that Ruth for all his childlike behavior was in no way blind to the economics of baseball: he is known to have asked for a percentage of his $125,000 selling price when the Red Sox deal was made that brought him to the Yankees.

Landis, the new boss, knew he must make his authority felt, and who better to batter down than the king of baseball, even if the weapon used was outdated and rarely employed.

> On the last day of the regular season, Landis stopped in the Yankee clubhouse to congratulate the club on their pennant. Ruth looked at him and asked, "Judge, what's all this talk about our being forbidden to barnstorm after the Series?"
> Landis repeated what the rule was and said it would be strictly enforced.
> "Well," Ruth shot back, "I'm notifying you that I am going to violate the rule and I don't care what you do about it" [Pietrusza, 230].

If challenged in the clubhouse, Landis could still bring to bear his new authority as the *Post-Dispatch* reported.

> Ten members of the Washington American League club are going to be called upon the carpet ... including Walter Johnson who recently played in a exhibition game in Chester, Pennsylvania. Certain Chester players, according to [sic] story are on baseball's ineligible list.

The Sporting News of October 27 went on to define the problem even further: "The Washingtonians ... would be liable to the penalties of baseball law for playing a team that contained or had contained ineligibles, whether

THE ST. LOUIS ARGUS, FRIDAY, SEPT. 30, 1921

BASEBALL
Monday, Oct. 3rd, Tues. 4th---Sunday 9th, Mon. 10th, Tues. 11th
AMERICAN LEAGUE PARK, Grand and Dodier

St. L. Cardinals vs St. L. Giants

NATIONAL LEAGUE BATTING CHAMPIONS   NAT. NEGRO LEAGUE BATTING CHAMPIONS

5 BIG
Post-Season
Games

Between The

RECOGNIZED STRONGEST CLUBS
IN TWO BIG LEAGUES

Seats For Everyone

Bleachers	- -	50c
Pavillion	- -	75c
Grand Stand	-	$1.00

GENERAL ADMISSION

Back Boxes   - - $1.33

INCLUDING GRAND STAND

Front Boxes - - $1.50

INCLUDING GRAND STAND
WAR TAX INCLUDED

Don't Miss The Opening Game Monday

PROBABLE BATTERIES
MONDAY, OCT. 3

Haines and Clemons,
Drake or Finner and Kennard

SEE THE BATTLE OF ACES

ALL GAMES CALLED 3 P. M.

UMPIRES: LEO BROWN
       JAMES POWERS
       HUGHIE MILLER

One Half of
Grand Stand

JUST BEHIND
GIANTS' BENCH

Reserved For
Colored Patrons

Best Seats
In The Park

BOX SEATS ON SALE
At

Giants' Headquarter

Leonard and Laclede
PHONE, BOM., 1043

Hours: 4 p. m. to 10:30 p. m.
Sunday, 1 p. m. to 5 p. m.

DAN KENNARD   *JOE HEWETT*   *WILLIAM DRAKE*   *CHARLES BLACKWELL*   *OSCAR CHARLESTON*

Advertisement in the *St. Louis Argus* for the series between the St. Louis Giants and the St. Louis Cardinals in 1921.

the ineligibles were actually in the game or not." The mania "for the welfare of the game" continued, but the game's health was whatever Landis decided was healthy.

That same issue's editorial stated the need for obedience to the will of Landis:

> It will make some ball players with Bolshevik tendencies hesitate, probably in their hinted intentions of definite and organized attempts to violate the rules. Some of these acts appear to have been premeditated and with intent to challenge the authority of the Commissioner.

The news of Landis' wrath spread quickly. *The Sporting News* noted that Eddie Ainsmith, Browns catcher, had been barnstorming but then one game planned at Jackson, Michigan, was canceled since the home Briscoes had ineligible players on their roster. "The Browns," their hometown newspaper suggested, "did not wish to risk suspension for five years."

Ruth abandoned his barnstorming tour; it was not all that successful anyway, and the Babe, urged by his owner, was ready to give in to Landis.

The new commissioner eventually fined Ruth all of his World Series money — more than $3,500 — and suspended him until May 20; his companions, Meusel and Piercy, got the same punishment. Part of Landis' power came from the fact that it was his office that decided when to release the checks for the World Series.

While this Ruthian controversy occupied the nation's newspaper sporting sections, the St. Louis Cardinals repeated their 1920 touring, starring Jess Haines and Pickles Dilhoefer. And as they had in 1920, the Cardinals played some games against the St. Louis Giants, contesting those games at the new home park of the Cardinals, who had moved over in 1920 from old Robison Field to the home of the Browns, Sportsman's Park.

Featuring rookie George Scales and starring the great Oscar Charleston, the thirteen-year-old St. Louis Giants team had finished third in the Negro National League in 1921. Likewise, the Cardinals had finished third at 87–66. Both Charleston and Hornsby led their leagues in hitting and so, the St. Louis black newspaper, the *Argus*, concluded,

> the games will prove or disprove the contention that the Negro league is as strong as the major organization. Thousands of white fans as well as colored are anxious to settle this big question.... It will also afford an opportunity for that class of white fans who have never seen the Colored players to learn that Negroes excel in baseball as well as in the prize ring or on the athletic field.

The white newspaper told its readers where the games were to be played:

> at Sportsman's Park which was rented for the five days by Bob Quinn, business manager of the Browns, to Alderman Ed Scholl.... Stands on the third base line are for the whites while those on the first base side for Negroes.

The *Argus* ran a six-column-wide advertisement for the games and posted prices of $1.50 for the front boxes, $1.33 for the back boxes, $1.00 for the grandstand, 75 cents for the right field pavilion, and 50 cents for the bleachers. Those tickets could be bought in advance at "No.6–1 South Leonard Avenue, corner Laclede" or by calling "Belmont 1043." The *Argus* went on to cover each game play by play.

The Cardinals took game one on October 3 by 5–4 but it took eleven innings. Faring better in game two, black Giants pitcher Dixie Drake, with the help of Oscar Charleston's homer and double, won over Pop Haines 6–2.

Then the Cardinals, returned from playing two games at Portage against the Brooklyn Nationals during fair time on October 5 and 6, again met the Giants in a Sunday doubleheader, which the Cardinals took by 12–3 and 9–6. The *Argus* led its story with "Colored Boys go up in the air and drop all their class when the National League sluggers start their heavy guns." Oscar Charleston was again the heavy gun the next day but Roy Dixie Walker won for the Cardinals 10–3 over Lefty Starks.

It was to be the last game against the Negro League team since the Giants announced that they would not play the Tuesday, October 11, game because the "gate receipts of Sunday's game were attached and, with the officials of the team not paying the players as a result, the boys did not report" (*St. Louis Globe-Democrat*, October 12, 1921).

Knowing that the game was canceled, the Cardinals entrained for Effingham, Illinois, a city served by 39 trains every day, but one which was still mostly a town without telephones. Advertisements in the *Effingham Record*, for example (milk 10 cents per quart), did not list phone numbers in the town of 4,000, while the ad for the Opera House promised a Mary Pickford movie for between 11 cents and 25 cents. The two hour train trip north from St. Louis brought the Cardinals into town via the Pennsylvania Railroad, arriving at 11 a.m. for the 2:30 p.m. game.

Covering the game on its first page, the *Record* took note of the team's willingness to pose for photos. Lou North pitched seven innings of the 10–4 win, after which first baseman Jack Fournier came on to pitch. It was at that point that the fans began to turn against the Cardinals because the manner in which the new pitcher "cavorted in the box ... didn't help to make the Cardinals a popular team in these parts or to popularize baseball." As for the Cardinals, being careful now after the Ruth uproar, they forbade the Effingham third baseman to play "on the grounds that he had exhibited in games against blacklisted players."

Traveling 100 miles south to Herrin for a Columbus Day game, the emphasis was on hometown boy Bobby Veach, though why he was a hometown boy is unclear since he was born in Kentucky. Still under contract with the Tigers, Veach played for his hometown, a city of 11,000. When it was his turn to bat in the second inning, Veach was presented with a gold watch and chain by Mayor Pace, on behalf of the local fans. The mayor said that the late Ray Chapman was also a Herrin boy, though he was also born in Kentucky, and the mayor "asked the vast audience to rise and stand uncovered a moment in memory of Chapman." The locals, even with Veach, were unable to overcome Jess Haines in the 5–1 game.

After the game, the big leaguers probably went back to St. Louis for a day off and to be close to their next game in Kirksville, Missouri, population 7,200, where future Hall of Fame pitcher Pop Haines again won by 5–1. Again returning to the city, they could easily travel on game day, October 15, to St. Peters, Missouri. There, in the last recorded game they won 14–1. Other games scheduled in the area were never played. "Then they departed for the South," the *St. Louis Globe Democrat* reported, and *The Sporting News*, in its "Caught on the Fly" column noted that the Cardinals

wound up their season last week in New Orleans.... So far, no penalties have been inflicted by Commissioner Landis on the players who are charged with associating with ineligibles during their post-season activities. Some of the players wanted to back out after they found out they were in a jam, but each had put up a forfeit to go through.

The debate over Ruth's troubles with Landis and over barnstorming in general was not finished since, as the *St. Louis Post-Dispatch* characterized the problem, the "Ruth Case Viewed as Important Test Of Owners' Rights." *The Sporting News* reacted to this controversy, while keeping in mind what it called "rebellious players" and the threat to start a new league, with, perhaps, Ruth in that new league. "The size of the World's Series' receipts [$900,000 that year] and signs of players in rebellion" could "lead to another baseball war." As memory of the Federal League remained fresh in the minds of the magnates, one way to quiet the players was to "amend or rescind the 'barnstorming' rule."

The *St. Louis Post-Dispatch* reported one of the effects of the Ruth case:

> Owing to Judge Landis' stand in the case of Babe Ruth, the scheduled game here between the All-Americans and the All-Nationals on October 17 in Ogden, Utah, was canceled today upon instructions of L. J. Galbreath, director of the tour, who wired that all remaining games of the players have been canceled.

Though this particular tour was largely ignored by large city newspapers, much discussion that followed in the nation's papers about Ruth specifically and barnstorming in general was based on rule paragraph B of section 8 of the World Series agreement which forbade barnstorming by both teams who had just contested for the world's championship.

Reporting from the St. Louis Cardinals' front office of Sam Breadon, Branch Rickey, and Clarence Lloyd, the *Post-Dispatch* on October 18, 1921, wrote that in barnstorming three things happen:

1. players are "without a firm hand"
2. "danger of injuries" is present
3. the "acquiring of bad habits" becomes likely.

This declaration conveniently ignores the fact that the Cardinals' front office approved of the team's barnstorming trip of that year, as well as in 1920.

Nine days later, *The Sporting News*, often understood as the trumpet of the commissioner, listed the reasons against barnstorming, "the very solid grounds ... designed to protect the reputation of the sport." These "solid" grounds included the substantial reasons that the players would be "enervated by a season of six months." Then too, they would be "lacking sufficient stimulus to exert themselves." They would by season's end "be wearied [of] the constant travel" during the season. Of course, the players also would make "painful exhibitions of themselves off the field."

In addition, the barnstormers would be "playing on indifferent or even dangerous diamonds." The players might let "the local lights get a lead out of sheer good fellowship." These are the things, *The Sporting News* feared: the dismay resulting from the damage to the game, those ravages to include having players "not deliver the goods expected by the fans who went to see the barnstorming in the bush," since, the paper assured the reader, "the best base-ball players extant could not be counted on to display more than 50 per cent of their true form when barnstorming." This would cause the fans to "accuse the stars of either faking or deliberately laying down on the job," an accusation which will "hurt the fair name of the sport" and "bring derision or suspicion upon the majors" and so disgust "the small town fan that he lost interest in his home team."

Though by 1921 there had been hundreds of games, with very few complaints, the fear of barnstorming remained and with it, fearful objections to the postseason play.

Or could it be something else?

The big city fans, or at least those in St. Louis, drew the attention of the front page of *The Sporting News* on October 13, 1921, writing that while the World Series was going on between the Giants and Yankees, with the help of third baseman Milton Stock,

> Cardinal players, representing nobody but themselves ... elected to ... pick up a few dollars playing a negro team before a scattering of colored enthusiasts.... The Cardinals who took part in the grand African show probably will hear about it next spring. In the eyes of the average white St. Louis fan the stunt was bad stuff.... "Who's to blame for letting these Cardinals play the negroes?" was a question frequently asked during last week.

The Sporting News looked back at those games a year later:

> The home of the Browns and Cardinals ... has been closed ... after the criticism last year when the park was rented to the Cardinals and a club of negroes.
> The whole matter brings to the fore the issue of what control club owners shall exercise over the players during the off-season.... There is much holler from the magnates about their players risking life and limb by taking chances on evil associations by playing these winter games.... There are hints that some players have been reckless enough to take part in game in which ineligible players have figured.

The Cultural Encyclopedia of Baseball took note of these St. Louis games, writing:

> Judge Landis ... more strictly enforced the rule [of 1914 against barnstorming] in part because Negro League teams were defeating Major League teams and Organized Baseball's all-white image was tarnished by the defeats [Light, 62].

Burk in his *More Than a Game* cites a "*Sporting News* story that criticized a barnstorming St. Louis Cardinals unit for playing an exhibition with 'colored players' asserting that it demeaned the former to be part of the 'grand African show'" (33).

If getting beaten by the black teams demeaned the white teams, then what did the victories do for the reputation of the black players on those teams? After all, in just two years, the Hilldale, the Kansas City Monarchs, the St. Louis Giants and the Atlantic City Bacharachs had met all-star white teams as well as touring white major league teams and held their own. Did those wins bring legitimacy to the black players, even parity with white major leaguers? Was it the parity that frightened many in baseball?

And yet, typical of the continuing barnstorming dispute and the divisions it precip-

A *Philadelphia Inquirer* cartoon from 1921 showing the effect of the Black Sox scandal.

itated among baseball people, John B. Sheridan's column, which appeared on the same page as the editorials in *The Sporting News,* thought the anti-barnstorming rule "un-American, unfair, unpopular and absurd." Sheridan was even able to distinguish between barnstorming and winter leagues, leagues popular now particularly in California. Sheridan admitted that ten weeks of playing in California might help a young ballplayer polish his craft, while weakening a veteran or star. A warning too, from Sheridan, was sounded about "Cuban trips and the menace of booze and gambling. I have some young friends going to play in Cuba this fall. I tremble for them" (November 17, 1921).

Was all this strife really about the Black Sox and Landis' new power? To be sure everyone knew about his powers when Landis assigned Benny Kauff to the ineligible list after he had been acquitted of auto theft. So Landis was willing to punish players even if they were not legally guilty, an action he would soon repeat in the Black Sox affair.

Not everyone shared respect for, or fear of, the new commissioner. Bob Meusel, as he passed through Chicago, where the commissioner had his office, was asked if he would visit Landis. "His reply was that he had no business with the Commissioner and that ... Landis could 'go jump in the lake.'"

1922

True, Ruth along with some ineligibles had been involved in Landis' recent decision, but post–World Series play itself was not. This lack is partly due to the stubborn independence of each magnate and each league.

The *Washington Post* observed the lack of firm action on barnstorming by the leagues and wrote that "the [Ruth barnstorming] rules case created as almost widespread discussion.... The consensus of opinion ... seemed to be that Ruth should be punished, but that the rule should be removed from the books."

By June 1922, the rule that both World Series teams must disband after the games was upheld by the National League owners, while the American League owners, on June 15, 1922, threw the rule out and replaced it with a curfew of October 31 for the last barnstorming game.

Under the stress of public sympathy aroused for Babe Ruth and Bob Meusel the previous spring, the bans against barnstorming by members of pennant-winning teams were lowered to the extent of giving them a chance to earn some money if they were given the permission of their club owners and the commissioner. Players on non-championship teams were also allowed to tour.

In fact, in July the *New York Times* carried a story that "a joint meeting of the two major leagues may be necessary to iron out difficulties over the anti-barnstorming rule."

By the August joint meeting of the two leagues, the disputed section, "Section 8-b," said that for the World Series players, what was needed was written permission from both Landis and the team owner in order for up to three men to tour, but did not mention the curfew date for all the rest of the players. By December, the October 31 curfew reappeared and was approved.

At the same time, 1922 marked the first year that the entire World Series was broadcast, casting its net over the whole country, which by now owned almost one million radio receivers.

Finishing seven games back in second place, the 1922 Reds divided $713.41 in World Series money and still "The Red barnstormers Monday [October 2, 1922] opened a two weeks jaunt through Ohio, Kentucky, Indiana, Illinois and West Virginia in style" by winning at a city of 22,000, Lawrenceville, Illinois, by 6 to 1, the interested *Cincinnati Post* wrote. Pete Donahue pitched and "a large delegation from Eddy Roush's hometown,

Oakland, Ind., was on hand and with the Lawrenceville Elks, who helped entertain the Reds in the evening."

Another dinner awaited the Reds the next night in the same town. After Rube Bressler pitched the game, Three Fingered Brown, the manager of the Lawrenceville team, hosted a fish fry for the Reds at his country home Tuesday night. After a game in Washington, Indiana, at which Eppa Rixey pitched and Jake Daubert and Ivy Wingo homered, the Reds had traveled to their third state. After the competition at Manchester, Ohio, the team again was treated to a chicken dinner, and knew that the expense of meals "had been nicely trimmed."

Well-fed, by tour's end, even with two rain-outs, each player was paid about $250. "They could have remained out another week, but didn't think it was worth while."

Still Landis' hobgoblin was in the news. *The Sporting News* of October 12, 1922, took note of a "team of Cincinnati players playing a series with a team over in Illinois that harbors at least one ineligible player and others classed as 'voluntary retired' who make themselves ineligible when they play ball as an occupation."

George Sisler was barnstorming in New England for an average rate of $1,000 an afternoon. This statement means Sisler was crafty enough to get guarantees for games. His squad included Muddy Ruel, Pat Collins at catcher and Bill Piercy pitching with Chick Shorten in center and Chick Galloway at shortstop. Sisler also pitched during this jaunt.

They came to Salem, Massachusetts, on October 4, 1922, at Donovan Field, and next in Fitchburg on October 5 at Summerset Grounds. By October 11, they had made their way to Warren, Rhode Island, in a game that matched them with Yankees teammates Carl Mays and his catcher, Wally Schang, for the Warren team.

After October 21, 1922, the last game in Sanford, Maine, a tour manager counted up the 15 games scheduled, 11 played, for an 8–3 record "and the players picked up a nice bit of money," particularly with the four rainouts guaranteed.

That other frequent group of barnstormers, the Pirates, hit the rails again in 1922 with three great stars of the day: Rabbit Maranville, Max Carey, and Pie Traynor. Paid scarce attention by the *Pittsburgh Sun*, the Pittsburgh team was smart enough to have as their third date Fremont, Ohio.

As they were arriving there for the game, the *Daily Messenger* speculated on the need for "eye tests for autoists" and advertised 111 cigarettes for 10 cents a package. They offered the townspeople the chance to see Norma Talmadge in an eight-reeler for a 10 cent matinee and Buck Jones in a western for the same price.

But far more important than those entertainments was the town's centenary celebration of ex-President Rutherford B. Hayes. Since Hayes opened his first law office in Fremont in 1845, he went on to be a congressman, governor and president of the United States. Streets were decorated, floats built, costumes ordered, military battalions and bands scheduled to march, and a grand parade and celebration organized. Motorcycle policemen and Boy Scouts would be in the line of march, as well as veterans of the Civil War and Spanish-American War. After the thirteen floats had passed by, nineteen men would come to the speaker's stand, among them senators, representatives and authors.

At the end of that display of local pride, the town's Kewpies met the Pirates at three in the afternoon before 5,000 fans. But with the three future Hall of Fame players, and manager Bill McKechnie, the Kewpies were so outclassed—the Pirates scored eighteen runs—for most of the game, that the team let Maranville pitch and so the locals scored a few runs at game's end.

Next for the Pirates was a game in Tiffin, Ohio, with 15,000 residents where one competitor for the team's entertainment was the Grand Theater which offered "a Paramount all-star," and "a Buster Keaton Comedy," as well as an orchestra, a group of "living models" and bargain prices that began at 10 cents. Still, 2,000 fans made their way to Armstrong Field where the Tiffin team was "saved from the disgrace of a shutout," as the *Daily Advertiser* saw it. "Of course," the paper continued, "the locals were badly outclassed, but that was to be expected." Making seventeen hits led to fourteen runs, helped by the three Tiffin errors. At least, for the fans' sake, "Rabbit Maranville furnished amusement throughout the practice session and during the game."

A stop near tour's end was Marion, Ohio—a city of 12,000—where pitcher Wilbur Cooper had begun his career. Cooper was given a diamond stickpin from the fans.

There was word too in baseball circles that Rogers Hornsby was touring Michigan and that the black St. Louis team was again taking on white major league competition. One white team featured Bob Veach and Fred Haney.

Still, the hand-wringing *Sporting News* did not cease: "Victory of Semipro Teams Over Nines in Which Major League Players Are Advertised Weakens Attraction of Good Baseball."

Sentiment among the major league club owners against post-season barnstorming may result in positive legislation against this practice at the winter meetings. The magnates have always taken the stand that the game and the players themselves derive no credit from unsupervised playing after the close of the season and some stories coming to their ears this fall support their contention. Reports of major leaguers playing against ineligibles have come to the attention of Commissioner Landis and it is understood that he is making an investigation. Several teams with prominent major leaguers have been beaten in the last week colored semipro teams and the showing made by the big league stars was said not to be first class.... When the magnates see their players, the season ended, playing Negro teams, bushwhacking, associating with gamblers, breaking legs and what not, they wonder if contracts giving them control of the players for the year around would not be advisable, then they would sigh heavily and say such contracts would not be practical.

And, in yet another act of disobedience against the owners, "An interesting thing about these games that are being played by barnstormers from the majors is the abandon with which they break the rules against associating with ineligibles." Ineligibles remained infected.

The *Washington Post* reported that, prior to sailing to the Far East, four men from the 1922 World Series got in at least one game in Vancouver, British Columbia. Commissioner Landis chose to investigate the breach of the rule by George Kelly and Irish Meusel of the Giants, and Joe Bush and Fred Hoffman of the Yankees.

At least one owner was willing to tell what he thought about barnstorming to John Kiernan of the *New York Tribune*: "Yankee Owner No Longer Keen to Permit Barnstorming Trips. Col. Huston Does Not Approve Major Leaguers Losing Farcical Games to Colored Teams; Altrock and Schacht Go Big at Scranton."

"I agree with the gentlemen," said Col. Huston, "who think this barnstorming business is getting past a joke. First I was all for the boys. I couldn't see why they should be deprived of earning the extra money in the fall, but, gee whillikens, some of the happenings in these barnstorming trips have made me sit up and take notice. Think of several teams of major leaguers losing farcical contests to colored teams. Either they ought to quit playing or at least draw the color line."

The *Sporting News* of December 6, 1923, wrote that "in Organized Baseball [there exists] a tacit understanding that a player of Ethiopian descent is ineligible — the wisdom of which we will not discuss except to say by such rule some of the greatest players the game has ever known have been denied their opportunity."

As far as the black teams are concerned, that wariness may have been somewhat justified. For example, John B. Holway, eminent Negro Leagues historian, said that between 1884–1948 black teams had a record of 266–166 against white teams.

Chiming in were many newspapers, the *Minneapolis Journal* typical enough: "The club owners figure that the result has been unsatisfactory and that the only thing to do to prevent discredit on the game is to stop all kinds of barnstorming in the future."

But the *New York Daily News* at the same time was reporting that Ruth expected to make $20,000 and Meusel $8,000 on the tour of Oklahoma and Kansas. Smelser, a Ruth biographer, claims $1,000 per game for Ruth and $800 for Meusel.

With money even near that level up for grabs, the owners had a hard time reining in their players, and so under the new rule, a certain amount of barnstorming was allowed up until November 1, by players who belonged to teams in the World Series.

From 1923 to 1933 there was little barnstorming, except, of course, for the biggest draw in all of sports, Babe Ruth. Ruth barnstormed a little in 1923, the year he was voted Most Valuable Player, had a fifteen game itinerary in 1924, and turned down $25,000 to tour Canada in 1925. In 1926 he barnstormed across the country to California, partly because he was signed to shoot a movie, *Babe Comes Home*, for First National in Hollywood.

After that, two years on the road with Lou Gehrig, a series of games in California in 1931, and then occasional trips to Hawaii and Japan. His last true exhibition game may have been against the Bushwicks in Dexter Park in New York City on October 20, 1935.

The dearth of touring beginning in 1923 for everyone other than Ruth had a number of causes. Not to be forgotten is the death of one of the great entrepreneurs of barnstorming, Frank Bancroft, just two years earlier.

The greatest cause for the slowdown seems to be the activities of the new commissioner of baseball. Landis, beginning his third year in office, had established himself, through his judgeship as well as his decisions as baseball commissioner, as a person Seymour describes with these words: "narrow, arbitrary and vindictive" as well as permitting "his personal dislikes to warp his judicial objectivity."

Landis saw to it that in 1921 alone, four players—Eugene Paulette, Ray Fisher, Benny Kauff, and Phil Douglas—were declared ineligible for reasons like "treachery." These men were clearly not stars of the game and the fact that Landis would decide to punish even lesser players could not fail to have a chilling effect on everyone in organized baseball. Some of this effect was a good thing; some players needed to be reminded of their responsibilities. But yet it does look as if the arbitrary aspect of Landis' decisions made players hesitate. "During his first several years," Harold Seymour reminds us in *The Golden Age*, "Landis blacklisted some fifteen players permanently, including the eight Black Sox" (372). It is often overlooked that none of these players had been convicted of anything.

And now, having even the great Ruth come pleading for permission to barnstorm certainly made recruiting players to tour even more difficult. On October 5, 1923, Landis announced that players could barnstorm until November 10 and that World Series players could also go out on the road so long as no more than three of those players were on a single team. In effect, this decision threw out the rule that he himself enforced with Ruth.

Even more puzzling was a note in the *New York Times* on November 22: "The barnstorm rule provides that 'no player shall participate in any exhibition game after October 31, unless in special instances and only then with the unanimous consent of the Advisory Council.'" This concerned Bill Piercy and Red Oldham who were "alleged to have played in Los Angeles last Sunday [November 19, 1923]." If Landis said until November 10, why was the rule now to be until October 31?

Even with this confusion some games went on. Limited in scope to exhibition games was a team led by Casey Stengel, and the Athletics played six games against the Hilldale.

It was even known that some banned Black Sox members barnstormed and when Dickie Kerr, a very good and very honest White Sox pitcher, played with them, he was suspended for two years.

1924

The next year, 1924, in addition to city series games, there was a seemingly short tour by Ed Holley's American Leaguers, with the newspapers paying attention to one game in Rochester, New York, on October 11 before 5,000, and another in Hazleton, Pennsylvania, on October 13, 1924. There two great stars, Walter Johnson and Lou Gehrig, arranged to join teammates George Mogridge, Joe Judge, Nick Altrock and Al Schacht of Washington and Joe Bush of New York. Also along were Charlie Jamieson of Cleveland, and Steve O'Neill and Howard Ehmke of the Red Sox.

But the most ambitious tour was by the Brooklyn Nationals, known as the Robins in 1924. The coverage of these games is scant, however, though stops were recorded in Kingston, New York, in Iowa, and in Montana. Unfortunately, the one stop on the tour that made the most news was an incident in Wenatchee, Washington, a village of 6,400. In additon to Burleigh Grimes and Charlie Hargreaves, playing there were Bernie Neis, Johnny Mitchell, Milton Stock and Elmer Brown. These men were accused, and convicted, of assaulting a local bellboy, William Weaver, as they were leaving for Seattle to play the Seattle Indians. The players were each fined $200, they paid the hotel $100 and they paid Weaver $750.

1925

It may have been that too many players had seen barnstorming plans go bust and in fact baseball itself was worrying about the problems of baseball in the autumn, as the *Washington Post* took note on October 21, looking at the impact of college football on baseball as well as "the usual autumn rainy season." Then too:

Landis and fellow officials also sought to regulate other forms of player conduct that threatened the productivity of the player or his economic dependence on his club. One form ... was ... off-season or twelve-month contracts that prohibited winter ball. In the uniform contract, management required players to maintain good physical condition, exhibit "sufficient" on-field skill, and "conform to high standards" of personal conduct on and off the diamond or risk fine and suspension for violating employment terms ... gain written consent for any public appearances, newspaper or magazine article deals, commercial sponsorships, radio appearances, or participation in any other sporting activities. These various conduct prohibitions proved far easier to enforce upon the vast majority of journeyman players than upon the game's stars [Burk, 11].

1926

The Sporting News on December 12, 1926, printed an amendment to the "National Association constitution that forbids future participation of players under reserve in baseball during the so-called off-season." Driven partly by the owners of Pacific Coast League teams, "the contention was that play at baseball ... gave the fans of the particular territory a surfeit of baseball and commonized play by these league players to the fans." This rule affected minor league players.

For major leaguers, salary changes were another effect of the boom of the 1920s and though most people might point to the $70,000 Ruth made on the 1927 Yankees, there were still two men on Ruth's club who were paid $2,500. Salaries were rising and so the need to take home extra money for the 200 days of cold weather began to diminish.

Also, as Seymour points out, the players in the twenties were living in a very materialistic decade, a consumer encouragement decade, while at the same time more players were better educated with "107 men representing 79 colleges [holding] one third of the regular positions on major league teams."

It was true in addition that "by 1930 a youngster's possibility of going to high school was five times greater than in 1900" and so the better educated players had more opportunities for off-season employment in jobs that offered higher pay.

The Athletics of Connie Mack, for instance, were handed $712 each for third place. And, it turned out, the son of Athletics manager Connie Mack, Earle Mack, was now, at age 34, about to make his mark on the history of barnstorming. A minor league player and manager, Earle was appointed as his father's coach in 1924. Years later he was a team vice-president and general manager of the Athletics, an important figure in the eventual sale of the team before it moved to Kansas City.

Why he decided to take a team out on tour is unknown, but many have speculated that it was a way to distinguish himself from his very famous father and a way to prepare himself for what seemed to be the inevitable taking over of the team from his father.

By the time the Athletics played their last game on September 29, 1926, Mack had signed up players that he would contract with repeatedly over the years, including stars from other teams, showing not only how good an organizer he was but also how he was able hold their loyalty. The Hall of Fame would eventually take in three of them: pitcher Lefty Grove, outfielder Heinie Manush of Detroit, and Goose Goslin of Washington.

As John Holway points out in his able description of some of these 1926 games, excellent black players of the time from the Hilldale team — Biz Mackey, John Beckwith, and the great Oscar Charleston — demonstrated their skills against the young Mack's team to audiences in Wilmington, Delaware; and Philadelphia and Bloomsburg, Pennsylvania. At small fields in Youngstown, Ohio, and Towanda, Pennsylvania, and at Forbes Field in Pittsburgh, the players from the Homestead Grays, like pitcher Smokey Joe Williams, ably comported themselves against the great white players on Mack's team from October 1 through October 8. Earle Mack's team went on to face other opposition in towns in Ohio as well. What seems to have been their last game was in Glouster, Ohio, as the *Enquirer* wrote of the game in the town of 3,200, "The stars will tackle Schaub's Camden Club on Saturday [October 16, 1926] at which time George Burns will be presented with an automobile by Al Rue, a close friend of the Cleveland star."

Holway's note on Grove's two losses to the black teams was this: "When asked about it 50 years later, he replied, 'I never pitched against black teams'" (220).

At least one player, Bill McKechnie, was not anxious about the winter: "'The winter's coal is bought, I'm fit and the hunting season is at hand. So why worry.'"

1927

The sole piece of news about barnstorming, always slight anyway, was that the *Washington Post* guessed that pitcher Al Zachary would join some Philadelphia and Detroit players out on the road. Ruth and Gehrig cashed in from exhibition games as they did in 1926.

1928

For those who needed to, there were still ways to make winter money. The Cubs made World Series money totaling $677 for finishing third and probably another $40 each for winning the city series with the White Sox. Paul and Lloyd Waner signed to go on the Loew's Vaudeville Circuit, paid at $3,000 per week.

In 1928, Ty Cobb went to Japan with a friend but not with any other players to play about ten games with college teams and to teach the Japanese his batting secrets.

The chief, maybe only, barnstormer was another of the Athletics, Jimmie Foxx. One of Foxx's biographers, Daniel, said Foxx was able to command $5,000 for his work in October. There were four games in Baltimore in which Foxx appeared, at times alongside his teammate Lefty Grove, against the Baltimore Black Sox.

Then he moved to Milwaukee to face his teammate Al Simmons for whom Milwaukee was home. Later, games in California followed.

1929

Again there was scattered and incomplete news of barnstormers. Someone toured Watertown, New York, and Reading, Pennsylvania. In four games in Chicago against the black Chicago American Giants, an Earle Mack team could boast of meeting future Hall of Fame players Heinie Manush, Bill Foster, and Willie Wells.

In Baltimore, Athletics pitchers Ed Rommel, Howard Ehmke, Cary Odgen and Ed Carrol played with the Baltimore Orioles of the International League against the Baltimore Black Sox.

The Kansas City Monarchs, after winning at San Antonio, Texas, against the San Luis Potosi Cubans of Mexico by 10–5 and 6–0, were now part of the California Winter League and there contested five games against Tony Lazzeri, Bob Meusel, Fred Haney, plus minor leaguers, at the time, Smead Jolley, Gus Suhr, Irish Meusel, Sloppy Thurston and Herman Pillette.

It seems that both Al Simmons and Jimmie Foxx were interested in adding to their $6,003 World Series payout and on October 19, 1929, they had a contest in Springfield, Illinois. These two engaged in a series of games without those being true barnstorming because only three of the named players on the team were current major leaguers.

After a game at Milwaukee, they went to California for exhibitions scheduled at Los Angeles, San Francisco and Sacramento.

The Sporting News of November 14 summed up: "Simmons and Foxx made a tour of many cities throughout the Middle West and West, taking part in games with local teams, one on one side and one on the other."

Exhibition Games

1920

In 1920, Charles A. Stoneham, owner of the New York Giants, saw it to be perfectly acceptable, as did the cartel, to buy a controlling interest in a Havana race track.

Not so comfortable with other gambling enterprises was the rest of baseball which helped to empanel a grand jury in late 1920 to investigate the 1919 World Series. New York Giants pitcher Rube Benton testified that he knew the series was fixed, naming White Sox players.

While this was playing out, the Reds finished their season on October 4, immediately arranging an exhibition game. On October 12, the Boston Braves with Rabbit Maranville came to Worchester, Massachusetts, meeting the Graton and Knight industrial baseball team. Facing another industrial team — the Pond Tool Works nine — were Al Schacht of the Washington team and his catcher, Val Pichinich, playing alongside of some minor leaguers in Plainfield, New Jersey. A third company team — the Bigelow-Hartford team challenged the Red Sox at Thompsonville, Connecticut, against pitchers Herb Pennock and Joe Bush with Wally Schang catching.

The Yankees—or at least Jack Quinn, Bob Meusel (who pitched) and Truck Hannah—found themselves in New Haven, Connecticut, on October 4. The locals had loaded up with Ross Young, Dave Bancroft, Joe Dugan and Cy Perkins.

Babe Ruth was not with his Yankee teammates, engaging in a game in New York City for which he was said by the *Cincinnati Enquirer* to have been paid $1,000. (Ruth supposedly had also been offered $2,500 for one exhibition and $5,500 for three consecutive games from October 8–10, 1920.) After the Babe finished games in Philadelphia, Ruth, Wally Schang, Carl Mays and Fred Hoffman toured in Oneonta, New York; Jersey City, New Jersey; and then in three more New Jersey spots, Perth Amboy, Camden, and Trenton.

"Babe Ruth denies that he broke his wrist in a barnstorming game," said *The Sporting News* on October 28. "He's doing a little bit of moving picture work in New York now, after which he will make a trip to Cuba." David Pietrusza writes that Ruth had legally earned an estimated $40,000 in exhibitions in 1920.

There must have been something about the amount of money Ruth was earning outside of baseball, the kind of money the Black Sox players had earned outside of baseball, that made the high commissioner of baseball pay attention. Two months after Landis banished the eight players from baseball for life he was going after Ruth for his barnstorming.

Did players have strong objections to the way the cartel treated them? The financial report of the 1920 World Series demonstrated that the players received 28 percent of the receipts and the team owners 26 percent. But, somehow, the players were allotted less money if they lost the Series, while the owners each received the same amount no matter who won.

Other games and other players did not attract so much of the new commissioner's attention perhaps because, as Landis said, they were not from a World Series team. Or they were for a good cause. Rogers Hornsby and George Sisler, for example, announced that they planned games on October 3 or 4 for disabled soldiers in St. Louis. (There had been a benefit game near season's end for Christy Mathewson who was "in the life battle he was fighting against the white plague at Saranac Lake," as the *New York Times* described Mathewson's plight.) Another benefit game was played in Scranton, Pennsylvania, at Athletic Park on October 19, 1921, for the ill Jimmy O'Neill of the Senators. The game attracted a crowd of 1,500 who saw not only Steve O'Neill and George Burns of Cleveland along with Chick Shorten of Detroit, but also there, but not on the field, were Wally Schang and Mike McNally of the Yankees along with Eddie Collins of the White Sox, and featherweight boxing champion Johnny Kilbane.

The Sporting News of October 20, 1921, told of how "A few of the Indians joined up with [outfielder] Elmer Smith and gave Smith's home folks down to Sandusky a glimpse of how regular ball players perform ... Tris Speaker and [catcher] Les Nunaker" took part. In Attleboro, Massachusetts, Patsy Gharrity and Walter Johnson played for the home squad while the Providence team listed Rabbit Maranville, Joe Dugan, Joe Judge, Sam Rice, Hank Gowdy, and pitcher Joe Oeschger before 4,000.

The *St. Louis Post-Dispatch* of October 19, 1921, wrote of a game which seemed to fly directly in the face of the new commissioner: ten Senators, including Walter Johnson, traveled to Chester, Pennsylvania, though Chester players were on the ineligible list.

1922

By the year after, the ban on playing postseason games was beginning to be overlooked, so that *The Sporting News* of October 26, 1922, mentioned a lineup of Giants and Braves playing ten days earlier at Oil City, Pennsylvania.

Mike Cvengros, Giants rookie, pitched against a group of Cardinals facing the team of Pana, Illinois, who had Bill Barnes on the mound. The *New York Times* reported that "Hornsby has signed up with Milton Stock" of the Cardinals infield to barnstorm. The American League all-stars, with Eddie Rommel pitching, won at Johnstown, Pennsylvania. Two weeks later an exhibition at Baltimore, Maryland, also featured Rommel.

Meeting other teams as well, said the *New York Times*, were the Brooklyn squad that defeated the Recreation Club semipro team in Plainfield, New Jersey, on October 2, 1922. The Associated Press, in a story published by the *Brooklyn Daily Eagle*, said that Carl Mays and Wally Schang would head another barnstorming party and the *New York Tribune* reported that the two were to tour Arizona and Oklahoma.

1923

Even Ruth, used to big paydays playing exhibitions, did not tour much in 1923. There had been contested a five innning exhibition on October 8, 1923, between the Washington Nationals and the Baltimore All-Stars at Oriole Park. Taking part were Nick Altrock, Goose Goslin, Sam Rice, and Bucky Harris. Four days later Bucky Harris, Goose Goslin and Tom Zachary were part of a team in New Haven, Connecticut.

Back on July 11, the *New York Times* reported that the Bastrop, Louisiana, semipros had on their roster four of the eight Black Sox players—Joe Jackson, Eddie Cicotte, Swede Risberg, and Buck Weaver—and this group "has walloped every club it has met in North Louisiana and South Arkansas." Apparently Cicotte was playing under the name of Moore.

1924

The tour that attracted the most attention in 1924 were the teams touring Europe, the Giants and White Sox, who played a few games in Quebec before leaving.

After finishing their schedule four days earlier, the New York Giants were covered by the *New York Times* for October 2, 1924, at

Ossining, NY, October 1. While a large crowd of prisoners and other spectators looked on, the New York Giants, champions for the fourth consecutive time of the National League, today played the baseball nine of the Mutual Welfare League on the prison field at Sing Sing.

Not far from the prison town, at Kingston, New York, the Brooklyn team, now called the Robins, met the city's Colonials before moving across the country. Listed was the Brooklyn battery of Burleigh Grimes and

Charlie Hargreaves, and postion players Milt Stock, Bernie Neis, and Ivy Olson. The Phillies visited in Wilkes-Barre on October 2 and some players went to California to play because that was where the baseball players golf tournament was to begin on October 30, 1924. In that state, Griff says that Walter Johnson pitched in games in Los Angeles on October 26 against Vernon, against a Babe Ruth aggregation on October 27, and on October 29 at Oakland in a game advertised as Joe Devine's Major-League All-Stars versus Walter "Duster" Mails' Coast League All-Stars.

But of all of Johnson's work in the postseason perhaps the most remarkable took place on October 11, 1924, in Rochester, New York, for a team known as Ed "Eldorado" Holley's American Leaguers. Joining Johnson there were teammates George Mogridge, Joe Judge, Nick Altrock, and Al Schacht. Also on the club were Charlie Jamieson from the Indians, Steve O'Neill and Howard Ehmke of the Red Sox, and Joe Bush of the Yankees along with his teammate, 21-year-old Lou Gehrig. The club next played in Hazleton, Pennsylvania, but was not heard of again.

1925

In the second week of October 1925, the Yankees and the Tigers were playing on the fairgrounds of Bloomsburg, Pennsylvania. Mentioned were Bob Shawkey and Wally Schang; Bob Mesuel pitched game two for the Yankees. Rip Collins, Oscar Stanage, Jess Doyle and Bob Fothergill were listed with Detroit. A three-game set was promised but just two games were recorded.

Later, *The Sporting News* of October 15, 1925, wrote about Bob Shawkey's "day" in his home town of Brockville, Pennsylvania, and with Wally Schang catching, the honoree pitched against neighboring Sykesville.

Echoes of the Black Sox remained. Happy Felsch and Swede Risberg signed with the town team in Scobey, Montana, for $600 a month, plus expenses, and Joe Jackson took part in an exhibition game with Waycross against Macon at Americus at the Americus Play Ground Diamond July 27–30, 1925.

Walter Johnson and Max Carey participated in two games for the American Legion at Daytona, Florida and the Cleveland Indians travled to Muncie, Indiana, to play its Athletics.

Meanwhile Commissioner Landis was still working his way through his thinking about postseason play. *The Sporting News* relayed talk of a Florida (or Miami) Winter League which would have "close to major league players." Frankie Frisch was said to manage the Croissant Park team, Stanley Harris of the champion Senators for another team in the league, and George Sisler at the head of the Miami Shores club, the league to run November 11 to February 22. A month and a half later *The Sporting News* reported that "Sisler, in conformity with the major league contract stipulation, will be a non-playing manager. In no case is a major league player permitted to play in an off-season league because of the wording of their contracts. Commissioner Landis laid down the rule on the matter some weeks ago when a number of big league players sought permission to play with the teams."

1926

By the next year, 1926, *The Sporting News*, took note that the Florida Winter League did not do so well in 1925 and might not play at all in 1926. In New York City's Dyckman Oval, Jeff Teserau's Bears played the New York Giants for two doubleheaders in two consecutive days.

Out west, Nebraska native — and hero of the 1926 World Series— Grover Cleveland Alexander pitched in Omaha "in a friendly game between two of Omaha's fastest amateur teams" and was hired "to pitch another sandlot game Sunday at Council Bluffs." That game apparently was followed by his own day at home in St. Paul, Nebraska, celebrated by 15,000 people. Alexander was given a Masonic watch charm and then pitched three innings. "After the ball game," the AP story reported, "the thousands feasted on seven beeves in a great barbecue and tonight attended a pavement dance."

After announcing his retirement in 1927 and just a few years from managing, Walter Johnson was in California looking to make it his permanent home while playing in three exhibition games. In the first game, the aging pitcher was paid $1,000 plus expenses to pitch for the White King Soap Company team. "Walter autographed 50 balls for charity, and was presented in return a ball autographed by 50 Hollywood movie stars," the C. W. Carey family web site claims (http://www.cwcfamily.org/wj/cc8.html).

Johnson had also pitched in mid-October in Warrenton, Virginia, at a Boy Scout benefit matching the Phillies against Walter Johnson, Sam Rice and Joe Judge playing for the Warrenton All-Stars (Griff, 300) and Johnson met Dazzy Vance in Denver shortly after.

1928

Ty Cobb, on his way to Japan, was convinced to appear in Seattle for a Dugdale Park exhibition, going 4 for 6. Continuing the tradition of playing in your home town after the season, Jess Haines, now often called "Pop," from Clayton, Ohio, pitched in a game between Brockville and a team near his home of Farmersville. "Sunny Jim Bottomley of the St. Louis Cardinals capitalized on his fame as a World's Series player on October 11, at Edwardsville, Ill., playing first base for the Edwardsville all stars against the local Edwardsville team. A tremendous crowd saw the game."

1929

As the effects of the Great Depression began to be felt across the world in 1929, Bottomley again signed on at Edwardsville for the annual Simon Kellerman baseball game and barbecue on October 13. At Montclair, New Jersey, on October 21, Mule Haas went on the field with his old Claremont squad. "He went home with a radio set, the gift of the fans." Down in Augusta, Georgia, a game was played with barnstormers Alvin Crowder of the Browns, Rick and Wes Ferrell, and Sammy Byrd, the Yankees' rookie outfielder called "Babe Ruth's legs." Jimmie Foxx and Al Simmons from the triumphant Philadelphia Athletics were signed to appear on Sunday, October 27, in Los Angeles.

Babe Herman went out on a vaudeville tour with Newark pitcher, and singer, Al Mamaux. Mamaux was a former Pirates and Dodgers pitcher during a twelve-year career.

CHAPTER FOUR

Barnstorming Tours and Exhibition Games, 1930–1939

FOR MOST OF THE 1930s, except for Earle Mack, barnstorming virtually disappeared. There were still some rare tours, but the influence of the Great Depression no doubt brought about reluctance on the part of both organizers and players. When salaries had dropped back by 60 percent to their pre-1920 level during this time, the uncertainty of barnstorming was being avoided.

But the decade saw the ascendancy of two pitchers. First, brash Dizzy Dean, with the help of promoter Ray Doan, offered his services to large venues after the season, most successfully after his, and his brother's, fabulous 1934 championship season. The second pitcher was Bob Feller, who at age 18 in the 1936 season, his first, was able to draw $4,000 in the postseason, also through the offices of Ray Doan.

Team owners agreed on an All-Star Game in 1933 as a way to spark interest, and attendance, in these hard times. But at year's end in 1939 a ten day limit, applicable only after the World Series was completed, was imposed on touring, effectively killing barnstorming until after World War II.

Barnstorming Tours

1930

Scattered reports continued from various sources. *The Sporting News* on October 16, 1930, said that Al Simmons, with Jimmie Foxx and George Earnshaw, played in Milwaukee on October 12, and then in Peoria and New Orleans on October 26. In 1930 or in 1931 or both, George Giles in *Black Diamonds* recounts, "We were playing Bill Terry's All-Stars, the Waner brothers, Heinie Meine, Babe Herman" (Holway, 63).

Giles also says that in the 1930s, "We played the Dean boys, the Waner boys, Billy Herman, Ruth, Gehrig, Waite Hoyt, Herb Pennock, Steve Swetonic, Max Carey, Pepper Martin, Jim Bottomley, Lefty Grove, Schoolboy Rowe, Tommy Bridges, George Earnshaw, Lefty O'Doul."

The tour for what would be Earle Mack's team began on October 2, 1930, meeting the Chicago American Giants for a series of games at the Giants Field on 39th Street and Wentworth Avenue. For now, the incomplete team included Charley Gehringer, Harry Heilmann and Lefty O'Doul. *The Sporting News* paid attention to that team's stops at Minneapolis and Sioux City. That game's date marked the end of the World Series, won by Mack's Athletics.

The next day, October 9, found the not-yet-complete team in Huron, South Dakota, a city of fewer than 11,000 people, but 11,000 fans packed the stands for the game. This city remained, as many cities did, a relatively rural area. Though Huron could claim just 13 percent of its roads paved, it was served by two railroads. The game itself was more or less over soon into the first few innings (it ended at 15–1) as Earl Whitehill of the Tigers and Art Shires of the Washington team pitched the game.

But the best part of the game came after seven-year-old South Dakotan Walter Green started walking home through the outfield in the ninth inning, seeing that the game was a blowout. Harry Heilmann, playing center field that day, started to chat with the boy and asked him if he wanted to cover center field for the major leaguers. Taking the glove, the boy bent over, hands on knees, as he had learned to do. Just then, a Huron player slammed a line drive right near the young center fielder who was being spoken to by Heilmann, squatting next to him. Harry grabbed the ball on the fly and since the boy, Walter, had been in the field wearing a glove, he was given credit for one of the twenty-seven putouts and then given the ball as well.

Likewise, the next stop was in a city of some size — 33,000 — though it would be typical of the time to see that although the city could claim it had 125 miles of streets, only 34 percent of those miles were paved. Serviced by five different railroads, it was from one of those that four new team members alighted, their World Series ended. The Philadelphia Athletics had won the Series four games to two on October 8 and by October 10, Lefty Grove, Rube Walberg, Bing Miller and Wally Schang, now a part-time player, arrived along with Earle Mack and Nick Altrock, "clown coach of the Senators." This was the first long trip for Earle Mack.

Grove, seeing all the reporters at the Sioux Falls station said, "I thought I got rid of you newspaper fellows in Chicago."

Barnstorming, apparently, was supposed to mean freedom from observation. Or perhaps to Grove it meant that he was so far out of the usual baseball world that he did not expect the same level of scrutiny or curiosity. That expectation may have been yet another of the pleasures of barnstorming. Seeing new places, playing games with the pressure removed, playing for fans who understood that what they were seeing was an exhibition being played, not a contest during, as it was called at the time, the championship season (just as spring training was called the training season). America was still not yet an automobile's country in 1930, since there were 694,000 miles of rural surfaced roads in the whole country and 2,315,000 miles not surfaced.

And this was still a country that counted Sunday as a day of rest so that Blue Laws forbade miniature golf, movies, driving the auto for pleasure, deliveries of bread, dance recitals, tin cans on bridal cars, swimming pools, ice sales, playing of outdoor games, operating trains, as well as baseball with admission charged. To encourage these restrictions, groups such as the Lord's Day Alliance and the Women's National Sabbath Alliance held some sway.

With the Mack team now complete, three Hall of Fame–level players were liable to be on the field at once:

Charlie Gehringer, Tigers—1949 Hall of Fame
Harry Heilmann, Tigers—1952 Hall of Fame
Lefty Grove, Athletics—1947 Hall of Fame

The team gathered in Sioux Falls at the American Legion field at Elmwood Park where 2,500 paid — tickets were priced at $1.10 and 85 cents— to see their opposition. That collection of men included players from two semipro clubs, the Sioux Falls Canaries and the Sioux Falls Cowboys, including Sam Dailey who had pitched for the Phillies in 1929. Altrock's "tomfoolery" kept the fans laughing and with the help of Art Shires, a boxer himself, presented "a boxing act in which Altrock knocked himself groggy. He climaxed it all by hitting a weak grounder ... and perching serenely on third base when the opposition looked about to see why he had not made his appearance at the proper station" (*Sioux Falls Daily-Argus Leader*, October 11, 1930).

Grove was called upon to pitch against a former Northern League team, the Fargo-Morehead Twins, in Fargo, North Dakota, a game followed by a contest in Bismarck in the same state. With a game being mentioned on October 14 in Yakima, Washington, the team was next heard of for four games in Los Angeles beginning on October 29 against the Royal Giants and two California Winter League teams.

Apparently some players left the group and some players—Max Bishop of Mack's Athletics, Spud Davis from the Phillies, and Johnny Neun of the Boston Braves—joined it. This team was managed by Earle Mack, son of Connie Mack, and barnstormed its way across the country. Against the

Commercial Club, the final game for the travelers on October 31, 1930, "the contest was one of the best of the series even if the All-Stars did have to restrain themselves in the tenth to let the winning run score and prevent another extra inning of toil.... The All-Star infielders, anxious to catch a 6 o'clock train for the East, came in so close [pitcher Art] Shires had room to wind up and that's all" the *Los Angeles Times*' writer Bob Ray reported. Then "Joe Mellano slapped a line drive and [Red] Kress reached up before he thought, but pulled his hands down just in time to let it whizz over his head." That brought home the winning run. "All of which shows how hard it is to end a ball game sometimes."

The game also marked the end of exhibition games for the year and the beginning of the California Winter League's schedule.

1931

In *Total Baseball*'s "The History of Major League Baseball," David Q. Voigt commented on the Great Depression's effect on baseball.

Major league baseball felt the effects of the gathering Depression in 1931, when the AL suffered losses while the NL barely broke even. Once engulfed by the economic storm, both major leagues were hard hit as attendance fell to 8.1 million in 1932 and hit rock bottom with an overall total of 6.3 million in 1933. Thereafter attendance improved, but not until 1940 did annual attendance totals reach 10 million.... In the AL ... after losing a total of $156,000 in 1931, the league suffered three desperate years during which overall losses topped $2 million.... Nor were conditions much better in the NL, which also lost heavily during the years 1932–1934.... Under such financial pressures, salaries of major league players were slashed.... Such cuts dropped the average player's salary to $6,000 in 1933, and the 1939 average salary of $7,300 still lagged behind the $7,500 figure of 1929.

In these hard times, Major League Baseball was asked for "a share of the World Series receipts [to] be devoted to relief for the needy of the Nation." By now, the sharply increasing number of unemployed — the number rose over 15 percent for the first time in 1931 — caused this request from the *Washington Post*. Responding, organized baseball appointed William Harridge, president of the league of which Washington was a part, to deal with the newspaper. Harridge pointed to seven charity games already contended at the end of the season in 1931, games which generated over $200,000 for the unemployed and President Heydler of the National League said that "baseball has made a very creditable showing in its charity efforts."

Landis at least chose to allow exhibition games after October 31 and until November 15, so long as "the entire receipts go to relief or charity funds."

As for the World Series receipts, after the shares to the players were disbursed two weeks later, there remained $633,363 to go the clubs and the commissioner.

Babe Ruth, still active in the postseason, went to Los Angeles for three games beginning Sunday, October 18, but as Ruth was fading from the barnstorming scene, another player came into it. Dizzy Dean was a star that year, but with the Houston, Texas, Buffaloes. True, he had pitched with the Cardinals after the Texas League season was over, but only for nine innings. Even so, Dizzy felt himself ready to entertain fans nearby to St. Louis and he returned to the city where he had played in 1930, St. Joseph, Missouri, of the Western League. Playing for that city he had earned $100 per month, this sum being less than an average worker outside of baseball who was being paid $104 each month.

With games lined up for Charleston, Missouri (3,400); Joplin, Missouri (34,000); and Atkins, Arkansas, a town of 1,400 in Dizzy's home state, reports show that really only one game was completed. In Charleston, Dean boasted that he would pitch half the game left-handed and still strike out fifteen. However, his rival pitcher, the ex-St. Louis Browns pitcher Elam Vangilder, the veteran from Cape Girardeau, led his team, the Caphas, and Vangilder struck out 22, allowing two hits enabling his team to take a 4–0 victory over Dean's team. Though Dizzy had negotiated to pitch in Joplin, Missouri, asking for $150, promoters thought it was too much to pay, and called off the game.

Too much may have been Lefty Grove's thinking too when he pitched an exhibition game in Newark, New Jersey, on Friday, September 25, against the Newark Bears, the second-place team of the International League. Max Bishop may also have played for Grove. Since the season had ended for the Bears five days earlier, this suggests the game was not a duty of Grove's during the run of his 1931 contract, but rather a money-making opportunity. His attraction to the Newark fans certainly would have been his thirty wins— so far — that year. The great Grove finished his contract on the last day of the season and went on to beat the Yankees for his thirty-first win, enough to earn him a Most Valuable Player Award.

The Sporting News of October 31 took note of players Art Shires, Karl Swanson (former White Sox infielder), and Lynn King (later of the Cardinals), among minor leaguers, who played on October 10 at the Des Moines, Iowa, Western League Park, "Art The Great Shires ... will receive all interviewers, photographers and sightseers" the local paper declared, at 9 a.m. on game day. About 200 people watched five innings in a light drizzle before the team moved on to Omaha, Nebraska. There, Mel Harder, who started on the sandlots of Omaha, pitched in a 4–4 tie for the Murphys, who opposed the team of Lefty Gomez, Rube Walberg, Earl Whitehill (with the Tigers in 1931), and Al Schacht.

There may have been a game in Wichita, Kansas, on the twelfth, but the next game certainly happened on October 20, a night game in Houston, Texas, at Buffalo Stadium opposing the Admiration Coffee company team, who were state amateur champions. Called on to pitch were Rube Walberg and Al Schacht, as was Earl Whitehill. With fans numbering 1,200, paying $1.75, 50 cents and 25 cents, they saw their hometown team lose 5–1, partly due to their four errors.

After a game to be played on October 21 in El Paso, Texas, as *The Sporting News* reported on November 5, the team moved to California where, with contests organized by Boots Weber and Oscar Reichow, they met such players as Babe Herman from Brooklyn and Wally Berger of the Braves, as well as former major leaguers Frank Shellenback, George Burns and Jigger Statz. Probably Fred Haney manned third. With the tour due to finish in California, here it is not clear who was on the team and who was opposing the team because now for the first time listed in these games are Ernie Orsatti, of the Cardinals, Bill Dickey and Benny Bengough of the Yankees, with Johnny Kerr of the White Sox.

At any rate, during the October 23 night game, won by Mack's team 8–0,

Nick Altrock and Al Schacht kept the fans in an uproar with their comedy throughout the contest. They put on a special act before the start of the game and then took the coaching lines over while the contest was in progress [*Los Angeles Times*, October 24, 1931].

The final game may have been in San Francisco on October 29.

1932

Unemployment grew to five million in 1930, and rose to thirteen million in 1932, a number representing 23.6 percent of the work force, the highest percent reached — so far — during the Great Depression. And no one knew when this calamity would be halted, or slow down, or if it would simply keep growing. Workers were often given three options: see your job disappear, take a 20 percent cut or take a 50 percent cut.

Up until now major league rosters had settled at 25 players each. But using the December 9, 1931, entry from Jim Charlton's book, we read: "Baseball owners, fearful of the effects of the Depression, vote to cut organizations from 25 players to 23." This means 32 fewer major league jobs on the 16 teams. As for the salaries in those jobs, for example, the World Series-winning St. Louis Cardinals cut the salary of the great star Frankie Frisch by 27 percent, from $28,000 to $18,500. Another great star, Bill Terry, was sent a contract that cut his salary from $22,500 to $13,500, a 40 percent cut. In the American League, one umpire's position was cut.

In his second year, having been credited with 75 homers in 1931, Josh Gibson was paid $275 per month in 1932, or $1,375 per season. It was his team that met the National League All-Stars in seven games in four cities from September 26 to October 7. Those Crawfords, besides their great catcher, also showed a lineup with Satchel Paige, Judy Johnson, and Oscar Charleston — four future electees to the Hall of Fame — while the National League All-Stars had signed Hack Wilson, Fred Frankhouse, and Roy Parmelee.

"A group of Negro players from the Royal Giants toured the country ... in 1932 and lost one of 24 games," according to the *Cultural Encyclopedia of Baseball.* White players calling themselves the St. Louis All Stars made a team with Paul Dean (in the minors in 1932) and brother Dizzy (18–15 in 1932, who had, among other things, collected the most National League strikeouts with 191. Once the St. Louis Cardinals finished their season on September 25, young pitcher Paul Derringer and catcher Jimmy Wilson joined the squad. But this was a team with not enough major leaguers to qualify as barnstorming, particularly after Jimmie Wilson left the team to be with his sick child.

But one game, in Carbondale, Illinois, has some interest now and had enough importance for the city's mayor for him to ask the merchants and businessmen to close their doors for the game. With Wilson gone, Dizzy called on his pal Pepper Martin to join him for this game. Then, Dean, Martin and Derringer played with the Carbondale Van Natta Aces, placing Paul Dean at second, Pepper Martin at first and in right field, Dizzy Dean in center who halfway through planned to switch with and replace starter Paul Derringer.

Arriving at noon, the traveling squad paraded to "give the fans a glimpse at them," the *Carbondale Free Press* wrote. The game drew "the largest crowd ever to witness a baseball game in Carbondale. Fans were treated to big league thrills when Pepper Martin made one of his famous diving shoestring catches and came back in the same inning to stretch a single into a double by diving headlong into second base." In addition, "several valuable souvenirs were given away to the holders of lucky numbers, which included autographed balls and bats, gloves, and shoes," so it seemed the crowd went home happy after the 2–1 Carbondale victory. Dizzy was also hired to pitch for the Pevely nine for the championship of Belleville, Missouri, against the St. Louis Dairys.

It was left up to Earle Mack to continue full barnstorming for the year. All that is known now is that the team visited Sioux Falls, South Dakota, on October 2, 1932, and on October 4, Jamestown, North Dakota. In that city of 8,187, the hometown Jamestown Jimmies hired three Negro League players: Charles Hancock (St. Louis Giants 1921), Red Haley (Cuban Stars 1933), Barney "Lefty" Brown (last with the Cuban Stars in 1931–32), then with the Minot Mallards. But the all-stars won 3–2 while the clowns, Altrock and Schacht, kept the crowd [of 1,800] in good humor ... and are worth the price of admission alone.... Their jokes and performance was as good as could be. They imitated Graham McNamee in a broadcast stunt, which was clever.

After the game, about 150 people attended the Gladstone Hotel banquet. After player introductions, there was some singing, some more jokes and entertainment by Altrock and Schacht. After the introductions of a few candidates for statewide office, the banquet concluded.

The next place to play was in Devils Lake (5,500) and "A group of fans from this city," the *Jamestown Sun* reported, "will journey to Jamestown [98 miles], where the Stars play tonight, and bring them here after the game in the Bluejay city. The members of the all-star team will spend Wednesday hunting" with members of the Isaak Walton League.

While the Stars pounded out 12 hits for five runs Thursday afternoon at Lakewood Park, the opponents made only three hits and no runs, even with Grove on the bench. Both Altrock and Schacht made an impression as they "entertained the crowd with their wisecracks from the coaching boxes, their slow motion hitting and pitching, and their pinch hitting in the ninth when each of the comedians singled," the *Sun* commented.

Though it was the last North Dakota game, the most populous of the cities— 28,619 — was saved for the final game. The October 9 event was contested at Moorhead League Park against the Fargo-Moorhead Twins at 3:30 P.M. Snow was beginning to fall all over the state and the game had to compete with a five-hour air show at Hector Field that started at 1:30 P.M. But the game went on in the cold and the all-stars won again, this time 12–8.

1933

Meanwhile, second baseman Frankie Frisch's salary, which had been cut from $28,000 to $18,500 in 1932, would be reduced further, to under $10,000, since the Cardinals team owner had a new rule: there would be no salaries over $10,000 for that year. Branch Rickey stood alone as the highest paid man in baseball at $49,470 in 1933.

Young Hank Greenberg said his pay was $3,300 in 1933. The mean major league player salary was $6,099. Commissioner Landis agreed to a 40 percent pay cut and even Babe Ruth took a 31 percent cut. The cuts made sense. Unemployment in 1933 reached 24.9 percent, eight times that of 1929. It was a sparse and hard year for everyone, even in the barnstorming.

Not much was printed about a trip to Mexico for ten games planned to begin on October 1, 1933, with Charlie Dressen and pitcher Tex Carleton, along with some Nashville players. Dressen had just finished his last year as a player and might have been interested in showing his leadership qualities and managerial ability in heading up the team. But the only mention of the team's play was a fight reported in Mexico City on October 22 when "more than forty police and gendarmes were required to break up a free-for-all fight today at the close of a baseball game" (*Los Angeles Times*) between the Azteca team and Dressen's team.

Occasional news about Jimmie Foxx reached the papers. Sticking to his home state of Maryland, Foxx, a player in the first All-Star game that year, played a few games but suffered a broken foot, discovering the injury only a week later.

Dizzy Dean and brother Paul again tried to pick up some money going out after the season's end, but Paul received an injured arm in Pasadena and their red ink amounted to $800 for their troubles.

1934

Earle Mack took a team out again to the Dakotas, but when the team arrived in Winnipeg headlines blared the news of Jimmie Foxx's beaning. Foxx remained in the hospital till the night of the ninth and then left for Regina to rejoin Mack's team.

Al Schacht wrote about this trip in his biography under the heading "Canadian Views":

> I had my own loudspeaker with me and I'd climb up to the roof of the grand stand and broadcast the game from there for the benefit of the fans who were looking right at it. You know, I'd give them the old stuff: "Ladies and gentlemen of the radio audience, the game is about to start. The weather is wonderful. The huge crowd is all excited. The pitcher is winding up. He throws! It's a terrific blow the batter hits— it's going over the fence — It's still climbing— it's a homer — no, pardon folks! The shortstop caught it just behind the pitcher's box; This is the National Flycasting Company, Silver-tongued Schacht speaking." ...
> At the end of the eighth inning I would announce: "Hold your seats, folks. I will now go down and pitch the ninth inning and you will see pitching that is pitching. I will let you listen to the applause that greets this announcement." I'd clap my hands in front of the microphone and, then shinny down off the roof with the contraption [Schacht, 134].

With the memory of Foxx's broken foot in 1933 and the beaning in 1934, President Harridge of the American League desired to ban all barnstorming, no matter how much fun it was for the players and the fans. The Associated Press on October 7 reported:

> Barnstorming Ban Urged by Harridge Cites Injuries to Foxx, Deans as Reasons for Proposal. CHICAGO, October 7 An absolute ban on all barnstorming by major league baseball players was advocated today by President Will Harridge, of the American League. President Harridge said action undoubtedly would be

taken on the subject at the annual winter meeting.... President Harridge said the only thing to do was to prohibit barnstorming altogether. "Baseball gives the player every possible protection during the regular session," President Harridge said. "The players are provided with the best of everything—food, hotels, railroads and playing fields. And then, as soon as the season ends, many of them immediately rush off to play exhibition games on poor fields, with poor accommodations and without proper supervision. Injuries are apt to result, and often do. In many cases, antics of wildcat promoters, whose interest, naturally, is not in baseball but in their personal pocketbooks, give the game a bad name. The magnate has an undeniable property right in the player's career which the player, by barnstorming, places in jeopardy without any compensation for the magnate.

And Heydler did chime in, not taking quite so strident a tone about his property. The Associated Press continued to report developments on October 9:

BARNSTORMING BAN SEEN AS UNLIKELY. Heydler doubts That Clubs of Major League Will Stop Post-Season Activities. He States Players Owe It to Themselves to Get Proper Rest. While not giving three cheers for the extra-curricular activities of big league baseball players, John A. Heydler, president of the National League, is inclined to doubt that club owners of the two major circuits will place a ban on post-season barnstorming.... Heydler said the National League is not likely to discuss barnstorming at its annual meeting unless the matter is brought up at the joint session of the leagues.

On October 17, President Heydler of the National League reiterated the fact that "the proposed ban on all barnstorming would have to be adopted jointly by both leagues and the contracts for players also would have to be jointly changed so as not to permit barnstorming."

The urge to ban postseason play when only the players got a cut of the money was still alive.

A 1934 *Brooklyn Daily Eagle* cartoon on President Harridge's diatribe against barnstorming.

Barnstorming with Jimmie Foxx in Grand Forks, North Dakota, in 1934. This advertisement appeared in the *Grand Forks Herald*.

Dean earned from exhibitions, not barnstorming, more than $9,000 at a time when bread cost a nickel and a quart of milk a dime. This amount may seem high but look at other 1934 salaries. Doctors averaged $3,500; $520 was the average for waitresses; congressmen had the highest average annual salary, $8,600. (Dean's postseason total of $9,591 in the year 1934 has the same purchasing power as $133,290 in the year 2003.) The postseason amount was also more than 50 percent of his salary and bonuses for the year.

The 275 separate dust storms in 1934 caused children to die of dust pneumonia and forced parents to make their children sleep with wet towels on their mouths. Hundreds of families left their homes for California. Unemployment stood at 21.7 percent.

But then, in the midst of poverty and suffering there were "the crack executives of National Distillers Products Corp. President Seton Porter's annual salary was upped from $51,000 to $75,000. Most of the vice presidents were boosted, including Daniel K. Weiskopf who was jumped from $15,640 to $47,286. Even Secretary & Treasurer Thomas A. Clark was raised from $13,806 to $17,886" (Derks, 246). Judy Garland's starting salary was $100 per week.

Was Dean paid too much?

In *The Glory of Their Times*, Hank Greenberg said his pay was $5,500 in 1934 (Ritter).

1935

Some new money had to be generated in baseball even if it meant taking a chance on broadcasting games. William Wrigley, Cubs president, became the first owner to allow all of his team's games to be heard on the radio in 1935. Burk points out that the major leagues were very profitable in the 1920s, when each club averaged $115,000 in annual profits. Players' salaries rose from $5,000 to $8,000 over the course of the decade, but by 1935 average salaries had dropped from $8,000 to $5,000.

Dizzy Dean would be hard pressed to match the money he made in 1934. Though his 1935 pitching record approached his 1934 record, his team did not win the pennant, and so he took home about $4,000 less in World Series share than in the Gas House Gang year. Therefore, most observers would conclude, his value as a barnstormer went down.

Dizzy didn't think so. He hired umpire George Barr to be in charge of a tour which was announced to include twice as many games as the year before. Some might judge this doubling as greed, others as ego. But if Cardinals owner Sam Breadon made $80,000 from his Cardinals stock, a player might think that his income also ought to approach that fabulous number.

In this year Dizzy's touring came very close to true barnstorming—unlike 1934, when just he and his brother toured — because the team included more major leaguers: brother Paul, pitcher Larry French, utility man Mike Ryba, retired Joe Hauser, retired Hack Wilson and — as a touring opposition team — Webster McDonald, Cool Papa Bell, Ted Page, Boojum Wilson, Jerry Benjamin, Josh Gibson, Buck Leonard and Satchel Paige. "According to Ted Page, the Negro team won seven of the nine games" (Staten, 146). With four future black Hall of Fame players, no one ought to be surprised at black men's dominance.

Again, large metropolitan areas were chosen as game sites and many times that option met with success. In Pittsburgh, Pennsylvania, 30,000 paid and in New York City's Yankee Stadium, 15,000–20,000 fans paid.

But this would be a year that Dizzy would give a black eye to barnstorming because this year Dizzy would refuse to appear if he deemed attendance was so low so as not to be worth his time.

For Babe Ruth and Dizzy Dean, so the pitcher clearly thought, the Springfield, Missouri, crowd of 4,300 was not really enough. When, on October 7, in Kansas City, Missouri's Muehlebach Field a crowd of fewer than 900 attended, that number was not high enough to make Paul stay on the tour but it was enough to prompt Dizzy to cancel some games at smaller venues, such as Belleville, Missouri.

Then Dizzy himself gave up on a proposed game at New Orleans' Heinemann Park on October 18 when only 200 were in the stands at game time. But worst of all, as the *New York Times* of October 18, reported, Dizzy walked out on a scheduled game at Chattanooga when 375 fans had showed up at game time, though more were due. Instead, two mill teams played for the crowd, the Peerless and the Dixie Spinners.

Dizzy was later pressured by Joe Engel, the Chattanooga manager, through Commissioner Landis, to give $400 to $500 to Engel's Christmas toy fund for poor children in Chattanooga. Dean's reason was that he had "only a verbal agreement." Dizzy offered to return to pitch but Engel refused this way as reported by *The Sporting News* on October 14:

> Your wire received October 19 offering apology and expressing regret for your behavior at exhibition game, Chattanooga, October 17. Under no circumstances would I permit you to appear before my fans in any capacity, at any future date.

This disaster was followed by pick up games in California, games where Dean was hired as another star mostly to oppose black teams rather than a barnstorming game.

Whether or not Dean's conduct was a causal factor or not, barnstorming remained a problem in the minds of some owners.

By November 20 Colonel Jacob Ruppert, owner of the New York Yankees, was quoted as saying that he would like "the major leagues to prohibit players from engaging in post-season exhibition games." He also thought that "the player's salary would be paid on a monthly basis over a period of twelve months and the club owner should have exclusive use of his baseball services. If he wants to engage in some other business during the off-season, that is all right." (If the occupation was more dangerous than playing ball, Ruppert seemed unconcerned.) It was the colonel's opinion that some of his men "played themselves out" during a trip to Japan, so that the Yankees finished three games behind the Tigers in 1935.

The nail in the coffin of barnstorming was pounded in on December 11, 1935. "Barnstorming activities of major league ball players have been drastically curbed. The players will be allowed to engage in exhibition games for a period of only ten days after the close of the championship season."

1936

For some players, the lost income from barnstorming (or even exhibitions) was very distasteful, because as the nation began to rise out of the Great Depression, players' salaries did not. In fact, protesting what they felt to be unfairness, fifty players held out in 1936.

That year the season ended on September 27, and barnstorming jaunts could stay out only until October 7. This meant that, for anyone planning to go out on the road, they would have to face direct competition from the World Series and the fact that any bad weather at all would greatly decrease their limited time to draw income. The effect of the 1935 edict was severe limitations on most barnstorming activities.

The Sporting News spoke of plans for Dizzy Dean and Pepper Martin to go barnstorming and an additional tour sponsored by Ray Doan for which "Mize, King, Ryba and Winford [four Cardinals players] are supposed to go on an exhibition tour of Kansas and neighboring states."

Ray Doan, who had managed the Dizzy Dean exhibitions in 1934, now signed Bob Feller, just turned eighteen and graduated high school. Feller was slated to receive $4,000 for appearing in ten games or less under his contract with Doan. The pitcher was free to go barnstorming until October 13, the deadline under his American League contract. He appeared in Minneapolis on October 6 for two innings and was next noticed on October 10 in Kansas City where Lon Warneke and Mace Brown finished up for him. Feller on this tour was being paid the equal of 25 percent of Warneke's annual salary.

But again there is confusion here. Seeing that there were reports of a team featuring white players Rogers Hornsby, Jimmie Foxx, and Johnny Mize, if this is Doan's team, there is an indication of it from John Holway, but this is denied by one of Feller's biographers, Sickels. At any rate, the Hornsby squad arranged a Midwest series of games in 1936 against the team of Negro Stars starring pitcher Satchel Paige. The two black position players— Oscar Charleston and Cool Papa Bell — hit over .400 in the five games, mostly played in Iowa. Holway records that black team as being 4–1 against pitchers Jim Winford, Mike Ryba, Jim Weaver, and Ray Caldwell.

Hornsby, Foxx and Feller joined, at varied times, Earle Mack's troupe (his tenth), a squad that that played in North Dakota, Montana and British Columbia, and eventually in Mexico. One game was in Fargo, North Dakota, against a team run by former Athletics pitcher Bruno Haas and featuring Bob Feller. Feller was still pitching when Bell, Cambell and Kress all hit home runs. Still, Mack's team won all eight games.

1937

After Landis prohibited bonuses being given by individual team owners at season's end, the commissioner demanded that there be "no more than three men from the combined membership of both teams" from the World Series to "be allowed to appear in any one exhibition game ... for more than ten days after the series." The squeeze by the owners continued.

The Sporting News of October 21, 1937, covered Rogell's Red Raiders on their ten day tour of Michigan cities featuring Tigers Billy Rogell, Roxie Lawson, and Pete Fox. The tour planned an admission which was 75 cents for men, 35 cents for women and 25 cents for kids, which was the same as the regular season prices.

Bob Feller's barnstorming earned him $4,000 for 10 games, the first in his hometown of Van Meter, Iowa, and then on the West Coast. This cash equaled "40 percent of his Cleveland salary for just two weeks of work" (Sickels, 73). "C.C. Slapnicka, vice-president of the Cleveland Club, said the 18-year-old pitching sensation was free to barnstorm until October 13, the deadline under his American League contract."

Playing four games against the Kansas City Monarchs (three in Feller's home state of Iowa), the fourth was a disastrous game in Minneapolis, headlined by the *Minneapolis Tribune* as "Negroes Win Farce from Stars, 10–0," the story went on to say that

> Post season baseball barnstorming may give the major leaguers a few extra pennies to keep them warm and fat during the winter, but demonstrations such as they gave at Holland Field ... should be called to the attention of someone who can do something about it.... Feller pitched one inning and then flew to Los Angeles where $1,200 awaited him for one exhibition game.

Feller would go on to exhibit in a number of games on the West Coast.

1938

The year 1938 marked a very steep decline in barnstorming. Exhibition games in ones and twos were sure to be contested, and *The Sporting News* wrote about the three DiMaggio brothers — Dom, Joe and Vince — playing together in California.

DiMaggio's income, in fact, is a fine case in point demonstrating the clout of the cartel. That year Joe demanded a raise from the Yankees to $40,000. That demand was then lowered to $30,000 as a satisfactory compromise, and DiMaggio was offered a $10,000 raise to bring his pay to $25,000. Baseball, with its reserve clause, had its way yet again and when the Yankees outfielder signed on April 20 for $25,000, he agreed to be penalized a day's pay until he was ready to go back into the lineup. The rate was "$148.81 for every day, which will add up to $1,636.91," so that he wasn't even making the $25,000. He was making $23,363.09

But the salary of baseball players are held to a different standard. That year, Judy Garland landed the choice role of Dorothy in *The Wizard of Oz*. She was paid $500 a week. No one said she was making too much money.

Sickels says Feller went barnstorming in 1938, but the newspapers were silent about that.

1939

The year 1939, the year of the first televised game, saw some more black-against-white games after the season. One man, George Giles, remembered "In 1939 ... we [the Kansas City Monarchs] were playing in Nebraska, against Dizzy Dean's All-Stars" (Holway, 67). Feller, eager for money while he could make it, threw some exhibition games in Des Moines (October 4), Los Angeles, and San Francisco on October 12.

Exhibition Games

1930

In 1930, the *Washington Post* listed some possible tours, but then, little information exists on them. Supposedly, George Earnshaw, Jimmie Foxx and Al Simmons were to go out on the road, probably to Toledo, on October 11, 1930, and then to Milwaukee, Simmons' home town, before moving "southward to Texas." Teammate Lefty Grove was hired to appear in Los Angeles near October's end.

Also mentioned was the Cy Perkins All-Star squad to challenge the strong Pottsville club at Cressona, Pennsylvania. This team had Perkins, Jack Quinn, Jack Boley, Howard Ehmke, Charley Gelbert and Sparky Adams. Gelbert also showed up in Baltimore on October 12. And there later, Frankie Frisch was spiked in the leg during a game with teammates Charley Gelbert and Johnny Neun.

Men who were in the habit of playing in the postseason continued as others were added. For instance, the annual game at Edwardsville, Illinois, added Andy High, from nearby Ava, to the regular Jim Bottomley. In Oklahoma, at Ada, near to his home in Harrah, Lloyd Waner went hitless in an exhibition.

In the *Long Island Daily Press* there were notices games on both October 5 and October 12 of Babe Herman's all-stars playing at Farmer's Oval in Ridgewood against the semipro Farmers. The group featured Andy High of the Cardinals, Fred Heimach of the Robins, as well as Babe Herman from that same Brooklyn team.

The New York Giants met the Hilldales in Philadelphia on October 3 and 15, with games in between on October 7, and on October 14 in Fairview, New Jersey. An all-star squad of National Leaguers opened on October 17 at Scranton, Pennsylvania, with four eventual Hall of Famers: Dazzy Vance, Pie Traynor, Mel Ott, and Chuck Klein.

1931

A game on October 4, 1931, in Kansas City, attended by 10,000, featured the Kansas City Monarchs facing former Pirates infielder Cot Tierney's team who had signed Bill Terry, the Waner brothers, and Babe Herman. These two squads appeared to have played five games at the Monarchs' home and in St. Louis.

Joe Judge of the Senators planned games with the team he fronted, and a sketchy report of an unnamed team exhibiting in 1931 in Wilkes-Barre, Pennsylvania. Babe Ruth and Lou Gehrig arranged some games close to New York City and then Ruth went on to play some exhibitions in Los Angeles.

Born in Lynchburg, Tennessee, John Stone, Tigers outfielder, played with Tullahoma, Tennessee, on October 6, 1931, versus Atkins Brake of Nashville. Ripper Collins agreed to be on the squad of his Nanty-Glo, Pennsylvania, team on October 18 against Johnstown. For the penitentiary team in Jackson, Mississippi, Benny Frey pitched, Jackson being his home town, and he was opposed by Guy Bush of the Cubs who pitched for Stockbridge and was born in Aberdeen, Mississippi. Bill Walker, from East St. Louis, Illinois, pitched for Anna-Jonesboro on October 18 at West Frankfort, Illinois, against the West Frankfort Athletics; facing Walker was pitcher Bob Weiland from Chicago of the White Sox, as were players Luke Appling, and Jackie Warner of the Brooklyn Robins.

Whereas Grover Cleveland Alexander had to go out on the road and play 176 games with the House of David in 1930, Babe Ruth made $10,500 for one game in Los Angeles in 1931 (Sobol, 234). Dazzy Vance was earning some money pitching regularly for his friend Max Rosner, owner of the famous Brooklyn Bushwicks team, and for two days the Bushwicks of Dexter Park played against a team with Moose Earnshaw and Jimmie Foxx in the lineup.

And in a rare piece of honesty, *The Sporting News* made clear that in one game "although Boyle of Brooklyn, and Durocher and Allen of St. Louis were the only National League players laboring under their own names, the entire nine were made up of players of the league that presents Bill Terry's New York Giants as its title winner."

1932

Although some may be surprised, in 1932 Lou Gehrig appeared on a vaudeville stage on November 4 in New Jersey. On nearby Staten Island, New York, the Phillies beat an island team at Thompson's Stadium by 7–4. Identified as the 1932 All-Americans by the *Philadelphia Inquirer*, this team played at Middleburg, Pennsylvania, on October 8, 1932. And as the nervous Middleburg club made nine errors, the All-Americans won 17–3. Stars of the team included Camera Eye Bishop and Chick Fullis, while pitching were Fred Frankhouse and Howard Ehmke.

Pitching star Dizzy Dean remained active too. He, Pepper Martin, and Jimmy Wilson met the West Frankfort Athletics with Red Sox catcher Benny Tate in Carbondale, Illinois, on October 6. World Series pitcher Burleigh Grimes pitched for New Haven, Missouri, against the club from Washington, Missouri.

A winter league organizing in Houston was covered in *The Sporting News* of October 27, a league that attracted organizer Eddie Dyer as well as Carey Selph of the White Sox. The peerless Bushwicks again courted a postseason all-star team and met one three days after the season ended. There in Dexter Park, the squad that featured Rube Walberg, Al Schacht, Joe Judge, and Bing Miller gathered for the game on September 28.

1933

The next year, on October 4, 1933, another team of stars came into Dexter Park to meet the Bushwicks. That stellar lineup included Jimmie Foxx,

Rube Walberg and Bing Miller of the Athletics; Marty McManus, Joe Judge and Al Walters of the Red Sox, Dick Porter and catcher Ed Madjeski of Cleveland, with Bing Miller serving as manager. Buddy Hassett, not yet in the big leagues, played left field before 8,000. On October 15, a semipro team called the Bay Parkways of Brooklyn, New York, signed for the game World Series stars Carl Hubbell, Hal Schumacher and Blondy Ryan in order to have them on their roster to play the Bushwicks. This game drew 20,000 fans to Dexter Park.

Because the Athletics dropped to third place in 1933, some of them were looking for winter's money and so Athletics teammate Jimmie Foxx's all-stars lost twice to the Glendale Farmers at Farmer's Oval in Queens, New York. Hank Greenberg was stationed at first in both games and Billy Jurges covered short.

Later, the *New York Times* of October 20, 1933, reported that Foxx had broken his left foot during another exhibition game in Baltimore, Maryland, somewhere around October 13. The team he was on, however, kept playing as Federalsburg, and another Athletics player, Rube Walberg, led the team. They met Milford, Maryland, the winning team as it turned out, that starred Lew Krausse and Bill Dietrich of the Athletics as well as Mule Haas of the White Sox, Mickey Cochrane and Goose Goslin from the Tigers. Another Athletics player, Al Simmons, played with the Milwaukee All-Stars against the Polish Triple-A All-Stars at Milwaukee on October 15.

Regarding the injury to Foxx and complaints from owners about exhibition injuries, the *Chicago Defender* on October 7, 1933, wrote that

> the all-star business is not new to the Waner brothers, since they have engaged in such a series each year, following the regular season. They have played in practically every part of the country as members of all-star teams and have not suffered any ill-effects from their playing.

In one of those home town games Red Ruffing and Jim Bottomley, the prides of Nokomis, Illinois, played for their home town team on October 15 against Pana before 1,800. Carl Hubbell, mostly a pecan farmer in the off-season of 200 days, pitched for his hometown, Meeker, Oklahoma, and Johnny Marcum, attired in a Philadelphia Athletics uniform, pitched for the Huff Furniture team of New Albany, Indiana, against O'Neill's Café club on October 15 at Jeffersonville, Indiana. (Marcum was born forty miles north in Campbellsburg, Kentucky.)

Some southern boys arranged a game on October 14 in Durham, North Carolina. Those players included Ben Chapman of the Yankees; Dixie Walker, a rookie teammate; Bill Werber, with the Red Sox; Garland Braxton, a Browns player; Wes Ferrell from the Indians; and Monte Weaver, a rookie with the Nationals. Also in the Tarheel State, four of the Ferrell brothers—Wesley, Marvin and George, in addition to Rick—played together. Brother Elmer

Dean tripled off his famous brother Dizzy and Paul's kin, during a benefit game in Houston, Texas, where Dizzy had played in the minors. Dizzy and Pepper Martin went on to California with minor leaguer Paul to play in White Sox Park in Los Angeles against the Philadelphia Royal Giants, facing Satchel Paige on the mound for the night game.

In 1934, Schoolboy Rowe, opponent of the Deans in the 1934 World Series, pitched in a game in his hometown of El Dorado, Arkansas, for a game at Rowland Field. Rowe's team lost to Mount Ida, Arkansas, led by Lon Warneke. Rowe later pitched a game in New Orleans against home town men and major leaguers Zeke Bonura (White Sox) and George Stumpf (Red Sox). Elden Auker, Rowe's teammate, born in Norcatur, Kansas, pitched for the Manhattan, Kansas, team against Emporia on October 27, 1934.

The Cubs were said to have visited Kalamazoo, Michigan, on October 5, 1934, and on October 15 in Greensboro, North Carolina, the four Ferrells again played, but this time with Garland Braxton, Jimmy Bucher, Bill Werber, Ben Chapman, Dale Alexander, and Pep Young with Max Bishop serving as manager. They faced an equally talented team with Buck Newsom, Alvin Crowder, Ossie Bluege, Pat Crawford, Lew Riggs, Dave Harris, Gerald Walker, Fred Sington, and Baxter Jordan, with Ray Hayworth as the manager.

Apparently unhappy with losing money touring, as they had in 1933, considerable plans were made early in the season for Dizzy Dean. The great pitcher signed on with Ray Doan to manage the junket. His deal with both Deans, as described by Bob Ray of the *Los Angeles Times*, was contracted in the spring when he agreed to pay each of the brothers $75 per barnstorming game plus 50 percent of the gate receipts, while he would take care of the expenses and take the remaining 50 percent of the tickets sold. With his home base in Muscatine, Iowa, Doan's colorful background included promoting Babe Didrickson's athletic talents, running a baseball school for boys in Hot Springs, Arkansas, and owning two traveling teams, both of which were called the House of David.

The two Deans had a remarkable year in 1934. In March, Dizzy announced that he and brother Paul would win 40–45 games between them for the Cardinals. They won 49, with Dizzy winning 30 games. In fact, the elder brother started 33 games and relieved in 17. In mid-season Dizzy went to the 1934 All-Star Game, and in the World Series the two brothers won all their team's games in their triumph over the Tigers.

While it is true that their exhibition games do not satisfy the definition of true barnstorming, they do set a precedent. This October 10 to October 24 trip became a model for trips to come and broke new ground for most United States excursions.

First in strategic choices was the decision by Doan to schedule games in major cities. Such was the fame of the Deans in 1934 that Doan was willing to pay premium prices for the leasing of large ballparks. It was certainly a major business risk to choose these diamonds, but there exists no doubt that these large parks appealed to Dizzy's large ego. And it was really Dizzy that fans would turn out to see. Paul, called "Daffy" in the press, was called "Harpo" by his teammates, due to his quiet demeanor, or at least so when contrasted with this flamboyant brother. This two-brother tour would also generate an enormous amount of money for the brothers and for Ray Doan.

The Deans got right to it. On the day of the victory parade in St. Louis, Dizzy accepted the plaudits of the crowd and then he and Paul boarded a plane for Oklahoma City, Oklahoma. They would be joined in that city of 186,000 by Paul Derringer for the 8:15 night game to meet the Negro League's Kansas City Monarchs, the opponent for the first six games. The fans in that city knew Dean since Dizzy had pitched in the Texas League against their team many times before.

Bus Ham of the *Daily Oklahoman* wrote,

> The stands were loaded before sundown and by the time the lights were turned on thousands had pushed their way out onto the diamond. Although police were called, all six of them, the cash customers refused to give an inch.... As some one remarked, "Any guy should be able to pitch with 7,000 infielders."

John Holway quotes Newt Allen, via Staten, that "the ball game quit in the fifth inning—had to—people were all out in the outfield and every inning they would press closer to try to see Dizzy." Dizzy pitched two innings and Paul three. And that was all.

Following a pattern established by the fame and greatness of Babe Ruth, the fans gobbled up every baseball, including those put into play. Dean's team, smartly called the Oklahoma All-Stars, won 4–0, and stopped the game after five-and-a-half innings, since all the baseballs had been grabbed by the crowd.

Here the admission prices went as high as $1.90, 65 cents and 25 cents and there were 15,000 paid. (A bleacher seat for the 1934 World Series in Detroit cost $1.10.) Immediately after that deluge of fans, the Deans successfully re-negotiated their deal with Doan and got back half of his half, so that the pitchers took $75 per game and 75 percent of the gate receipts. (Doan had earlier paid Dizzy $250 for two weeks of instruction work at Ray Doan's All-Star Baseball School in Hot Springs, Arkansas.)

Dizzy understood money, ballplayer money. In 1930 he was paid $100 a month in a five-month contract for the year. The next year his pay was raised to $2,400 a month. With a bonus he made $8,000 for 1934. Dean came from poverty in Lucas, Arkansas, and like many others he knew how short his career might be. How many players had come up through the minors and gone down that way too? Dizzy was, of course, very right about the brevity of his major league career.

Next, in Kansas, the *Wichita Morning Eagle* said no rain checks would be issued and the Deans were guaranteed $2,500 "with a privilege of 50 per cent of the gross gate receipts.... A donkey game ... will follow the baseball game." There in that Kansas city of 112,000 the Dean boys beat the Monarchs 8–3 before 9,000 "at the Lawrence Stadium, a record turnout for baseball in Wichita if not for any sport event." Two pitchers followed the Deans to the mound, as the contract between Doan and the Deans continued to be flexible.

On Columbus Day, 14,000 Kansas City fans came to watch Dizzy (and Paul) pitch for the semipro Kansas City Mills against the Satchel Paige Monarchs. After a planned stop in Des Moines, they moved on to Chicago for an October 14 game at Mills Field. Due to the fans' numbers, 20,000, the *Chicago Tribune* wrote:

> The pocketbook of Mrs. Jerome (Dizzy) Dean, treasurer of the firm of Dean and Dean ... was bulging with $5,000 more yesterday after the pair went through the motions of pitching a few innings each to help the Chicago Mills semipro team defeat the Deans' barnstorming companions, the Kansas City Monarchs 13–3.

Fans even climbed up on the railroad tracks as Paul pitched two innings and sat. Dizzy pitched three and then moved out into left field. Kansas City's pitchers were Chet Brewer and Cooper, plus Ted Trent of the New York Black Yankees. The *Tribune* claimed that the Deans had made $14,000 so far.

Covered even in the *New York Times*, that paper of October 16 printed this story about the game in Milwaukee, a city of 579,000: "The Dean brothers ... were loudly jeered today and disappointed fans raised such a roar that police units appeared at Borchert Field." The local *Milwaukee Sentinel* reported that two riot squads had to be called to deal with the hundreds of patrons who wanted their money back and had gathered outside of the box office.

This furor was caused by the Dean brothers leaving after five and a half innings to go the box office to collect their money from a gate of 3,300. Dizzy pitched two innings and played left for four more; Paul, with a sore arm, just covered right field until their time to bat in the sixth. Catcalls and boos started at the shortness of the game and of Dizzy's brief mound appearance but the Deans had picked up $750.

In Pittsburgh, a locale of 670,000 souls, where he was scheduled to divide nine innings of an exhibition game, Dizzy pitched just two innings and Paul none. Both left the field at the halfway point. On October 25, 1934, *The Sporting News* reported, "A few minutes later some of the fans followed the pair to the box office" where they went "to collect their portion from the gate of about $3,300." When some fans demanded a refund, riot police were called to "quell the vociferous." Paul's sore arm was a precursor to a dead arm in 1936.

The next day, October 16, Dizzy Dean and Paul Dean arrived in Camden, New Jersey, and appeared at a softball game in Atlantic City that afternoon and then traveled north to Philadelphia, Pennsylvania, a metropolis of two million, for a doubleheader (losing 8–0 and 4–3) against the black Philadelphia Stars. At Shibe, again Paul did not pitch and played but six innings in right in game one; Dizzy just pitched two innings to start game two.

With a guarantee of $1,000 each for the Sunday game at Dexter Park in New York City, against the Black Yankees, the Deans and teammate (and future Hall of Famer) Joe Medwick agreed to sign on with the peerless semi-pro Bushwicks against the Black Yankees. Another large crowd, 10,000, turned out at that Brooklyn ballpark to see Dizzy pitch three innings, to see Paul Dean in right field, and watch Medwick at third base. Catcher Chet Thomas of the Black Yankees stole home on Dean and pitcher Lefty Page shut out the Deans 6–0. "The fans, always particularly demonstrative at Dexter Park," wrote the *Brooklyn Daily Eagle*, "gave Dizzy and Paul and Joe Medwick a great going-over as they trooped into the dressing-room."

A game in Paterson, New Jersey, not reported in the local paper, partly because there was no Sunday edition, was followed by the October 19 night game in Baltimore. Here just 2,215 of the city's 805,000 people chose to show up. Dean pitched for the Cloverland team for two innings and played right for the rest of the game. Paul agreed to cover left in a 4–0 loss for the Deans.

By now both men were exhausted and ready to quit, especially Paul. The *Sun* wrote:

> Both were besieged at every step by autograph hunters, until halfway through the ball game they had to call it a halt. Dizzy visited St. Mary's Industrial School in the afternoon and led the boys' band at the alma mater of Babe Ruth, but Paul remained at the hotel to rest.

Against the legendary Pittsburgh Crawfords at Cleveland's League Park before almost 12,000 fans, Dizzy was outpitched by Satchel Paige for three innings. (Paige first made it to the pros on May 1, 1926, in the Negro Southern League for Chattanooga.) Paige beat Dizzy again with his six innings of work, as he had on the fourteenth. The Deans, playing for the Cleveland Rosenblums, stationed Paul in right for just three innings in the fifth, sixth and seventh innings while Dizzy pitched. Dizzy had played the first three innings in right and then warmed up in the fourth. Nevertheless, the Deans were said to have made $3,000 for the game.

It is only fair to point out that much of the draw for that game was Paige. One reason was his remarkable performance on July 4, 1934: after pitching a no-hitter against the Homestead Grays in Pittsburgh, he drove to Chicago and pitched a twelve inning shutout that same night.

In Columbus, Ohio, a city of 291,000 where Paul pitched in 1932, the brothers were heard on radio station WBNS at 6:15 P.M. before going on to Red Bird Stadium for the night game. Here let Holway speak from his *Complete Book of Baseball's Negro Leagues*:

> The Craws won 4–3, but the game is best remembered for a wild fight on the field.... Vic Harris ("I was a little fiery"), angry at a close call, pulled the umpire's mask out and snapped it back on his face. A riot broke out, with players and fans swinging wildly. Oscar Charleston was punching away enthusiastically. Even the happy-go-lucky Josh Gibson, his shirt pulled out, had a headlock on Dean's catcher, George Susce.... Dean and Ted Page ran over to try to pull Josh away, but he just shrugged them off. The struggle ended with handshakes and backslaps all around. It took [owner] Cum Posey's friend, Steelers owner Art Rooney (a former minor league star baseball player), to get the judge to waive the charges.

Though this was the last game, still vaudeville awaited the brothers at the Roxy theater in New York City beginning on October 26 for a week for $2,500.

What follows only adds to the saga of Dizzy Dean because, as in a saga, the account seems not to be all that specific. One report claimed $5,714 for Dizzy Dean alone. The *St. Louis Post-Dispatch* on October 18, wrote that "Paul and Dizzy are going to share $30,000 profits on this tour." Vince Staten's book (157) claims $7,000 for Dizzy. *The Sporting News* in 1969 asserted that "In 13 days, the Deans made $13,000 and so did Doan."

Writing to *The Sporting News* in part to give exact figures, Ray Doan stated that "each one of the Dean boys received $5,716 apiece and expenses ... I also signed Dizzy and Paul for a one-reel short in which they received $4,500 net ... I also know that they got $3,250 between them for their appearance for one week at the Roxy theater."

All this was added to Dizzy's bank account of $18,000 from salary, bonuses and World Series money. The $9,591 beyond salary and bonuses would be instructive to any player who was trying to decide whether to play in the 200 days or not. Even 10 percent of what Dean made might satisfy many players.

Summed up in verse in the column "Sport Salad" in the *St. Louis Post-Dispatch*, L. C. Davis pointed out the price that might be paid for the barnstorming:

> D. Dean Speaking
> From Mickey, it was noted.
> John Heydler says he doesn't plan
> To favor a barnstorming ban
> As Harridge has suggested;
> He aims to let the heathen rage
> Around the sticks, or, on the stage
> His actions unprotested.

And so for six months in the year,
When fall and winter months are here,
The slave can go unshackled.
But Brother Paul and Brother "Diz"
Will tell the world barnstorming is
The toughest job they've tackled.

Promoter Ray Doan stayed active in postseason baseball by offering Babe Ruth $35,000 to play with the House of David; by now Doan was sending three House of David teams on the road.

1935

Almost as if the rest of baseball was overwhelmed by Dean's success, the number of exhibtions dropped off dramatically after 1934. There is a note that Dick Bartell's team played briefly in 1935 in Oakland, California, and then there was the game as the result of a bet. The owner of the Philips Delicious Tomato packing company in Cambridge, Maryland, was offered a bet of $500 from a Buick dealer in the same city that the car seller's aggregation would win a match with the packer's team. The Tomato squad, nothing but ringers, included Cubs outfielder Bill Nicholson, the Reds' Wally Roetger, Maxie Bishop with the Red Sox, Bud Thomas who had worn the uniform of the Senators, Jimmie Foxx with the Athletics, and Billy Werber, the origin of this story, said that Dick Porter called Joe Medwick, since Porter had been chosen to get Philips' team together.

1936

There was an early benefit game two days after the season ended in 1936 for Monte Cross' widow. The teams matched were the two Philadelphia teams since Cross had played for both teams from 1895–1907. The news of 1936 ended with a game in Los Angeles on October 5, when 10,000 fans saw Dizzy Dean, Pepper Martin, Jack Rothrock, and Buster Mills play what the *Los Angeles Times* called "a meaningless exhibition" against the Coast League all-stars. Clearly Dean, for example, was given three easy throws to hit. Martin pitched for a while and moved to third.

Though Dean was involved in the exhibition business on a very small scale, the man who would supplant Dean as a postseason phenomenon, Bob Feller, could claim that the first exhibition games that he played in as a major leaguer were in 1936. After completing the season, Feller came home to Van Meter, Iowa, and played in a fundraising game for the city. The game raised enough money to build the Community Building in the heart of downtown Van Meter.

1937

In 1937, another young star of the game, Joe DiMaggio, signed for a charity game on October 24 in San Francisco with his brother Dom, Tony Lazzeri, Cookie Lavagetto, Alex Kampouris, Eddie Joost, Lefty Gomez, and Lefty O'Doul. On the West Coast as well was Feller, pitching on a team that also starred Babe Herman. On Arky Vaughan's roster were Dolph Camilli and Vince DiMaggio. Some days later in Los Angeles, on October 13 a contest took place between the named American League stars and the National League stars. Here Feller pitched five innings at Wrigley Field before 6,000. The American League team included Molo Almada, Red Sox outfielder; Jess Hill and Earle Brucker, Athletics; and Bill Knickerbocker of the Browns. The National League club was Arky Vaughan of the Pirates; Dolph Camilli of the Phillies; Vince DiMaggio, a rookie with the Braves; Bill Brubaker of the Pirates; Joe Gonzales of the Red Sox and Lee Stine of the White Sox and Reds.

1938

Only New York City seemed to have exhibitions in the next year. Hank Greenberg played at Dexter Park against the Bushwicks for the Bay Parkways and on October 9 Leo Durocher's team of Tony Cuccinello, Goody Rosen, and Bill Lohrman played against the Farmers at Farmer Stadium in Brooklyn.

Father and son played in Mobile, Alabama. O. T. Trucks and son Virgil, who was two years from playing in the big leagues, lost a doubleheader. Bob Feller was in action again. On October 6, 1939, Bob and his Coast League all-stars met Sacramento of the Pacific Coast League. Feller then flew to San Diego for his next game. Three weeks later a game was reported on October 29, opposing the major leaguers with minors at San Francisco starring Vince and Joe DiMaggio, Ernie Lombardi, Joe Cronin, Eddie Joost, Alex Kampouris, and Dick Bartell.

Lastly for the year, a benefit game was arranged on October 29 for a pitcher from the Sacramento Valley League who had lost an arm in a hunting accident. Played at Chico, the game saw the services of Ducky Medwick and Myril Hoag.

CHAPTER FIVE

Barnstorming Tours and Exhibition Games, 1940–1949

RAY DOAN WAS ABLE TO ORGANIZE a barnstorming group in 1945 but the blossoming of post-war play waited for a former Navy man. Players were eager to replace money lost during their time in the service. Joe DiMaggio, for example, went from being paid $37,500 for his play in 1941, to being paid $21 a month in the Army.

The former Navy man was pitcher Bob Feller, who approached the problem with the most foresight and with the best-organized tour — certainly the most ambitious tour — in the history of barnstorming. His signing of Satchel Paige was a guarantee of closely-watched games for the 1946 itinerary that took them from Pittsburgh to Los Angeles. Four other squads went out on the road as well that year, though Feller was the gold standard.

Though Paige was not to put on a white major league uniform until 1948, Jackie Robinson signed with the Dodgers in October of 1945. His influence and the influence of the rest of the players signed right out of the Negro leagues was felt not only in white baseball but black baseball as well. By the end of 1948, the Negro leagues were dead, the players bought or stolen by owners of the white professional organizations.

By 1949, there were ten teams traveling in Nebraska, Canada and Mexico. Meanwhile, the Cardinals were the most frequent visitors to the World Series in the decade of the 1940s, just before the Brooklyn Dodgers and the Yankees began their control of the time around mid-century. It was the tours featuring Dodgers players that were frequently the most successful, tours that imitated the scope of the 1946 Feller barnstorming trip.

Barnstorming Tours

1940–1943

By 1940, the war news, the war disasters, were everywhere. The terrible news from the bloody attacks by Japan had been in the news since 1937 and after September 1, 1939, Nazi Germany's murderous ambitions became clear.

After December 7, 1941, the country was completely involved in and affected by the declaration of war. Everyone in the country was expected to contribute in many ways. Everything was directed toward survival first and victory at the last.

Part of this effort meant that automobile tires were rationed, and there were to be no new automobiles, and parts would be hard to find as the industry's factories turned out jeeps and tanks and trucks for the war. Without tires, gasoline and useable cars, there would be no barnstorming.

Ballplayers, to keep out of the draft, were allowed to return to their teams but only after an off-season in a defense industry. For example, Joe Medwick was hired to be a personnel counselor at the Curtiss-Wright St. Louis plant on the 1 to 8 a.m. shift. The war, swiftly affecting baseball, called on Hank Greenberg in 1940 to be inducted into the armed forces.

At the end of 1940, one lone band of barnstormers still kept on. *The Sporting News* of October 10, 1940, wrote of the resurrected barnstormer Earle Mack and his team that included Tom Carey, Johnny Mize, and Bob Feller. They played in Montana, in the towns of Little Falls, Billings, Great Falls and Missoula, then into North Dakota at Fargo. But that was the end of it. Occasionally there would be exhibitions starring Babe Ruth, for one, to raise money for the war effort but no postseason touring at all.

Perhaps no other statistic better expresses the extent to which the military put its stamp on professional baseball during World War II than the one which appeared in the *New York Times* in the spring of 1945: as of January of that year, 5,400 of the 5,800 pro baseball players in the country at the time of Pearl Harbor were in the service.

1944

Without special permission, barnstorming was limited until October 11, 1944. *The Sporting News* of September 28, 1944, announced the beginning of the first barnstorming tour since 1940, clearly *with* special permission. With more men to be added by Charles De Witt, secretary of the Browns, the tour was supervised by barnstorming veteran Ray Doan and he saw to it that sixteen major leaguers were approved for the junket, with Tommy Holmes being the biggest name. With the first stop in Davenport, Iowa, on October 2, the tour ended in Yakima on October 11. The trip proved to have only fair results, with box seats costing $3, reserved at $1.75 and general admission for $1.75 or $1.50.

In addition to the change in touring, SABR member Dennis Vanlangen has noted that Sportsman's Park was the last major league park to end segregated seating. In 1944, black fans were allowed to buy tickets in other sections of the park.

And in 1945 there were six TV stations on the air. Both of these changes — in racial equality and in broadcast media — would come to affect barnstorming.

1945

At the normal time of year for the 1945 All-Star Game, the Office of Defense Transportation had so limited travel that the *Boston Globe* headlined "War Fund Ball Games Replace All-Star Tilt." For the Braves, a July 10 game at Fenway against the Red Sox, took the place of the All-Star Game.

But around that time players began to return from military service and the column "Mustered Out" began appearing in *The Sporting News*:

> On August 24, 1945, after forty-four months in the Navy, Bob Feller made his first start against the Tigers in Cleveland ... Hank Greenberg heralded his return to the Tigers on July 1, 1945, by hitting a home run against the Athletics before 48,000 hometown fans. On the final day of the season, his grand slam home run in the rain against the Browns clinched the American League pennant for Detroit. Tiger righthander Virgil Trucks was discharged from the Navy less than a week before the 1945 season ended. He started the Tigers' pennant-winning 6–3 victory over St. Louis and followed that up with a 4–1 complete-game win over the Chicago Cubs in the second game of the World Series [Crissey].

All three of those baseball men had been drawing considerable salaries *before* the war, even before salaries had been frozen *during* the war. An important person in post-war barnstorming would be Bob Feller. One of Feller's biographers, Gene Schoor, writes that "the war cost Feller, as he calculated about $250,000, he said discussing the war with [his wife] Virginia one evening. 'The trick is to make it up.'"

Robert C. Cole, in his groundbreaking barnstorming essays, sums up Feller's 1945 activities:

Ambitious and self-disciplined, Feller had got rich off his fastball and fast curve. As he was always willing to say, he knew his strong right arm was a perishable asset and he wanted to cash in on it while he could. As soon as he returned to baseball in 1945, [release August 21] he asked the new commissioner, Happy Chandler, to change the rule that allowed players to schedule only 10 days of exhibition games after the season ended. Feller appealed for 30 days, and finally prevailed by arguing that returning war veterans should be given the chance to recoup financial losses the war had cost them [Cole, "Ersatz," 90].

With an important player and war hero like Feller asking for a favor, other tours were allowed to go out as well in 1945.

Charley Dressen scheduled games not only with white stars but against black men who were only a few years away from their own stardom, Roy Campanella and Monte Irvin.

A disaster was averted when a barnstorming team of American League All-Stars escaped unhurt in a railroad wreck north of Great Falls, Montana, and Ray Doan organized a tour of American Leaguers against National Leaguers. "Although minus some of the glint of pre-war barnstorming troupes, the two major league outfits will, nevertheless, trout [sic] out a number of tested aces," reported the *Daily Oklahoman* on October 6, 1945.

In 1945, Chet Brewer's team, including Jackie Robinson and Satchel Paige, regularly defeated major league competition. In late September Robinson hooked up with Chet Brewer's Kansas City Royals, a postseason barnstorming team which toured the Pacific Coast, competing against other Negro League teams and major and minor league all-star squads [Tygiel].

And Feller? Feller faced Satchel Paige in one October game that drew 20,000 in St. Louis and in a November game that attracted 23,000 in Los Angeles.

And Robby? On October 23, 1945, Brooklyn Dodgers owner Branch Rickey announced the signing of Jackie Robinson.

1946

"When the freeze on salaries continued through 1946, it stirred strong unionist sentiments among grousing players that erupted in the first postwar season" (Voigt, "The History of Major League Baseball: Part 2").

One way to add to their income, of course, that had always been useful to players was barnstorming and there was a post-war boom in the jaunts.

There were still games that drew less that were still for fun. Earle Mack's American League All-Stars ventured into Alberta and Montana.

Jackie Robinson, fresh from his triumphs with the Montreal Royals, winners of the Little World Series, decided that he too would barnstorm. It was a flop. Robinson had guaranteed $5,000 to his group but all the checks

Satchel's All-Stars and their Flying Tiger, 1946. On the ground, from left: Hilton Smith (Kansas City Monarchs), Howard Easterling (Homestead Greys), Barney Brown (Philadelphia Stars), Sam Jethroe (Cleveland Buckeyes), Gentry Jessup (Chicago American Giants), Hank Thompson (Monarchs), Max Manning (Newark Eagles), Othello Renfroe (Monarchs), Refus Lewis (Eagles), Gene Benson (Stars), Buck O'Neil (Monarchs), Frank Duncan (Monarchs), Artie Wilson (Birmingham Black Barons), Quincy Trouppe (Buckeyes). On steps: Dizzy Dismukes, the All-Stars' business manager. In doorway: Satchel Paige (right) and his valet. *(Courtesy Phil Dixon)*

The Satchel Paige All-Stars posing before their DC-3 airplane during the 1946 Paige-Feller tour. (National Baseball Hall of Fame Library, Cooperstown, New York.)

bounced and Jack had to "lay out $3,500 of his own money, his bonus sign-ing money from Rickey" (Falkner, 54). Even with stars like Roy Campanella, Buck Leonard, Ted Strong, and Larry Doby, the tour failed.

The most famous of the interracial barnstorming tours occurred in 1946, when Cleveland Indian pitcher Bob Feller organized a major league All-Star Team, rented two Flying Tiger aircraft and hopped the nation accompanied by the Satchel Paige All-Stars. With Feller and Paige each pitching a few innings a day, the tour proved extremely lucrative for promoters and players alike and gave widespread publicity to the skills of the black athletes [Tygiel].

Bob Feller did not forget the crowds that he and Satchel Paige drew in 1945 and he began thinking about a 1946 tour even before he had permission to actually guarantee his tour dates.

Before spring training Feller volunteered to conduct "an instructional school for returning veterans" (Gilbert, 137). At January's end, Feller along with Rollie Hemsley, Tommy Bridges and Bucky Walters worked on what was called a free baseball school for returning veterans, even as Danny Gardella began a small exodus from the major leagues to join the Mexican League.

Feller incorporated himself as Ro-fel, Inc., partly to cover his work on his own radio show. He planned to use his own money for the 1946 postseason jaunt. Working with Feller were his wife, Virginia; his lawyer, Russell Craft; secretary Bob Gill; and trainer Lefty Weisman. (Feller later supposed that the cause for the extension for barnstorming was his pre-spring training work.)

The most ambitious tour of major cities since Dizzy Dean's exhibitions in 1934, Feller's re-introduced the scheduling of large cities, this time by chartering two DC-3 airplanes from Flying Tiger Lines. It was the airplanes that scared the owners of the teams of Ted Williams and Hal Newhouser who were each paid $10,000 not to tour with Feller, because of the airplanes, though "I was paying first class salaries," Bob Feller says, "ranging from $1,700 for the month to $6,000."

This excursion was announced as early as July 10, and on August 8, new commissioner Happy Chandler allowed touring up to 30 days after season's end, so that Feller could arrange for 35 games in 27 days in 31 cities in 17 states.

Signed on besides Feller, were three future Hall of Fame players: Ralph Kiner, Bob Lemon and Phil Rizzuto. Mickey Vernon was the 1946 hitting champion at .353.

Feller wisely chose, then, a team headlined by Satchel Paige, a club often called the Colored Stars in press reports. Paige himself had been 24–2 with the Monarchs in 1946. It did take some time for Paige to make it to the majors himself as it did for other men on the team: Henry Thompson of Paige's Kansas City Monarchs; Sam Jethroe, from the Cleveland Buckeyes; and Buck O'Neil, also from the Kansas City Monarchs.

Other players would appear as they became available. Also with the teams was baseball clown Jackie Price. Price's act included chasing fly balls in a jeep and batting balls while standing on his head and hanging by his feet from the screen behind home plate.

Landing in the major league cities, Feller's teams had lined up contests in Pittsburgh, Cleveland, Cincinnati, Chicago, New York (twice) and St. Louis. They also flew to cities where there were high minor league franchises: Newark, Kansas City, Louisville, St. Paul, and then in many of the Pacific

Coast League cities. Those cities and states have been definitely established as was the travel through thirteen states from September 30 to October 26. But there continues to be debate over exactly how many cities and how many games were played. Sickels writes that the games against local teams—eleven of them—were not reported (154.) Up until the twenty-fifth game in Los Angeles on October 16, the list of games is clear.

Still the numbers for those major metropolitan area games are most impressive for any team or teams:

21,131 at Comiskey Park in Chicago
21,291 at Yankee Stadium
13,000 in Newark, New Jersey
27,462 back in Yankee Stadium again
22,577 in Los Angeles.

Intent on making the most from these coast-to-coast games, Feller had even arranged for two games to be played on four of the dates. That much is known. But after the October 16 game in Los Angeles, reports become cloudy.

Reports are equally murky about how many of these games featured Paige against Feller. John Holway claims thirteen. We do know that there were at least three games not against Paige: the first of those games was number 13, with 5,000 attending, against Billy Herman's Louisville, Kentucky, Satellites on October 9. The Triple-A team from Louisville had just lost in the Little World Series to the Montreal Royals. Two games were not contested: game 17 in St. Paul was canceled due to bad flying weather and game 20 in St. Louis, Missouri, on October 13 was called off so as not to compete with the St. Louis team in the World Series.

One notable game in these games was the one designed for Versailles, Kentucky, on October 3. Why that town? It was Happy Chandler's home town.

In the midst of this hectic schedule, on October 11, 1946, Feller was sued in Davenport, Iowa, for $42,500 by Ray Doan, Feller's former barnstorming partner, probably for not letting Doan in on the tour.

Two other games are known to not be against the pitching of Satchel Paige: game 23 at Denver, Colorado, on October 15 reported fans numbering 2,000 who watched an American Legion team take on the Fellers team and the next game, that night in the same place, had 3,000 see the Rogers Jewelers team play. Those games were the last outside of the West Coast.

The October 16 date for the Wrigley Field game in Los Angeles also meant that Stan Musial could join the tour, his World Series championship being won the day before. His payday for the series, however, was not all that large. Since the two parks for the World Series contestants averaged about 35,000 each, the winning team's full share of $3,742 had dropped to a level not seen since 1917.

That game, number 25 on Feller's itinerary, was to be completed once the plane with the squad of sixteen landed from Denver, about noon, local time. The game once again put Satchel Paige on the mound but this time for a different aggregation — Chet Brewer's Kansas City Royals, a team not a Negro National or Negro American League team, but one that was made up for California Winter League purposes.

And now the confusion began as players came and went and teams were constituted, torn down, rescheduled. Some of these opposition teams, in addition to Chet Brewer's, were Earle Mack's, a PCL all-star outfit and a team organized by Feller's Cleveland teammate Bob Lemon.

It was that Feller team that opposed Chet Brewer's team, now featuring Jackie Robinson, who was home in California. First, Robinson led his Montreal Royals to the championship of the Little World Series and then went out on his own barnstorming journey as the leader of Jackie Robinson's Stars. That team had played in Chicago, Illinois, October 19, 1946, against Hans Wagner's All-Stars.

In this Los Angeles game with Brewer, Robby needed to loudly argue ball and strike calls. This seems also to be the game in which Cool Papa Bell, now 43, scored from first on a sacrifice bunt. The game did draw 12,140 but it was not Feller who cashed in.

Further games are hinted at on October 17 at San Diego and in San Francisco the next day. Part of the confusion can be laid at the doorstep of the *Los Angeles Times*, which, on October 19, wrote that Musial was "still touring."

Then on October 21, "A non–Paige exhibition." in Sacramento. The story in the October 30th issue of *The Sporting News*, chronicled:

> Feller's early start in Sacramento so he could catch a plane for the East, an arrangement which saw the big attraction leaving the park while some of the spectators still were coming in, was a one time isolated incident, due to factors over which Bob had no control. But it showed, at least, that it is possible for a barnstormer to run into complications which can do the game no good among its followers in the hinterlands.

When Feller came back from his $2,000 milk convention appearance in Atlantic City, he returned to another game on October 22 and maybe one at San Diego, California, October 24. The next day was a Friday and a game was to be played in Wrigley Field again on October 25 as announced in the *Los Angeles Times*, with Feller meeting, yet again, Satchel who would throw for Chet Brewer's Colored Royals. But apparently it ended up with Jackie Robinson putting together an outfit, without Paige, that played Feller and Musial and the rest of his all-stars. Brooklyn Dodgers manager Leo Durocher was on hand to closely watch Jack, sure to be his player in 1947.

The last of Feller's games seems to have been at Long Beach, probably on October 25 since Feller was said to be leaving for Honolulu after the game.

There may have also been a game in Canada's British Columbia the next day without the tour's organizer.

Much of this confusion comes from the desire for as many players as possible to cash in on Feller's phenomenal success. *The Sporting News* of October 29, 1947, calculated that the 1946 tour drew 271,645 fans.

"Each [of fifteen] players received $100 plus expenses per game, bringing the total haul for most players over $3,500" (Sickels, 156) for 35 games in 27 days, playing in 31 cities in 17 states and British Columbia before 271,645 customers. Musial made about $200 less than his World Series share.

In the *Washington Post*, Shirley Povich's column of June 20, 1947, had Feller claim that Vernon made $9,000 for the regular season (165 days) and $3,000 for 30 days of barnstorming. Feller made $80,000 (Sickels, 156).

There are those who want to say that Feller exploited his black opponents. Buck O'Neil said he made in one month what he normally made in six. Sickels writes, "While some of the Negro barnstormers he faced felt that he was taking advantage of them for financial gain, others were happy to showcase their abilities, and gave Feller credit for making it possible."

The Sporting News on November 6, 1946, could not let this important landmark in baseball history pass without comment:

> There is ample reason to re-examine the decision to allow the athletes a full month of post-season performance. ...
> For one thing, the paltry purses paid to the Cardinals and the Boston Red Sox after the World Series emphasized the financial folly of playing with a comparatively small park. ...
> There is an obvious answer to this objection. The World Series rewards should be larger.

The Sporting News article insisted on pointing out Jackie Robinson:

> With the lone exception of Jackie Robinson's wrangling ... at Los Angeles there has been no evidence that any of the 1946 barnstormers behaved in a manner which would bring discredit on the game. But here, again, is an aspect which cannot be shrugged away. Subject only to the discipline of the tour conductor ... the boys conceivably could do a little kicking over of the traces.

The same weekly newspaper chimed in with the oldest of all objections to barnstorming, the objection based on the property rights of the owners:

> The risk of injury on sometimes poorly-lighted minor league diamond is an awesome thought to stockholders who have invested many thousands of dollars in the players involved. There is obviously some connection between the club's interest in the athlete and the latter's responsibility to keep himself out of the hospital during the fall and winter months.

For his 1946 enterprise, Feller brought along a trainer, as well as selecting games in excellent major and at minor league parks at the highest level. But the argument by the magnates is still specious. If the players get hurt, who will come to their rescue? The owners? How many of these players carried disability insurance? Any? If they are hurt badly, the owners will discard them and replace them with minor league players who can work at a lower salary.

It is important to realize that players were playing in postseason barnstorming games for the money. Some of it was fun, some of the games were even relaxing, and many of the games provided pleasurable camaraderie, but most men would not have played if they were not getting paid for that play.

And still *The Sporting News* would insist that " the owners be given maximum protection." Their protection, not the players, was the only way to be sure of not "cheapening the great American game."

Cheap? Except for four owners—of the Detroit Tigers, Cincinnati Reds, Philadelphia Athletics, and Phillies—major league ticket prices were raised.

1947

The year after the Pirates almost struck a game against the New York Giants in order to gain recognition of the American Baseball Guild, the owners' cartel agreed to a minimum salary of $5,000, a few fringe benefits and the first pension plan. For the first time, players would have money put into their hands for the work they did during spring training, sometimes called "Murphy Money."

SUNDAY JUNE 29

BASEBALL

WEST KITTANNING FIELD

2:30 P.M., DST

Sponsored by Armstrong County
Amateur Baseball Federation

FEATURING

PIE TRAYNOR AND HIS COCHRANE STARS

Vs. KITTANNING INDIE LEAGUE ALL-STARS, with Dotty Kovalchick, Armstrong county's only girl baseball player.

Pie Traynor in an exhibition game in 1947, just before his induction into the Hall of Fame. (National Baseball Hall of Fame Library, Cooperstown, New York.)

The Sporting News of October 1 in its column "From the Ruhl Book": "Barnstorming plans have fallen off this year because of the new rule delaying the jaunts ... Johnny Rigney who took a group of American Leaguers through Michigan, Illinois, Indiana last fall has abandoned his projected jaunt." Yet 11 teams went out, Feller drawing the most notice.

So much so that brouhaha was the order of the day in Cleveland when, on August 13, Feller announced he would be playing in the 1947–48 Cuban Winter League for $18,000. As Sickels points out (173), the *Cleveland News* decided to publish "a pro-con feature entitled 'Should Bob Feller Barnstorm,'" shortly after Commissioner Happy Chandler pronounced his prohibition on playing with the Cuban national team.

Feller had won a "mere" 14 games by mid-August. (He would win 20 that year and keep his ERA below 2.7.) His strikeouts reached a high in 1946 at age 28, a level that he would never reach again, and in fact, he would not strike out even more than 200 ever again. It is simply true that 1946 for Feller was his highest achievement for one year as every player can point to a single year as the year of his highest achievement.

Still, when it was clear that he would not again win 26 games in 1947 as he had in 1946, causes were being sought. The conventional wisdom of 1947, as it is in every year, is to look toward the obvious. Barnstorming, as it had for decades, became the whipping boy for many ills in the game. Sickels sees clearly on this point and writes that the critics chose to ignore Feller's back injury in 1947 and "the other charge, that Feller's business dealings and preparations for the '47 tour were inhibiting his performance for the Indians, was clearly unfair. Business preparations had not interfered during his excellent '46 season" (174).

Using the popular logic, it is equally possible to conclude that his business preparations caused his excellent season, if his critics are willing to say that his business preparations caused his less-than-excellent 1947 season. As for the team, the Indians' team record rose from 68–86 in 1946 to 80–74 in 1947. If Feller's 26 wins in 1946 didn't help the team to succeed, then what ought to be concluded about his 20 wins in 1947?

> Bob Feller of the Cleveland Indians said today that if Commissioner Happy Chandler gives him permission to pitch in the Cuban Winter League he will donate all money from the venture, about $18,000, to the American Major League Players' Baseball Pension Fund. ...
> "I want to prove ... the right of any ballplayer to work at his chosen profession" [*Washington Post*, August 17, 1947].

There were other criticisms stemming from barnstorming, but not about Feller. For example, the decades-old charges that crude diamonds and weak lighting would lead to injuries. There are two injuries to be seen here within a few years. On October 21, 1948, in Grand Falls, New Brunswick, Stuffy Stirnweiss pulled a tendon and was taken to the local hospital as his All-Stars won again 4–2. The next year at age 30 he played in 70 games and hit nine points higher than the previous season. Also in 1948 Ray Mueller, catcher for the Reds, suffered a broken thumb in the first inning on a foul tip during a barnstorming game. He caught 88 games in 1949, more than the 74 games that he had been behind the plate in 1948.

And yet complications kept popping up that would affect decisions about postseason touring. The influx of greater World Series money, plus the prohibition about the tour not beginning until ten days after regular season ended, or when the World Series was over, might have put off some barnstormers. Warren Giles, Reds' president, was quoted as saying that the owners hadn't forgotten their objections to barnstorming.

"From the Ruhl Book," a column in *The Sporting News*, let readers know that Johnny Rigney, who took a group of American Leaguers through Michigan, Illinois, and Indiana the previous fall, had abandoned his projected jaunt.

Also in this mix was the looming influence of television. Larry MacPhail began weekly television broadcasts of the Dodgers in 1940. The first televised World Series was the 1947 games.

In addition, many taverns installed air conditioning. The great black players of the Negro leagues, an increasing number of them, were now playing on television, which could be watched in a neighborhood tavern for the price of a glass of beer, then 10 cents, without traveling in the heat on the subway to a ballpark where a beer itself would be liable to cost five times that dime.

If the Cuban trip caused too many problems for Feller, he did not seem all that discouraged. Feller's 1947 postseason plan was even more ambitious than in 1946: a longer tour and games in Mexico (October 23–30). The team, less star-filled than in 1946, would again travel by chartered airplane, and include more entertainment, Jackie Price and Max Patkin, comedian-coaches of the Indians. Price's act included unzipping his fly and catching 80-mph fastballs in his pants. It was the same act, more or less, performed as one of two clown coaches for Bill Veeck's 1947 Indians.

Helping out were trainer Max Wiseman of the Indians and business manager Bob Gill, from the Spartanburg team of the Tri-State League. The business manager was in place to take some of the load off Feller.

But this tour was a much leaner undertaking than 1946. If for no other reason, expenses were cut in half because Feller did not bring along the opposing team.

After the Series that ended on October 6, Feller's team was ready to go, adding pitcher Allie Reynolds of the Yankees; Bob Lemon also joined at some point.

Spending just six days outside of California and Mexico, an early game in Birmingham saw Harry Walker's all-stars with Virgil Trucks and Murry Dickson shut out the Fellers by 3–0. But the October 29 issue of *The Sporting News* wrote that Feller's team was 13–4 with Feller pitching 59 innings and the team drawing 93,191 or 5,482 fans on average. Bob Feller's All-Stars were matched with the Coast League All-Stars for games in Guadalajara in Mexico on October 28, 1947, drawing 12,000, and then they flew to Tampico for another game.

In early November, in Los Angeles, Feller's team was matched with the Kansas City Royals starring Piper Davis, Buster Haywood, Charlie Neal, and Paige. Paige beat Feller's team 8–0, as he struck out 15 throwing a four-hitter. Feller also went the full nine innings before a crowd of 9,145. The next day, November 3, Feller's tour ended with games against Chet Brewer's Kansas City Royal barnstormer team. Sickels reports that Feller lost $5,000 (178).

"Attendance was down some 100,000 from 1946, which Feller blamed on a later start. Once the World Series was over, it was hard to get people interested in baseball as attention quickly turned to the gridiron. 'Unless the rule is amended,' Feller told *The Sporting News* on November 12, 'there is no use in making tours.'" Even tours with half the expenses of the year before.

1948

At the same time as there were more television stations on the air in 1948 — 17 — there were revised barnstorming rules. The barnstorming period was not to extend more than 30 days after the World Series; no barnstorming club could include more than three players from any one major league team, or more than three from the two World Series teams combined. The withdrawing of the players from the World Series games took away a major attraction, an important advertising element from the possible success of barnstorming.

And yet Feller pitched in California, Birdie Tebbetts caught in Maine, Jackie Robinson toured the South and booking agents such as Ed Gottlieb and Eddie Loesch began to ply their trade very strenuously.

But there was much more to barnstorming than the money. It was hard to argue against the companionship, the chance to visit new towns, the warm reception by fans, the virtually free vacation that these trips afforded, and the pressure-free baseball. Along with the money to take a player through the winter, or part of the off-season, barnstorming was clearly a delight for many players.

The year 1948 was the first year for a new column in *The Sporting News,* a feature called "Barnstorming Notes," that weekly deciding the phenomenon was finally important enough to justify a section of the paper.

Feller decided apparently that enough money could be made just in California while Jackie Robinson and teammate Roy Campanella made their way through good-sized cities in the South and Southwest. But not all of the big leaguers wanted to travel large distances or to make a pile of money, so many of them went to much smaller locales.

Featuring an infield made up of four brothers, a team known as the Schoendienst Stars scheduled exhibition games in Illinois. This team enlisted

Pete Reiser and Yogi Berra. Rex Barney took a team to small cities in Nebraska, and Bobby Thomson and Ralph Branca traveled to small spots in the Midwest. Danny Litwhiler's schedule took him to Roaring Springs, Pennsylvania, and Birdie Tebbetts explored northern New England and Canada with his squad.

Major League Stars

NIGHT BASEBALL

At Washington Park, Peru

MONDAY, OCT. 11

National League Stars
Vs.
Peru Merchants

Game Time—8 P. M.

This team of National League stars includes Peru's Russell Meyer, Chicago Cubs, who will pitch. This marks the biggest attraction of the season, the grand climax of the 1948 season. Come out and see the various big-time performers.

Admission: Adults, $1.25, grandstand; 74c, field. Both admissions include the tax.

Dick Sisler's team arrived at a typical stop for them, in Peru, Illinois, on October 11. Pitcher Russ Meyer was the hometown boy, and after arriving in Peru he heard from the local four-

A 1948 advertisement for a Peru, Illinois, game between National Leaguers and a squad of locals.

county newspaper, *The Daily News-Tribune*, that he had just been traded from the Cubs to the Phillies. The paper also advertised that to pitch were George Munger of the Cardinals and Ken Trinkle of the Giants. To start at 8 p.m. in Peru's Washington Park, the 1,500 patrons "left their favorite radio jackpot programs or a friendly game of euchre [to] brave an evening that wasn't exactly conducive [sic] to baseball." The Tuesday night game was won by the all-stars 10–5, Baumholtz, Dusek and Marchsall having multi-hit games, and Andy Seminick playing first base to back up the pitching of Meyer, Branca and Wilks. After that game, Meyer left the tour to return to school at Western Illinois University.

Tebbetts' northward-bound enlistees traveled in seven private automobiles. Tickets were 20 cents to $5 as Birdie's team won in Burlington, Vermont, on October 12 before 5,400 against a team that named itself the Vermont All-Stars. The *New York Times* on October 13 took note of the casual atmosphere of the jaunt:

Pitchers Frank (Spec) Shea of the Yankees and Joe Coleman of the Athletics were loaned to the Vermonters, along with Catcher Gus Niarhos, also of the Yankees, and Tebbetts. The major leaguers employed local talent for their battery. Tebbetts said that procedure would be followed during all of his team's New England and New Brunswick tour.

Danny Litwhiler's involvement in barnstorming was well-documented in Cole's essay "Ersatz Octobers":

> While working as a substitute physical education teacher at Scott Township High School near Bloomsburg, Pennsylvania, he got the idea to form his own team for the fall of 1948. ... In those days of lower salaries, part of the motive for barnstorming was the need most players had for winter income. ... Although he was a two-time batting champion, Mickey Vernon played for the poor-paying Washington Senators and had to work winters at everything from an oil refinery to a haberdashery shop.

The odd fact that "Litwhiler recruited 14 players" echoes the roster of big league teams set for the year 1901, thus harkening back to an earlier era. "Litwhiler also would arrange games in small towns in his area where major leaguers lived who were not on his touring team, and then contract to have such a player join the All-Stars for a single game in his hometown," Cole continues.

> For example, he would schedule a game at Brownsville, Pennsylvania, because Pat Mullin lived there ... Litwhiler said his standard financial arrangement was a 70–30 split with the local promoter, the 70 per cent coming off the top to the touring team. If it rained, Litwhiler collected $1,000 a game.

The Sporting News let its readers know after the World Series had ended that 7.7 million viewers watched the games on 466,000 receivers. There was even a B-29 plane, labeled "Stratovision," relaying a signal to Cleveland. "A series telecast," the forecast bravely stated, "within a few years, may be witnessed by one tenth of the nation's population."

Baseball, on the radio in many places for thirty weeks a year, was often the most listened to show on the radio.

But the Negro leagues which had supplied much of the quality opposition, as well as gate draw, were dead.

1949

Salaries increased steadily after the war, and by 1949 the average major league salary was up to $15,000, and that year saw Joe DiMaggio sign for the first six-figure contract in the history of Major League Baseball. To understand the contrast, in 1905 rookie Al Bridwell said that he was paid $2,100, an amount that would buy as much as $5,646 in 1949 money according to

EH.net. Still, this was the year that the highest number of barnstorming teams would arrange games.

In 1946, the country had fewer than 17,000 television sets. Three years later, 1949, consumers were taking home 250,000 sets a month. As the number of sets in use grew, so did the number of stations broadcasting. Television stations in New York City now numbered seven, with a viewing audience of 1,392,469, according to Weed and Company, which called itself a "radio and television station representative." The Boston Braves advertised that they intended to install television under the stands. The medium was here to stay and to affect the game dramatically.

The year 1949 would mark Bob Feller's last tour and his barnstorming games, now not beginning until October 17, were a jumble. Also in the mix of postseason games was an outfit organized loosely by Bob Lemon, fellow Cleveland pitcher, as well as the Kansas City Royals. Dodgers pitcher Don Newcombe came in to throw one game and flew back to be with Jackie Robinson's team again. It appears that Feller averaged just 3,000 fans per game for most of his games, but by November 6 the game in Tijuana, Mexico, attracted a mere 125 fans.

It is possible to suggest that the fact that the number of TV stations almost tripled in one year (17 to 50) in 1949 was beginning to affect attendance. In the regular season, a five-year attendance spurt was at an end and that year the majors lost 705,477 fans from the 1948 total.

Jackie Robinson's great club was asking ticket prices of $1.50, $1.30, $1.65 and 35 cents to see his black against black games that starred Buck Leonard, Roy Campanella and Don Newcombe, as well as Larry Doby. (An upper reserved seat at the Polo Grounds, home to the New York Giants, cost $1.75 in 1949.) The team, ending with a record of 25–6 after 29 games, as *The Sporting News* reported, drew more than 240,000, or 8,275 per game.

Birdie Tebbetts once again patrolled New England and drew 45,341 fans for ten games; Tebbetts counted about 200 more fans per game than in his trip in 1948.

Exhibition Games

1940

The year 1940 listed six exhibition games. First was a charity game in New Orleans, with Mel Ott and Howie Pollet that matched Hal Anderson's All-Stars against Hoerner's Pros at Pelican Stadium and another game on October 12 matched St. Louis Browns player Jack Kramer and his All-Stars with the Gelbke All-Stars. The game that featured pitcher Paul Derringer on

October 13 was arranged in Georgetown, Kentucky, where Derringer had attended college.

Another pitcher, Preacher Roe, pitched for a team in Arkansas, Roe's home state. The South Fork team played the Gainesville club on October 10. Ash Flat, Roe's hometown, is now identified on the map; the other two places are not. Roe was working on making it back into the major leagues after his cup of coffee in 1938 with the Cardinals. There was a CYO game at San Francico on October 20 with Dom DiMaggio, Joe Orengo, and Bill Posedel. The game at the Joliet, Illinois, prison involved a team with Ray Schalk as manager and Ted Lyons as catcher with Nick Etten and Bob Kennedy in the field against a convict team.

1941

Just before America's entry into World War II, Dizzy Dean, who had pitched an inning with the Cubs in 1941, pitched against former New York Giants player Randy Reese's team — the Tupelo, Mississippi, Tornadoes — at Russwood Park in Memphis. Jimmie Foxx and Ted Williams were to play on the West Coast for "a brief hurried exhibition tour." One game was on October 8 with Lou Novikoff against Chet Brewer's club. Dom DiMaggio also played in Los Angeles on October 4, 1941, a week before the Los Angeles Winter Baseball League opened its season.

And Bob Feller, celebrated again in his home town of Van Meter, pitched two innings on October 2 before going to the mound on October 5 in St. Louis. He won 25 big league games that year, but would not win another until his wartime service was over.

1942–1944

The war effort included games to encourage fans to buy bonds, two of them being early in the 1942 season that had Satchel Paige and Dizzy Dean once again meeting on May 24 and June 5. Ending that year, as well as George Barr's umpire school, were the games called City Series. They halted forever in Chicago where the White Sox victory gave the Sox their nineteenth Chicago championship in twenty-five tries over the Cubs.

Prison games in Illinois were called off for October 10 and October 11, 1942, at Statesville and Joliet due to a prison break at Statesville. Signed to play were Ted Lyons, Nick Etten, Lou Boudreau, and Mule Haas. Early in Novemeber there was a contest between major and minor league players in the Alameda, California, Elks Christmas Charity fund game on October 25 featuring Joe Hatten and Jim Tobin of the Braves; Dick Bartell, Giants; Joe

DiMaggio, Yankees; Augie Galan and Cookie Lavagetto, Dodgers; and Ernie Lombardi from the Boston Braves. The crowd the game drew at the Oakland Park — 7,000 — was the largest in the charity event's 14-year history.

And the Bushwicks semipros continued to welcome all-star teams in doubleheader play. Against the Bushwicks on October 11 was an all-star team that included Hank Borowy, Yankees pitcher; Buddy Hassett, Yankees first baseman and this squad's manager; and Whitey Kurowski of the champion Cardinals. The next week the all-stars featured Bill Lohrman of the Giants, Tom Hennessey of the Phils, and his teammate Johnny Podgajny.

It was all Bushwicks in 1943. Lefty Gomez, ex-Yankee, pitched for the Bushwicks at home against Larry French, then a Navy lieutenant, pitching for the South Orange, New Jersey, American Legion team. Neighborhood man Phil Rizzuto, on leave, signed with the Bushwicks in one game of a doubleheader against ex–Giants Babe Young's squad, the New London Coast Guards, and he also played the next week against the New London Diesels at Dexter Park on October 3. Rizzuto's former teammate, Lefty Gomez, pitched the first seven innings for the Bushwicks for the win.

Three games can be mentioned in 1944. Two New Orleans men who pitched in the World Series, Al Jurisich (Cardinals) and Jack Kramer (Browns) pitched in a benefit game at New Orleans for Jax Buddies against the Bookies. October 10 had some major leaguers playing against Red Ruffing's Service All-Stars in a night game at Los Angeles, and 24 major leaguers were allowed to play in a benefit game on October 22 in Los Angeles for the Serviceman's Rehabilitation Fund.

1945

The war was now over. In mid–October, *The Sporting News* took close notice that three pitchers, Bob Feller, Satchel Paige and Jack Salveson, a Cleveland reliever, pitched in Wenatchee, Washington, the night of October 8. The three portray an interesting mix. Salveson was just finishing his career in the big leagues, Feller was returning to his, and Paige, though now 39 years old, had not yet begun his time in the majors. Salveson was a teammate of Feller's, and Paige would be in 1948. These three worked on the West Coast and attracted 57,500 fans in four games. A smaller crowd showed up to watch Dave Ferriss of the Red Sox and Walt Dubiel of the Yankees continue their duel at Hartford, Connecticut, matching the Savitt Gems and the New Britain Codys. In two consecutive Sundays, visting Dexter Park were Aaron Robinson of the Yankees, Nap Reyes of the Giants and Anton Karl of the Phillies on October 7, and on October 14 Tigers teammates Hank Greenberg, Eddie Mayo, and Doc Cramer with Danny Gardella from the Giants.

1946

Like those memorable games in 1910 and 1911, before the 1946 World Series, while the Brooklyn-St. Louis playoff games were still underway, "The [Red] Sox kept their hands in by thumping a 14-carat collection of American League All-Stars two games out of three in an exhibition series at Fenway Park," the *Brooklyn Eagle* reported. This all-star team that included Hank Greenberg, Luke Appling, Joe DiMaggio, and Hal Newhouser took part in three exhibition games.

Then DiMaggio formed an all-star team with teammates Snuffy Stirnweiss and Randy Gumpert and New York City National Leaguers Carl Furillo of the Dodgers, Wes Westrum, Mickey Witek, Buddy Kerr, Dick Lajeski, and Mickey Grasso, as well as pitcher Randy Gumpert along with infielder Babe Young. This team traveled from New York City up the Hudson River to Kingston, New York, to meet those semipros well-known in the area and reported on by the Kingston *Daily Freeman*. Fans were assured that the Cardinals-Red Sox game would be broadcast during the exhibition. Photos of the game show Furillo wearing his Dodgers away uniform as were Stirnweiss and DiMaggio. There were ten hits in the 2–0 win by the all-stars. Furillo drove in a run and DiMaggio tripled for two of the team's seven hits.

1947

In 1947, two pitchers threw games out on the road. Dizzy Trout played at South Range, Michigan, on October 13 before 4,000. Orval Grove pitched to his regular catcher, Mike Tresh of the White Sox, and Preacher Roe worked for the Piggott Ramblers on October 17 at Piggott, Arkansas, in a game that also featured Johnny Sain from Havana, Arkansas.

The Sporting News of October 15, 1947, said that Cubs catcher Clyde McCullough had arranged to lead a team through Virginia and North Carolina. Signed up with McCullough were Cubs pitcher Russ Meyer; pitcher Chuck Stobbs of the Red Sox; Allen Gettel, a pitcher; and Dom DiMaggio, Red Sox outfielder. But the paper gave no other information about the tour or even if it took place at all.

What was certain in the paper was that there were a group of games contested against the Bushwicks. Ralph Branca of the Dodgers and the World Series Stars met the Bushwicks on October 12 and then a planned doubleheader was rained out on October 19. These World Series Stars, including Eddie Stanky and Tommy Holmes of the Braves and Larry Doby of the Indians, lost the first game of a doubleheader 1–0 in 14 innings to the semipro team and were behind 2–0, when the nightcap was called after one and one-half innings because of darkness. A crowd of 9,500 turned out at Dexter Park for the attraction. Sam Nahem, formerly of the Phillies, and Eddie, later Whitey, Ford, a Yankee farmhand with Norfolk of the Piedmont League working then for the Bushwicks, dueled the long route on the mound. Doby walked twice and made two hits in four times at bat.

Speaking of Series stars, Al Gionfriddo, he of the memorable catch in Yankee Stadium's left-center field, gave an exhibition in his home town of Dysart, Pennsylvania, a town of 1,000. There 5,000 showed up to see him play with Dysart in a game against the Coalsport Moose.

1948

Cleveland pitchers Bob Feller, Bob Lemon and Gene Bearden were involved with games against teammate Satchel Paige on the West Coast in 1948.

On November 9, 1948, came the announcement of the disbanding of the Newark Eagles, an important team in Ruppert Stadium since 1935. Effa Manley was furious at Branch Rickey for what she considered the bankrupting of the Negro leagues, lashing out at the "gullibilty and stupidity of Negro baseball fans themselves in believing that he has been interested in anything more than the clicking of the turnstiles" (Associated Press). The turnstiles would also be affected in exhbition games now that the Negro leagues were a dying institution.

1949

Important news for baseball all over the country was the fact that 15,000 fans took in five World Series games on television at the Fabian Fox Theater in Brooklyn. All those fans chose a venue with a controlled temperature and comfortable seats either because they did not own a television — yet — or simply liked the idea of watching it at a cheaper price with friends.

In New Orleans on October 13 and 16, home town boy Mel Parnell drew them to the two games. A game sponsored by the Knights of Columbus was booked for Stockton, California, on October 23. Among the major leaguers listed were Mike McCormick of the Dodgers, Tom Glaviano of the Cardinals, Lloyd Hittle of the Senators, Frankie Crosetti of the Yankees and Lloyd Merriman of the Reds. A team of major league stars was announced to play a minor league all-star team at Long Beach, California, October 29. Among the big leaguers reported on were Cliff Mapes of the Yankees, Bob Lemon of the Indians, Vern Stephens of the Red Sox, Jade Graham of the Browns, and Eddie Bockman of the Pirates. Jimmie Dykes' team of Gerry Priddy, Vern Stephens,

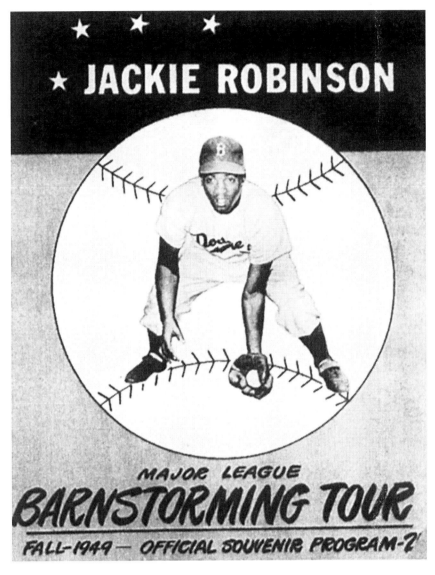

Scorecard for Jackie Robinson's tour in 1949. (National Baseball Hall of Fame Library, Cooperstown, New York.)

Gus Zernial, and Duke Snider played against a Casey Stengel team of movie stars Dennis Morgan, Jack Carson, Gordon McCrea and Mike O'Shea at Glendale, Queens, for a playground charity on October 23, 1949. Also in Queens the week before (October 16) another of the World Series All-Stars teams came in to play the Bushwicks: from the Dodgers were Ralph Branca, Gene Hermanski, and Cal Abrams, and the Yankees were represented by shortstop Phil Rizzuto.

CHAPTER SIX

Barnstorming Tours and Exhibition Games, 1950–1962

THE PERIOD BETWEEN 1950 AND 1962 began with veterans of the barnstorming enterprise, Danny Litwhiler and Birdie Tebbetts. But the most dominant figures were three Brooklyn Dodgers players: Gil Hodges, Roy Campanella and Jackie Robinson. After all, by 1955, the Dodgers had finished first or second every year since 1946. These three had the most ambitious tours, following, as most extensive tours did, the East coast to Florida, the Gulf Coast to Texas, and playing the final games in California. While Litwhiler would stay mostly in Pennsylvania and Tebbetts in a few states in New England, the Dodgers players would schedule month long tours of twenty-five games or more.

But this period of grand tours was short. In 1955, there were but five teams out in the postseason. In 1962, one.

Barnstorming Tours

1950

Now television, in its stations and in its receivers, began to gather speed. The number of TV stations almost doubled in one year (50 to 97) in 1950 and there were now 10.4 million homes with TV sets. The year also marked the first All-Star Game to be telecast. *The Sporting News* advertised the World Series as being televised "over NBC, CBS, ABC and Mutual Networks." By 1950 that Series was beamed as far west as Omaha so that 38 million watched. Regular season attendance, down by three-quarters of a million in one year during 1949, declined by *two* and three-quarter million in 1950. In fact, attendance, which averaged 1,263,460 customers per team in 1949, would not get that high again until 1966 when attendance for the 20 teams was 25,182,209, an average of 1,259,110.

Also televised was the beginning of the Korean War. *The Sporting News* began a column titled "Call to Colors," listing the players becoming part of the military.

Of the barnstorming team starring Johnny Mize, Luke Appling and Warren Spahn, *The Sporting News* wrote on September 27, 1950, that "in addition to their games along the route, the Harrismen will attend banquets and autograph sessions in business establishments and clubs, visit hospitals, schools, etc., free of charge for the promoters and sponsors of the contests."

The tour of the team led by pitcher Allie Reynolds, now being paid $25,000 by the Yankees, had many of the same types of experiences traveling through small town Oklahoma. For example, after helping to "dedicate a new 7, 000-seat amphitheater named Civic Center Stadium in Sulphur, members of the all-star were guests of R. T. Brown at Bill's Café after the game for a steak dinner."

In Durant, "the major leaguers kept things interesting by easing up on the basepaths," while pitcher Cal McLish, then of the minor league Los Angeles Angels, pitched both left and right handed. In Seminole, on October 12, the town where Reynolds started his career, the 541 paid saw a treat: the Petroleum team batboy went to bat, bunted and Al Benton let the ball go through his legs for a hit. In Ada, on October 15 the 2:30 game at Hereford Park included Cardinals pitchers Harry Brecheen and Freddie Martin on the opposing team. A great name just back from managing in Florida, Oklahoma native Pepper Martin, played half the game in center field to the delight of the crowd of 820.

Not quite so happy was the John Jachym–Bobby Riggs entourage of 18 players. John J. Jachym was a young businessman who owned, briefly, a piece of the Washington Senators, and Bobby Riggs was the famous tennis hustler who in 1973 played a series of heavily promoted and televised net matches against women.

Jachym told *The Sporting News* that "we need about $5000 per game to break even and we're traveling first class all the way. We're using trains in the North but once we tour the South we'll travel by plane ... helping to cover the $150,000 nut." Before too long "Riggs hastened to Miami and asked the players to take a 45 per cent pay cut.... Most agreed to slice their salaries 25 per cent."

Lasting only until October 22, the tour ended in New Orleans after 13 games, fewer than half those planned, probably with a $64,000 loss; many of the 38 major leaguers signed did not show up or would play only part of the game. The *New Orleans Time-Picayune* reported that

> Promoter Bobby Riggs announced Sunday night [October 22] that [it] was the last game of the tour.... Bad weather on the Canadian leg of the tour, and more foul weather in Chicago and in Syracuse and the falling off of attendance caused Riggs to make the decision ... [a] few hundred people viewed the game.

The management and players agreed to settle for 50 percent of their contracts.

With Roy Gregory of Bridgeport, Connecticut, in charge of the Tebbetts tour, a tour that included the comedy of Max Patkin, none but local teams and small cities were on the schedule. Games began on October 11, perhaps so as to be able to count on the pitching of Yankees starters Tom Ferrick and Spec Shea, who were not finished with the World Series against the Phillies until October 7. This was a jaunt that asked the players to lay out the money for their own expenses and to drive their own cars. Going along as the money minder was Bud Smith, who often watched as the fans paid their way into the ballparks. This close money minding allowed each player to be paid right after the game in cash in his own envelope.

On October 20 the team ventured far north to Augusta, Maine, where they played before 2,500 customers, a "chilled crowd." As John Murphy of the *Kennebec Journal* saw it,

> Perhaps the best defensive play of the game came at the end of the ninth. The kids had been mobbing the Tebbetts's team dugout and the players all during the game in quest of autographs. The All-Stars very quietly had all their equipment taken out of the dugout and when Bowman struck out to end the game, the entire squad turned about and ran full tilt for the gate and their cars.

They hurried south to Burlington, Vermont, that city being chosen because that was where Tebbetts' wife-to-be lived. It turned out to be a good choice because the team drew 3,500.

Then back they drove to Maine, to Portland, where Eddie Lopat and Spec Shea faced teammate Joe Page who pitched for the host team, the Maine All-Stars. The Tebbetts men won 8–0, with Phil Rizzuto going 4–5.

Driving 300 miles north for the October 23 game in Presque Isle, they were greeted by snow but played anyway, though the game was called after five-and-a-half innings. After the game, fans and players went to a dinner at the city fire station where Rizzuto and Dropo presented trophies to players from the Maine-New Brunswick League and the Northern Aroostock League. The Presque Isle fire auxiliary staged the dinner.

But the next day in Bangor cold canceled both the game and the rest of the tour.

1951

On October 1, 1951, the first coast-to-coast televised baseball game was sent out over the airwaves when the Dodgers beat the Giants 3–1 in their first playoff game that year. That year fifty-two stations signed up to telecast the Giants and the Yankees in the World Series. There was no turning back from baseball telecasts and there was a price to be paid for the coverage. In the last three years of major league attendance, the number of fans had decreased by 4,794,166. Owners began to wonder if the television revenue would balance out the books for the missing fans at the gate.

Even worse for baseball, in all of the minor leagues, attendance dropped by seven million in 1950 and another seven million in 1951. In a ten-year span during the 1950s, thirty-seven minor leagues would disappear.

For the players, the 1951 World Series checks were higher, no doubt influenced by television rights fees, now at one million dollars per year: the Yankees took home $6,446.04 and the Polo Grounders $4,951.03. From then on, down from the pennant finishers the championship money declined rapidly as it did every year. For example, the Braves for fourth place in 1951 made $51.51.

Still, winning the World Series by now would bring about $6,000 to every full share recipient.

> During the 1950s, 75 percent of player salaries ranged from $10,000 to $25,000 a season. However, three superstars— Joe DiMaggio, Ted Williams, and Stan Musial — received annual salaries of $100,000 a season.... But if organized players showed signs of gaining wealth and power, the powers of baseball commissioners were waning. Indeed, when Landis died in 1944, it soon became apparent that the owners would not abide another powerful commissioner. Thus Landis' successor, Commissioner Chandler, was denied a second term in 1951.... The flamboyant Chandler was replaced by Ford Frick, who served for fourteen years as the compliant tool of the owners [Voigt].

The year of Bobby Thomson's home run saw barnstorming dominated by three Dodgers players. Jackie Robinson traveled his way south and west, though the Dodgers' second baseman's 1950 contract for $35,000 had made him the highest paid Brooklyn Dodger ever. Catcher Roy Campanella chose the East and South, and first baseman Gil Hodges, who planned on a modest 16 games. Fewer than ten teams would travel during the postseason.

The Hodges' team and the Campanella team met each other at least for a while. With Jim Crow still reigning in some parts of the country, this black and white blend of players could mean trouble. And so *The Sporting News* of October 31, 1951, recorded "Louisville Nixes Game; Mixed Teams Play For First Time in Augusta. Under Kentucky state law, the two races must be segregated at the ball park." But the NAACP decided to picket the park if that segregation rule was implemented and rather than to get snared in controversy or anger anyone, the game was canceled. Making people mad and causing controversy would not end for some time.

At any rate, the first 13 games of the joint meetings of the Hodges and Campanella tours attracted 43,895 fans, meaning that each player would have made about $112 per game (minus expenses and promoter's fee). Attendance had a high of 6,200 and a low of 595.

As for teammate Jackie Robinson, "Promoter Ted Worner said that this year's tour did not draw as well as the 1949 and 1950 jaunts by Robinson," and that the overwhelming majority of attendees were Negroes.

Deciding to pay attention to his third tour of the New England cities, Birdie Tebbetts, now owned an insurance business in Manchester, New Hampshire. Almost thirty years old, the veteran catcher was a thirteen-year veteran of the big leagues and was apparently thinking not only of an off-season job as well but also, by managing barnstorming teams, of running tours. It does seem as if he proved his managerial ability at least in part by taking these teams out and within two years of the end of his major league career in 1952 he was appointed manager at Cincinnati.

An oddity of his 1951 postseason games was that as Tebbetts was touring in New England, so were the NBA's Boston Celtics, playing exhibition games in Maine against the Baltimore Bullets on October 15 and October 16, 1951. Tebbetts' team followed those basketballers into the towns of August and Bangor in Maine.

Another oddity happened during a game in Portland on October 21, the 1:30 p.m. game on Magnate Hale Day at Portland High Stadium where 3,000 watched a 17–3 win with Sal Maglie, Mike Garcia and Joe Coleman pitching. The Portland, Maine, *Express-Herald* reporter Vern Putney wrote,

> Surrounded by autograph seekers in the ninth as the game dwindled to less than exhibitions stature, [Bobby] Thompson [sic] paused in the middle of a signature upon spotting Archer's drive to center. He politely excused himself, turned for the fence, and reached up for the backhand, going-away stab that rewarded onlookers who were staying until the final out.

At October's end *The Sporting News* quoted Birdie in an article titled "Tebbetts' Barnstormers Latest Victim of Video."

> After the last game in Houlton, Maine, Tebbetts said "Barnstormers will be able to draw crowds in areas not affected by television but any place that has good reception of TV, these post-season tours are a thing of the past." Jack Fleischer, who wrote the column was aware that, "the Tebbetts team wound up with seven games instead of its usual schedule of 12 or 14 contests."

Satchel Paige (now a member of the St. Louis Browns after rejoining Bill Veeck), and teammate Ned Garver lined up a tour beginning at Jackson, Michigan, October 11. After moving quickly into Ontario, they visited the home of the fabled House of David teams in Benton Harbor, Michigan, on October 14, almost an homage. Paige had faced House of David teams many times in the past. Now, backed by Browns players first baseman Hank Arft, outfielder Jim Delsing, shortstop Bill Jennings, and utility man Jack Maguire, with some minor league players, Paige and Garver continued to play in small and medium-sized cities.

In some of the games, Browns' players like Garver were written into the lineups of a team from the All-American Girls Professional Baseball League. For instance, the two star pitchers were to perform for the girls' team at Ballwin, Missouri, on October 18.

Creative baseball was one thing that promoter Fido Murphy was known for, but imagination has to be discounted when the advertised players did not appear. None of his World Series participants showed up and Roberto Avila of Cleveland was missing. Mike Garcia of the Indians was slated to join the tourists on the late date of October 21. The tour was a disaster.

By the end of the barnstorming period for 1951, *The Sporting News* was beginning to print "Series TV Blamed as Barnstormers Lose Gate Appeal."

Because barnstorming had appeared to become an uncertain postseason choice for many players, though some players toured for a while, the *Chicago Daily Tribune* caught sight of off-season jobs of the Cubs. Phil Cavarretta, for example, ran a

Kiddieland Park in Dallas, while Dee Fondy and Johnny Klippstein worked as mailmen. Frankie Baumholtz sold clothing in Cleveland and Hank Sauer ran a gas station in Los Angeles. On the other end of the continent, Hal Jeffcoat worked carving tombstones in Gloucester, Massachusetts.

Workers in two other industries caught the attention of the press as the hot summer of 1951 cooled into the autumn. Those hot summer evenings turned into the cool of the evening, the cool delivered by air conditioning. "After World War II, window unit air conditioners appeared, with sales escalating from 74,000 in 1948 to 1,045,000 in 1953." In the other industry, by 1951, 17,000,000 television sets had been sold. Television counted 50,000,000 fans viewing the 1951 World Series, many more than the sum of all of the fans who ever attended all the World Series games back to 1903. For the first time in history, there were more than 100 TV stations. In three more years there would be 349 stations. Almost 80 percent of households in urban areas owned a television.

As for the family changing, "Consumer spending on spectator sports in 1949 was around $280 million.... But for the decade of the 1950s the annual average was $282 million." Though a higher dollar figure, "there was a shift from inner-city public forms of recreation to private, home-centered forms of recreation" (Rader, 33) and a shift to playing softball as well.

Feller, quoted in the fine book by Sickels, "mourned the death of barnstorming" saying that one team had lost $70,000 while "tracing the decline in the popularity" of barnstorming to the "integration of the major leagues," since "black vs. white games produced such hard-fought contests."

John Holway wrote about those hundreds of interracial games:

> As for comparisons between black and white big leaguers, this is a conjectural area, and there is no absolute answer. Campanella and others maintained their power numbers after moving to the white bigs. In fact, Campy's and Doby's improved greatly. And, generally speaking, the blacks had passed their primes by the time they made the transition. In barnstorming games against white big league pitchers, some black batters did better, some did worse, but most were consistent against both opponents. Black pitchers, overall, beat white big leaguers slightly more than they beat black big leaguers, about 53 to 47 percent vs. whites, 50–50 vs. blacks. Paige, who was 1–1 in his last year in the black league, was 6–1 in his first year in the American League. At the age of 44. Which race was stronger? Nobody knows for sure. Least of all me. But it's food for thought, isn't it. And your great-great grandfathers missed some terrific baseball in what was then called the "major" leagues [private correspondence].

Integration in barnstorming teams would have to wait for two more years by, who else and of course, Jackie Robinson.

1952

> Out of the 1952 barnstorming picture were Bob Lemon, Cleveland pitcher, always a drawing card on the Pacific Coast; Danny Litwhiler and Birdie Tebbetts, who annually led teams through eastern territory, abandoned the tours this fall. Fido Murphy, who had an ambitious schedule wrecked by poor attendance last fall, also was missing [*The Sporting News*].

And yet, that same *Sporting News* issue headlined "Barnstorm Bonanza Burning Out; 5 Clubs Drawing Fair Crowds.... Because of the cancellation of Paige's appearances the plans of another team headed by manager Paul Richards of the White Sox had to be abandoned." Richards' team was to have included Allie Reynolds, Billy Pierce, and Warren Spahn.

Success was made certain for Roy Campanella when he added Joe Black to his team and their journeys wound up drawing 62,500 fans in 25 games, traveling from North Carolina, through the South, then westward through Alabama and Mississippi to Louisiana and Texas.

With less grandiose plans, eight games all in upstate New York, Hal White's tour seemed to have fun in mind rather than big paydays. It surely resembled the tours at the turn of the twentieth century more than the megatours of the Dodgers players Robinson, Campanella and Hodges.

Having from one small city, Utica, New York, two Harolds—Hal White, who was then in his tenth year with the Tigers—along with another Harold, a moneyman called Harold "Bud" Smith, who for many years owned a tavern — became a handy way to run a tour. Art Mills, one more Utica native and formerly a Detroit coach for five years, was one more piece of the barnstorming puzzle, and once local celebrity and national baseball comedian Billy Mills, Art's son, joined in, all the elements for success were completed. Agreed on were ticket prices for most games of $1.50, $1.25 and 60 cents.

Hal White was known for his play in upstate New York — at Rome and in Buffalo too — and he gathered men he knew, mostly American Leaguers, to travel with him. One of the big names on this tour would have to be Virgil Trucks because the Tigers pitcher had thrown two no-hitters in 1952. From the champion New York Yankees came Joe Collins and Bob Kuzava, who held the Dodgers in check in the last three innings of game seven in 1952. Utica-born too was Ted Lepcio, rookie Red Sox infielder, who played alongside of Sibbi Sisti of the Braves, another upstate New Yorker agreeing to tour as well. This was not a tour of stars. Never to be chosen an All-Star were Trucks, Collins, Sisti, and Lepcio. Lollar would be picked, but not for three years; Wertz was a three-time All-Star (but in 1952 he hit .246 for the Tigers before he was sentenced to play with the Browns); and Ennis had been twice selected and would be once again.

If there were a few stars on this trip, they were not at the level of Roy Campanella, but stars nevertheless and many baseball fans remember frontline players like Lollar, Wertz and Ennis. Whitey Ford planned to be on the touring group, but he was still awaiting his Army discharge.

Assigned to be the field manager was White, while Smith and Art Mills lined up games, sent out contracts, negotiated percentages and guarantees. Art Mills probably served as the advance man, coming to a town before a game, and Smith traveled with the team, making certain that the team was paid properly.

The twelve players paid their own expenses and drove their own cars. With their clubs' permission, all the Phillies players were shown in the home uniforms, Boston and New York in away uniforms. Each man had the advantage of being paid right after each game in cash in an envelope.

Many of the places these major leaguers were about to visit had phone numbers that were still two digits (dial "97") and some used party line numbers ("Call 1276-j-1"). In less than ten years, much of their travel might have been along the New York State Thruway that now runs north from New York City to Albany where it turns west through Schenectady, Utica, Syracuse, Rochester and Buffalo. But in 1952 the team traveled on two-lane roads, like U.S. Route 20, in their cars, the journey beginning about mid-state in Little Falls, New York, a city of 9,500.

There the October 10 game was under the sponsorship of the local American Legion Post. That organization asked things of the players and also provided them with the chance to make some money. Another bonus for the players was that the veterans group fed them at lunch and at dinner as well.

So, first, at 11:30 A.M., the players showed up at an autograph session for children at Burwell Field, an activity followed by a 12:45 buffet lunch at the American Legion home.

The players then dressed and were shown to the park. There, ticket prices were listed at 60 cents for children, general admission at $1.50, and reserved seats for $1.75. "Prior to the game," the city's *Evening Times* wrote,

> Billy Mills entertained briefly. His two selections included, "Elmer Fudd, the rookie pitcher working with the bases loaded" and the immortal Babe Ruth "hitting his homer against the Cubs in the 1932 World Series." Both were well received by the crowd.

Next, a Marine Corps color guard marched onto the field for the playing of the national anthem. First to take the field before 2,000 fans were the barnstormers' opposition, players from the Mohawk Valley League. They committed five errors. Bob Kuzava, on the other hand, struck out nine in three innings, resulting in a 7–0 shutout by the big leaguers.

The game was played as many barnstorming games were allowed to proceed. Kids ran onto the field to grab a ball hit down the left field line before the fielder could get to it. Often, a player would be sought out between innings to sign the ball.

After the game came a visit by the players to the Little Falls Hospital "where they will mingle with the patients and entertain the people confined there, who [were] unable to attend the game in the afternoon." The players distributed souvenirs at 7 p.m. during an open house at the Legion post and following that the players sat down for dinner.

The next morning the players drove south for about an hour and a half to Norwich, where the sponsors, the local Elks, had decided to charge admissions of $2.00, $1.50, with teenagers for 75 cents, and under 13 free. Included in the admission were souvenir booklets for the October 11 game. Pulling into the city of 8,800 at 11 A.M., the team accepted a key to the city from the mayor at the Elks club. When the clash with the high school football game time was noticed, the school agreed to change its kickoff to 3 P.M. The Saturday game for the benefit of Elks youth at Veterans' Park had to keep its time at 1 P.M.

Celebratory seemed to be the mood for the 1,200 paid. "The famed Oneonta Elks Clown Band entertained at the field also with a pre-game program and numbers throughout the game," as the *Norwich Sun* reported and

> a sparkling pre-game show was offered by the King of Pantomime and one of the best diamond entertainers in the nation today, Billy Mills. He presented "A Day At the Races," "Elmer Fudd, the Screwball Rookie of the Year," and "Ruth's Immortal Homer."

Once again the players signed autographs before the game.

The game itself featured the opposition managed by Steve Peek, a pitcher who was 4–2 with the Yankees in 1941. But his guidance made no difference; the All-Stars won 11–2. With the game over in less than two hours, the fans could then walk over to the high school field and see the football game.

Later that day, at 6:30, an Elks banquet took place, a father-son affair, at the Elks Lodge.

The next day the team drove north on Route 12 to McConnell Field in Utica, then a city of 101,000, for the 2 p.m. game. This game had been very seriously promoted; municipal buses began shuttling fans from the Busy Corner to McConnell Field at noon for the game with the Municipal League All-Stars.

And the game drew well, 4,200 paid, and in a pre-game entertainment Sibbi Sisti clowned by having the two bat boys come out and have one pitch to the other. Then Sisti pitched to one and as he did he removed jacket after jacket with each pitch, all of which the second bat boy carried. Then Kuzava came out and carried boy and jackets into the dugouts.

Also before the game, pitcher Hal White was honored by his home city of Utica — he was in his twelfth year in the majors — and he turned out to be the winning pitcher that day. The major league barnstorming troupe met Frank Soscia's Area All-Stars, and the 3,500 fans who turned out saw stars like Utican Ted Lepcio, Whitey Ford (he then just another player after his second year in the majors), Joe Garagiola and Sherm Lollar go on to victory by 8–4.

Fifteen miles was the short distance to the Rome State School, the city of Rome being home to 42,000, 2,000 of whom paid to see the Rome Colonels meet the travelers. Rome had lost its team in the Canadian American League after the 1951 season when sixteen leagues had folded. As usual, the players were asked to appear at a banquet afterwards at the Commander Hotel.

The next day, October 14, the team was scheduled to play an exhibition at the Auburn prison but this game was either not covered or rained out. But a night game before 1,200 was played at Geneva, another small city that had lost its minor league team.

Back roads were followed to the city of Oneonta, to a park that still stands, a park that Babe Ruth barnstormed in after the 1920 season. That ballpark, then called Neahwa Park, now called Damasche Field, has stood on the same site since 1903 in the city of 14,000. In that park three additional big leaguers staffed the opposing team on October 15: Jim Konstanty of the Phillies, Dick Fowler of the Athletics, and former Giants player Ken Chase all agreed to play in the 7:30 p.m. game. But though the *Oneonta Star* head-lined "Virgil 'No-Hit' Trucks and Vic Wertz," only 855 "customers huddled in top coats and blankets" watched the 7–2 win by the all-stars. "Because of the cold and possibility of injury to players on both clubs, the game was called at the end of seven innings."

Perhaps because of that cold, two days passed without games. But it is known that after an off-day on October 16 — Thursday — a party took place at Caroga Lake's Nick Stoner Golf Club the next day on October 17. Caroga Lake is just north of the usual east-west routes across the middle of New York and a convenient stopoff while heading another 150 miles north to Saranac Lake, that village of 7,000 where the next-to-last game was played on October 18 before 1,700.

Tour's end was in Schenectady, the second largest city on the tour. The *Schenectady Gazette* named Schenectady Stadium at 2 p.m. for the policeman-fireman cerebral palsy benefit game. The stars had a 9–0 victory "before an overcoat crowd of 1,000 [or 945] paid fans."

"The game was called at the end of eight innings in order to give the major all-stars a chance to make train connections." But not all went home; some of the upstate New York residents among the barnstormers were the guests of the former Giants hurler Hal Schumacher, now in the employ of a Dolgeville, New York, company, McLaughlin-Millard Manufacturing, the company later to be known as Adirondack Bats.

Attendance for the seven games turned out to be on average 1,720 per game, with a total of 12,045. In contrast, Campanella's expansive tour averaged 2,500 per game in 25 contests.

1953

Changes had arrived in the world in 1953: the Korean War ended; specifications for mass-produced color televisions were adopted.

On television, the first appearance of the baseball Game of the Week quickly garnered very high ratings. Though banned in all major league cities, the weekly game captured 75 percent of all sets in use not in big league cities.

In the previous year *The Sporting News* of October 29, 1952, announced that, "All But Campy Cancel Tours Due to Poor Weather, Crowds." In 1953 only three teams would go on the road in the United States.

And yet barnstorming continued to have its appeal for players: *The Sporting News* wrote,

> The 1953 barnstorming season, one of the most elaborate arranged in recent years, with three teams signed up for Pacific Ocean trips, got under way on October 8, when the New York Giants, Eddie Lopat's all-stars, and Roy Campanella's tourists started on their extensive exhibition travels.

Pacific trips or extensive trips through the warmer parts of the South, these three jaunts followed the racial formula as they had since the beginning.

No matter that by 1953 there was some progress in the hiring of blacks for major league jobs (seven teams employed twenty black players by 1953), it was still clear that more than half of the big league franchises did not choose to sign black players.

And why should they? Well, in the National League, Jackie Robinson had placed fifth in the MVP voting in 1947, the year he won Rookie of the Year; his teammate Roy Campanella won the first of his three MVP awards in 1951; Monte Irvin and Campanella took RBI crowns prior to 1953; Robinson and Bill Bruton would be stolen base champions; Jim Gilliam led in triples once and took 100 walks in 1953; Don Newcombe led in lowest opponents batting averages one year and tied for the lead in shutouts and strikeouts in another. Big Newk won the Rookie of the Year award the same year that Robinson was the MVP, 1949

Still, many teams refused to hire black players and not until 1959 did the Red Sox sign a black man.

America was still a country vastly de facto segregated — Jim Crow laws, the sit-in-the-back-of-the-bus rules— were still firmly enforced. The power of Jim Crow was so pervasive that in 1965 Congress had to enact the Voting Rights Act, allowing American citizens to vote.

Was there nationwide integration, meaning equal rights, evident in the country? All those areas that received the baseball Game of the Week with the Arkansas drawl of Dizzy Dean broadcasting certainly saw and heard the excellence of black players in a vastly white game, because the powerful Dodgers of Robinson and Campanella and Newcombe and the almost as powerful New York Giants, with black men Mays, Thompson and Irvin, appeared on those television screens all the time.

Campanella's barnstorming team in 1953 included black players Jim Gilliam, Joe Black, and Don Newcombe.

But it was Jackie Robinson, who else and of course, who called on four white players to travel with him making up a fully integrated team: Bobby Young of the Orioles; Gil Hodges, his teammate; Ralph Branca, his former teammate, now pitching for the Tigers; and Al Rosen, the American League's Most Valuable Player who had just lost out on winning the Triple Crown.

Robinson's tours in 1950 and 1953 were close to identical. Start in Baltimore and Virginia, travel southward through the Carolinas and Georgia, and then turn westward through Alabama, Mississippi, Louisiana and Texas. True, Jack had replaced Florida games with games in Mexico, but the trip did not avoid the Deep South. The barnstorming organizers were Lester Dworman, a money man from New York, with Ted Worner again assigned as promoter. (Worner was the promoter for all five of Jack's tours.)

In addition to Jackie Robinson and the four white players, the group included Luke Easter and Bob Trice of the Athletics. Filling out the squad were black farmhands of the Dodgers organization such as Charlie Neal, whose contract then belonged to the team at Newport News (he would make it to the big club in 1956); Maury Wills, then a Miami pitcher who found his spot with the Dodgers in 1959 after eight years in the minors, and accepted the National League's Most Valuable Player in 1962. Signed to appear later were Larry Doby, a future Hall of Famer, and Minnie Minoso. It is known that Branca and Hodges played their games in Brooklyn home uniforms.

Most times the team that the Robinsons were matched with was made up of players from the Indianapolis Clowns, a team that maintained a midget mascot, Spec Bebop, and another baseball clown, King Tut (Richard King) who performed various pantomime routines, as Billy Mills did.

Part of Robinson's optimism for the success of his tour was based on the fact that radio still had its reach: the 1953 Brooklyn Dodgers Radio Network signed up 117 stations.

Just after the opening game in Baltimore, October 9, the black newspaper, the *Pittsburgh Courier*, appeared on October 10, 1953, stating the importance of Robinson's venture: "For the first time in modern baseball history a Negro all-star team will include two white major league stars."

The historic team's first game was on October 9 in Baltimore, a 6–2 win over a Negro League all-star outfit before 1,500. Luke Easter hit two doubles and a home run in Westport Stadium. The game resulted in an eight line item in the *Baltimore Sun*.

The next game in Wilmington, Delaware, ended in a 4–4 tie, but at Myers Field in Norfolk, Virginia, Robinson's integrated squad won 11–3 before 3,700 in a game that saw first baseman Gil Hodges pitch three innings. The regular pitching had to be held back since a game followed in Newport News that night. With a quick trip to North Carolina for a game at Winston-Salem, the team bounced back up to Lynchburg, Virginia, on October 13 for a 9–3 win before 1,200.

In North Carolina for three dates, the night game at Griffith Park in Charlotte attracted the largest crowd so far as the big leaguers were defeated 11–5. Drawing well at Asheville's McCormick Field — it was the largest crowd of the year at the field with 2,659 paying — Robby won 5–3, but before the game started Rosen said he had hurt his back so badly, probably in Charlotte, that he had to leave the tour, to heal at his home. After a quick stop in a hamlet of 1,200, Conover, it was on to Chattanooga and then to Birmingham, Alabama, on October 18.

As early as October 3, 1953, disturbing reports were coming in. The *Washington Post* on the ninth ran a story that began "Police Commissioner Eugene Connors ... said ... an all Negro game would be all right. Birmingham has a city ordinance which prohibits 'mixed athletic events.'" (In just a few years, the country would know policeman Connors by his nickname — "Bull."

His actions against blacks would not be confined to city ordinances. In May of 1963 the whole country knew him as the man who ordered powerful fire hoses and police attack dogs to be used against unarmed, nonviolent protest marchers.)

The *Pittsburgh Courier* of October 3, 1953:

> City officials [in Birmingham on] Tuesday, Sept. 22, backed down on their announced plan to modify Birmingham's sports segregation ordinance 798-F so that Negro and white ballplayers could lawfully compete against each other. ...
>
> A spot paid advertisement by the Civic Protection committee ... urg[ed] citizens to appear at City Hall to protest the change. About 100 showed up.

The book *Great Time Coming* (251) says that the chief deputy to Bull Connors visited Worner and said, "'Listen jewboy, if they white show up at Rickwood Field on Sunday, you and Robbison's gonna be in jail before the game starts." (Ted Worner remembers the incident happening in 1954.) Jack fought the prohibition but Hodges, Branca and Young were worried.

In the *New York Age* in December, Robinson discussed the incident:

> "Everyone knows how I feel about discrimination," Jackie began. "I was just a hired hand on the barnstorm tour.... I accepted Ted Worner's offer this year when he agreed to pay me well.... Worner had been assured that there would be no trouble in Birmingham."

But Hodges, Branca and Young were being threatened with arrest. Could the Jim Crows laws be fought? When Worner talked to some of the city leaders, they believed that

> Bull Connors, a fighter for white supremacy, would use the incident as fuel in his campaign to be elected sheriff. Worner, factoring in the promotional money that his Birmingham partners had spent, decided to play the game to an eager Birmingham audience.

To replace a white player, Willie Mays was signed to play in Birmingham while on a weekend pass from his service duty at Fort Eustis, Virginia, 700 miles to the north. For the 2:30 game, Willie Mays and Artie Wilson replaced Gil Hodges and Bobby Young. "A special section has been reserved for white fans, " the *Birmingham News* reported on October 17, 1953. Robby's team won 10–4 with Mays making two hits and stealing home in the sixth before 6,000 fans.

During the game, "two of the cops stormed into the dugout and ordered Jack to remove the white kid [i.e., Willie Mays] playing center field. Maury Wills almost hemorrhaged from laughing" (Falkner, 251).

And though the *Chicago Defender*'s page one headline read, "Dixie Bars Jackie's All-Star Team" on October 17, 1953, a letter written to the *News* praised Birmingham's hospitality shown during the Alabama-Tennessee football game.

Wedged in between two games in Tennessee was a game without incident in either Decatur or Florence, Alabama. At Sulphur Dell in Nashville at eight o'clock 1,200 came to the park to see Jack's team win 12–1.

But concerning the October 21 game at Martin Stadium in Memphis, a meeting was scheduled at City Hall to discuss Negroes and whites playing together. Once again Ted Worner conducted the negotiations and met with the city attorney to see if there was an ordinance prohibiting play. The Memphis paper said it this way: "Ted Worner, of Yonkers, NY, the promoter, agreed with city officials ... not to press the point ... that the white players sit out the game." The United Press syndicate clarified the point.

> "There was no talk about an ordinance," Worner said, "it was merely suggested that that it would be better if the matter were not pressed".... Worner said Hodges, Young and Branca will be introduced from the stands during the game, but will not play.

This meant, for their money, the 5,600 fans watched only Robinson and Easter as major league players, Robby's team winning 10–4. Once again Jim Crow prevented admission-paying fans from seeing the best the game had to offer. For decades this meant that Josh Gibson and Cool Papa Bell were never to be seen by major league fans. This time it was the white players.

Little Rock, Arkansas, did make sure that a section of Traveler's Field on October 18 would "be reserved for white fans." Black and white fans numbering 4,137 saw Easter hit two homers in a 7–6 win. Play continued in other spots in Arkansas, as well in Louisiana and Texas.

In Jasper, Texas, 2,000 saw Branca win the 22nd game of 27 for Robinson, and Branca the next day, November 1, won again throwing a one-hitter in Houston, winning the game with the help of Gil Hodges' home run. It was Maury Wills throwing a four-hitter in Jacksonville, Florida, on November 4 that led to a 5–5 tie, ending the games for the club in the United States.

Jack received feelers to play in Mexico and agreed to a three-game series in Mexico City. The famous attempt by Jorge Pasquel to have a league in Mexico at the level of the majors finally ran out of money in 1953. But the northern clubs of Pasquel's league merged into the Arizona-Texas and Arizona-Mexico leagues of 1953–57, and it was those leagues that supplied much of the opposition for Robinson.

On November 7, 1953, in Mexico City, Jack's team played before 13,000 in Parque Delta when they faced the Mexico City Aztecas of the Winter Baseball League, with Sonny Dixon of the Washington Senators on the mound for the Mexicans. Branca took the loss against Dixon though Easter hit two homers and two singles in the 6–3 defeat. On November 9, 1953, again in Mexico City, Cuban Gil Guerra defeated Jack's team 3–1, when a balk was called on pitcher Wills with the bases loaded. Robby lost the rubber game 3–1 to the Aztecas, dropping the team to 1–2 in Mexico.

In sum, the barnstorming team's record, traveling from Baltimore to Mexico City was 23–7–1.

Four years later: Atlanta, February 14, 1957 — "Georgia's Senate unanimously adopted a bill to outlaw interracial athletics." This law was deemed necessary, the *New York Times* reported a Georgia lawmaker saying, because "it is not possible for races to be thrown into interracial social contact without both races thereby being corrupted."

1954

Television's impact increased exponentially: the number of stations on the air more than doubled in one year (from 125 to 349) in 1954. At the same time, perhaps affected by the rise in television rights payments to teams, the minimum salary level for major leaguers was set at $6,000, about $42,000 today. And the World Series payoff that year set a record: the victorious New York Giants each made $11,147, a clear record by almost $3,000. Those changes were reflected, too, in the moving of the St. Louis Browns to Baltimore to become the Orioles, and the Athletics barely holding on in Philadelphia.

Though Commissioner Ford Frick prohibited one trip to due to financial disagreements in 1953, three ambitious tours are worth noting. Though Roy Campanella planned a barnstorming venture, the catcher had to withdraw due to a very serious hand injury. Eddie Lopat's team, to play in places such as Las Vegas and in California, was the subject of a story quoting Frank Scott in *The Sporting News* on November 3, 1954, called "More Leis Than Bucks In Hawaii; Tourists Now Eye New Trip." The story began:

> "The major leaguers had expected to net $6,000 for their visit, but left the islands without any cash for their exhibition appearances." Scott said "You have to remember that these people are used to seeing the players on World Series TV. They get it a little late, but they're getting it, and that's important because in the past people would come out just to see what the players looked like."

The players seemed to have made about $300 from the trip, mostly from games on the West Coast.

Even more of a disaster was Ned Garver's excursion, as covered in the same issue: "Rain, Poor Crowds Kayo Kretlow Tour," a trip which averaged just 547 admissions per game.

> The twin handicaps of insufficient advance publicity and bad weather wrecked the barnstorming tour of Ned Garver's major league all-stars.... The enterprise blew up with a bang ... when the club disbanded after drawing only 2,738 fans for five games.... Only four members of the team were willing to continue the tour.

Campanella's squad fared batter, by playing 26 games throughout the South and by scheduling seven games in major California cities. In Los

Angeles the *Times'* advance coverage of the game of November 4 identified Campanella's squad—the team with Henry Aaron, Willie Mays, Henry Thompson, and Ernie Banks, in addition to tour star Joe Black—as "Colored Stars."

Playing in smaller places were the squads of Spec Shea and Russ Meyer.

And playing once more was the tour that in 1952 played in upstate New York. There were new members of the squad that year, all from the American League, including, from the Yankees, Gil McDougald, Gene Woodling, and Ralph Houk. Hal White, who pitched for the Tigers, Browns and Cardinals (1941–1954) and finished the past season with Oakland of the superior Pacific Coast League, again signed comedian Billy Mills to accompany his barnstormers. Harold "Bud" Smith, Utica restaurateur, again was the business manager of the club, with Bill Oliver serving as scorer and press liaison.

As these particular barnstormers chose, they started with a big payday— two games on the same day—so that by the time October 8 was over they had drawn 1,500 fans for the 3:30 game in Montgomery Blair High Stadium in Silver Springs, Maryland, and in the same state they drew 1,600 that same night in Hagerstown. Directly north they drove for about seven hours to reach a city of 49,716, Elmira, New York, for an afternoon game at 3 p.m. on a Saturday. There they faced the stars of the semipro Tri-County League and former stars of the Elmira Pioneers. The ad for the game pronounced that all seats at Dunn Field would cost $1.50 and pictured in the publicity photo were McDougald, Billy Hunter and Cleveland pitcher Art Houtteman. The pre-game show included the clowning of Billy Mills as well as the music of the Moose Band. The players were honored at the Moose club after the game.

As was so often true in baseball, the biggest draw for a team would always be on a Sunday and that Sunday the team was in Offermann Stadium in Buffalo, New York, then a city of 580,000. Home to the AAA Bisons, a team for which barnstormer Hal White had played, 3,000 admissions had been sold, even though just 2,000 showed up for the benefit game for muscular dystrophy. (With a game-time temperature in low 60s, it was the rain that kept people away from the game.) A team sponsored by the Simon Pure Brewery was named as the rival team and included pitcher Marion Fricano, then in his third year in the majors with the Athletics. Briefly mentioned too was Danny Ozark, now 31, who spent many years as a player-manager in the minors before he was selected to be the manager of the Phillies from 1973–1979, as well as with the Giants in 1984. Sibbi Sisti, after his last major league year, during which he had been in over 1,000 games, was from Buffalo and he served as third baseman and coach for the Simon Pures as well as being the recipient of the gift of a suitcase. Billy Mills was returning to the city where he had been the team mascot when his father managed the hometown Buffalo Bisons. Perhaps the greatest baseball man was in the stands for

BASEBALL TODAY

MAJOR LEAGUE All-Stars

— vs. —

SIMON PURE BREWERY

3 P. M. - OFFERMANN STADIUM - 3 P. M.

Watch —
MARION FRICANO — SHERM LOLLAR — STEVE
GROMEK — GENE WOODLING and TED LEPCIO
and BILLY MILLS, BASEBALL CLOWN, and "SIBBY
SISTI DAY"

Presentation By Romulus Club!

ADMISSION —$2-$1.50-50c

BOX   GRANDSTAND   CHILDREN

OFFERMANN BOX OFFICE OPEN at 12 NOON

BENEFIT GAME FOR ERIE COUNTY CHAPTER,
MUSCULAR DYSTROPHY ASSNS. of AMERICA —
"GIVE HOPE TO THE HOPELESS"

Announcement of a game in Buffalo, New York, 1953, for Hal White barn-stormers.

the game: former manager Joe McCarthy, the winner of seven of the nine World Series his Cubs and Yankees had played in. Farming acreage near Buffalo for many years, McCarthy was three years away from election to the Hall of Fame.

From nearby Niagara Falls came Sal Maglie, "the Barber," who had won game one of the World Series that year, and who was determined to contribute, even with a sore back, even though he could have appeared on Ed Sullivan's weekly CBS television show (*Toast of the Town*) that same night. Sibbi Sisti drove in the winning run for the Simon Pures in the ninth.

Back through Elmira and then south the team drove to what was called Sunbury, Pennsylvania, in the itinerary. With 950 spectators on hand, the major leaguers faced the team from Krebs' Electric on Columbus Day. The next day they played in Ralston, Pennsylvania, where 600 paid to see their Lycoming Avco team meet the barnstormers. After the game, townspeople could attend a $1.50 buffet and dance, with the players agreeing to stay until midnight.

They agreed to the late time because the next game was a night game (6:30 P.M.) though the distance was a winding 200 miles away. Herkimer, New York, population 9,400 had called upon the Crowley-Barnum American Legion Post to sponsor the event. Having 2,400 come though the turnstiles, the event featured a one-inning game between the major leaguers and the Herkimer Little Leaguers. In the main game Jim Aiello pitched, he who had worn the uniform of the Yankees farm team in 1954 while assigned to Grand Forks, North Dakota, of the Northern League.

But the quintessential barnstorming game was played in little Lowville, New York, a village of about 3,700 people. Just 70 miles north of Herkimer, the coverage in Lowville was in the hands of the weekly *Journal & Republican* ("$3.00 per year subscription if paid in advance") which noted that the game at the fairgrounds could be seen that Friday by all the schoolchildren in town since school was to be closed early that day at 2 P.M. Eighteen percent of the village's population showed up for the game as their Lowville Area All-Stars took the field.

Did it matter who won? The local newspaper saw fit to expend about twelve words on the game itself. It only mattered that the game was played, that people had fun, that the players made a little money, that kids collected some autographs.

Scheduled after the game was a banquet at 6 p.m. to honor the Lowville Athletics, baseball champions of the Lewis County League, as well the barnstormers. Following a reception in the Elks lodge in town, the banquet, hosted by Court of Claims judge Fred Young, began in St. Peter's church hall. Attended by 250 people, the banquet's coverage concentrated on the local players with special attention being given to the cooks for the banquet, the members of St. Therese's Guild.

Before all the players were introduced, baseball clown Billy Mills entertained the crowd with jokes and pantomimes done to recordings. After an orchestra of local students played, Judge Young presented Mills and the all-stars with gifts of Lewis County cheese.

Next was a game at far northern New York, at Hogansburg on the St. Regis Indian Reservation, where 900 fans paid to see the Border All-Stars face the barnstormers. And the last game for the touring squad was scheduled on October 17, twelve days after the first games in Maryland, before a crowd of 1,500–2,500 at Murnane Field in Utica, New York. The 2 p.m. game was covered by Doc Merna in the local *Observer-Dispatch*. Merna told his readers that six dozen baseballs were brought to the game but the 72 were not enough as

> many youngsters in the crowd ... located a bonanza along the left field line where every ball hit resulted in a pileup of some 50 youngsters seeking a pellet. That the barnstormers would beat the Utica Municipal League all-stars was a foregone conclusion.

Following the tour, on Sunday night, the players were once again the guests of Hal Schumacher, former Giants' pitcher and now vice-president of McLaughlin-Millard, manufacturers of Adirondack bats.

So in 1954 what can be known centers on four teams:

The Lopat team had a good time but came home virtually empty-handed.
The Garver outfit managed 547 admissions per game.
The Campanella named tour averaged 2,300, with a team that averaged 2,000 more fans per game in 1953 than in 1954.
White's team drew an average of 1,447 average for nine contests.

If we can speculate that an admission equaled about $1.25 and if we can also imagine that the money men took 50 percent of the receipts while paying expenses, then we can say that each player on the Campanella team made about $100 per game; players on the White team made about $70 per game. A player at minimum salary in 1954 made about $1,100 per month, or $36 a day during the regular season.

The Sporting News editorial on November 3, 1954, took note that "There's Been Changes, for Barnstormers."

> Barnstorming, like so many other attractions in the entertainment field, depends heavily on the element of novelty.... Radio and television have ranged so far into the outlands that many potential customers no doubt have had their fill of baseball by the time the season comes to a close.

1955

The salaries in the mid-fifties ranged from $10,000 to $25,000 on average but superstars—DiMaggio, Williams and Musial—were paid $100,000. Again that largesse seems to be tied to television revenue.

> By 1955 only three teams didn't televise (the Braves, Pirates, and A's). On the other hand, the Cubs, Dodgers, Yankees, and Giants broadcast every home game, the Indians and Cards every road game. The Reds televised all weekday after-

noon home games; the Phillies showed 29 home and 27 road games; Baltimore showed 65 contests; even the Red Sox and Senators had TV on their schedule; six stations in Michigan showed 42 Tigers games; WGN televised every day game from Comiskey Park [Adomites].

One station, TBS, says on its Web site that Willie Mays' 1955 barnstormers were considered by Henry Aaron to be the greatest he would ever play for. The team, put together by traveling secretary Curtis A. Leake and by Mays, included Ernie Banks, Roy Campanella, Monte Irvin, Joe Black and Don Newcombe. Having Hank Thompson, Minnie Minoso, and Junior Gilliam on your side did not hurt either. This squad didn't lose a single game as they meandered first to Chapel Hill, North Carolina, and then south to Georgia, next west to Alabama, Louisiana, Texas, the barnstorming tour ending in California. The 32 game tour ended on November 6 with more than 100,000 paid admissions with $95,588.79 in total receipts. If we grant 50 percent to the promoter and with the usual twelve players on the team, each man could take home about $4,000 each.

While the team of Spec Shea of the Senators— still composed of white players as Mays' was still all black —chose to go to medium-sized cities in New England, the all-white team led by Al Kaline played ten games drawing 8,000 fans with just 56 paid at Baltimore for the last game. *The Sporting News* of November 9, 1955, after speaking to Kaline, said that the Detroit outfielder would tour again "despite the flop of the recent junket," adding,

> Kaline feels the chilly nights, the size and lighting of the parks and the unfamiliarity of the way of other players detracts somewhat. "I know that I was a little afraid to dig in up there at the plate when I couldn't see as well as in an American League park and didn't know how wild the pitcher might be," he said. "You just can't give your best under those conditions."

The conditions for Sherm Lollar's team depended on how well the contracts to play were written — a good thing. For most of the tour, they rarely drew one thousand or more at the gate. In Macon, Georgia, only 375 paid to see the game, though the thermometer read 70 degrees. But Lollar's business manager saw to it that the agreements were to play for a guarantee rather than a percentage and so in money terms the team made out well, even though the club averaged only 588 fans in each of 17 contests.

Russ Meyer and Ned Garver wanted to go out on the road, but prospects looked so bleak that they canceled their plans.

In the midst of all this talk about money, let us not forget the fun. Here is a story by Ted Kubiak, a major league infielder for many years, whose father-in-law was Irv Noren, and concerns Mickey Mantle one of those 1958 players:

> Needless to say, my father-in-law, who roomed with Mickey, had to get him safely back to his room many a nights after their night on the town; Irv did not drink so he was the designated chauffer.

About 1955 or '56, my father-in-law, Irv Noren, and Mickey, roommates that year, decided to drive together to the West Coast. Irv lived in Pasadena and Mickey in Oklahoma.

Pretty soon they went through a small town and saw a group of young boys playing baseball behind a school. They thought it would be a good idea to have some fun so they stopped to watch. Irv asked the boys if he could pitch to his buddy because his buddy said he could not strike him out. The boys did not want these "old guys" to take up their time so they said no. After bribing the boys with some new baseballs they had in the car, Irv began throwing to Mickey who hit everything and, of course, was hitting the balls over the school much to the surprise of the boys. Finishing up, Irv asked them if they knew who Mickey Mantle was, and they did. "Well, this is Mickey!"

"No way," they said. Mickey had to eventually show them his driver's license; they left the boys the new balls and got on their way. What a story for those kids to tell their kids! [Kubiak, personal communication].

1956

If salaries were rising, why did players continue to barnstorm? Could it be that the fun, the camaraderie was still a strong pull? One powerful reason might be the frustration over both the lack of justice in being paid your worth plus the continual heavy-handedness of the club when dealing with player compensation. For example, when Mickey Mantle, after his triple crown 1956 season, asked for a big raise, the club responded by telling him that if he continued to insist on more money, the owner might have to show his wife a private detective's report about his active night life.

Oscar Kahan covered the trip organized by Willie Mays and Don Newcombe, with help again of traveling secretary Curtis A. Leake. This year Alex Pompez, a Giants scout, would be the team backer. Pompez has a long and colorful history in baseball, from running the numbers to owning a semipro team, the Cuban Giants, to scouting, to being on the committee that determined the admission of Negro League players to the National Baseball Hall of Fame. One of his players, Monte Irvin, served as field manager on the tour and he could look out and see what some consider to be the greatest outfield in the history of baseball: Willie Mays, Henry Aaron and Frank Robinson.

And even though the team was a powerhouse, playing from October 11 through November 11, a drop in fan interest was noticeable at almost every stop:

At Memphis, 4,123 vs. 8,527 in 1955, a drop of 4,400.

At Birmingham, 900 in 1956 vs. 4,963 in 1955.

After 12 games, attendance in 1956 dropped 42 percent from 1955.

At Houston, a one game decrease of 20,000 paid.

At Corpus Christi, Texas, Mays stole home, but 820 paid in 1956 after 5,000 had paid in 1955.

When Suitcase Simpson broke his finger in a game, he was replaced by George Crowe. Simpson, speaking to *The Sporting News* on October 31, 1956, reflected on the low turnout:

> "We hit some towns in Texas where they had television down there for the first time this year ... I guess they got a little too much baseball....

Ticket to a 1956 Fort Smith, Arkansas, game with Willie Mays. (National Baseball Hall of Fame Library, Cooperstown, New York.)

Imagine that, people getting tired of baseball. I just can't understand it.... We need some of the Dodger guys who were on the tour with us last year.... Those Dodger guys pull in the fans everywhere. We really missed 'em."

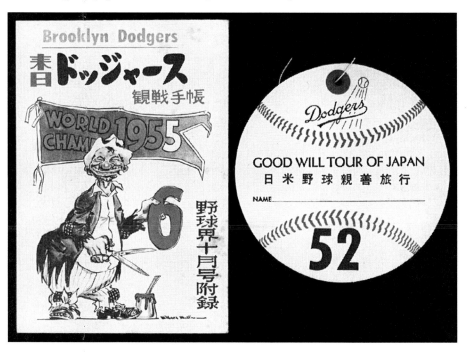

Advertisement for the Brooklyn Dodgers tour of Japan in 1956. (National Baseball Hall of Fame Library, Cooperstown, New York.)

Curtis Leake was heard to remark that the 1956 trip was the worst trip in his nine years of working with the barnstormers. He blamed "excessive admission, lack of local advertising, and too low a percentage of the gate as reason why the tour was not as successful as previous ones" (*The Sporting News*, October 31, 1956).

Each player made $1,226.31 minus the $400 in expenses, but that amount has to factor in the hurriedly-scheduled games on the West Coast which added over 18,000 fans to the attendance figures. The first major games saw a drop in attendance equaling 58 percent.

At the end of October, *The Sporting News* wrote that "Courtney's Players Receive $450 Each" after drawing 8,000 paid in ten games in Texas and New Mexico.

> The all-stars, accustomed to the plush of Pullman and plane travel in the majors, had a taste of the rigors of the road when they drove almost all night to reach Tucumcari at 3:30 a.m. after playing under the lights at Wichita Falls, Texas [340 miles northwest].

An earlier column by Oscar Kahan reported on Al Kaline who decided not to tour. "He said he didn't think there was much future in it, or money, either" and on October 24 Spec Shea said that "the fans have become familiar with big league players during the season. Before television, it was a novelty when big leaguers came to town. No more."

By November the paper said that barnstorming attendance was off by 50 percent in 1956. In 1956 only four teams barnstormed after the season.

1957

Only Nellie Fox, Frank Bolling, Charley Maxwell and Willie Mays risked the barnstorming trail in 1957.

Frank Bolling's team with a skein of six reported games in Texas, New Mexico, Arizona and Mexico drew 9,275. Nellie Fox's all-stars playing mostly for fun, wound up with about $200 apiece for their efforts. They were 4–1–1 in six games, with the average attendance at about 1,500, the same as Bolling's group.

Charley Maxwell was the playing manager for Bud Smith's team. When *The Sporting News* wrote that "Maxwell's Troupe Successful Despite Inclement Weather," one of those inclement dates was on October 20 in Utica, New York, where 120 paid to watch the game in 50-degree weather. But Tris Speaker was introduced from the stands and the game still maintained an enjoyable atmosphere:

> The Utica Sports Boosters Association entertained the major leaguers at a dinner after the game. Trucks' wife, Vicki, was chosen the most attractive woman at the affair, and was presented an orchid corsage as a prize.

The last group, bossed by Willie Mays of the Giants, tried its luck in Mexico—two games canceled there—and traveled to the Dominican Republic and Panama, before moving 3,000 miles west to California. This was the first year that the black team failed to play a schedule of games in the southern United States, and that decision might have been due to the Giants' recent move to San Francisco. Adding 3,000 miles of travel was a very costly item for the barnstormers.

In 24 games in 1957 the team drew 141,301 (an average crowd was 5,887), a number to cheer the hearts of both Mays and Leake. Attendance was no doubt helped by the opposition, a

> Mexican all-star team, featuring Bobby Avila of the Indians from Mexico.... The barnstormers will follow their itinerary as originally announced, playing in the Dominican Republic, Nicaragua, Panama, and on the Pacific Coast, November 1 to 12 [*The Sporting News*, October 22, 1958, p. 8].

The first fifteen games, all played in Latin countries, drew 117,000 paid, a wonderful average of 7,666. The games on the West Coast only added to the income for the team. (Apparently, Bob Lemon, born in San Bernardino, put together opposing teams in Los Angeles whenever an all-star team came through as far back as 1946.)

1958

In early October 1958, *The Sporting News* once again let it be known that "Few Barnstorm Tours This Fall, Pickings Lean." Harold J. "Bud" Smith, Nellie Fox, and Frank Bolling all decided not to tour this year but Nellie Fox and Dick Groat agreed to travel through Pennsylvania, and Charley Maxwell played a few games in Michigan. "The barnstorming trail once glittered with gold for major league players, who criss-crossed the country after the regular season, but the extra bucks aren't there any more."

Or at least not in the States. Mays went below the U.S. border again in 1958, again playing Bobby Avila's team. For the twenty-one games that took in money, the trip attracted 128,560 fans. This average of 6,121 per game was down from 1957, but the still high numbers meant that the players took home about $500 per week.

A contributor to the downfall of barnstorming was the growth and sophistication of television. Beginning in 1955, the World Series had been sent out in color. Though color television receivers were still few in number, it was a development that could only gain momentum in the next decade. Then, too, the televising of the National Football League games had become a staple of American viewing beginning in 1956 when the CBS network took over the games; in 1958, the first ever sudden-death championship game only increased the popularity of the sport. And this sport took place at the same time as the barnstorming tours would have been looking for fans. More and more, spectating meant seeing a sport from home.

1959

For the first time in history more than 500 TV stations could be counted on the air in 1959. Barnstorming, therefore, began to concentrate on playing in Mexico. Joe Tubiolo of Sports Attractions, Inc., in Washington was promoting the all black trip which was supposed to feature the future Hall of Fame players Henry Aaron, Willie McCovey, and Bob Gibson with Harmon Killebrew and Jim Bunning on an opposing team.

By the time the first game in the tour was finished, Henry Aaron (later fined $500 by the commissioner), Willie McCovey, Jim Gilliam and Charley Neal were no longer with the team. This was after Mays dropped out after advice from Giants owner Horace Stoneham. When John Roseboro left after a few games in Mexico, he too was fined $500.

Killebrew's team played nine games before 16,785, or 1,865 per game. In Mexico, the teams drew 43,598 for twenty games, or 2,180 per game. Some games were canceled by the Mexican promoter.

Perhaps basketball promoter Eddie Gottleib was more convincing. He signed up Willie Mays, Willie McCovey, Henry Aaron, Mickey Mantle, Whitey Ford, Richie Ashburn, Ernie Banks, Bill Mazeroski and Hoyt Wilhelm, all future Hall of Fame players. You could even say that this touring aggregation could field a team of nothing but Hall of Fame players. Lesser stars—Gil Hodges, Johnny Podres and Junior Gilliam from the Dodgers, for example—played too. The first game was played in Yankee Stadium on October 12, three days after the World Series ended on October 9. (Yankees players in these games, Mantle, Billy Martin, Elston Howard, and Whitey Ford, were paid $8,579 for their Series work.) When a crowd of 21,129 came to the game, promoters Frank Forbes and Julie Issacson paid each player $300 plus expenses. Comedian Jackie Gleason pitched to both Mays and Mantle.

The second match was played in Connie Mack Stadium, featuring a home run contest before the game and Gil Hodges, with three home runs, was awarded a plaque by the South Philadelphia Optimists Club, and 6,876 saw Mays hit a grand slam in the fourth inning.

After that game the players boarded buses to travel to Syracuse in upstate New York for the next game, a contest promoted by boxer Carmen Basilio. In that game, 7,986 paid, making for receipts of $20,000. No matter the profit for players, the games ended there.

1960

Jack Horner covered the botched tour of two black all-star teams that began in Durham, North Carolina, October 14. In that Carolina city, the local promoter complained to Ford Frick that Henry Aaron, Wes Covington, and Lee Maye of the Braves, Maury Wills and Charley Neal of the Dodgers, Vada Pinson of the Reds, Bill White of the Cardinals and Don Newcombe from Cleveland failed to make their advertised appearances. All but Aaron, Maye of the Braves, Wills, and Neal were excused by Frick. (Later, Al Smith of the White Sox and Bennie Daniels of the Pirates also were in trouble with the commissioner.) Aaron was fined $1,000 and Neal and Wills were fined $500 each, "all offenders had been given the alternative of joining the tour or facing a minimum fine of $500" the *Los Angeles Times* reported on November 3, 1960.

After the two games in Jersey City and Syracuse, the rest of the team included Newcombe of the Indians and his teammate Jim Grant; Earl Wilson, Pumpsie Green and Willie Tasby of the Red Sox; Lennie Green and Earl Battey of the Senators; Bob Boyd of the Orioles and Jesse Gonder of the Yankees. The remainder of the roster was filled by minor leaguers.

The success of the barnstormers seemed to be based on visiting places ignored for years by barnstormers, many places having under 100,000 residents. But when the data was known of the first ten games, and when the attendance totaled only 12,420, the absence of all those players was beginning to be understood. Ending in Texas, the team drew 453 for their last game on November 7. For all 28 games, the attendance averaged less than 1,000 per game, at $1.50 each.

This lackluster performance may have prompted *The Sporting News* for November 16, 1960, to suggest in an editorial that it was "Time to Ban Barnstormers." The column read in part: "Time was that the visit of a team of major leaguers after the season was an occasion of some importance in minor league cities. Now, when you can get a good look on television, these trips have become almost needless."

Other factors killing barnstorming, beside the cultural changes of television's growth and the rise of salaries that have been pointed out so many times, included the banning of American professional baseball in Cuba, the death of quality semipro baseball to provide opposition (the Bushwicks stopped playing after the 1951 season) and playing fields, the end of the Negro leagues as a force in 1948, and the inauguration of the Instructional Leagues in Florida, which in effect extended the season into Florida.

In addition, baseball in these smaller cities and towns was dying as well. In 1960, there were 118 minor league teams, a 56 percent decline in the number of teams from 1946.

1961

When the time came for the 1961 barnstorming season, Willie Mays was not heard from, since he was in the middle of working out of some serious indebtedness. In fact, "in 1960 [Mays] stood ... on the brink of filing for bankruptcy" (Einstein, 128). The *New York Times* on August 10, 1961, said that because of a suit filed by Mrs. Mays, Willie let it be known that he had already received salary advances of $65,200 for 1961. Since 1957, Mays had ten suits filed against him for indebtedness and currently owed $8,641 in state and federal taxes. And Mays "had been drawing advances on his salary since 1957."

What replaced barnstorming for 1961 was a home run tour with three players scheduling exhibitions solely of home run hitting. In other words, it was the television show *Home Run Derby* brought to ballparks in North Carolina. In the telecast version, a pair of sluggers hit in the empty Wrigley Field in Los Angeles. Only their home runs counted; otherwise an out was recorded in the nine inning contest.

The 1961 touring version featured two sluggers, each with 46 home runs that year — Jim Gentile and Harmon Killebrew — and Roger Maris, he of the 61 homers. North Carolina apparently was chosen because that state was the home of Clyde King, the designated thrower for the contests. After drawing 616 fans in Charlotte and 490 in their last stop, Winston-Salem, it was easy enough to declare the idea a flop.

1962

It was a very ambitious barnstorming tour that was planned for 1962, with 30 major leaguers signing on, fifteen from each league. Buck O'Neil was chosen manager and Satchel Paige the coach of the National League with Earl Battey managing the American Leaguers. George Leonard was the business manager of the squads and selected as promoter was Whitey Larkin, then the business manager of the Nashville Vols. In charge of the first game was Mack Massingale of the Kansas City Monarchs who said that everyone but Mays would get $100 per game, Mays to get more. Massingale said he would need $30,000 in net receipts to cover the costs of the tour — that is about 20,000 fans to attend, at ticket prices of $1 to $2.50. The biggest attraction was clearly Willie Mays.

Why Mays, one of the highest paid players in the game? *The Sporting News* explained in a November issue. Mays' reported salary for 1962 was $90,000, or $545 per game for a 165 game season, not counting spring training.

But, as Mays' first alimony payment came due, the Giants asked the star to return the money he had been previously advanced by the club and, as Mays tells it, "proposed that instead of them writing me my check [for his $90,000 salary] they just withhold the money from my salary that year.... Which put me in the position of having to pay not only going expenses but my new expenses, plus the taxes on $90,000 salary — all this on an actual income of no more, possibly, than $35,000" (Mays, 253).

Though the center fielder received $7,291.49 in World Series money, that sum was clearly not enough to cover Mays' indebtedness. But, because of the World Series, Mays, McCovey, Pinson and Wilson missed the first game in Lawton, Oklahoma, a city of 62,000. There, 900 fans in ABC Park saw Satchel Paige, now 55, pitch for the American Leaguers, who lost 9–1.

For the second game, Mays and Willie Davis were photographed in road uniforms. Wes Covington said he bought his Phillies uniform for $12 from the club and Mays was surprised to hear that he had to pay at all. At least game two was in a city of some size. The October 17 contest was played 240 miles from game one in Wichita, Kansas, in Lawrence Stadium. With 255,000 residents in the city, the team drew much better than in game one — 6,500 — with Paige again on the mound.

The next game was scheduled for the next day in Monroe, Louisiana. Because the players were driving to games, this meant that somehow they would travel more than 650 miles to play in a town of 53,000. It is likely that the game was canceled once the distance between games was clearly understood. Much more sensible was the decision to travel 200 miles from Wichita to Kansas City for the third game, to a city that was one of the largest (476,000) in the country. But with fewer than 1,000 attending, the barnstormers made short work of their game. Paige pitched the first four innings.

Game four on October 19 was played in Little Rock, Arkansas, 425 miles from Kansas City. And after another hard drive for the players, just 2,000 fans showed up for the game.

And that ended it. The decision was made to cancel the four or five remaining games and pay off the players. Everybody was supposed to get $100 but it was probably closer to $50 with Mays getting more.

The Sporting News of November 3 spoke of the tour in show business language: "Barnstorm Tour Floppo at Gate, Folds En Route."

And that ended barnstorming. In 1962 the major leaguers had put teams in Houston, New York, Los Angeles and Washington, D.C. These cities had all been important stops for barnstormers, guaranteed paydays for teams who might play most of their schedule in much smaller cities and towns.

Exhibition Games

1950

Something had changed drastically in both major league and minor league baseball as the 1950s began. Attendance in the majors declined 13 percent just from 1949 to 1950. Brooklyn, which came in second only on the last day of the pennant race, lost almost 450,000 fans.

Would exhibition games reflect this downturn? The exhibition game at Comiskey for Friday night, October 13, was to be star laden with American League All-Stars Al Rosen, Gus Zernial, Vern Stephens, Al Zarilla, Sam Chapman, Jerry Coleman, Sherman Lollar, Mickey Grasso, Dizzy Trout, Bill Wright, Early Wynn, Mel Parell and Lou Brissie. The team was managed by Buster Mills, White Sox coach. The National League All-Stars boasted of Ralph Kiner, Gil Hodges, Red Schoendienst, Willie Jones, Sid Gordon, Al Dark, Ted Kluszewski, Sam Jethroe, Duke Snider, Clyde McCullough, Wes Westrum, Howie Pollett, Larry Jansen, Bill Werle, Howie Fox, and Cliff Chambers. The manager for the game was Johnny Riddle. Even with all these stars, the game drew only 3,030. Maybe the other exhibition games being played around the same time, the games in the NBA, NHL and NFL which were now attracting lots of ink, could have something to do with the low baseball turnout.

For fun or for charity, or for both, there were still smaller games. Yankees pitcher Tommy Brynes pitched in Salisbury, North Carolina, against former and future big leaguer Clyde Kluttz who was born in nearby Rockwell for the all-star team of Senators pitcher Al Evans on October 21. World Series player Milo Candini and Dodgers catcher Bruce Edwards took part in a charity game in Stockton, California, on October 22, 1950.

Through the generosity of Merrie Fidler, All-American Girls Baseball League historian and author of *The Origins and History of the All-American Girls Professional Baseball League* (McFarland, 2006), much information has been disclosed about a part of a season of the All-American Girls Professional Baseball League, an exhibition season — 90 games scheduled, 46 played as of August 4.

Two teams that started the beginning of the 1948 season, the Springfield Sallies and the Chicago Colleens, had lost their franchises in mid–1948 and 1949, respectively. They became traveling teams touring the country playing each other in exhibition games and searching for new talent.

The beginning of the contract for the girls read this way:

Whereas two of the clubs formerly associated with said All-American Girls Baseball League have disbanded and their franchises been forfeited, and the Corporation [the All-American Girls Baseball League Management Corporation]

Birdie Tebbetts and his team in their uniforms. Front row: two unidentified bat boys. Second row, left to right: Eddie Pellagrini, Bob Savage, Vic Wertz, Vern Stephens, Snuffy Stirnweiss, Ray Scarborough, Spec Shea and Birdie Tebbetts. Back row, left to right: Jimmie Piersall, Cal Steib, Joe Coleman, Tony Lupien, Red Barrett, and Gus Niarhos. (National Baseball Hall of Fame Library, Cooperstown, New York.)

Advertisement from the All American Girls Professional Baseball League barnstorming trip in 1950. (National Baseball Hall of Fame Library, Cooperstown, N.Y.)

for the purpose of giving employment to the players formerly associated with said two clubs proposes to conduct an exhibition tour.

During the tour the girls were given $3 a day expense money and player salaries ranged from $55 to $100 per week. The *News* of Lynchburg, Virginia, on June 14, 1950, reported that the space between bases for these games was

72 feet and the mound was 55 feet from home. The weight of the ball was almost exactly the same as the men's but slightly larger in size, giving the girls a little bigger target to hit and field (Gregorich). An overhand pitching delivery began in the AAGPBL in 1948, after one year of sidearm.

The summer's tour began on June 3 in Illinois and covered much of the country. Quoted ticket prices in one spot were 74 cents for adults and 30 cents for children; in another, a night game advertised tickets costing $1 for adults, 50 cents for children and 50 cents for the "colored bleachers." The tour ended in Cleveland, Ohio, on September 4, games having been played on almost every day.

The year 1950 also marked the end of a mostly annual event called the Baseball Pheastival which took place in Huron, South Dakota, a locale known as the "Pheasant Hunting Paradise of America." In 1940, for example, coming for the baseball game and hunting expedition were pictured Phil Cavarretta and Doyle Lade of the Cubs, Blix Donnelly from the Phillies, Andy Anderson and Paul Lehner, the Browns' Murry Dickson and Pete Castiglione of the Pirates, and Frank Papish, Indians. "Their host and guide was Jim Meghan, a Huron civic leader and energetic baseball fan" who came up with the idea of having the visitors compete in a game (Hoepf). The game became the centerpiece of other events, including golf outings, dances, banquets, and parades focused on the local hospital. In 1943 after attracting players and hunters Paul Derringer, Bill Nicholson, Paul Waner, and Kiki Cuyler, the Pheastival went into full swing in 1944. That year the "Huron Armour Packers amateurs lost to the major leaguers, 9–0, in the inaugural Pheastival game" with 3,000 watching at the South Dakota State Fairgrounds. The players, Paul Derringer, Jimmie Foxx, Paul Waner, and Andy Pafko as well as coach Kiki Cuyler, hunted pheasant in the area for the next week. The next year, 1945, the game showcased Phil Cavarretta, Bill Nicholson, Paul Derringer, Paul Gillespie and Dewey Williams of the Cubs; Dizzy Trout of the Tigers; Emil Verban and Johnny Hopp of the Cardinals; Charlie Keller of the Yankees, and Paul Waner for an October benefit game for Huron's playgrounds and clinic for children.

The Pheastival of 1948 bragged about Ralph Houk, Joe DiMaggio, and Joe Page of the Yankees; Doyle Lade and Phil Cavarretta of the Cubs; Blix Donnelly and Bill Nicholson of the Phillies; Enos Slaughter of the Cardinals; Ken Raffensberger of the Reds; and Dizzy Trout of the Tigers. Opposing them was a group of players from the Pacific Coast League. Joe DiMaggio returned to Huron in 1949 and *The Sporting News* of October 12, in its "Caught On the Fly" column, also listed Joe Page, Johnnny Lindell, Willard Marshall, Pete Castiglione, George Metkovich, Phil Cavarretta, Paul Lehner, Sheldon Jones, and Frank Papish.

The event ended forever in 1950 when a meager pheasant population kept the hunters away.

1951

By 1951, as so many high organized barnstorming groups were on the road, there remained a few big leaguers with less travel and less time taken to be played. *The Sporting News* reported on the five Schoendienst brothers in one game at Athens, Illinois, on October 14. On the same day, Red Schoendienst's rival in the National League, Pee Wee Reese, played an exhibition game in Lousiville with outfielder Gus Bell before 1,100 customers. Also that day, Yogi Berra and teammate Phil Rizzuto, managed by Tommy Holmes, played the comedy baseball team called the Georgia Chain Gang at Hartford, Connecticut. Berra's two other teammates, Tom Morgan and Art Shallock, participated in a benefit game in Oakland, California, two weeks later.

In Oklahoma in 1951, Warren Spahn was out earning extra money. He faced fellow Oklahoman Allie Reynolds on October 21, 1951, in Oklahoma City before 7,517. Spahn also pitched on October 28 in Hollywood, California, and gave up a homer to Gus Zernial as the stars from the National League were matched with stars from the American League. At Gilmore Field there was the same matchup on November 1 with Enos Slaughter and Duke Snider on the National League team joining Zernial.

1952

The exhibition games now pass by rapidly. A benefit game took place in Oklahoma City on October 19, 1952, with Allie Reynolds and Warren Spahn, with the help of George Kell, Lou Kretlow, Ransom Jackson, Jim Busby and Cliff Mapes. With no games mentioned in 1953, again Spahn and Reynolds arranged games in Tulsa and Oklahoma City with Mike Garcia, Harry Brecheen, Dale Mitchell, Randy Jackson, Joe Frazier, and Dave Philley.

Virgil Trucks appeared in 1954 in Silver Spring, Maryland. At Gilmore Field in Hollywood on October 17, 1954, Leo Durocher and Fred Haney managed Rocky Bridges, Billy Consolo, and Bob Lemon. Against these formidable opponents were Forrest Tucker, Dennis Morgan, and Vince Barnett of the movies. The game, watched by 1,500, was marked by "buffonery and tomfoolery." But the first annual Variety Boys Club charity game in Oakland, California, on October 24 kept the contest more serious, this game starring Ted Kluszewski, Gus Grissom, Andy Carey, Joe DeMaestri, Bobby Adams, Jim Mangan, and Jackie Jensen against minor leaguers.

The year 1955 saw an October 9 exhibition game in Youngstown, Ohio, for the Heart Fund. Participating in this contest were Ed Wright and Paul Minner, Cubs; George Shuba, Dodgers; Chuck Tanner, Braves; Mike Kume, Athletics; Tigers players Jack Phillips, Steve Gromek and Jim Delsing; with the Red Sox sending Milt Bolling and Willard Nixon and the Indians Gene Woodling and Bobby Young.

The year 1956 had only a Modesto, California, exhibition on October 14 with Roy Smalley, Gene Mauch, Marv Grissom, Billy Martin, Frank Robinson, Duane Pillette, Larry Jackson, Jim Davis and Troy Heriage. Yogi Berra, Gil McDougald and Whitey Ford of the Yankees, along with sportscaster Red Barber, made some extra cash by appearing on televison's *Sgt. Bilko* show in 1957, but Morrie Martin and Bob Miller of the Cardinals with Bob Weisler of the Senators exercised smaller choices by exhibiting in Washington, Missouri.

Two games in 1958 continued a tradition. The Youngstown, Ohio, Heart Fund game was repeated on October 12 with Dick Groat before a crowd of 3,500 and 1957's Modesto game was repeated in 1958 on October 19, attracting 6,000 fans to see Johnny Briggs, Stu Miller, John McCall, Jim Gentile, Hank Sauer, and Jim Davenport. There were also three benefit games played that year. On October 20 in Sacramento's Redmonds Field, a benefit was arranged for scout Ken Penner. Signing up for the game were players Dick Stuart of the Pirates, and Hank Sauer and Mike McCormick from San Francisco. Sauer also agreed to a game in Long Beach, California, on October 12 with attractions Ron Fairly, Bob Lemon and Chuck Dressen. Finally in St. Louis on October 19 a benefit game with Del Rice, Don Lenhardt, Harry Hanebrink, and Chuck Diering.

With no games listed in 1959, it seemed to be true that a team may have one or two good crowds and then the drop-off would be significant. One example was the game in Jersey City on October 14, 1960, matching the Ernie Banks National League All-Stars against the Roger Maris American League All-Stars before 6,000 at Roosevelt Stadium. That total is not discouraging but the next stop, Syracuse, New York, suffered from a morning rain, resulting in receipts of about $9,000 compared with the $13,000 that Mantle's team had generated not that long ago in the same city. The promoter guessed that they lost $6,000 on the game.

And this was a team with eight 1958 All-Stars and seven future Hall of Fame players.

Only one other game in 1960 was covered. An exhibition in Houston on October 23 before 4,582 that brought in many big leaguers. Houston had been a farm team of the Cardinals for many years (1919–42, 1946–58) and many of these players had spent time playing for the local Buffaloes. Solly Hemus (installed in the Texas Baseball Hall of Fame), Larry Jackson, Don Cardwell, Bill Henry, Ryne Duren, Billy Muffett, Jim Umbricht, Texan Ernie Banks, Bill White, the Throneberry brothers, Pete Runnels, Dick Gernert, Roy Sievers, Gene Freese, Dick Williams, Russ Nixon, Ken Boyer (who had played for the 1954 Houston Texas Leaguers), Walt Moyrn, Charley James,

Carl Sawatski, Don Zimmer, Richie Ashburn, Alvin Dark, Norm Cash and Russ Snyder all came to play.

Though nothing was played in 1961, another Houston game took place in 1962. A fine group of players participated: Curt Flood (born in Houston), Johnny Keane (31 years in the Cardinals organization), Pete Runnels, Bob Aspromonte (Astros 1962), Earl Wilson, Bill White, Dal Maxvill, Ruben Amaro, and Tom Sturdivant. That game marked the end of exhibition games in the postseason.

Postscript

Extending this study by two years found a telling game scheduled to be played in New York City on October 12, 1963, in connection with the Latin-American Hall of Fame and the Hispanic-American Baseball Federation. The following were mentioned as participants: Pedro Ramos, Hector Lopez, Felipe Alou, Vic Power, Zoilo Versailles, Vic Davalillo, Felix Mantilla, Joe Christopher, Chico Fernandez and Ed Bauta. The report on the game itself mentioned a home run hitting contest prior to the game. To be inducted in that Hall of Fame were Adolfo Luque, Hiram Bithorn, Frank Coimbre, and a player whose son would represent him. For on that field was that son, Orlando Cepeda, and three others who would join him in the National Baseball Hall of Fame in Cooperstown: Luis Aparicio, Juan Marichal, and Roberto Clemente. Aparacio and Cepeda, for example, were being paid more than $40,000 a year. Soon the names Rodriguez, Gonzalez and Martinez would dominate All-Star teams.

Clearly, the sport no longer belonged just to white major leaguers and as time passed more and more changes would be felt in professional baseball. The longer season extended by almost a month the time the games would be played. Higher pay for the players, along with a pension plan, made winter work days unnecessary.

These modifications extend now even to a time when it is possible to have games for fun, games for a vacation from the pressure of the pennant races.

Baseball itself has given up on serious exhibition games. The annual Hall of Fame Game, one familiar exhibition game, is now an event that mostly matches players from the minor league affiliates of the big league opponents for the year. Sometimes, even the coaches play.

And now there was domed baseball, artificial grass baseball. There were more teams than any one fan could keep track of. The idea of major leaguers going out on the road at season's end into small towns in North Carolina or Maine or Arkansas or North Dakota for fun, for camaraderie, for a few dollars, was one more death in baseball.

Afterword

There were still some baseball travelers out there on the road, just no major league players. Occasionally, those that followed baseball could read about a few players playing beyond their retirement for organized baseball.

Once out of the majors, Johnny Podres barnstormed in upstate New York. There were a few men — Bill Lee, Bob Stanley, George Foster, Ferguson Jenkins and others— who toured in the early 1990s as the New England Grey Sox playing to raise money for burn centers and for the Boston-based Jimmy Fund.

The Colorado Silver Bullets, a new women's professional baseball team, played 185 games in its four-year history, playing exclusively against men's teams, minor league, semiprofessional and college teams.

In 1995, when owners and players might have had to face a season without any games, Reebok considered negotiating with the Major League Baseball Players Association to recruit the top 100 players to form some sort of league which would have to use ballfields other than Major League Baseball's, from which they would be locked out, and almost certainly from any minor league parks as well. Whether this would truly be barnstorming or not does not matter, because such an arrangement was never agreed to and the 1995 season was played.

The clearest indication of the final end of barnstorming came in the *New York Times* on June 20, 1983. There an article about the Indianapolis Clowns appeared, as they tried to play 90 games in 90 days over 30,000 miles playing against semipro, college and pick-up teams. Owner George Long was quoted as saying, "The USA ought to be able to support one traveling team." But apparently the country would not, recognizing that the team wasn't of particularly high quality. If the country would not support a team with very great stars, a team with no stars could not succeed.

Appendix A:
Major Leaguers Appearing in Exhibition Games

1901

Rube Waddell
Addie Joss
Doc Newton
Duke Farrell
Bill Dahlen
John Gochnaur
Willie Keeler
Joe Kelley
Patrick "Cozy" Dolan
Bill Donovan

1905

Jimmy Dygert
Sam Mertes
Eddie Grant
Sammy Strang
Harry McIntyre
Harry Davis
Joe McGinnity
Boileryard Clarke
Eddie Plank
Eddie Cicotte
Tom Doran

1906

Roger Bresnahan
Christy Mathewson
Tris Speaker
Harry Hooper
Eddie Cicotte

1907

Christy Mathewson
Joe Tinker
Johnny Evers
Johnny Kling
Nick Altrock
Lou Fiene

1909

Chief Bender
Jim Scott
Christy Mathewson
Joe McGinnity
Willie Keeler
Hughie Jennings
Hal Chase

1910

Charley Wagner
Tris Speaker
Duffy Lewis
Harry Hooper
Clyde Engel
Jake Stahl
Clyde Milan
George McBride
Kid Elberfeld
Walter Johnson
Doc Big Ed Walsh
Bris Lord
Ty Cobb
Doc White
Billy Sullivan
Gabby Street
Germany Schaefer
Eddie Collins
Home Run Baker
Eddie Plank
Chief Bender
Larry Doyle
Larry Gardner
Cy Seymour

Billy Gilbert
Rube Manning
Ray Fisher

1911

Clyde Milan
Ty Cobb
Doc Gessler
Hal Chase
Kid Elberfeld
Larry Gardner
George McBride
Gabby Street
Smoky Joe Wood
Bull Henry
George Mullin
Chief Bender
Eddie Plank
Jack Coombs
Walter Johnson
Ray Collins
Germany Schaefer
Bill Schardt
Elmer Steele
Elmer Knetzer
Otto Miller
Tex Erwin
Joe McGinnity

1912

Hal Chase
Walter Johnson
Larry Cheney
Casey Stengel
Larry Doyle
Arlie Latham
George Wiltsie
Tobe Thompson
Louis Drucke
Cy Seymour
Josh Devore
Nick Altrock
Germany Schaefer
Buck O'Brien
Hugh Bradley
Marty McHale
Chief Meyers
Fred Snodgrass

Art Shafer
Duffy Lewis
Harry Hooper
Howard Cravath
Ray Collins
Charley Hall
Frank Allen

1913

Harry Hooper
Clyde Engle
Steve Yerkes
Larry Gardner
Casey Stengel
Max Carey
Wild Bill Donovan
Earl Yingling
George Cutshaw
Bill Fisher
Otto Miller
Jake Daubert
Pat Ragan

1915

Babe Ruth
Donny "Ownie" Bush
Chief Bender

1916

Walter Johnson
Zach Wheat
Grover Cleveland
   Alexander
Hal Chase
Casey Stengel
Max Carey

1917

Walter Johnson
George Sisler
Mack Wheat
Zach Wheat
Grover Cleveland
   Alexander
Max Carey
Hal Chase
Casey Stengel

Rogers Hornsby
Chief Bender
Ralph Young
Amos Strunk
Wally Schang
George Burns
Roy Grover
Chief Meyers
Joe Bush
Bob Shawkey
Donny "Ownie" Bush
Hooks Dauss

1918

Rogers Hornsby
Babe Ruth
Wally Schang
Amos Strunk
Joe Bush
Wally Mayer
Rube Marquard
Al Demaree
Red Causey
Ralph Stroud

1919

Babe Adams
Dutch Zwilling
Joe Kelly
Caddy Cadore
Ernie Krueger
Babe Ruth
Al Schacht
Lew Malone
Allen Russell
Dick Rudolf
Johnny Enzmann
Frank Gilhooley
Rube Marquard
Steve O'Neill
Joe Judge
Joe Wood
Joe Dugan
George Bancroft
Chick Shorten
Sam Rice
Nick Altrock
Jesse Barnes

Lew McCarthy
Pancho Snyder
Benny Kauff
Frank Woodward
Larry Gardner
Bill Klem

1920

Rabbit Maranville
Al Schacht
Val Pichinich
Jack Quinn
Bob Meusel
Truck Hannah
Ross Youngs
Dave Bancroft
Joe Dugan
Cy Perkins
John McGraw
George Kelly
Herb Pennock
Joe Bush
Wally Schang
Babe Ruth
Carl Mays
Fred Hoffmann

1921

Elmer Smith
Tris Speaker
Les Nunaker
Patsy Gharrity
Walter Johnson
Rabbitt Maranville
Joe Dugan
Joe Judge
Sam Rice
Hank Gowdy
Joe Oeschger
Steve O'Neill
George Burns
Chick Shorten

1922

Mike Cvengros
Bill Barnes
Eddie Rommel

1923

Nick Altrock
Goose Goslin
Sam Rice
Bucky Harris
Tom Zachary
Joe Jackson
Eddie Cicotte
Swede Risberg
Buck Weaver

1924

Burleigh Grimes
Charley Hargreaves
Milt Stock
Bernie Neis
Ivy Olson
Walter Johnson
Babe Ruth
George Mogridge
Joe Judge
Nick Altrock
Al Schacht
Charlie Jamieson
Steve O'Neill
Howard Ehmke
Joe Bush
Lou Gehrig

1925

Wally Schang
Bob Shawkey
Bob Meusel
Rip Collins
Oscar Stanage
Jess Doyle
Bob Fothergill
Happy Felsch
Swede Risberg
Joe Jackson
Walter Johnson
Max Carey

1926

Grover Cleveland
    Alexander

1927

Walter Johnson
Sam Rice
Joe Judge
Dazzy Vance

1928

Ty Cobb
Jess Haines
Sunny Jim Bottomley

1929

Sunny Jim Bottomley
Mule Haas
Alvin Crowder
Rick Ferrell
Wes Ferrell
Sammy Byrd
Jimmie Foxx
Al Simmons

1930

George Earnshaw
Jimmie Foxx
Al Simmons
Lefty Grove
Cy Perkins
Jack Quinn
Jack Boley
Howard Ehmke
Charley Gelbert
Sparky Adams
Frankie Frisch
Johnny Neun
Andy High
Jim Bottomley
Lloyd Waner
Babe Herman
Fred Heimach
Dazzy Vance
Pie Traynor
Mel Ott
Chuck Klein

1931

Cot Tierney

Bill Terry
Paul Waner
Lloyd Waner
Babe Herman
Joe Judge
Babe Ruth
Lou Gehrig
John Stone
Ripper Collins
Benny Frey
Guy Bush
Bill Walker
Bob Weiland
Luke Appling
Jackie Warner
Dazzy Vance
Moose Earnshaw
Jimmie Foxx

1932

Camera Eye Bishop
Chick Fullis
Fred Frankhouse
Howard Ehmke
Dizzy Dean
Pepper Martin
Jimmy Wilson
Benny Tate
Burleigh Grimes
Rube Walberg
Al Schacht
Joe Judge
Bing Miller

1933

Jimmie Foxx
Rube Walberg
Bing Miller
Marty McManus
Joe Judge
Al Walters
Dick Porter
Ed Madjeski
Carl Hubbell
Hal Schumacher
Blondy Ryan
Hank Greenberg
Billy Jurges
Lew Krausse

Bill Dietrich
Mule Haas
Mickey Cochrane
Goose Goslin
Al Simmons
Paul Waner
Lloyd Waner
Red Ruffing
Jim Bottomley
Johnny Marcum
Ben Chapman
Dixie Walker
Bill Werber
Garland Braxton
Wesley Ferrell
Monte Weaver
Dizzy Dean
Pepper Martin
Rick Ferrell

1934

Schoolboy Rowe
Lon Warneke
Zeke Bonura
George Stumpf
Elden Auker
Garland Braxton
Wesley Ferrell
Rick Ferrell
Jimmy Bucher
Bill Werber
Ben Chapman
Dale Alexander
Pep Young
Max Bishop
Buck Newsom
Alvin Crowder
Ossie Bluege
Pat Crawford
Lew Riggs
Dave Harris
Gerald Walker
Fred Sington
Baxter Jordan
Ray Hayworth
Dizzy Dean
Paul Dean

1935

Dick Bartell

Bill Nicholson
Wally Roetger
Maxie Bishop
Bud Thomas
Jimmie Foxx
Billy Werber
Joe Medwick

1936

Dizzy Dean
Pepper Martin
Jack Rothrock
Buster Mills
Bob Feller

1937

Joe DiMaggio
Dom DiMaggio
Tony Lazzeri
Cookie Lavagetto
Alex Kampouris
Eddie Joost
Lefty Gomez
Lefty O'Doul
Arky Vaughan
Dolph Camilli
Vince DiMaggio
Babe Herman
Bob Feller
Molo Almada
Jess Hill
Earle Brucker
Bill Knickerbocker
Bill Brubaker
Joe Gonzales
Lee Stine

1938

Joe DiMaggio
Dom DiMaggio
Tony Lazzeri
Cookie Lavagetto
Alex Kampouris
Eddie Joost
Lefty Gomez
Lefty O'Doul
Babe Herman
Hank Greenberg

Leo Durocher
Tony Cuccinello
Goody Rosen
Bill Lohrman
Bob Feller
Vince DiMaggio
Ernie Lombardi
Joe Cronin
Dick Bartell
Joe Medwick
Myril Hoag

1940

Mel Ott
Howie Pollett
Jack Kramer
Paul Derringer
Preacher Roe
Dom DiMaggio
Joe Orengo
Bill Posedel
Ray Schalk
Ted Lyons
Nick Etten
Bob Kennedy

1941

Jimmie Foxx
Ted Williams
Lou Novikoff
Dom DiMaggio
Bob Feller

1942

Joe Hatten
Jim Tobin
Dick Bartell
Joe DiMaggio
Augie Galan
Cookie Lavagetto
Ernie Lombardi
Hank Borowy
Buddy Hassett
Whitey Kurowsi
Bill Lohrman
Tom Hennessey
Johnny Podgajny

1943

Larry French
Phil Rizzuto

1944

Al Jurisich
Jack Kramer
Red Ruffing

1945

Bob Feller
Jack Salveson
Dave Ferriss
Walt Dubiel
Aaron Robinson
Nap Reyes
Anton Karl
Hank Greenberg
Eddie Mayo
Doc Cramer
Danny Gardella

1946

Hank Greenberg
Luke Appling
Joe DiMaggio
Hal Newhouser
Snuffy Stirnweiss
Randy Gumpert
Carl Furillo
Wes Westrum
Mickey Witek
Buddy Kerr
Dick Lajeski
Mickey Grasso
Babe Young

1947

Dizzy Trout
Orval Grove
Mike Tresh
Preacher Roe
Johnny Sain
Clyde McCullough
Russ Meyer
Chuck Stobbs
Allen Gettel

Dom DiMaggio
Ralph Branca
Eddie Stanky
Tommy Holmes
Larry Doby
Al Gionfriddo

1948

Bob Feller
Bob Lemon
Gene Bearden
Satchel Paige

1949

Mel Parnell
Mike McCormick
Tom Glaviano
Lloyd Hittle
Frankie Crosetti
Lloyd Merriman
Cliff Mapes
Bob Lemon
Vern Stephens
Jade Graham
Eddie Bockman
Gerry Priddy
Gus Zernial
Duke Snider
Ralph Branca
Gene Hermanski
Cal Abrams
Phil Rizzuto

1950

Al Rosen
Gus Zernial
Vern Stephens
Al Zarilla
Sam Chapman
Jerry Coleman
Sherman Lollar
Mickey Grasso
Dizzy Trout
Bill Wright
Early Wynn
Mel Parnell
Lou Brissie
Ralph Kiner
Gil Hodges

Red Schoendienst
Willie Jones
Sid Gordon
Al Dark
Ted Kluszewski
Sam Jethroe
Duke Snider
Clyde McCullough
Wes Westrum
Howie Pollett
Larry Jansen
Bill Werle
Howie Fox
Cliff Chambers
Tommy Brynes
Clyde Kluttz
Al Evans
Milo Candini
Bruce Edwards

1951

Red Schoendienst
Pee Wee Reese
Gus Bell
Yogi Berra
Phil Rizzuto
Tommy Holmes
Tom Morgan
Art Shallock
Warren Spahn
Allie Reynolds
Gus Zernial
Enos Slaughter
Duke Snider

1952

Allie Reynolds
Warren Spahn

1954

George Kell
Lou Kretlow
Ransom Jackson
Jim Busby
Warren Spahn
Allie Reynolds
Mike Garcia
Harry Brecheen

Dale Mitchell
Randy Jackson
Joe Frazier
Dave Philley
Virgil Trucks
Rocky Bridges
Billy Consolo
Bob Lemon
Ted Kluszewski
Gus Grissom
Andy Carey
Joe DeMaestri
Bobby Adams
Jim Mangan
Jackie Jensen

1955

Ed Wright
Paul Minner
George Shuba
Chuck Tanner
Mike Kume
Jack Philips
Steve Gromek
Jim Delsing
Milt Bolling
Willard Nixon
Gene Woodling
Bobby Young

1956

Roy Smalley
Gene Mauch
Marv Grissom
Billy Martin
Frank Robinson
Duane Pillette
Larry Jackson
Jim Davis
Troy Heriage

1957

Morrie Martin
Bob Miller
Bob Weisler

1958

Dick Groat

Johnny Briggs
Stu Miller
John McCall
Jim Gentile
Hank Sauer
Jim Davenport
Dick Stuart
Mike McCormick
Ron Fairly
Bob Lemon
Del Rice
Don Lenhardt
Harry Hanebrink
Chuck Diering

1960

Ernie Banks
Roger Maris
Larry Jackson
Solly Hemus
Don Cardwell
Bill Henry
Ryne Duren
Billy Muffett
Jim Umbricht
Bill White
Marv Throneberry
Pete Runnels
Dick Gernert
Roy Sievers
Gene Freese
Dick Williams
Russ Nixon
Ken Boyer
Walt Moyrn
Charley James
Carl Sawatski
Don Zimmer
Richie Ashburn
Alvin Dark
Norm Cash
Russ Snyder

1962

Curt Flood
Johnny Keane
Dal Maxvill
Ruben Amaro
Tom Sturdivant

Appendix B:
Exhibition Games,
1901–1962

Information is incomplete for some games, for one or more of the following reasons:

1. There was an itinerary printed, but no dates were given.

2. There was only a very brief mention for that year ("The Cubs came back from Michigan...").

3. Tours often added and subtracted games in mid-journey.

4. There were "open" dates but games were probably played.

5. At times, only two games are listed, but other games were hinted at.

6. The names of players were often omitted, misspelled, or lacking first names or team affiliations. The difficulty of identifying players by name is compounded by the fact that many players were out of their usual positions.

Year	Date	City / State	Year	Date	City / State
1901	1 Oct.	Johnstown PA	**1907**	13 Oct.	Reading PA
	20 Oct.	Racine WI		17 Oct.	Chicago IL
1905	1 Oct.	Newark NJ	**1909**		New Orleans LA
	8 Oct.	Brooklyn NY		6 Oct.	New York NY
	15 Oct.	Paterson NJ		13 Nov.	El Paso TX
	16 Oct.	Trenton NJ	**1910**	4 Oct.	Bronx NY
1906	5 Oct.	Portland ME		10 Oct.	New York NY

Year	Date	City / State
	11 Oct.	Philadelphia PA
	Allstars vs. Athletics 3 game series	
	16 Oct.	New York NY
1911	8 Oct.	Newark NJ
	9 Oct.	Washington DC
	Allstars vs. Athletics 4 game series	
	13 Oct.	Morristown NJ
	15 Oct.	New York NY
1912	10 Oct.	Newark NJ
	20 Oct.	New York NY
	27 Oct.	Coffeyville KS
	27 Oct.	New York NY
	7 Nov.	Humboldt KS
	9 Nov.	CA
	Coast all-stars	
1913	5 Oct.	New York NY
	19 Oct.	New York NY
1915	24 Sep.	New York NY
	24 Oct.	Baltimore MD
	29 Oct.	Indianapolis IN
1916	29 Nov.	Kansas City MO
1917	19 Oct.	Indianapolis IN
	20 Oct.	Chester PA
	21 Oct.	Kansas City MO
1918	29 Sep.	Lebanon PA
	12 Oct.	Lebanon PA
	20 Oct.	Lebanon PA
1919		Mount Moriah MO
	5 Oct.	Brooklyn NY
	9 Oct.	Rutland VT
	12 Oct.	Brooklyn NY
	13 Oct.	New Haven CT
1920	4 Oct.	New Haven CT
	4 Oct.	Thompsonville CT
	7 Oct.	Lancaster PA
	12 Oct.	Worcester MA
	12 Oct.	Plainfield NJ
	?	Camden NJ
	?	Jersey City NJ
	?	Oneonta NY
	?	Perth Amboy NJ
	?	Trenton NJ
1921	19 Oct.	Scranton PA
		Attleboro MA

Year	Date	City / State
		Chester PA
		Jackson MI
		Sandusky OH
1922		Baltimore MD
		Johnstown PA
		Pana IL
1923	8 Oct.	Baltimore MD
	12 Oct.	New Haven CT
		Bastrop LA
1924	1 Oct.	Kingston NY
	11 Oct.	Rochester NY
	26 Oct.	Los Angeles CA
	27 Oct.	Los Angeles CA
	29 Oct.	Oakland CA
	?	Hazleton PA
1925	9 Oct.?	Bloomsburg PA
	27 Oct.	Americus GA
	?	Brockville PA
	?	Daytona FL
	?	Scobey MT
1926		Council Bluffs NE
		Omaha NE
		St. Paul NE
1927		Denver CO
		Warrenton VA
1928		Edwardsville IL
		Farmersville OH
		Seattle WA
1929	13 Oct.	Edwardsville IL
	21 Oct.	Montclair NJ
	27 Oct.	Los Angeles CA
		Augusta GA
1930	17 Oct.	Scranton PA
	17 Oct.	Toledo OH
		Ada OK
		Cressona PA
		Edwardsville IL
		Los Angeles CA
		Queens NY
1931	4 Oct.	Kansas City MO
	series against the Monarchs	
	6 Oct.	Tullahoma TN
	18 Oct.	Nan-Y-Glo PA
	18 Oct.	West Frankfort IL

Year	Date	City / State
		Jackson MS
		Los Angeles CA
		New York NY
		Wilkes-Barre PA
1932	28 Sep.	New York NY
	vs. Bushwicks	
	6 Oct.	Carbondale IL
	8 Oct.	Middleburg PA
		New Haven MO
1933	4 Oct.	New York NY
	vs. Bushwicks	
	14 Oct.	Durham NC
	15 Oct.	Jeffersonville IN
	15 Oct.	Milwaukee I
	15 Oct.	New York NY
	vs. Bushwicks	
	15 Oct.	Nokomis IL
		Baltimore MD
		Los Angeles CA
		Meeker OK
		Milford MD
		Queens NY
		NC
1934	5 Oct.	Kalamazoo MI
	15 Oct.	Greensboro NC
	27 Oct.	Manhattan KS
		El Dorado AR
		New Orleans LA
1935		Cambridge MD
		Oakland CA
1936	5 Oct.	Los Angeles CA
		Van Meter IA
1937	24 Oct.	San Francisco CA
		Los Angeles CA
1938	6 Oct.	Sacramento CA
	9 Oct.	New York NY
	29 Oct.	Chico CA
	29 Oct.	San Francisco CA
		New York NY
	vs. Bushwicks	
		San Diego CA
1940	10 Oct.	AR
	20 Oct.	San Francico CA
		Georgetown KY
		Joliet IL
		New Orleans LA

Year	Date	City / State
1941	4 Oct.	Los Angeles CA
	5 Oct.	St. Louis MO
		Van Meter IA
1942	11 Oct.	New York NY
	vs. Bushwicks	
	18 Oct.	New York NY
	vs. Bushwicks	
	25 Oct.	Alameda CA
1943	3 Oct.	New York NY
	vs. Bushwicks	
1944		Los Angeles CA
		New Orleans LA
1945	7 Oct.	New York NY
	vs. Bushwicks	
	8 Oct.	Wenatchee WA
	14 Oct.	New York NY
	vs. Bushwicks	
		Hartford CT
1946		Boston MA
	World Series tune up	
		Kingston NY
1947	12 Oct.	New York NY
	vs. Bushwicks	
	13 Oct.	South Range MI
	17 Oct.	Piggott AR
	to tour VA and NC	
		Dysart PA
1948		CA
1949	13 Oct.	New Orleans LA
	16 Oct.	New Orleans LA
	16 Oct.	New York NY
	vs. Bushwicks	
	23 Oct.	Queens NY
	23 Oct.	Stockton CA
	29 Oct.	Long Beach CA
1950	13 Oct.	Chicago IL
	21 Oct.	Salisbury NC
	22 Oct.	Stockton CA
1951	14 Oct.	Athens IL
	14 Oct.	Hartford CT
	21 Oct.	Oklahoma City OK
	28 Oct.	Hollywood CA
	28 Oct.	Oakland CA
	1 Nov.	Hollywood CA
		Lousiville KY

Year	Date	City / State
1952	19 Oct.	Oklahoma City OK
1954	17 Oct.	Hollywood CA
	24 Oct.	Oakland CA
		Oklahoma City OK
		Silver Springs MD
		Tulsa OK
1955	9 Oct.	Youngstown OH
1956	14 Oct.	Modesto CA
1957		Washington MO

Year	Date	City / State
1958	12 Oct.	Long Beach CA
	19 Oct.	Modesto CA
	19 Oct.	St. Louis MO
	20 Oct.	Sacramento CA
		Youngstown OH
1960	14 Oct.	Jersey City NJ
	23 Oct.	Houston TX
1962		Houston TX

Appendix C:
Major Leaguers Appearing
in Barnstorming Games

1901

ALL-AMERICANS

Sugden
Katoll
Bresnehan
Bernhardt
Hahn
Bergen
Lerver
Smith
Young
Phillips
Zimmer
Joss
Sullivan

BROOKLYN

Jimmy Sheckard

REDS

Lou Wolfson
Dick Harley
Jack Dobbs
Henry Peitz
Jack Sutthoff

Tom Corcoran
George Magoon
Billy Fox
Billy Bergen

ALL-NATIONALS

Barrett
Donlin
Seymour
Lajoie
Beckley
Mercer
Bradley
Sullivan
Bernhard
Carrick
Davis

1902

ALL-NATIONALS

Charlie Irwin
Bill Dahlen
Claude Ritchey
Jake Beckley

Willie Keeler
Duff Cooley
Sam Crawford
Kahoe
Jack Chesbro
Jesse Tannehill
Will Bill Donovan

ALL-AMERICANS

Bradley
Monte Cross
Nap Lajoie
Harry Davis
Hartsel
Fielder Jones
Dick Harley
William Sullivan
Bill Mercer
Addie Joss
Cy Young

1903

NY GIANTS

G. Browne

D. McGann
Davis
Van Haltren
C. Babb
Dunn
B. Gilbert
C. J. Warner
P. Cronin
J. Warner
Van Haltren
D. Taylor
J. McGraw
Christy Mathewson

1904

REDS

Admiral Schlei
Heinie Peitz
Harry Dolan
Miller Huggins
Harry Steinfeldt
Orville Woodruff
Fred Odwell
Cy Seymour
Frank Hahn
Bob Ewing

NY GIANTS

G. Browne
D. McGann
Davis
Van Haltren
C. Babb
Dunn
B. Gilbert
C. J. Warner
P. Cronin
J. Warner
Christy Mathewson
John McGraw

BROOKLYN

N. Hanlon
Jacklitch
D. Jordan
C. Babb
Dude McCormick
J. Sheckard
Batch

Ritter
B. Bergen
P. J. Cronin

1905

PIRATES

D. Howard
P. S. Leever
P. C. Case
M. Lynch
O. Clymer
Bob Ganley
T. Leach
H. Wagner
Steamer Flanagan
Ritchey
Patsy Flaherty
George Gibson
Deacon Phillippe
M. F. Clarke

REDS

Bob Ewing
Tom Walker
Charley Street
Admiral Schlei
Miller Huggins
Harry Steinfeldt
Tom Corcoran
Fred Odwell
Al Bridwell
Cy Seymour

NY GIANTS

P. J. McGinnity
G. Browne
D. McGann
Mertes
Strang
Dahlen
Devlin
B. Gilbert
C. J. Warner
P. Cronin
Clark
Bresnahan
P. Wiltsie
Mathewson
John McGraw

1906

YANKEES

Ira Thomas

PHILLIES

M. H. Duffy
K. Bransfield
Kid Gleason
M. Doolan
E. Courtney
Sherry Magee
Duffy
J. Titus
R. Dooin
Neuer

ATHLETICS

Connie Mack
Chief Bender
D. Murphy
Oldring
T. Hartsel
Eddie Plank
S. Seybold
C. Powers
Jack Coombs
P. R. Waddell

PIRATES

F. Clarke
J. Nealon
C. Ritchey
Tommy Leach
T. Sheehan
L. Leifield
Ginger Beaumont
B. Ganley
G. Gibson
S. Leever
Lefty Leifield
Claude Ritchey
Bob Ganley

1907

PIRATES

Anderson
Leach

Sheehan
Phelps
Gibson
Smith
McKechnie
Leifield
Sam Leever
Wagner
Phillippe
Maddox
Goat Anderson
Barney Dreyfuss

White Sox

Ed Hahn
George Rohe
Donahue
Billy Sullivan
Lee Tanehill
Hub Hart
Charlie Armbruster
Nick Altrock
Frank Owen

Tigers

Donohue
Schaefer O'Leary
Coughlin
Flick
Crawford
Cobb
Donovan
Mullin
Tannehill
Criger
Sullivan

1908

Reds

Hoblitzel
Huggins
Lobert
Hulswitt
Kane
Dubec
Spade
Campbell
Schlei
McLean

1909

Cubs

Tinker
Brown

Athletics

C. Mack
H. Davis
E. Collins
J. Barry
T. Hartsel
Heine Heitmueller
Coombs
R. Oldring
D. Murphy
Simon Nicholls
R. Oldring
I. Thomas
Lapp
E. Plank
C. Bender
Cy Morgan

Athletics, All NL

Frank Bancroft
Johnson
Marquard
Curtis
Moore
Meyers
Bliss
Konetchy
Larry Doyle
Ed Lennox
Dick Egan
Belcher
Hummel
Ellis
Snodgrass

All-Americans

Lajoie

1910

All-Stars

Speaker
Cobb

Ed Walsh
Walter Johnson

Pirates

B. Byrne
McKechnie
T. Leach
Hyatt
C. Wilson
McCarthy
G. Gibson
Powell
Phillippe
Maddox

1911

Reds

Smith
McLean
Clark
Frome
Benton
Keefe
Hobby
Egan
Esmond
Mitchell
Bates
Bescher

1912

Pirates

Marty O'Toole
Jack Ferry
Max Carey
Hugh Bedient

1913

All-Stars to Orient

The players enrolled
by Manager McGraw:

Meyers
Wingo
Mathewson
Tesreau

Fromme
Wiltse
Heart
Merkle
Doyle
Doolan
Lobert
Magee
Snodgrass
Thorpe
Donlin

ALL OF THESE PLAYERS
WENT AROUND THE
WORLD, BUT MOST OF
THEM DID NOT GO ACROSS
THE CONTINENT.

James J. Callahan
Benz
Scott
Weaver
Daley
Schalk
Slight
Crawford
Schaefer
Bliss
Leverenz
Eagan
Evans
Chase
Russel
White
Berger
Rath

BROOKLYN SUPERBAS

Jake Daubert
Herbie Moran
Casey Stengel
George Cutshaw
Bob Fisher
Red Smith
Bill Fisher
Pat Ragan
Earl Yingling
Cliff Curtis
Otto Miller

1914

ALL-AMERICANS

Doc Hoblitzel
Lute Boone
George Moriarty
Ben Chapman
Duffy Lewis
James Walsh
Eddie Murphy
Ira Thomas
George McAvoy
Joe Bush
John Henry
Leonard Cole
Bill James

ALL-NATIONALS

Fred Snodgrass
Tom Clark
Doc Hoblitzel
John Milier
Bobby Byrne
Arthur Fletcher
Max Carey
Cozy Dolan
George Burns
William Killifer
Tommy Clark
Jeff Tesreau
Grover Alexander
Jim Vaughan

1915

CUBS

B. Fisher
A. Phelan
F. Schulte
Jimmy Archer
G. Pearce

AMERICAN LEAGUE

Klepfer
Ayers
James
Harper
Henry

Cady
Hoblitzell
Mullen
W. Schang
Shanks
Walker
Roth
Strunk
Pipp

NATIONAL LEAGUE

Coombs
Alexander
Pfeffer
Vaughan
Miller
McCarty
Daubert
Evers
Groh
Fisher
Carey Killifer
Magree
Walter Johnson
George Foster

1916

PIRATES

PLAYERS NAMED
WITHOUT A BOXSCORE:

W. Wagner
Jacobs
Schmidt
Evans
Mamaux
Cooper
Baird
Hinchman
McCarthy
Miller

1919

CUBS

Bill McCabe
C. Hollocher
B. Killefer

D. Paskert
Fred Lear
Bob O'Farrell
Turner Barber
Dode Paskert

1920

RED SOX

Pennock
Bush
Schong

ST. L CARDS/GIANTS

Lyons

CARDINALS

Schultz
Milt Stock
Doc Lavan
Jack Fournier
Cliff Heathcote
Austin McHenry
Hal Janvrin
Verne Clemons
Pickles Dilhoefer
Schultz
Ferdie Schupp
Elmer Jacobs
Lou North
Bill Sherdel
George Lyons

PIRATES

Charlie Grimm
George Cutshaw
Barbare
Nicholson
Billy Southworth
Carson Bigbee
Max Carey
Walter Schmidt
Carlson
Cooper

GIANTS

Lyons
Hewitt
Charleston

Blackwell
Dudley
Kennard
Day
Holt
Wallace
Mackey
Drake
Finer

PHILLIES

Gene Paulette
Johnny Rawlings
Emil Meusel
Stengel
Walt Tregressor
Lee Meadows
Tony Boeckel
Posum Whitted
Bob Meusel

NY GIANTS

John McGraw
Lefevre
Dave Bancroft
Larry Doyle
George Kelly
Smith
Gonzales
C. F. Snyder
Ryan
J. Barnes

AL ALL-STARS

Pep Young
Dykes
Galloway
Dugan
Griffin
Bigbee
Roy Moore
Myatt
Harris
Dave Keefe
Rollie Naylor

HILLDALES

Chacon
Francis

Briggs
Santop
Johnson
White
Allen
Cockrell
Brown

ATHLETICS

Jumping Joe Dugan
Rollie Naylor
Chick Galloway
Jimmie Dykes
Ivy Griffin
Dave Keefe
Lyle Bignbee
Glenn Myatt
Slim Harriss
Pep Young

PHILLIES

Gene Paulette
Johnny Rawlings
Emil Meusel
Stengel
Walt Tregressor
Lee Meadows
Tony Boeckel
Posum Whitted
Bob Meusel
O' Doul
Hoffman
Ruth
Schang
Mays
Sheers
Hesse
Starke
R. Brown

1921

ST. L CARDS/GIANTS

Jack Smith
Jack Fournier
Milt Stock
Joe Schultz
Austin McHenry
Doc Lavan

Pickles Dilhoefer
Verne Clemons
Lou North
Roy Walker
Jess Haines
Pertica
Day
Wallace
Mackey
Finner
Blackwell
Hewitt
Chaleston
Kennard
Dudley
McAdoo
Scales
Holt
Brooks
Drake
Bennett

1922

REDS

Pete Donahue
Eddy Roush
Rube Bressler
Eppa Rixey
Jake Daubert
Ivy Wingo

PIRATES

Rabbit Maranville
Max Carey
Carson Bibbee
Cotton Tierney
Pie Traynor
Charlie Grimm
Johnny Gooch
Johnny Morrison
Hal Carson

ALL STARS

George Sisler
Muddy Ruel
Pat Collins
Bill Piercy
Chick Shorten
Chick Galloway

1924

BROOKLYN

Johnny Mitchell
Elmer Brown
Burleigh Grimes
Charley Hargraves
Milt Stock
Bernie Neis
Ivy Olson
Jack Fournier
Dazzy Vance

ED HOLLEY'S

Walter Johnson
Geoge Mogridge
Joe Judge
Nick Altrock
Al Schacht
Charlie Jamieson
Steve O'Neill
Howard Ehmke
Lou Gehrig
Joe Bush

1926

MACK

Perkins
Quinn
Grove
Dykes
Padgett
Manush
Gosling
Burns
Miller
McCann
Heimach

1928

MAISEL & FOXX

Crush Holloway
Jesse Hubbard
Robert Clarke
Laymon Yokeley
Luther Farrell
Dick Lundy

Oscar Charleston
Walter Cannady
Frank Warfield
Josh Beckwith
Fritz Maisel
Dick Porter
Johnny Neun
Max Bishop
Lefty Grove
Eddie Rommel
Jack Ogden
Jimmie Foxx

1929

GEHRINGER

Cool Papa
Willie Wells
Bill Foster
Frog Hosley
Jelly Gardner
Jim Brown
Mule Suttles
Buck Miller
Jimbo Jackson
Charlie Gehringer
Al Simmons
Heinie Manush
Bing Miller
Bill Sweeney
Harry Heilman
Steve O'Neill
Art Shires
Red Kress
Wally Schang
Willis Hudlin
Jake Miller
George Uhle
Earl Whitehill

1930

EARLE MACK

Art Shires
Bill Sweeney
Lefty O'Doul
Charlie Gehringer
Bing Miller
Nick Altrock

Red Kress
Harry Heilmann
Steve O'Neill
Rube Walberg
Grove
Wally Schang
Ted Lyons

1931

[NAME UNKNOWN]

Lou Gehrig
Rabbit Maranville
Lefty O'Doul
Franke Frisch
Mickey Cochrane
Al Simmons
Lefty Grove
George Kelly
Larry French
Muddy Ruel
Tom Oliver
Ray[?] Cunningham

NYG/VERGEZ

Johnny Vegez
Ethan Allen
Chick Fullis
Bill Hennefield
Al Spohrer
Denny Sothern
Freddy Heimach
Owen Carroll

TIERNEY'S ALL-STARS

Bill Terry
Bill Akers
Paul
Waners
Babe Herman
Hub Walker
Joe Kuhel
Ollie Marquardt
Bill Akers
Bill Walker
Heine Meine

EARLE MACK

Bing Miller
Lew Fonseca

Sweeney
Red Kress
Van Camp
Thomas
Bill Dickey
Benny Bengough
Al Schacht
Nick Altrock
Rube Walberg
Lefty Gomez
Alphone Thomas
What-a-man Shires

1932

EARLE MACK

Charlie Gehringer
Eric McNair
Rube Walberg
Joe Judge
Heine Manush
Earl Whitehill
Luke Sewell
Bing Miller
Clint Brown
Babe Herman
Lefty Grove
Walter Johnson
Red Kress
Nick Altrock
Al Schacht

NL/CRAWFORDS

Chick Fullis
Woodie English
Hack Wilson
Doc Taylor
Tom Paden
Al Todd
Larry French
Johnny Frederick
Rabbit Warstler
Bill Swift
Fred Frankhouse
Roy Parmelee
Satchel Paige
Judy Johnson
Oscar Charleston
Josh Gibson

1934

EARLE MACK

Jimmie Foxx
Heine Manush
Ted Lyons
Mike Higgins
Dick Porter
Soup Campbell
Luke Sewell
Marty Hopkins
Earl Whitehill
Ted Lyons
Tommy Thomas
Rube Walberg
Al Schacht
Doc Cramer

1935

DIZZY DEAN

Paul Dean
Dizzy Dean
Larry French
Mike Ryba
Joe Hauser
Hack Wilson
Webster McDonald
Cool Papa Bell
Ted Page
Boojum Wilson
Jerry Benjamin
Josh Gibson
Buck Leonard
Satchel Paige

1936

EARLE MACK

Alphonse Thomas
Monte Weaver
Dave Keefe
Charley Berry
Billy Sullivan
Chibby Dean
Boze Berger
Red Kress
Bob Feller
Beau Bell

Heine Manush
Wally Moses
Bruce Campbell

HORNSBY & BELL

Lynn King
Harland Clift
Rogers Hornsby
Johnny Mize
Gus Suhr
Ival Goodman
Heine Mueller
Todd
Jim Weaver
Cool Papa Bell
Sammy Hughes
Oscar Charleston
Bill Perkins
Bill Wright
Chester Williams
Felton Snow
Jimmie Crutchfield
Leroy Matlock
Bob Griffith
Satchel Paige
Pullman Porter
Jim West
Biz Mackey
Sammy Bankhead

ROGELL

Billy Rogell
Roxie Lawson
Pete Fox
Roy Hughes
Bruce Campbell
Dennis Galehouse
Tom Carey
Beau Bell

FELLER

Don Gutteridge
Ival Goodman
Johnny Mize
Gus Suhr
Vince DiMaggio
Alex Kampouris

Heine Mueller
Rollie Hemsley
Mike Ryba
Lon Warneke
Bob Feller
Lou Fette
Jim Weaver

1940

EARLE MACK

Tom Carey

1944

DOAN

Eddie Miller
Steve Mesner
Tommy Holmes
Phil Masi
Butch Nieman
Jim Tobin
Fritz Ostermueller
Pete Coscarart
Bob Elliot
Charley Schanz
Milo Candini
Russ Christopher
Don Black
Roy Partee
George Metkovich
Hershel Martin

1945

DRESSEN

Hal Gregg
Ralph Branca
Eddie Stanky
Goodie Rosen
Frenchy Bordagaray
Clyde Kluttz
Buddy Kerr
Whitey Kurowski
Jim Russell
Johnny Barrett
Virgil Trucks

WALKER

Spud Davis
Truett Sewall
Tommy O'Brien
Lamar Newsome
Leon Culbertson
Johnny Rucker
Ace Adams
Marty Marion
Emil Verban

[NAME UNKNOWN]*

Jeff Heath
Allie Reynolds
Steve Gromek
Frank Hayes
Bobo Newsom
Buddy Rosar
Sam Chapman
Bert Shepard
Jim Bucher

GRAY

Pete Gray
Jerry Priddy
Johnny Lindell
Red Adams
Newt Kimball
Lou Novikoff
Ernie Bonham
Red Adams
Newt Kimball
Tom Seats

DOAN

Babe Dahlgren
George Hausman
Eddie Miller
Pete Coscarart
George Kell
Ray Schalk
Phil Masi
Danny Gardella
Butch Nieman
Jahhny Lazon
Nick Etten
Bob Muncrief

*This team was in a train wreck reported in the newspapers; no team name was given.

Vernon
Kennedy
Herschel Martin
Tex Shirley
Fritz Ostermueller
Earl Caldwell
Clem Hausman
Russ Christopher
Frank Mancuso
Milt Brynes

1946

ROBINSON

Jackie Robinson
Roy Campanella
Buck Leonard
Ted Strong
Larry Doby
Al Campanis
Frankie Gustine
Al Gionfriddo
Hank Camelli
Joe Beggs
Eddie Lukon
Bob Malloy
Eddie Miller
Stan Ferrens
Pete Suder
Hank Sauer

EARLE MACK

Denny Galehouse
Ralph Kress
Doc Cramer

RICHARDS

Hank Helf
Frank Mancuso
Tex Shirley
Al Benton
Buster Mills
Allen Benton

FELLER & PAIGE

Bob Feller
Bob Lemon
Jim Hegan
Stan Musial
Mickey Vernon

Dutch Leonard
Ralph Kiner
Sam Chapman
Bob Savage
Charlie Keller
Spud Chandler
Phil Rizzuto
Eddie Lopat
Satchel Paige
Barney Brown
Art Wilson
Henry Thompson
Sam Jethroe
Gentry Jessup
Max Manning
Howard Easterling
Buck O'Neil
Johnny Davis
Quincy Trouppe
Stolez[?]

NATIONAL LEAGUE

Ken Gables
Ray Baker
Max West
Bobby Adams
Dain Clay
Clyde McCullough
Ray Prim
Vic Lombardi
Charley Schanz
Mike Budnick
Vandeer Meer

AMERICAN LEAGUE

Bob Muncrief
George Caster
Floyd Bevens
Eddie Lake
John Lindell
Vern Stephens
Jim Bloodworth
Thurman Tucker
Walter Judnich
Tuck Stainback
Ken Silvestri
Al Evena
Bob Muncrief
George Caster
Gordon Maltzberger

Clarence Marshall
Dario Lodoigiani

1947

FELLER

Ed Lopat
Phil Marchildon
Bill McCahan
Ferris Fain
Gerry Priddy
Eddie Miller
Ken Keltner
Jim Hegan
Matt Batts
Andy Pafko
Ralph Kiner
Jeff Heath
Paul Lehner
Jackie Price
Max Patkin
Max Wiseman
Bob Gill
Jackie Robinson
Allie Reynolds

GLENNON

Marty Marion
Whitey Kurowski
Murry Dickson
Harry Walker
Emil Verban
Skeeter Newsome
Bert Haas
Walker Cooper
Willard Marshall
Bama Rowell
Virgil Trucks
Jim Bagby

LEWIS

Ray Scarborough
Al Evans
Rudy York
Bob Gillespie
Taft Wright
Ralph Hodgin
Dick Culler
Mickey Livingston

Kirby Higbe
Tommy Byrne
Jimmy Brown

BLACKWELL

Ewell Blackwell
Al Zarilla
Bob Dillinger
Jess Flores
Johnny Lindell
Peanuts Lowery
Johnny Berardino
Roy Partee
George Metkovich
Bobby Sturgeon

1948

BARNEY

Rex Barney
Johnny Hopp
Richie Ashburn

ROBINSON

Jackie Robinson
Roy Campanella

SISLER

Dick Sisler
Russ Meyer
Andy Seminick
Erv Dusak
Ted Wilks
Bob Thomson
Buddy Blattner
Willard Marshall
Frank Baumholtz
Johnn Wyrostek
Ralph Branca

TEBBETTS

Joe Coleman
Bob Savage
Carl Scheib
Frank Shea
George Stirnweiss
Gus Niharos
Tebbetts

Vern Stephens
Vic Wertz
Ray Scarborough
Eddie Pellagrini
Tony Lupien
Piersall
Dropo
Johnny Barrettter
Earl Torgeson

LEMON & BEARDEN

Bob Lemon
Gene Bearden
Cliff Mapes
Al Zarilla
Johnny Berardino
Roy Partee
George Vico
Eddie Bockman
Nippy Jones
Don Lang

LITWHILER

Ron Northey
Vern Bickford
Curt Simmons
Bill McCahan
Danny Murtaugh
Carl Furillo
Billy Cox
Rocky Rhawn
Ray Mueller

[NAME UNKNOWN]

Bill Kennedy
Tommy Bryne
Billy Johnson
Billy Goodman
Stan Spence
Jake Early
Gil Coan
Al Evans
Ralph Hodgin
Floyd Baker
Jimmy Brown

[NAME UNKNOWN]

Al Schoendienst
Elmer Schoendienst

Joe Schoendienst
Julius Schoendienst
Yogi Berra
Pete Reiser
Joe Garagiola
Chuck Diering

1949

LITWHILER

Ken Heintzelman
Ron Northey
Hank Borowy
Del Ennis
Carl Furillo
Ray Mueller
Vern Bickford
Bobby Shantz
Charley Kress
Ken Raffensberger
Danny Murtaugh
Carl Scheib

LEWIS

Al Evans
Mickey Livingston
Billy Goodman
Jimmy Brown
Floyd Baker
Willie Jones
Stan Spence
Whitey Lockman
Buddy Lewis

ROBINSON

Jackie Robinson
Roy Campanella
Don Newcombe
Larry Doby
Buck Leonard

SISLER

Dick Sisler
Ken Heintzelman
Russ Meyer
John Wyrostek
Joe Garagiola
Chuck Diering
Lou Klein

Yogi Berra
Bob Hofman
Ellis Kinder
Boris Martin

TEBBETTS

Birdie Tebbetts
Johnny Pesky
Dom DiMaggio
Gus Niarhos
Frank Shea
George Stirnweiss
Art Houtteman
Vic Wertz
Eddie Pellagrini
Dick Kokos
Ray Scarborough
Sherry Robertson
Joe Coleman
Earl Torgeson
Mickey Vernon
Bob Savage

TROUT

Dizzy Trout
Virgil Trucks
Bob Kuzava
Cass Michaels
Mike Tresh
Pete Suder
Elmer Valo
Roy Sievers

BARNEY

Rex Barney
Richie Ashbum
Johnny Hopp

EASTER

Luke Easter
Dan Bankhead

CAVARETTA

Sheldon Jones
Murry Dickson
Pete Castiglione
Andy Anderson
Paul Lehner
George Metkovich
Joe Tipton

Phil Cavarretta
Frank Papish

LEMON

Bob Lemon
Johnny Berardino
Vic Lombardi
Del Crandall
Vern Stephens
Eddie Bockman
Hank Sauer
Ed Sauer
Cliff Mapes
George (Sam[?]) Vico

FELLER

Jack Graham
Red Embree
Gus Zernial
George Metkovich
Gene Mauch
Herman Reich
Ray Boone
Orestes Minoso
Lou Stringer
Bob Feller

1950

HARRIS

Johnny Mize
Sherry Robertson
Luke Appling
Alvin Dark
Allie Clark
Hoot Evers
Sam Mele
Gene Woodling
Joe Dobson
Ellis Kinder
Sam Zoldak
Warren Spahn
Mickey Harris
Bob Swift
Gus Niarhos
George Myatt
Del Crandall (caught a
    few games)
Harris

REYNOLDS

Bobby Morgan
Dale Mitchell
Cot Deal
Ray Murray
Allie Reynolds
Al Benton
Lou Kretlow
Cal McLish

JACHYM & RIGGS

Ted Lyons
Lou Brissie
Sam Chapman
Gerry Coleman
Walt Dropo
Mike Garcia
Ned Garver
Mickey Grasso
Don Kolloway
Sherman Lollar
Duane Pillette
Al Rosen
Dizzy Trout
Bill Wight
Early Wynn
Al Zarilla
Gus Zernial
Lou Brissie
Sherm Lollar
Dom DiMaggio
Buster Mills
John Riddle
Cliff Chambers
Alvin Dark
Howie Fox
Sid Gordon
Gil Hodges
Larry Jansen
Sam Jethroe
Willie Jones
Ralph Kiner
Ted Kluszewski
Clyde McCullough
Howie Pollet
Al Schoendienst
Duke Snider
Bill Werle
Wes Westrum
Jackie Price

TEBBETTS

Walt Dropo
Snuffy Stirnweiss
Phil Rizzuto
Johnny Pesky
Johnny Groth
Vic Wertz
Bob Kennedy
Ray Scarborough
Fred Hutchinson
Art Houtteman
Maury McDermott
Ed Ford
Ed Lopat
Joe Coleman
Tebbetts
Jim Hegan
Tom Ferrick

LITWHILER

Danny Litwhiler
Danny Murtaugh
Danny O'Connell
Granny Hamner
Del Ennis
Carl Furillo
Ron Northey
Sibbi Sisti
Vern Bickford
Russ Meyer
Ken Raffensberger
Monte Kennedy
Harry Perkowski
Ray Mueller
Bob Rhawn

DIGBY

Mel Parnell
Matt Batts
Howie Pollet
Ted Wilks
Red Munger
Bubba Church
Earl Torgeson
Connie Ryan
Grady Hatton
Joe Adcock
Lou Klein
Tom Wright
Jim Russell

ROBINSON

Jackie Robinson
Roy Campanella
Don Newcombe
Larry Doby

LEMON

Jess Flores
Ray Boone
Eddie Bockman
Bill Wilson
Clif Mapes
Jack Graham
Irv Noren
Chuck Stevens
Dick Cole
Del Crandall
Rocky Bridges

WALKER

Harry Brecheen
Eddie Miller
Carl Erskine
Al Walker
Hank Sauer
Roy Smalley
Pete Castiglione
Ken Heintzelman
Kirby Higbe
John Wyrostek

1951

LITWHILER

Sibbi Sisti
Nelson Fox
Eddie Miksis
Litwhiler
Carl Furillo
Bill Nicholson
Bill Howerton
Ken Raffensberger
Frank Smith
Carl Scheib
Ray Mueller
Monte Kennedy

HODGES

Gil Hodges
Randy Gumpert

Eddie Robinson
Chuck Stobbs
Billy Goodman
Allie Clark
Whitey Ford
Ralph Houk
Gene Woodling
Sid Gordon
Frank Hiller
Gene Hermanski
Cal Abrams
Bob Porterfield
Tommy Byrne

CAMPANELLA

Roy Campanella
Don Newcombe
Monte Irvin
Willie Mays
Luke Easter
Suitcase Simpson

TEBBETTS

Sal Maglie
Bobby Thomson
Gil McDougald
Joe Coleman
Mike Garcia
Jim Hegan
Al Rosen
Walt Dropo
Johnny Pesky
Maurice McDermott
Johnny Groth
Vic Wertz
Eddie Pellagrini
Frank Shea

WALKER

Harry Brecheen
Al Brazle
Johnny Wyrostek
Ted Kluszewski
Howard Fox
Rube Walker
Clyde McCullough
Pete Castiglione
Ken Heintzelman
Dick Sisler
Granny Hamner
Harry Walker

MURPHY

Alex Kellner
Duane Pillette
Jim McDonald
Lou Kretlow
Bob Dillinger
Johnny Berardino
Irv Noren
Merrill Combs
Charles Silvera
Mike MeCormick
Cliff Mapes
Clarence Maddern

1952

CAMPANELLA

Roy Campanella
Joe Black
Monte Irvin
Henry Thompson
Suitcase Simpson
Larry Doby
George Crowe

WHITE

Hal White
Clyde Kluttz
Sherman Lollar
Virgil Trucks
Bob Kuzava
Joe Collins
Ted Lepcio
Connie Ryan
Sibby Sisti
Del Ennis
Vic Wertz
Steve Souchock
Art Mills
Billy Mills

WALKER

Harry Walker
Herman Wehmeier
Pete Castiglione
Clyde McCullough
Russ Meyer
John Wyrostek

Warren Hacker
Pick Sialw
Hal Rice
Ken Silvestri
Solly Hemus

BEARDEN

Gene Bearden
Bob Cain
Dave Philley
Ray Murray
Jim Dyck
Fred Hatfield
Faye Throneberry
Mickey McDermott
Willard Nixon
Whitey Lockman
Don Mueller

1953

CAMPANELLA

George Crowe
Junior Gilliam
Jim Pendleton
Larry Doby
Bob Boyd
Bill Bruton
Harry Simpson
Roy Campanella
Othello Renfro
Joe Black
Dave Hoskins
Connie Johnson
Jim Tugerson
Pat Scantlebury
Don Newcombe

ROBINSON

Jackie Robinson
Gil Hodges
Luke Easter
Bob Trice
Bobby Young
Ralph Branca
Charley Neal
Maury Wills
Lou Louden
Ray Neal

Frank Ensley
Jim Lewis
Bill Holden
Dick Hairston
Speed Merchant
Fate Sims
Ted Honey Richardson
Tom Pee Wee Jenkins
Al Priston
King Tut
Spec Bebop

WHITE

Hal White
Billy Hunter
Sibbi Sisti
Steve Bilko
Virgil Trucks
Joe Garagiola
Whitey Ford
Willard Marshall
Ted Lepcio
Turk Lown
Johnny Groth
Sherm Lollar
Johnny Logan
Mickey Vernon
Vic Wertz

1954

WHITE

Gil McDougald
Gene Woodling
Ralph Houk
Sherman Lollar
Willard Marshall
Billy Hunter
Eddie Waitkus
Steve Gromek
Ted Lepcio
Joe Coleman
Willard Nixon

CAMPANELLA & IRVIN

Larry Doby
Dave Hoskins
Monty Irvin
Hank Thompson

Junior Gilliam
Don Newcombe
Jim Pendleton
Charlie White
Minnie Minoso
Brooks Lawrence
Gene Baker
Bob Trice
Joe Black

SHEA

Wes Westrum
Billy Gardner
Art Houtteman
Sam Dente
Sam Mele
Jim Piersall
Sid Gordon
Walt Dropo
Johnny Pesky
Bob Porterfield
Maury McDermott
Danny O'Connell
Vic Raschi

MEYER

Russ Meyer
Dee Fondy
Clyde McCullough
Warren Hacker
Ray Jablonski
Rip Repulski
Rube Walker
Jim Hughes
Johnny Logan
Roy McMillan
Johnny Wyrostek

GARVER

Ned Garver
Bob Turley
Lou Kretlow
Bob Kennedy
Clint Courtney
Joe Presko
Jerry Snyder
Roy Sievers
Bill Tuttle
Jim Delsing

Bill Skowron
Randy Jackson
Walker Cooper
Satchel Paige
Ernie Banks
Chuck Harmon
Curt Roberts
Artie Wilson
Sam Hairston
Bill Pope
Willard Brown
Harry Simpson
John Ritchey
Bill Greason
Jim Tugerson
Ernie Johnson

LOPAT & SCOTT

Carl Erskine
Duke Snider
Whitey Ford
Bob Grim
Del Crandall
Eddie Matthew
Sammy White
Billy Goodman
Harvet Kuenn
Hank Sauer
Red Schoendienst

1955

MAYS & NEWCOMBE

Willie Mays
Don Newcombe
Ernie Banks
George Crowe
Hank Thompson
Minnie Minoso
Charley White
Henry Aaron
Junior Gilliam
Joe Black
Brooks Lawrence
Connie Johnson

SHEA

Spec Shea
Ed Fitz Gerald
Ed Yost

Ted Lepcio
Norm Zauchin
Jim Piersall
Clem Labine
Don Hoak
Jim Busby
Walt Dropo
Dick Donovan
Chet Nichols

ASHBURN

Richie Ashburn
Willard Schmidt
Ken Boyer

KALINE

Al Kaline
Mickey Vernon
Gus Triando
Ray Moore
Hal Smith

LOLLAR

Sherm Lollar
Virgil Trucks
Bob Porterfield
Johnny Groth
Clint Courtney
Billy Mills

1956

COURTNEY

Roy Sievers
Jim Lemon
Milt Bolling
Willard Nixon
Frank Bolling
Morrie Martin
Dave Philley
Les Moss

TRUCKS

Bob Buhl
Johnny Groth
Jack Harshman
Sherman Lollar
Fred Hatfield

Earl Torgeson
Ted Kazanski
Steve Gromek
Frank Holuse
Charlie Maxwell

MAYS

Monte Irvin
Gene Baker
Al Smith
Suitcase Simpson
Hank Thompson
Elston Howard
Charley White
Willie Mays
Hank Aaron
Frank Robinson
Sam Jones
Joe Black
Brooks Lawrence
Connie Johnson
Don Newcombe

SHEA

Moe Drabowsky
Dick Donovan
Art Ditmar
Frank Sullivan
Sammy White
Ted Lepcio
Dale Long
Frank Thomas
Billy Gardner
Don Hoak
Rocky Colavito
Walt Dropo
John Pollidoro

1957

MAXWELL

Charley Maxwell
Virgil Trucks
Bob Buhl
Al Cicotte
Billy Klaus
George Zuverink
Gene Woodling
Sherman Lollar

Earl Torgeson
Fred Hatfield
Johnny Groth
Frank House

BOLLING

Frank Bolling
Milt Bolling
Bill Tuttle
Jim Bunning
Tom Brewer
Willard Nixon
Gus Triandos
Les Moss
Roy Sievers
Jim Lemon

MAYS

Willie Mays
Wes Covington
Brooks Lawrence
Frank Barnes
Felipe Alou
Ozzie Virgil
Joe Pignatano
Connie Johnson
Gene Baker
Joe Black
Harry Simpson
Elston Howard
Humberto Robinson
George Crowe
Al Smith
Jim Pendleton

FOX

Nellie Fox
Dick Groat
Ronnie Kline
Roy Face
Chuck Tanner
Jerry Lynch
Joe Lonnett

1958

FOX & GROAT

Nellie Fox
Dick Groat
Roy Face

Jerry Lynch
Chuck Tanner
Bobby Del Greco
Paul Smith

MAXWELL

Al Kaline
Charlie Maxwell
Johnny Grother
Billy Hoeft
Jim Rivera
Ike Delock
Joe Ginsberg
Ted Kazanski

NIEMAN

Bob Neiman
Gus Triandos
Mickey Vernon
Rocky Colavito
Tito Francona
Gale Harris
Lou Sleater
Hal Smith
Leo Kiely
Dick Gernert
Lum Harris
Ed Rommel

1959

KILLEBREW

Hal Smith
Frank Bolling
Bobby Morgan
Jim Lemon
Jim Piersall
Dick Williams
Russ Nixon
Cal McLish
Jim Bunning
Bud Daley
Paul Foytack
Bob (Riverboat) Smith
Harmon Killebrew
Henry Aaron
Willie McCovey
Jim Gilliam
Al Smith

Charlie Neal
Bill White
Harry Simpson
Bob Boyd
John Roseboro
Earl Battey
Don Newcombe
Bob Gibson
Marshall Bridges
Bennie Daniels
Connie Johnson
Frank Barnes
George Crowe

GOTTLIEB

Willie Mays
Willie McCovey
Hobie Landrith
Henry Aaron
Don Newcombe
Gil Hodges
Jim Gilliam
Johnny Podres
Ken Boyer
Bill Mazeroski
Elroy Face
Smoky Burgess
Mickey Mantle
Whitey Ford
Elston [Howard?]
Ed Yost

Harvey Kuenn
Rocky Colavito
Tito Francona
Bob Nieman
Gus Triandos
Hoyt Wilhelm
Frank Malzone
Bob Shaw

1960

MAYS

Willie Mays
Henry Aaron
Wes Covington
Lee Maye
Maury Wills
Charley Neal
Vada Pinson
Bill White
Don Newcombe
Jim Grant
Earl Wilson
Pumpsie Green
Willie Tasby
Lennie Green
Earl Battey
Bob Boyd
Jesse Gonder

1962

MAYS

Buck O'Neil
Willie Davis
Tommy Davis
Leon Wagner
Willie McCovey
Vada Pinson
Charley Neal
Sammy Drake
Al Jackson
Wes Covington
Don Demeter
Daryl Spencer
Dick Farrell
Cal McLish
Barnes
Jess Gonder
Earl Battey
Earl Wilson
Bill Tuttle
Lennie Green
Whitey Herzog
Jerry Adair
Leon Wagner
Dick Farrell
Al Smith
Floyd Robinson
Norm Siebern
Jerry Lumpe
Ed Rakow
Joe Morgan
[?] Evans

Appendix D: Barnstorming Games, 1901–1962

Information is incomplete for some games, for one or more of the following reasons:

1. There was an itinerary printed, but no dates were given.

2. There was only a very brief mention for that year ("The Cubs came back from Michigan...").

3. Tours often added and subtracted games in mid-journey.

4. There were "open" dates but games were probably played.

5. At times, only two games are listed, but other games were hinted at.

6. The names of players were often omitted, misspelled, or lacking first names or team affiliations. The difficulty of identifying players by name is compounded by the fact that many players were out of their usual positions.

Date	City / State	Team	Date	City / State	Team
1901				Marlboro MA	Boston AL
1 Oct.	Worcester MA	All-Americans	10 Oct.	Torrington CN	Boston NL
5 Oct.	Cincinnati OH	All-Americans	11 Oct.	Leominister MA	Boston NL
7 Oct.	Pittsburgh PA	All-Americans	12 Oct.	Worchester MA	Boston NL
8 Oct.	Pittsburgh PA	All-Americans		OH?	Lajoie's
11 Oct.	Cleveland OH	All-Americans			All-Stars
12 Oct.	Cleveland OH	All-Americans		Vincennes IN	All-Nationals
1 Oct.	Columbia PA	Brooklyn		Olney IL	All-Nationals
12 Oct.	Jamestown NY	Pirates		Evansville IN	All-Nationals
14 Oct.	Greensburg IN	Reds		Cairo IL	All-Nationals

Date	City / State	Team
22 Oct.	Memphis TN	All-Nationals

1902

	Louisville KY	Reds
	Indianapolis IN	Reds
12 Oct.	Chicago IL	All-Nationals/
		All-Americans
13 Oct.	Cedar Rapids IA	
14 Oct.	Des Moines IA	
15 Oct.	Sheldon IL	
16 Oct.	Lamar IA	
17 Oct.	Sioux City IA	
18 Oct.	Omaha NE	
19 Oct.	Omaha NE	
20 Oct.	St. Joseph MO	
21 Oct.	Kansas City MO	
22 Oct.	Kansas City MO	
23 Oct.	Topeka KS	
24 Oct.	Sabine KS	
25 Oct.	Denver CO	
26 Oct.	Denver CO	
27 Oct.	Colorado Springs CO	
28 Oct.	Pueblo CO	
29 Oct.	Trinidad CO	
30 Oct.	Las Vegas NM	
31 Oct.	Santa Fe NM	
1 Nov.	Albuquerque NM	
2 Nov.	at El Paso TX	
3 Nov.	at Benson AZ	
4 Nov.	at Tucson AZ	
5 Nov.	Phoenix AZ	
6 Nov.	San Bernardino CA	
7 Nov.	open	
8 Nov.	open	
9 Nov.	Los Angeles CA	

1903

Date	City / State	Team
30 Sept.	Elmira NY	NY Giants
5 Oct.	Trenton NJ	NY Giants
	Buffalo NY	NY Giants
	Jersey City NJ	NY Giants
	Williamsport PA	Detroit
	Jersey City NJ	Brooklyn
	Bayonne NJ	Brooklyn
5 Oct.	Harrisburg PA	Brooklyn
7 Oct.	Williamsport PA	Brooklyn
12 Oct.	Osgood IN	Reds
13 Oct.	Charleston WV	Reds
14 Oct.	Charleston WV	Reds
15 Oct.	Catlettsburg KY	Reds

Date	City / State	Team
16 Oct.	Catlettsburg KY	Reds
17 Oct.	Wellston OH	Reds
18 Oct.	Zanesville OH	Reds

1904

Date	City / State	Team
10 Oct.	Irontown? OH	Reds
11 Oct.	Youngstown[?] OH	Reds
12 Oct.	Ashland KY	Reds
13 Oct.	Mason City WV	Reds
14 Oct.	Newark or	
	Zanesville OH	Reds
15 Oct.	Springfield OH	Reds
16 Oct.	Dayton OH	Reds
12 Oct.	Reading PA	NY Giants
13 Oct.	York PA	NY Giants
14 Oct.	Harrisburg PA	NY Giants
15 Oct.	Plainfield NJ	NY Giants
18 Oct.	Hazleton PA	NY Giants
20 Oct.	Scranton PA	NY Giants
23 Oct.	Hoboken NJ	NY Giants
	Trenton NJ	Athletics
	Hoboken NJ	Brooklyn
	Staten Island NY	Brooklyn
	Atlantic City NJ	Brooklyn
	Maquette Field	
	NY	Brooklyn
	Elizabethport NJ	All-Nationals

1905

Date	City / State	Team
10 Oct.	Canton OH	Pirates
13 Oct.	Salem OH	Pirates
14 Oct.	Youngstown OH	Pirates
15 Oct.	Zanesville OH	Pirates
2 Oct.	NY	NYY
9 Oct.	NY	NYY
	Newark NJ	Detroit
	Providence RI	Boston AL
9 Oct.	Cleveland OH	Reds
10 Oct.	Mt. Vernon OH	Reds
11 Oct.	Youngstown OH	Reds
12 Oct.	Marion OH	Reds
13 Oct.	Wapakonete OH	Reds
14 Oct.	Springfield OH	Reds
15 Oct.	Dayton OH	Reds
17 Oct.	Catlettsburgh KY	Reds
18 Oct.	Zanesville OH	Reds
16 Oct.	Trenton NJ	NY Giants
20 Oct.	Wilkes-Barre PA	NY Giants
22 Oct.	Trenton NJ	NY Giants
15 Oct.	Ridgewood NY	NY Giants

Date	City / State	Team
8 Oct.	Brooklyn NY	Athletics
15 Oct.	Paterson NJ	Athletics

1906

Date	City / State	Team
8 Oct.	Elizabethport NJ	NYY
15 Oct.	Hoboken NJ	NYY
10 Oct.	Reading PA	Phillies
11 Oct.	Williamsport PA	Phillies
12 Oct.	Lock Haven PA	Phillies
13 Oct.	Frankford PA	Phillies
19 Oct.	Pottsville PA	Phillies
7 Oct.	Hoboken NJ	Athletics
8 Oct.	Hartford CN	Athletics
12 Oct.	Chester PA	Athletics
19 Oct.	Camden NJ	Athletics
10 Oct.	West Liverpool OH	Pirates
11 Oct.	Beaver Falls PA	Pirates
15 Oct.	Fairmount WV	Pirates
16 Oct.	Mannington WV	Pirates
17 Oct.	Wheeling WV	Pirates
18 Oct.	West Liverpool OH	Pirates
19 Oct.	Rochester PA	Pirates
20 Oct.	Wheeling WV	Pirates
23 Oct.	Bruin PA	Pirates
24 Oct.	Witherup PA	Pirates
25 Oct.	Etna PA	Pirates
17 Oct.	Joliet IL	White Sox
19 Oct.	Kenosha WI	White Sox

1907

Date	City / State	Team
7 Oct.	Wilkes-Barre PA	NY Giants
	Reading PA	
	Reading PA	Athletics
	Lexington OH	Reds
8 Oct.	Alliance OH	Pirates
9 Oct.	Salem OH	Pirates
10 Oct.	Ford City PA	Pirates
11 Oct.	Butler PA	Pirates
12 Oct.	Tarentum PA	Pirates
13 Oct.	Wheeling WV	Pirates
14 Oct.	Charleroi PA	Pirates
15 Oct.	Coraopolis PA	Pirates
16 Oct.	Carnegie PA	Pirates
17 Oct.	Millvale PA	Pirates
18 Oct.	Meyersville PA	Pirates
19 Oct.	Clarksburg WV	Pirates
20 Oct.	Aliance OH	Pirates
21 Oct.	Canton OH	Pirates

Date	City / State	Team
22 Oct.	Salem OH	Pirates
23 Oct.	Ford City PA	Pirates
24 Oct.	Smithton PA	Pirates
25 Oct.	Carnegie PA	Pirates
		Browns
		Nap Rucker
11 Oct.	Chicago IL	White Sox
14 Oct.	Chicago IL	White Sox
15 Oct.	Joliet IL	White Sox
	IL	Tigers
	WI	Tigers
	CA	Tigers

1908

Date	City / State	Team
14 Oct.	Shamokin PA	Athletics
16 Oct.	PA	Athletics
24 Oct.	Pottsville PA	Athletics
15 Oct.	Newburgh NY	NY Giants
	Perth Amboy NJ	NY Giants
	Middletown NY	NY Giants
22 Oct.	vs Tigers	NY Giants
23 Oct.	vs Tigers	NY Giants
24 Oct.	vs Tigers	NY Giants
4 Oct.	Parkerburg WV	Reds
7 Oct.	Gallipollis OH	Reds
8 Oct.	Charleston WV	Reds
9 Oct.	Montgomery WV	Reds
10 Oct.	Scarboro WV	Reds
11 Oct.	Dayton OH	Reds
17 Oct.	Hamilton OH	Reds
7 Nov.	Tampa[?] FL	Reds
8 Nov.	Tampa[?] FL	Reds
	CT	Philadelphia
	Chicago IL	Cubs
20 Oct.	Terre Haute IN	Cubs
1 Oct.	Greenburg PA	Boston

1909

Date	City / State	Team
24 Oct.	Chattanooga TN	Tigers
25 Oct.	Chattanooga TN	Tigers
26 Oct.	Jacksonville MS	Tigers
27 Oct.	Jacksonville MS	Tigers
28 Oct.	Tampa FL	Tigers
20 Oct.	Beloit IL	Cubs
21 Oct.	Chicago IL	Cubs
22 Oct.	Chicago IL	Cubs
23 Oct.	Chicago IL	Cubs
24 Oct.	Chicago IL	Cubs
5 Oct.	Hartford CT	Athletics

Date	City / State	Team
6 Oct.	Trenton NJ	Athletics
7 Oct.	Perkasie PA	Athletics
8 Oct.	Camden NJ	Athletics
9 Oct.	Easton PA	Athletics
10 Oct.	New York NY	Athletics
11 Oct.	Sunbury PA	Athletics
12 Oct.	Milton PA	Athletics
13 Oct.	Danville PA	Athletics
14 Oct.	Nanticoke PA	Athletics
15 Oct.	Ashland PA	Athletics
16 Oct.	Reading PA	Athletics
17 Oct.	Shamokin PA	Athletics
18 Oct.	off	Athletics
19 Oct.	Chicago IL	Athletics, All NL
20 Oct.	off	Athletics
21 Oct.	Billings MT	Athletics, All NL
23 Oct.	Helena MT	Athletics, All NL
24 Oct.	Spokane WA	Athletics, All NL
25 Oct.	Spokane WA	Athletics, All NL
26 Oct.	Walla Walla WA	Athletics, All NL
27 Oct.	Seattle WA	Athletics, All NL
28 Oct.	Seattle WA	Athletics, All NL
29 Oct.	Tacoma WA	Athletics, All NL
30 Oct.	Portland OR	Athletics, All NL
31 Oct.	Portland OR	Athletics, All NL
1 Nov.	off CA	Athletics, All NL
2 Nov.	Sacramento CA	Athletics, All NL
3 Nov.	Los Angeles CA	Athletics, All NL
4 Nov.	San Francisco CA	Athletics, All NL
5 Nov.	Los Angeles CA	Athletics, All NL
6 Nov.	Los Angeles CA	Athletics, All NL
7 Nov.	San Francisco CA	Athletics, All NL

Date	City / State	Team
	Bakersfield CA	Athletics, All NL
3 Nov.	Los Angeles CA	Athletics
	Philadelphia PA	stay behinds
24 Oct.	Phoenixville PA	stay behinds
30 Sept.	Louisville KY	All-Americans
1 Oct.	Louisville KY	All-Americans

1910

Date	City / State	Team
15 Oct.	South Philadelphia PA	Phillies
16 Oct.	Ridgewood NY	Phillies
16 Oct.	NYC's Bronx Oval NY	Brooklyn
16 Oct.	NYC's Olympic Field NY	Speaker & Johnson
19 Oct.	NYC's Olympic Field NY	NYG
20 Oct.	NYC's Olympic Field NY	NYG
23 Oct.	NYC's Bronx Oval NY	NYG
4 Oct.	NYC's Bronx Oval NY	Speaker
10 Oct.	NYC's Olympic Field NY	Donlin
22 Oct.	NYC's Olympic Field NY	all-stars
23 Oct.	NYC's Olympic Field NY	all-stars Cubs
	Hot Springs[?] WV	Reds
19 Oct.	Athens WV	Reds
20 Oct.	Gallipolis WV	Reds
21 Oct.	Huntington WV	Reds
22 Oct.	Charleston WV	Reds
23 Oct.	Charleston WV	Reds
24 Oct.	Glen Jean WV	Reds
25 Oct.	Beckley WV	Reds
26 Oct.	Hinton WV	Reds
7 Oct.	first stop PA	Pirates
19 Oct.	Sharon PA	Pirates
12 Oct.	Huntington WV	Pirates
17 Oct.	Irwin PA	Pirates
18 Oct.	Beaver Falls PA	Pirates
19 Oct.	Sharon PA	Pirates
20 Oct.	Uniontown PA	Pirates
21 Oct.	last date PA	Pirates

Date	City / State	Team
1911		
	OH	Reds
	KY	Reds
	IN	Reds
	WV	Reds
1912		
	Charleston WV	Reds
	Gloucester VA	Reds
	Racine VA	Reds
	Caldwell VA	Reds
	Mariette VA	Reds
	Portsmouth VA	Reds
	14 games	
	Shenandoah PA	Athletics
	New Brunswick NJ	Athletics
	Renovo PA	Athletics
	squad split	
	Clarksburg WV	
7 Oct.	Lexington KY	Pirates
9 Oct.	Portsmouth OH	Pirates
10 Oct.	Ironton OH	Pirates
	Johnstown OH	Pirates
18 Oct.	Scottdale PA	Pirates
20 Oct.	Steubenville OH (last game)	Pirates
	Dixon IL	White Sox
	South Bend IN	White Sox
	Whiting IN	White Sox
	Lenox Oval NY	Larry Doyle's All Giants Cardinals
1913		
18 Oct.	Cincinnati OH	All-Stars to Orient
19 Oct.	Chicago IL	All-Stars to Orient
20 Oct.	Springfield IL	All-Stars to Orient
21 Oct.	Peoria IL	All-Stars to Orient
23 Oct.	Ottumwa IA	All-Stars to Orient
24 Oct.	Sioux City IA	All-Stars to Orient
25 Oct.	Blue Rapids KS	All-Stars to Orient

Date	City / State	Team
26 Oct.	St. Joseph MO	All-Stars to Orient
27 Oct.	Kansas City MO	All-Stars to Orient
28 Oct.	Joplin MO	All-Stars to Orient
29 Oct.	Tulsa OK	All-Stars to Orient
30 Oct.	Muskogee OK	All-Stars to Orient
31 Oct.	Bonham TX	All-Stars to Orient
1 Nov.	Dallas TX	All-Stars to Orient
2 Nov.	Beaumont TX	All-Stars to Orient
3 Nov.	Houston TX	All-Stars to Orient
4 Nov.	Marlin TX	All-Stars to Orient
5 Nov.	Abilene TX	All-Stars to Orient
6 Nov.	El Paso TX	All-Stars to Orient
7 Nov.	Douglas AZ	All-Stars to Orient
8 Nov.	Bisbee AZ	All-Stars to Orient
9 Nov.	Los Angeles CA	All-Stars to Orient
10 Nov.	Los Angeles CA	All-Stars to Orient
11 Nov.	San Diego CA	All-Stars to Orient
5 Oct.	Brooklyn NY	Gallagher's All-Stars
5 Oct.	Long Island City NY	Boston AL with Hooper
5 Oct.	Schenectady NY	Walter Johnson
5 Oct.	Brooklyn NY	Brooklyn Superbas
6 Oct.	Hartford CT	Brooklyn Superbas
11 Oct.	Lykens PA	Brooklyn Superbas
12 Oct.	Millersville or Pottsville PA	Brooklyn Superbas
18 Oct.	Ebbets in Brooklyn NY	Brooklyn Superbas

Date	City / State	Team
19 Oct.	Dexter in Queens NY	Brooklyn Superbas
21 Oct.	Charlottesville VA	Brooklyn Superbas
22 Oct.	Greenville SC	Brooklyn Superbas Pirates
	NYC NY	

1914

Date	City / State	Team
	Versailles PA	Reds
	Charleston WV	
	Sistersville WV	Pirates
	Pomeroy OH	
20 Oct.	Forsythe MT	Mack & Bancroft
21 Oct.	Helena MT	Mack & Bancroft
23 Oct.	Hamilton MT	Mack & Bancroft
24 Oct.	Missoula MT	Mack & Bancroft
25 Oct.	Spokane WA	Mack & Bancroft
26 Oct.	Potlach ID	Mack & Bancroft
27 Oct.	Lewiston ID	Mack & Bancroft
28 Oct.	Walla Walla WA	Mack & Bancroft
29 Oct.	Seattle WA	Mack & Bancroft
30 Oct.	Bellingham WA	Mack & Bancroft
31 Oct.	off	Mack & Bancroft
1 Nov.	Portland OR	Mack & Bancroft
2 Nov.	Medford OR	Mack & Bancroft
3 Nov.	San Francisco CA	Mack & Bancroft
4 Nov.	San Francisco CA	Mack & Bancroft
5 Nov.	San Francisco CA	Mack & Bancroft
6 Nov.	San Francisco CA	Mack & Bancroft
7 Nov.	off CA	Mack & Bancroft

Date	City / State	Team
8 Nov.	Oakland CA	Mack & Bancroft
8 Nov.	San Francisco CA	Mack & Bancroft
9 Nov.	[?] CA	Mack & Bancroft
10 Nov.	San Jose CA	Mack & Bancroft
11 Nov.	off CA	Mack & Bancroft
12 Nov.	Los Angeles CA	Mack & Bancroft
13 Nov.	Los Angeles CA	Mack & Bancroft
14 Nov.	off CA	Mack & Bancroft
15 Nov.	Los Angeles CA	Mack & Bancroft
16 Nov.	Pasadena CA	Mack & Bancroft
17 Nov.	Modesto CA	Mack & Bancroft
18 Nov.	Sacramento CA	Mack & Bancroft
19 Nov.	Petaluma CA	Mack & Bancroft
20 Nov.	off CA	Mack & Bancroft
21 Nov.	San Francisco CA	Mack & Bancroft
22 Nov.	Oakland CA	Mack & Bancroft
22 Nov.	San Francisco CA to Hawaii	Mack & Bancroft Mack & Bancroft
23 Dec.	Fresno CA	Mack & Bancroft
24 Dec.	Bakersfield CA	Mack & Bancroft
25 Dec.	off CA	Mack & Bancroft
26 Dec.	San Diego CA	Mack & Bancroft
27 Dec.	San Diego CA	Mack & Bancroft

1915

Date	City / State	Team
	Versailles PA	Reds
	Charleston WV	Reds

Date	City / State	Team
	Sistersville WV	Pirates
16 Oct.	Oil City PA	Pirates
	East Liverpool OH	Pirates
14 Oct.	Benton Harbor MI	Cubs
14 Oct.	Laporte IN	Whales
24 Oct.	Chicago IL	Whales
20 Oct.	Oshkosh WI	All Nationals/ Americans
22 Oct.	Minneapolis MN	All Nationals/ Americans
23 Oct.	Sioux City IA	All Nationals/ Americans
24 Oct.	Omaha NE	All Nationals/ Americans
25 Oct.	Lincoln NE	All Nationals/ Americans
26 Oct.	Columbus NE	All Nationals/ Americans
27 Oct.	Grand inland NE	All Nationals/ Americans
28 Oct.	North Platte NE	All Nationals/ Americans
29 Oct.	Greeley CO	All Nationals/ Americans
30 Oct.	Denver CO	All Nationals/ Americans
31 Oct.	Denver CO	All Nationals/ Americans
1 Nov.	Colorado Springs CO	All Nationals/ Americans
2 Nov.	Pueblo CO	All Nationals/ Americans
3 Nov.	Cheyenne WY	All Nationals/ Americans
4 Nov.	Rocky Swings WY	All Nationals/ Americans
5 Nov.	Ogden UT	All Nationals/ Americans
6 Nov.	Salt Lake UT	All Nationals/ Americans
7 Nov.	Salt Lake UT	All Nationals/ Americans
8 Nov.	Pocatello ID	All Nationals/ Americans
9 Nov.	Twin Falls MT	All Nationals/ Americans
10 Nov.	Shosone ID	All Nationals/ Americans

Date	City / State	Team
11 Nov.	Boise ID	All Nationals/ Americans
12 Nov.	Baker ID	All Nationals/ Americans
13 Nov.	Pendleton OR	All Nationals/ Americans
17 Nov.	Seattle OR	All Nationals/ Americans
18 Nov.	Seattle OR	All Nationals/ Americans
20 Nov.	San Francisco CA	All Nationals/ Americans
21 Nov.	San Francisco CA	All Nationals/ Americans

1916

Date	City / State	Team
		Speaker & Dubuc
3 Oct.	Daytona OH	Pirates
4 Oct.	St. Marys OH	Pirates
5 Oct.	Delaware OH	Pirates
8 Oct.	Sandusky OH	Pirates

1919

Date	City / State	Team
		New York Giants
		Pirates
3 Oct.	Peru IN	Cubs
6 Oct.	Hammond IN	Cubs
9 Oct.	Beloit WI	Cubs

1920

Date	City / State	Team
4 Oct.	Thompsonville CT	Red Sox
6 Oct.	Huntington WV	Brooklyn?
2 Oct.	St. Louis MO	Phil NL
4 Oct.		St. L C/Giants
6 Oct.	Portage WI	St. L C/P Pirates
7 Oct.	Portage WI	St. L C/P Pirates
8 Oct.	Portage WI	St. L C/P Pirates
11 Oct.	St. Louis MO	St. L C/Giants
12 Oct.	Hermann MO	St. L C/Giants
	St. Louis	St. L C/Giants
	Effingham IL	St. L C/Giants
16 Oct.	Harrisburg IL	St. L C/Giants
18 Oct.	Springfield IL	St. L C/Giants
19 Oct.	Lawrenceville IL	St. L C/Giants

Date	City / State	Team
20 Oct.	Ganesville IL	St. L C/Giants
21 Oct.	Oscaloosa IA	St. L C/Giants
22 Oct.	Chicago IL	St. L C/Giants
23 Oct.	off	St. L C/Giants
24 Oct.	St. Louis MO	St. L C/Giants
24 Oct.	Brooklyn NY	Phil AL
12 Oct.	Pontiac MI	Pirates
3 Oct.	St. Louis MO	Stengel
	Fort Wayne IN	Stengel
4 Oct.	Parkersburg PA	Stengel
	Kansas City MO	Stengel
	Los Angeles CA	Stengel
7 Oct.	Lancaster PA	New York Giants
3 Oct.	Philadelphia PA	A.L. All-Stars
4 Oct.	Philadelphia PA	Hilldales vs. Athletics
5 Oct.	Philadelphia PA	Stengel
6 Oct.	Philadelphia PA	Stengel
7 Oct.	Philadelphia PA	Ruth
8 Oct.	Philadelphia PA	Ruth
24 Oct.	Brooklyn NY	Athletics

1921

Date	City / State	Team
	Chester PA	Senators
	Jackson MI	Ainsworth/Browns
3 Oct.	St. Louis IL	St. L C/Giants
4 Oct.	St. Louis IL	St. L C/Giants
5 Oct.	Portage WI	Cardinals/Robins
6 Oct.	Portage WI	Cardinals/Robins
9 Oct.	St. Louis IL	St. L C/Giants
10 Oct.	St. Louis IL	St. L C/Giants
12 Oct.	Herrin IL	St. Louis Cardinals
11 Oct.	Effingham IL	St. Louis Cardinals
14 Oct.	Kirksville MO	St. Louis Cardinals
15 Oct.	St. Peters MO	St. Louis Cardinals
16 Oct.	Harrisburg MO	St. Louis Cardinals
17 Oct.	Troy MO	St. Louis Cardinals

1922

Date	City / State	Team
2 Oct.	Lawrenceville IL	Reds

Date	City / State	Team
4 Oct.	Washington IN	Reds
5 Oct.	Manchester OH	Reds
	Piqua OH	Reds
8 Oct.	Chillicothe OH	Reds
3 Oct.	Muncie IN	Pirates
	Vanwert OH	Pirates
	Fremont OH	Pirates
	Tiffin OH	Pirates
	Laporte IND	Pirates
8 Oct.	Minneapolis MN	Pirates
9 Oct.	Minneapolis MN	Pirates
10 Oct.	Milwaukee WI	Pirates
	Sidney OH	Pirates
	Sturgis MI	Pirates
	St. Mary's OH	Pirates
	Springfield OH	Pirates
	Marion OH.	Pirates
	MI	Hornsby
	New England	Sisler
	Johnstown PA	AL All-Stars
	Oil City PA	Rosy Ryan
2 Oct.	Plainfield NJ	Brooklyn
23 Oct.	Baltimore MD	Rommell
15 Oct.	Harrison NJ	WS All-Stars
4 Oct.	Salem MA	Sisler All-Stars
5 Oct.	Fitchburg MA	Sisler All-Stars
11 Oct.	Warren RI	Sisler All-Stars
21 Oct.	Sanford ME	Sisler All-Stars
	AZ and OK	Mays & Schang

1923

Date	City / State	Team
25 Oct.	Detroit[?] Chicago[?]	Tigers/CA Giants

1924

Date	City / State	Team
1 Oct.	Kingston NY	Brooklyn
9 Oct.	Mason City IA	Brooklyn
10 Oct.	Eau Claire WI	Brooklyn
11 Oct.	Chippewa Falls WI	Brooklyn
18 Oct.	Great Falls MT	Brooklyn
19 Oct.	Wenatchee WA	Brooklyn
22 Oct.	Vancouver BC	Brooklyn
23 Oct.	Seattle WA	Brooklyn
24 Oct.	Seattle WA	Brooklyn
11 Oct.	Rochester NY	Ed Holley's
13 Oct.	Hazelton PA	Ed Holley's
1 Oct.	Ossining NY	NYG

1926

Date	City / State	Team
1 Oct.	Wilmington DE vs. Hilldales	Mack

Date	City / State	Team
2 Oct.	Darby PA	Mack
	vs. Hilldales	
3 Oct.	Youngstown OH	Mack
	vs. Hilldales	
4 Oct.	Pittsburgh PA	Mack
	vs. Hilldales	
5 Oct.	Pittsburgh PA	Mack
	vs. Hilldales	
6 Oct.	Bloomsburg PA	Mack
	vs. Hilldales	
7 Oct.	Bloomsburg PA	Mack
	vs. Hilldales	
8 Oct.	Bloomsburg PA	Mack
	vs. Hilldales	
11 Oct.	Coshocton OH	Mack
14 Oct.	Glouchester OH	Mack
16 Oct.	Camden NJ	Mack

1928

Date	City / State	Team
3 Oct.	Baltimore MD	Maisel & Foxx
4 Oct.	Baltimore MD	Maisel & Foxx
5 Oct.	Baltimore MD	Maisel & Foxx
7 Oct.	Baltimore MD	Maisel & Foxx
18 Oct.	Milwaukee MD	Maisel & Foxx
27 Oct.	Los Angeles CA	Maisel & Foxx
28 Oct.	Sacramento CA	Maisel & Foxx
29 Oct.	Long Beach CA	Maisel & Foxx

1929

Date	City / State	Team
	Augusta GA	Crowder
5 Oct.	Pittsburgh PA	Pirates
		Gehringer
		Foxx
	Watertown? NY	
	Reading? PA	

1930

Date	City / State	Team
3 Oct.	Chicago IL	Earle Mack
4 Oct.	Chicago IL	Earle Mack
5 Oct.	Chicago IL	Earle Mack
6 Oct.	Chicago IL	Earle Mack
8 Oct.	Sioux City IA	Earle Mack
9 Oct.	Huron SD	Earle Mack
10 Oct.	Sioux Falls SD	Earle Mack
	Bismarck ND	Earle Mack
29 Oct.	Los Angeles CA	Earle Mack
	Yakima WA	Earle Mack

1931

Date	City / State	Team
	Wilkes-Barre PA	

Date	City / State	Team
	Japan	
	Charleston MO	Dizzy Dean
	Joplin MO	Dizzy Dean
	Atkins AR	Dizzy Dean
	Houston TX	Dizzy Dean
	New Orleans LA	Dizzy Dean
	Joplin MO	Dizzy Dean
3 Oct.	Philadelphia PA	NYG/Vergez
	vs. Hilldales	
	Fairview NJ	NYG/Vergez
14 Oct.	Fairview NJ	NYG/Vergez
15 Oct.	Philadelphia PA	NYG/Vergez
	vs. Hilldales	
17 Oct.	Scranton PA	Vance
4 Oct.	KC MO	Tierney
	St. Louis MO	Tierney
8 Oct.	Winnepeg Can.	Earle Mack
9 Oct.	Winnepeg Can.	Earle Mack
10 Oct.	Winnepeg Can.	Earle Mack
10 Oct.	Des Moines IO	Earle Mack
11 Oct.	Omaha NE	Earle Mack
12 Oct.	Wichita KS	Earle Mack
20 Oct.	Houston TX	Earle Mack
21 Oct.	El Paso TX	Earle Mack
24 Oct.	Los Angeles CA	Earle Mack
25 Oct.	Los Angeles CA	Earle Mack
26 Oct.	Los Angeles CA	Earle Mack
28 Oct.	Stockton CA	Earle Mack
29 Oct.	San Francisco CA	Earle Mack
	Baltimore MD	Foxx

1932

Date	City / State	Team
4 Oct.	Charleston MO	Dizzy Dean
6 Oct.	Carbondale IL	Dizzy Dean
10 Oct.	Boonville MO	Dizzy Dean
18 Oct.	Herculaneum MO	Dizzy Dean
1 Oct.	Edmonton ALB	Earle Mack
2 Oct.	Sioux Falls SD	Earle Mack
4 Oct.	Jamestown ND	Earle Mack
6 Oct.	Devils Lake ND	Earle Mack
9 Oct.	Fargo ND	Earle Mack
	York PA	NL/Crawfords
	Greenlee in Pitts PA	NL/Crawfords
	Altoona PA	NL/Crawfords
	Cleveland OH	NL/Crawfords

1933

Date	City / State	Team
15 Oct.	Queens NY	Foxx

Date	City / State	Team
16 Oct.	Milford DE	Foxx
19 Oct.	Baltimore MD	Foxx
	Houston TX	Dizzy Dean
	Los Angeles CA	Dizzy Dean

1934

Date	City / State	Team
11 Oct.	Oklahoma City OK	Dizzy Dean
12 Oct.	Wichita KS	Dizzy Dean
	KC MO	Dizzy Dean
	Hollywood? CA	Dizzy Dean
	Chicago IL	Dizzy Dean
	Milwaukee WI	Dizzy Dean
	Philadelphia PA	Dizzy Dean
	Queens NY	Dizzy Dean
	Baltimore MD	Dizzy Dean
	Paterson NJ	Dizzy Dean
	Columbus OH	Dizzy Dean
4 Oct.	Grand Forks ND	Earle Mack
	Valley City ND	Earle Mack
	Bismarck ND	Earle Mack
	Jamestown ND	Earle Mack
	Winnepeg Can.	Earle Mack
	Regina Can.	Earle Mack
15 Oct.	Seattle OR	Earle Mack
16 Oct.	Portland OR	Earle Mack

1935

Date	City / State	Team
2 Oct.	Springfield MO	Dizzy Dean
6 Oct.	St Joseph MO	Dizzy Dean
7 Oct.	KC MO	Dizzy Dean
	Belleville IL	Dizzy Dean
14 Oct.	NY	Dizzy Dean
17 Oct.	NY	Dizzy Dean
18 Oct.	Chattanooga TN	Dizzy Dean
19 Oct.	New Orleans LA	Dizzy Dean
	York PA	Dizzy Dean
	Pittsburgh PA	Dizzy Dean
	Oakland CA	Dizzy Dean
27 Oct.	Los Angeles CA	Dizzy Dean
31 Oct.	Los Angeles CA	Dizzy Dean

1936

Date	City / State	Team
	ND	Earle Mack
	MT	
	BC	
8 Oct.	Los Angeles CA	Dizzy Dean
2 Oct.	Des Moines IA	Hornsby & Bell
4 Oct.	Davenport IA	

Date	City / State	Team
5 Oct.	Denver CO	DH
7 Oct.	Des Moines IA	

1937

Date	City / State	Team
4 Oct.	Port Huron MI	Rogell
5 Oct.	Elkton MI	
6 Oct.	Cairo MI	
6 Oct.	Minneapolis MN	Feller
	Cedar Rapids IA	Feller
	Kansas City MO	Feller
	Tulsa OK	Feller
	Oklahoma City OK	Feller
21 Oct.	Los Angeles CA	Feller
	10 games	

1938

Date	City / State	Team
	San Francisco[?]	3 DiMaggios

1939

Date	City / State	Team
	NE	Dizzy Dean

1940

Date	City / State	Team
	Little Falls MT	Earle Mack
	Billings MT	Earle Mack
	Great Falls MT	Earle Mack
	Missoula MT	Earle Mack
	Fargo ND	Earle Mack

1944

Date	City / State	Team
2 Oct.	Davenport IA	Doan
3 Oct.	Omaha NE	Doan
5 Oct.	Salt Lake City UT	Doan
6 Oct.	Pocatello ID	Doan
7 Oct.	Boise ID	Doan
8 Oct.	Pendleton ID	Doan
9 Oct.	Tacoma WA	Doan
10 Oct.	Wenatchee WA	Doan
11 Oct.	Vancouver BC	Doan

1945

Date	City / State	Team
1 Oct.	Wilmington DE	Dressen
3 Oct.	Lawrence MA	Dressen
4 Oct.	Hartford CN	Dressen
7 Oct.	Brooklyn NY	Dressen
10 Oct.	Newark NJ	Dressen
3 Oct.	Knoxville TN	Walker
5 Oct.	Memphis TN	Walker
7 Oct.	Birmingham AL	Walker

Date	City / State	Team
8 Oct.	Talladega AL	Walker
9 Oct.	Atlanta GA	Walker
10 Oct.	Savannah GA	Walker
11 Oct.	Jacksonville FL	Walker
12 Oct.	Mobile AL	Walker
14 Oct.	New Orleans LA	Walker
11 Oct.	Great Falls MT	(train wreck)*
3 Oct.	Hollywood CA	Gray
	Oakland CA	Gray
	Los Angeles CA	Gray
	San Diego CA	Gray
8 Oct.	Hollywood CA	Gray
	San Francisco CA	Gray
	Sacramento CA	Gray
1 Oct.	Dayton OH	Doan
2 Oct.	South bend IN	Doan
3 Oct.	Davenport IA	Doan
4 Oct.	David City NE	Doan
5 Oct.	Oxford NE	Doan
6 Oct.	Ponca City OK	Doan
7 Oct.	Oklahoma City OK	Doan
8 Oct.	Texas	Doan
9 Oct.	Fort Worth TX	Doan
10 Oct.	Houston TX	Doan

1946

Date	City / State	Team
14 Oct.	Cleveland OH	Robinson
6 Oct.	Cincinnati OH	Robinson
7 Oct.	Youngstown OH	Robinson
19 Oct.	Chicago IL	Robinson
	"Kingston, NY"	DiMaggio
9 Oct.	"Edmonton," ALB	Earle Mack
10 Oct.	"Edmonton," ALB	Earle Mack
	State Line MT	Earle Mack
9 Oct.	Dallas TX	Richards
11 Oct.	Dallas TX	Richards
16 Oct.	San Francisco CA	Richards
17 Oct.	Sacramento CA	Richards
18 Oct.	San Jose CA	Richards
19 Oct.	Oakland CA	Richards
30 Sept.	Pittsburgh PA	Feller & Paige
	Youngstown OH	Feller & Paige
	Cleveland OH	Feller & Paige
	Chicago IL	Feller & Paige
	Versailles KY	Feller & Paige
	Cincinnati OH	Feller & Paige
6 Oct.	Yankee Stadium NY	Feller & Paige

Date	City / State	Team
	Newark NJ	Feller & Paige
	Baltimore MD	Feller & Paige
	Columbus OH	Feller & Paige
	Dayton OH	Feller & Paige
	Louisville KY	Feller & Paige
	Richmond IN	Feller & Paige
	Davenport IA	Feller & Paige
11 Oct.	Des Moines IA	Feller & Paige
	St. Paul MN	Feller & Paige
	Omaha Neb	Feller & Paige
	Wichita KS	Feller & Paige
	St. Louis MO	Feller & Paige
	Kansas City MO	Feller & Paige
	Denver CO	Feller & Paige
	Los Angeles CA	Feller & Paige
26 Oct.	British Columbia Canada	Feller & Paige
3 Oct.	KC MO	Vander Meer
6 Jan.	Denver CO	Vander Meer
8 Jan.	Ogden UT	Vander Meer
9 Jan.	Pocatello ID	Vander Meer
10 Jan.	Twin Falls ID	Vander Meer
16 Oct.	San Francisco CA	Vander Meer

1947

Date	City / State	Team
9 Oct.	Birmingham AL	Feller
10 Oct.	Memphis TN	Feller
11 Oct.	Pittsburgh PA	Feller
11 Oct.	New Orleans LA	Feller
12 Oct.	Houston TX	Feller
12 Oct.	Dallas TX	Feller
13 Oct.	Oklahoma City OK	Feller
14 Oct.	San Diego CA	Feller
15 Oct.	El Centro CA	Feller
15 Oct.	Los Angeles CA	Feller
16 Jan.	Oakland CA	Feller
17 Jan.	San Francisco CA	Feller
18 Jan.	Long Beach CA	Feller
18 Jan.	San Diego CA	Feller
19 Jan.	Los Angeles CA	Feller
19 Jan.	Bakersfield CA	Feller
20 Jan.	San Jose CA	Feller
21 Jan.	Ventura CA	Feller
23 Jan.	Mexico City Mexico	Feller
24 Jan.	Mexico City Mexico	Feller

The newspapers reported that a team was in a train wreck on this day, but the team was not named.

Date	City / State	Team
25 Jan.	Mexico City Mexico	Feller
26 Jan.	Mexico City Mexico	Feller
27 Jan.	Open Mex.	Feller
28 Jan.	Tampico Mex.	Feller
28 Jan.	Guadalajara Mexico	Feller
29 Jan.	Monterrey Mex. Mexico	Feller
30 Oct.	Torreon Mex.	Feller
	Birmingham AL	Glennon
	New Orleans LA	Glennon
	Jacksonville FL	Glennon
19 Oct.	Columbus GA	Glennon
	Americus GA	Glennon
	Albany GA	Glennon
	Moultrie GA	Glennon
	Savannah GA	Glennon
8 Oct.	Washington NC	Lewis
23 Oct.	Lumberton NC	Lewis
	Durham NC	Lewis
15 Oct.	Los Angeles CA	Blackwell
19 Oct.	Los Angeles CA	Blackwell
23 Oct.	Los Angeles CA	Blackwell
26 Oct.	Los Angeles CA	Blackwell
1 Nov.	Los Angeles CA	Blackwell
6 Nov.	Los Angeles CA	Blackwell

1948

Date	City / State	Team
12 Oct.	Odell NE	Barney
14 Oct.	Tilden NE	Barney
15 Oct.	Spencer NE	Barney
17 Oct.	Omaha NE	Barney
18 Oct.	Hastings NE	Barney
19 Oct.	North Platee NE	Barney
20 Oct.	Alma NE	Barney
24 Oct.	Wausa NE	Barney
13 Oct.	Memphis TN	Robinson
17 Oct.	New Orleans LA	Robinson
22 Oct.	Shreveport LA	Robinson
11 Oct.	Peru IL	Sisler
15 Oct.	Springfield IL	Sisler
17 Oct.	Johnson TN	Sisler
26 Oct.	Belleville IL	Sisler
12 Oct.	Burlington VT	Tebbetts
	New Bedford MA	Tebbetts
	Nashua NH	Tebbetts
	Laconia NH	Tebbetts

Date	City / State	Team
	Lancaster NH	Tebbetts
	Waterville ME	Tebbetts
	New Brunswick Canada	Tebbetts
	St. John Canada	Tebbetts
	Grand Falls one. Canada	Tebbetts
	Presque Isle ME	Tebbetts
24 Oct.	Lebanon NH	Tebbetts
17 Oct.	Los Angeles CA	Lemon & Bearden
29 Oct.	Oakland CA	Lemon & Bearden
31 Oct.	Los Angeles CA	Lemon & Bearden
7 Nov.	Los Angeles CA	Lemon & Bearden
11 Oct.	Bloomsburg PA	Litwhiler
12 Oct.	York PA	Litwhiler
13 Oct.	open PA	Litwhiler
14 Oct.	Greencastle PA	Litwhiler
15 Oct.	Williamsport PA	Litwhiler
16 Oct.	Paterson NJ	Litwhiler
17 Oct.	Wilkes-Barre PA	Litwhiler
18 Oct.	New Castle PA	Litwhiler
19 Oct.	Roaring Spring PA	Litwhiler
20 Oct.	Brownsville PA	Litwhiler
21 Oct.	North Berwick? PA	Litwhiler
22 Oct.	Portsmouth OH	Litwhiler
23 Oct.	Hamburg OH	Litwhiler
24 Oct.	Charleston WV	Litwhiler
25 Oct.	Dayton OH	Litwhiler
26 Oct.	Charleston WV	Litwhiler
27 Oct.	Bristol VA	Litwhiler
28 Oct.	Bluefield WV	Litwhiler
29 Oct.	Buena Vista VA	Litwhiler
	Winston-Salem NC	Litwhiler

1949

Date	City / State	Team
12 Oct.	Bloomsburg PA	Litwhiler
	Hazleton PA	Litwhiler
	Williamsport PA	Litwhiler
	Mahonoy City PA	Litwhiler
	Greencastle PA	Litwhiler
	Mt. Carmel PA	Litwhiler
	Berwick PA	Litwhiler

Date	City / State	Team
11 Oct.	Harrisonburg VA	Lewis
12 Oct.	Rocky Mount NC	Lewis
13 Oct.	Washington NC	Lewis
14 Oct.	Benson NC	Lewis
15 Oct.	Wilmington NC	Lewis
16 Oct.	Mt. Olive NC	Lewis
17 Oct.	Henderson and NC	Lewis
17 Oct.	Red Springs NC	Lewis
18 Oct.	Durham NC	Lewis
19 Oct.	Burlington NC	Lewis
20 Oct.	Charlotte NC	Lewis
21 Oct.	Albemarle NC	Lewis
22 Oct.	Kannapolis NC	Lewis
23 Oct.	Columbia NC	Lewis
24 Oct.	Spartanburg NC	Lewis
11 Oct.	Newport News VA	Robinson
12 Oct.	Norfolk VA	Robinson
12 Oct.	Richmond VA	Robinson
13 Oct.	Greensboro NC	Robinson
14 Oct.	Charlotte NC	Robinson
15 Oct.	Atlanta GA	Robinson
16 Oct.	Montgomery AL	Robinson
17 Oct.	Birmingham AL	Robinson
17 Oct.	Nashville TN	Robinson
24 Oct.	Memphis TN	Robinson
25 Oct.	Little Rock AR	Robinson
26 Oct.	Open	Robinson
27 Oct.	New Orleans LA	Robinson
28 Oct.	Baton Rouge LA	Robinson
29 Oct.	New Orleans LA	Robinson
30 Oct.	Alexandria LA	Robinson
31 Oct.	Shreveport LA	Robinson
1 Nov.	Oklahoma City OK	Robinson
2 Nov.	Fort Worth TX	Robinson
3 Nov.	Beaumont TX	Robinson
4 Nov.	Houston TX	Robinson
5 Nov.	Houston TX	Robinson
6 Nov.	New Iberia LA	Robinson
7 Nov.	Columbus MS	Robinson
8 Nov.	Columbus GA	Robinson
9 Nov.	Thomasville GA	Robinson
10 Nov.	Albany GA	Robinson
11 Nov.	Savannah GA	Robinson
12 Nov.	Augusta GA	Robinson
13 Nov.	Charleston SC	Robinson

Date	City / State	Team
14 Nov.	Jacksonville FL	Robinson
	Miami FL	Robinson
	Tampa FL	Robinson
	Macon GA	Robinson
	Columbia SC	Robinson
12 Oct.	Tamaroa IL	Sisler
14 Oct.	Springfield IL	Sisler
16 Oct.	Springfield IL	Sisler
17 Oct.	Peru IL	Sisler
18 Oct.	Jackson TN	Sisler
19 Oct.	Jackson TN	Sisler
20 Oct.	Milan TN	Sisler
21 Oct.	Milan TN	Sisler
22 Oct.	Alamo TN	Sisler
23 Oct.	Lexington TN	Sisler
11 Oct.	Stamford CN	Tebbetts
11 Oct.	Bridgeport CN	Tebbetts
13 Oct.	Torrington CN	Tebbetts
14 Oct.	Hartford CN	Tebbetts
15 Oct.	Rochester NH	Tebbetts
16 Oct.	Berlin NH	Tebbetts
18 Jan.	Presque Isle ME	Tebbetts
20 Jan.	Portland ME	Tebbetts
23 Oct.	Montpelier VT	Tebbetts
		Trout
	NE	Barney
		Easter
		Cavaretta
	LA(4 games)	Lemon
17 Oct.	San Diego CA	Feller
18 Oct.	Fresno CA	Feller
19 Oct.	Open CA	Feller
20 Oct.	Open CA	Feller
21 Oct.	Bakersfield CA	Feller
22 Oct.	Open CA	Feller
23 Oct.	San Diego CA	Feller
24 Oct.	Sacramento CA	Feller
25 Oct.	Hollywood CA	Feller
26 Oct.	Open CA	Feller
27 Oct.	LA CA	Feller
28 Oct.	Open CA	Feller
29 Oct.	Sacramento CA	Feller
30 Oct.	Stockton CA	Feller
30 Oct.	Las Vegas NV	Feller
31 Oct.	Open	Feller
1 Nov.	Open	Feller
2 Nov.	Open	Feller
3 Nov.	Open	Feller
4 Nov.	Open	Feller
5 Nov.	Open	Feller

Date	City / State	Team
6 Nov.	Tijuana Mexico	Feller
		Paige & Bearden
		Walker

1950

Date	City / State	Team
	Rochester NH	Harris
11 Oct.	Auburn ME	Harris
12 Oct.	Portland ME	Harris
13 Oct.	Bristol CT	Harris
14 Oct.	New Haven CT	Harris
15 Oct.	Manchester NH	Harris
16 Oct.	Bridgeport CT	Harris
17 Oct.	Torrington CT	Harris
18 Oct.	Berlin NH	Harris
19 Oct.	Springfield MA	Harris
20 Oct.	open MA	Harris
21 Oct.	Long Island NY (2 games)	Harris
22 Oct.	Hartford CT	Harris
10 Oct.	Sulphur OK	Reynolds
11 Oct.	Durant OK	Reynolds
12 Oct.	Seminole OK	Reynolds
13 Oct.	Open OK	Reynolds
14 Oct.	Guthrie OK	Reynolds
15 Oct.	Ada OK	Reynolds
16 Oct.	Pauls Valley OK	Reynolds
17 Oct.	Woodward OK	Reynolds
18 Oct.	Open OK	Reynolds
19 Oct.	Open OK	Reynolds
20 Oct.	Open OK	Reynolds
21 Oct.	Hugo OK	Reynolds
22 Oct.	Broken Bow OK	Reynolds
23 Oct.	Oklahoma City OK	Reynolds
24 Oct.	Oklahoma City OK	Reynolds
25 Oct.	Broken Bow OK	Reynolds
26 Oct.	Open OK	Reynolds
27 Oct.	Open OK	Reynolds
28 Oct.	Idabel OK	Reynolds
10 Oct.	Montreal QU	Jac. & Riggs
11 Oct.	Syracuse NY	Jac. & Riggs
12 Oct.	Toronto ON	Jac. & Riggs
13 Oct.	Chicago IL	Jac. & Riggs
14 Oct.	Cincinnati OH	Jac. & Riggs
15 Oct.	Pittsburgh PA	Jac. & Riggs
15 Oct.	Columbus OH	Jac. & Riggs
16 Oct.	Hamilton ON	Jac. & Riggs
17 Oct.	Brantford ON	Jac. & Riggs
17 Oct.	Rochester NY	Jac. & Riggs

Date	City / State	Team
18 Oct.	Richmond VA	Jac. & Riggs
19 Oct.	Columbia SC	Jac. & Riggs
19 Oct.	Charleston SC	Jac. & Riggs
20 Oct.	Tampa FL	Jac. & Riggs
21 Oct.	Miami FL	Jac. & Riggs
22 Oct.	New Orleans LA	Jac. & Riggs
23 Oct.	Nashville TN	Jac. & Riggs
24 Oct.	Birmingham AL	Jac. & Riggs
25 Oct.	Mobile AL	Jac. & Riggs
25 Oct.	Birmingham AL	Jac. & Riggs
26 Oct.	Memphis TN	Jac. & Riggs
27 Oct.	San Antonio TX	Jac. & Riggs
28 Oct.	Houston TX	Jac. & Riggs
29 Oct.	Fort Worth TX	Jac. & Riggs
29 Oct.	Dallas TX	Jac. & Riggs
30 Oct.	San Diego CA	Jac. & Riggs
31 Oct.	San Diego CA	Jac. & Riggs
1 Nov.	Los Angeles CA	Jac. & Riggs
2 Nov.	Los Angeles CA	Jac. & Riggs
3 Nov.	Hollywood CA	Jac. & Riggs
4 Nov.	Fresno CA	Jac. & Riggs
4 Nov.	Sacramento CA	Jac. & Riggs
5 Nov.	Oakland CA	Jac. & Riggs
5 Nov.	San Francisco CA	Jac. & Riggs
11 Oct.	Bridgeport CT	Tebbetts
12 Oct.	Hartford CT	Tebbetts
13 Oct.	Naugatuck CT	Tebbetts
14 Oct.	Fall River MA	Tebbetts
15 Oct.	Worcester MA	Tebbetts
16 Oct.	Hartford CT	Tebbetts
17 Oct.	Southbridge MA	Tebbetts
18 Oct.	Open MA	Tebbetts
19 Oct.	Bangor ME	Tebbetts
20 Oct.	Augusta ME	Tebbetts
21 Oct.	Burlington VT	Tebbetts
22 Oct.	Portland ME	Tebbetts
23 Oct.	Presque Isle ME	Tebbetts
24 Oct.	Bangor ME	Tebbetts
11 Oct.	Bloomsburg PA	Litwhiler
12 Oct.	York PA	Litwhiler
13 Oct.	Open PA	Litwhiler
14 Oct.	Greencastle PA	Litwhiler
15 Oct.	Williamsport PA	Litwhiler
16 Oct.	Paterson NJ	Litwhiler
17 Oct.	Wilkes-Barre PA	Litwhiler
18 Oct.	New Castle PA	Litwhiler
19 Oct.	Roaring Spring PA	Litwhiler
20 Oct.	Brownsville PA	Litwhiler

Date	City / State	Team
21 Oct.	Portsmouth OH	Litwhiler
22 Oct.	Charleston WV	Litwhiler
23 Oct.	Dayton OH	Litwhiler
24 Oct.	Charleston WV	Litwhiler
25 Oct.	Bristol VA	Litwhiler
26 Oct.	Bluefield WV	Litwhiler
27 Oct.	Open WV	Litwhiler
28 Oct.	Buena Vista VA	Litwhiler
29 Oct.	Winston-Salem NC	Litwhiler
9 Oct.	Montgomery AL	Digby
10 Oct.	Montgomery AL	Digby
11 Oct.	Birmingham AL	Digby
12 Oct.	Cullman AL	Digby
13 Oct.	Open AL	Digby
14 Oct.	Meridian MS	Digby
15 Oct.	Hattiesburg MS	Digby
16 Oct.	Ponchatoula LA	Digby
17 Oct.	Baton Rouge LA	Digby
18 Oct.	Monroe LA	Digby
19 Oct.	Greenville MS	Digby
20 Oct.	Manila AR	Digby
21 Oct.	Alexandria LA	Digby
22 Oct.	Lake Charles LA	Digby
22 Oct.	Port Arthur TX	Digby
23 Oct.	Baton Rouge LA	Digby
9 Oct.	Baltimore MD	Robinson
10 Oct.	at Norfolk VA	Robinson
11 Oct.	Richmond VA	Robinson
12 Oct.	Durham NC	Robinson
12 Oct.	Raleigh NC	Robinson
13 Oct.	Charlotte NC	Robinson
14 Oct.	Charleston SC	Robinson
15 Oct.	Columbia SC	Robinson
16 Oct.	Augusta GA	Robinson
17 Oct.	Atlanta GA	Robinson
18 Oct.	Birmingham AL	Robinson
19 Oct.	Montgomery AL	Robinson
20 Oct.	Jackson MS	Robinson
20 Oct.	Greenville MS	Robinson
21 Oct.	Pine Bluff AR	Robinson
21 Oct.	Little Rock AR	Robinson
22 Oct.	Memphis TN	Robinson
23 Oct.	Jackson MS	Robinson
23 Oct.	Greenville MS	Robinson
24 Oct.	Houston TX	Robinson
25 Oct.	Houston TX	Robinson
26 Oct.	Austin TX	Robinson
27 Oct.	Open TX	Robinson
28 Oct.	Natchez MS	Robinson

Date	City / State	Team
29 Oct.	New Orleans Houma LA	Robinson
30 Oct.	New Orleans LA	Robinson
31 Oct.	Mobile AL	Robinson
1 Nov.	off AL	Robinson
2 Nov.	Pensacola FL	Robinson
3 Nov.	Macon GA	Robinson
4 Nov.	Tampa FL	Robinson
4 Nov.	Lakeland FL	Robinson
5 Nov.	Miami Beach FL	Robinson
6 Nov.	Daytona Beach FL	Robinson
7 Nov.	Jacksonville FL	Robinson
12 Oct.	Santa Maria CA	Lemon
15 Oct.	LA CA	Lemon
16 Oct.	LA CA	Lemon
17 Oct.	Bakersfield CA	Lemon
18 Oct.	San Bernardino CA	Lemon
19 Oct.	San Diego CA	Lemon
21 Oct.	Long Beach CA	Lemon
22 Oct.	LA CA	Lemon
?	Visalia CA	Lemon
?	Porterville CA	Lemon
29 Oct.	Palm Springs CA	Lemon
1 Nov.	LA CA	Lemon
2 Nov.	Oakland CA	Lemon
19 Oct.	Memphis TN	Easter
20 Oct.	Little Rock AR	Easter
21 Oct.	Houston TX	Easter
22 Oct.	Galveston TX	Easter
24 Oct.	Austin TX	Easter
27 Oct.	Corinth MS	Walker
28 Oct.	Dexter MO	Walker
29 Oct.	Jackson TN	Walker
	many other games	Walker

1951

Date	City / State	Team
10 Oct.	Roaring Springs PA	Litwhiler
11 Oct.	Reading and PA	Litwhiler
11 Oct.	Altoona PA	Litwhiler
12 Oct.	Altoona and Bloomsburg PA	Litwhiler
13 Oct.	Harrisburg PA	Litwhiler
14 Oct.	York PA	Litwhiler
16 Oct.	Wilkes-Barre PA	Litwhiler
17 Oct.	Everett MD	Litwhiler

Date	City / State	Team
18 Oct.	Frederick MD	Litwhiler
19 Oct.	Carbondale PA	Litwhiler
20 Oct.	Bath NY	Litwhiler
21 Oct.	Hazelton PA	Litwhiler
11 Oct.	Frederick MD	Hodges
11 Oct.	Baltimore MD	Hodges
12 Oct.	Roanoke VA	Hodges
13 Oct.	Richmond VA	Hodges
13 Oct.	Petersburg VA	Hodges
14 Oct.	Norfolk VA	Hodges
14 Oct.	Newport News VA	Hodges
15 Oct.	Inn NC	Hodges
16 Oct.	Goldsboro NC	Hodges
17 Oct.	Durham NC	Hodges
18 Oct.	Charlotte NC	Hodges
19 Oct.	Atlanta GA	Hodges
20 Oct.	Rome GA	Hodges
21 Oct.	Augusta GA	Hodges
22 Oct.	Nashville TN	Hodges
23 Oct.	Louisville KY	Hodges
11 Oct.	Baltimore MD	Campanella
	Richmond and Petersburg VA	Campanella
	Norfolk VA	Campanella
	Newport News VA	Campanella
	Winston-Salem NC	Campanella
	Goldsboro NC	Campanella
	Durham NC	Campanella
	Salisbury NC	Campanella
	Charlotte NC	Campanella
	Atlanta GA	Campanella
20 Oct.	Augusta GA	Campanella
	Ft. Benning GA	Campanella
	Columbus GA	Campanella
	Macon GA	Campanella
	Nashville TN	Campanella
26 Oct.	Louisville KY	Campanella
31 Oct.	Houston TX	Campanella
2 Nov.	Shreveport LA	Campanella
3 Nov.	Natchez MS	Campanella
4 Nov.	New Orleans LA	Campanella
5 Nov.	Little Rock AR	Campanella
6 Nov.	New Orleans LA	Campanella
8 Nov.	Valdosta GA	Campanella
8 Nov.	Jacksonville FL	Campanella
30 Oct.	Lake Charles LA	Robinson
30 Oct.	Port Arthur TX	Robinson

Date	City / State	Team
31 Oct.	San Antonio TX	Robinson
1 Nov.	Dallas TX	Robinson
2 Nov.	open TX	Robinson
3 Nov.	open TX	Robinson
4 Nov.	Los Angeles CA	Robinson
5 Nov.	Bakersfield CA	Robinson
6 Nov.	San Diego CA	Robinson
7 Nov.	Los Angeles CA	Robinson
8 Nov.	Oakland CA	Robinson
9 Nov.	Oakland CA	Robinson
12 Oct.	Hartford CT	Tebbetts
13 Oct.	Waterbury and Bridgeport CT	Tebbetts
14 Oct.	Fall River MA	Tebbetts
15 Oct.	Portland ME	Tebbetts
16 Oct.	Augusta ME	Tebbetts
17 Oct.	Bangor ME	Tebbetts
18 Oct.	Houlton ME	Tebbetts
13 Oct.	Hamilton ON	Paige
14 Oct.	Benton Harbor MI	Paige
15 Oct.	West Frankfort IL	Paige
16 Oct.	Vincennes IN	Paige
17 Oct.	Cape Girard MO	Paige
18 Oct.	Ballwin MO	Paige
19 Jan.	Belleville IL	Paige
21 Jan.	Kansas City MO	Paige
22 Jan.	Jefferson City MO	Paige
26 Jan.	San Antonio TX	Paige
28 Jan.	Corpus Christi TX	Paige
11 Oct.	Tamaroa IL	Walker
12 Oct.	Columbia TN	Walker
13 Oct.	Cobden IL	Walker
14 Oct.	Anna IL	Walker
15 Oct.	Cario IL	Walker
16 Oct.	Milan TN	Walker
17 Oct.	Dyersburg TN	Walker
18 Oct.	Lawrence TN	Walker
18 Oct.	Waynesboro TN	Walker
19 Oct.	Savannah TN	Walker
20 Oct.	Alamo TN	Walker
21 Oct.	Jackson TN	Walker
21 Oct.	Bolivar TN	Walker
22 Oct.	Corinth MS	Walker
23 Oct.	Columbus MS	Walker
24 Oct.	New Albany MS	Walker
11 Oct.	Omaha NE	Murphy

Date	City / State	Team
12 Oct.	Topeka KS	Murphy
13 Oct.	Open KS	Murphy
14 Oct.	Denver CO	Murphy
15 Oct.	Albuquerque NM	Murphy
16 Oct.	El Paso TX	Murphy
17 Oct.	Tucson AZ	Murphy
18 Oct.	Mexicali MX	Murphy
19 Oct.	Yuma AZ	Murphy
20 Oct.	El Centro CA	Murphy
21 Oct.	San Bernardino CA (day)	Murphy
21 Oct.	Riverside CA (night)	Murphy
22 Oct.	Bakersfield CA	Murphy
23 Oct.	Fresno CA	Murphy
24 Oct.	Stockton CA	Murphy
25 Oct.	Visalia CA	Murphy
26 Oct.	Open CA	Murphy
27 Oct.	Porterville CA	Murphy
28 Oct.	Hollywood or Bakersfield CA	Murphy
29 Oct.	Upland and	Murphy
29 Oct.	Ontario CA	Murphy
30 Oct.	Open CA	Murphy
31 Oct.	Open CA	Murphy
1 Nov.	Hollywood CA	Murphy
4 Nov.	San Diego CA	Murphy
6 Nov.	Globe-Miami AZ	Murphy
8 Nov.	Mexicali MX	Murphy
10 Nov.	Mesa AZ	Murphy
11 Nov.	Phoenix AZ	Murphy

1952

Date	City / State	Team
10 Oct.	Charlotte NC	Campanella
11 Oct.	Knoxville TN	Campanella
12 Oct.	Birmingham AL	Campanella
13 Oct.	Atlanta GA	Campanella
14 Oct.	Birmingham AL	Campanella
15 Oct.	Decatur AL	Campanella
16 Oct.	Florence AL	Campanella
17 Oct.	Chattanooga TN	Campanella
18 Oct.	Nashville TN	Campanella
19 Oct.	Memphis TN	Campanella
20 Oct.	Little Rock AR	Campanella
21 Oct.	Greenville MS	Campanella
22 Oct.	El Dorado AR	Campanella
23 Oct.	Greenwood MS	Campanella

Date	City / State	Team
24 Oct.	Mobile AL	Campanella
25 Oct.	open	Campanella
26 Oct.	Shreveport LA	Campanella
27 Oct.	New Orleans LA	Campanella
28 Oct.	Baton Rouge LA	Campanella
29 Oct.	New Orleans LA	Campanella
30 Oct.	Port Arthur TX	Campanella
31 Oct.	Houston TX	Campanella
1 Nov.	Galveston TX	Campanella
2 Nov.	Houston TX	Campanella
3 Nov.	Waco TX	Campanella
10 Oct.	Little Falls NY	White
11 Oct.	Norwich NY	White
12 Oct.	Utica NY	White
13 Oct.	Rome NY	White
14 Oct.	Auburn NY	White
15 Oct.	Oneonta NY	White
16 Oct.	off NY	White
17 Oct.	off NY	White
18 Oct.	Saranac Lake NY	White
19 Oct.	Schenectady NY	White
11 Oct.	Streator IL	Walker
12 Oct.	Peru IL	Walker
13 Oct.	Cairo IL	Walker
14 Oct.	Milan TN	Walker
15 Oct.	Solivar TN	Walker
16 Oct.	Dyersburg TN	Walker
17 Oct.	Sayannah TN	Walker
18 Oct.	Huntsville AL	Walker
19 Oct.	Florence AL	Walker
20 Oct.	Corinth MS	Walker
21 Oct.	Jonesboro AR	Walker
9 Oct.	Jefferson City MO	Bearden
10 Oct.	Salina KS	Bearden
15 Oct.	Coffeyville KS	Bearden
16 Oct.	Ardmore OK	Bearden
18 Oct.	Longview TX	Bearden
18 Oct.	Greenville TX	Bearden
19 Oct.	Paris TX	Bearden
19 Oct.	Gilmer TX	Bearden

1953

Date	City / State	Team
11 Oct.	Memphis TN	Campanella
12 Oct.	Nashville TN	Campanella
13 Oct.	Louisville KY	Campanella
14 Oct.	Chattanooga TN	Campanella
15 Oct.	Birmingham AL	Campanella
16 Oct.	Atlanta GA	Campanella
19 Oct.	Honolulu HI	Campanella

Date	City / State	Team
20 Oct.	Honolulu HI	Campanella
21 Oct.	Honolulu HI	Campanella
22 Oct.	San Francisco CA	Campanella
23 Oct.	Los Angeles CA	Campanella
24 Oct.	Long Beachor San Diego CA	Campanella
25 Oct.	Los Angeles CA	Campanella
26 Oct.	Houston TX	Campanella
27 Oct.	Beaumont TX	Campanella
28 Oct.	Houston TX	Campanella
29 Oct.	Dallas TX	Campanella
30 Oct.	Little Rock AR	Campanella
31 Oct.	Greenwood MS	Campanella
1 Nov.	New Orleans LA	Campanella
2 Nov.	Hammond LA	Campanella
3 Nov.	New Orleans LA	Campanella
4 Nov.	Lake Charles LA	Campanella
5 Nov.	Mobile AL	Campanella
6 Nov.	Pensacola FL	Campanella
9 Oct.	Baltimore MD	Robinson
10 Oct.	Wilmington DE	Robinson
11 Oct.	Norfolk VA	Robinson
11 Oct.	Newport News VA	Robinson
12 Oct.	Winston-Salem NC	Robinson
13 Oct.	Lynchburg VA	Robinson
14 Oct.	Charlotte NC	Robinson
15 Oct.	Asheville NC	Robinson
16 Oct.	Conover NC	Robinson
17 Oct.	Chattanooga TN	Robinson
18 Oct.	Birmingham AL	Robinson
19 Oct.	Nashville TN	Robinson
20 Oct.	Decatur AL	Robinson
20 Oct.	Florence AL	Robinson
21 Oct.	Memphis TN	Robinson
22 Oct.	Hot Springs AR	Robinson
22 Oct.	Little Rock AR	Robinson
23 Oct.	Shreveport LA	Robinson
24 Oct.	Natchez MS	Robinson
25 Oct.	New Orleans LA	Robinson
25 Oct.	Baton Rouge LA	Robinson
26 Oct.	open LA	Robinson
27 Oct.	Hattiesburg MS	Robinson
27 Oct.	Laurel MS	Robinson
28 Oct.	Mobile AL	Robinson
29 Oct.	Port Arthur TX	Robinson
30 Oct.	Lake Charles LA	Robinson
31 Oct.	Galveston TX	Robinson

Date	City / State	Team
1 Nov.	Houston TX	Robinson
8 Oct.	Portland ME	White
11 Oct.	Augusta (2) ME	White
12 Oct.	Bangor ME	White
14 Oct.	Watertown NY	White
15 Oct.	off NY	White
16 Oct.	Dolgeville NY	White
17 Oct.	Buffalo NY	White
18 Oct.	Utica NY	White

1954

Date	City / State	Team
8 Oct.	Silver Springs MD	White
9 Oct.	Hagerstown MD	White
10 Oct.	Elmira NY	White
11 Oct.	Buffalo NY	White
12 Oct.	Sunbury PA	White
13 Oct.	Ralston PA	White
14 Oct.	Herkimer NY	White
15 Oct.	Lowville NY	White
16 Oct.	Hoganburg NY	White
17 Oct.	Utica NY	White
8 Oct.	Baltimore MD	Camp. & Irvin
9 Oct.	Richmond VA	Camp. & Irvin
10 Oct.	Portsmouth VA	Camp. & Irvin
10 Oct.	Newport News VA	Camp. & Irvin
11 Oct.	Greensboro NC	Camp. & Irvin
12 Oct.	Winston-Salem NC	Camp. & Irvin
13 Oct.	Charlotte NC	Camp. & Irvin
14 Oct.	Knoxville TN	Camp. & Irvin
15 Oct.	Atlanta GA	Camp. & Irvin
16 Oct.	Birmingham AL	Camp. & Irvin
17 Oct.	Memphis TN	Camp. & Irvin
18 Oct.	Nashville TN	Camp. & Irvin
19 Oct.	Louisville KY	Camp. & Irvin
20 Oct.	Greenwood MS	Camp. & Irvin
21 Oct.	Little Rock AR	Camp. & Irvin
22 Oct.	Los Angeles CA	Camp. & Irvin
23 Oct.	San Diego CA	Camp. & Irvin
24 Oct.	Los Angeles CA	Camp. & Irvin
25 Oct.	Bakersfield CA	Camp. & Irvin
26 Oct.	San Francisco CA	Camp. & Irvin
27 Oct.	Sacramento CA	Camp. & Irvin
28 Oct.	Oakland CA	Camp. & Irvin
29 Oct.	Los Angeles CA	Camp. & Irvin
30 Oct.	Waco TX	Camp. & Irvin
31 Oct.	Houston TX	Camp. & Irvin

Date	City / State	Team
1 Nov.	Houston TX	Camp. & Irvin
2 Nov.	Biloxi MS	Camp. & Irvin
3 Nov.	Baton Rouge LA	Camp. & Irvin
4 Nov.	Houma LA	Camp. & Irvin
5 Nov.	Pontchatoula LA	Camp. & Irvin
6 Nov.	Mobile AL	Camp. & Irvin
7 Nov.	New Orleans LA	Camp. & Irvin
7 Oct.	Springfield MA	Shea
8 Oct.	Waterbury CT	Shea
9 Oct.	Newport RI	Shea
10 Oct.	Pawtucket RI	Shea
11 Oct.	Attleboro MA	Shea
12 Oct.	Nashua NH	Shea
13 Oct.	Portsmouth NH	Shea
17 Oct.	Edmunston ON	Shea
18 Oct.	Houlton ME	Shea
22 Oct.	Attleboro MA	Shea
24 Oct.	Springfield MA	Shea
	cancelled	
9 Oct.	Richmond IN	Meyer
10 Oct.	Toledo OH	Meyer
11 Oct.	Wausau WI	Meyer
12 Oct.	Duluth MN	Meyer
13 Oct.	Port Arthur Ont	Meyer
14 Oct.	Hibbing MN	Meyer
15 Oct.	open MN	Meyer
16 Oct.	Lannon WI	Meyer
17 Oct.	Aurora IL	Meyer
18 Oct.	Peru IL	Meyer
19 Oct.	Dubuque IA	Meyer
20 Oct.	Clinton IA	Meyer
8 Oct.	Pueblo CO	Garver
9 Oct.	Denver CO	Garver
10 Oct.	Denver CO	Garver
11 Oct.	McCook NE	Garver
12 Oct.	Omaha NE	Garver
13 Oct.	St. Joseph MO	Garver
14 Oct.	Des Moines IA	Garver
15 Oct.	Storm Center (tent.) IA	Garver
16 Oct.	Easterville IA	Garver
17 Oct.	Cedar Rapids IA	Garver
10 Oct.	Las Vegas? NV	Lopat & Scott
22 Oct.	San Bernardino CA	Lopat & Scott
23 Oct.	Palm Springs CA	Lopat & Scott
24 Oct.	Palm Springs? CA	Lopat & Scott

Date	City / State	Team
1955		
7 Oct.	Chapel Hill NC	Mays & Newc.
8 Oct.	off NC	Mays & Newc.
9 Oct.	Memphis TN	Mays & Newc.
10 Oct.	Little Rock AR	Mays & Newc.
11 Oct.	Dallas TX	Mays & Newc.
12 Oct.	El Dorado-Pine Bluff AR	Mays & Newc.
13 Oct.	Greenville MS	Mays & Newc.
14 Oct.	Memphis TN	Mays & Newc.
15 Oct.	Columbus GA	Mays & Newc.
16 Oct.	Birmingham AL	Mays & Newc.
17 Oct.	Chattanooga TN	Mays & Newc.
18 Oct.	Asheville NC	Mays & Newc.
19 Oct.	Atlanta GA	Mays & Newc.
20 Oct.	Montgomery AL	Mays & Newc.
21 Oct.	Columbus GA	Mays & Newc.
22 Oct.	Mobile and Biloxi MS	Mays & Newc.
23 Oct.	New Orleans LA	Mays & Newc.
24 Oct.	Lafayette or Hazelhurst MS	Mays & Newc.
25 Oct.	New Orleans LA	Mays & Newc.
26 Oct.	Shreveport LA	Mays & Newc.
27 Oct.	Longview TX	Mays & Newc.
28 Oct.	Waco TX	Mays & Newc.
29 Oct.	Port Arthur TX	Mays & Newc.
30 Oct.	Houston TX	Mays & Newc.
31 Oct.	Austin TX	Mays & Newc.
1 Nov.	Corpus Christi/ Victoria TX	Mays & Newc.
2 Nov.	San Antonio/ San Angelo TX	Mays & Newc.
3 Nov.	El Paso TX	Mays & Newc.
4 Nov.	Los Angeles CA	Mays & Newc.
5 Nov.	Los Angeles CA	Mays & Newc.
6 Nov.	Los Angeles CA	Mays & Newc.
8 Oct.	Webster MA	Shea
9 Oct.	Pawtucket RI	Shea
10 Oct.	Manchester CT	Shea
13 Oct.	Woonsocket RI	Shea
14 Oct.	West Haven CT	Shea
15 Oct.	Woonsocket or Pawtucket RI	Shea
16 Oct.	Portsmouth NH	Shea
18 Oct.	Lewiston ME	Shea
20 Oct.	Petersburg ONT	Shea
22 Oct.	Ottawa ONT	Shea

Date	City / State	Team
9 Oct.	Tilden NE	Ashburn
10 Oct.	Jefferson City MO	Ashburn
13 Oct.	Leoti KS	Ashburn
15 Oct.	Colby KS	Ashburn
16 Oct.	Victoria KS	Ashburn
8 Oct.	Cambridge MD	Kaline
9 Oct.	Baltimore MD	Kaline
rain	York PA	Kaline
10 Oct.	Lancaster PA	Kaline
12 Oct.	Sunbury MD	Kaline
13 Oct.	Hickory & Salisbury MD	Kaline Kaline
rain	Baltimore MD	Kaline
15 Oct.	Richmond VA	Kaline
16 Oct.	Norfolk VA	Kaline
17 Oct.	Suffolk VA	Kaline
8 Oct.	Silver Spring MD	Lollar
9 Oct.	Hagerstown MD	Lollar
10 Oct.	Durham NC	Lollar
11 Oct.	Rocky Mt. NC	Lollar
12 Oct.	Statesville NC	Lollar
13 Oct.	Charlotte NC	Lollar
14 Oct.	Open NC	Lollar
15 Oct.	Greensboro NC	Lollar
16 Oct.	Asheville NC	Lollar
17 Oct.	Wytheville VA	Lollar
18 Oct.	Johnson City TN	Lollar
19 Oct.	Waycross GA	Lollar
20 Oct.	Valdosta GA	Lollar
21 Oct.	Open GA	Lollar
22 Oct.	Columbus MS	Lollar
23 Oct.	Montgomery AL	Lollar
24 Oct.	Biloxi MS	Lollar
25 Oct.	Selma AL	Lollar
26 Oct.	Macon GA	Lollar
27 Oct.	Macon GA	Lollar

1956

Date	City / State	Team
12 Oct.	Victoria TX	Courtney
13 Oct.	Corpus Christi TX	Courtney
14 Oct.	Brownsville TX	Courtney
14 Oct.	Harlingen TX	Courtney
15 Oct.	San Angelo TX	Courtney
17 Oct.	Tyler TX	Courtney
18 Oct.	Wichita Falls TX	Courtney
20 Oct.	Tucumcari NM	Courtney

Date	City / State	Team
21 Oct.	Hobbs NM	Courtney
11 Oct.	Bessemer MI	Trucks
	St. Louis MI	Trucks
	Fennville MI	Trucks
12 Oct.	Hancock MI	Trucks
13 Oct.	Douglas MI	Trucks
14 Oct.	St. Ignace MI	Trucks
15 Oct.	Alma MI	Trucks
16 Oct.	Alpena MI	Trucks
17 Oct.	Kalamazoo MI	Trucks
18 Oct.	off MI	Trucks
19 Oct.	Ionia MI	Trucks
20 Oct.	Coldwater MI	Trucks
21 Oct.	Portland MI	Trucks
11 Oct.	Charlotte NC	Mays
12 Oct.	Knoxville TN	Mays
13 Oct.	Nashville TN	Mays
14 Oct.	Memphis TN	Mays
15 Oct.	Sikeston MO	Mays
16 Oct.	Fort Smith AR	Mays
17 Oct.	Greenville MS	Mays
18 Oct.	Little Rock AR	Mays
19 Oct.	Memphis TN	Mays
20 Oct.	Chattanooga TN	Mays
21 Oct.	Birmingham AL	Mays
22 Oct.	Columbus GA	Mays
23 Oct.	Birmingham AL	Mays
24 Oct.	Montgomery AL	Mays
25 Oct.	Columbus MS	Mays
26 Oct.	Greenwood MS	Mays
27 Oct.	Shreveport LA	Mays
28 Oct.	Houston TX	Mays
29 Oct.	Austin TX	Mays
30 Oct.	San Antonio TX	Mays
31 Oct.	Corpus Christi TX	Mays
1 Nov.	Brownsville TX	Mays
2 Nov.	off TX	Mays
3 Nov.	Beaumont TX	Mays
4 Nov.	New Orleans LA	Mays
5 Nov.	Mobile AL	Mays
6 Nov.	New Orleans LA	Mays
7 Nov.	Hazlehurst MS	Mays
8 Nov.	Baton Rouge MS	Mays
9 Nov.	Biloxi MS	Mays
10 Nov.	Thomasville GA	Mays
11 Nov.	Jacksonville FL	Mays Shea

1957

Date	City / State	Team
12 Oct.	Douglas MI	Maxwell

Date	City / State	Team
13 Oct.	Grand Rapids MI	Maxwell
14 Oct.	Kalamazoo MI	Maxwell
15 Oct.	Sheboygan MI	Maxwell
15 Oct.	Alpena MI	Maxwell
16 Oct.	Durand MI	Maxwell
17 Oct.	Niagara Falls NY	Maxwell
18 Oct.	Lowville NY	Maxwell
19 Oct.	Auburn NY	Maxwell
20 Oct.	Utica NY	Maxwell
21 Oct.	Auburn NY	Maxwell
22 Oct.	Lowville NY	Maxwell
23 Oct.	Ralston PA	Maxwell
12 Oct.	El Campo NM	Bolling
13 Oct.	McAllen NM	Bolling
13 Oct.	Brownsville NM	Bolling
14 Oct.	Eagle Pass NM	Bolling
15 Oct.	McCamey NM	Bolling
16 Oct.	Perryton NM	Bolling
17 Oct.	Carlsbad NM	Bolling
18 Oct.	Roswell NM	Bolling
19 Oct.	Prescott NM	Bolling
20 Oct.	off NM	Bolling
21 Oct.	Winslow NM	Bolling
22 Oct.	Las Cruces NM	Bolling
23 Oct.	Amarillo TX	Bolling
24 Oct.	San Antonio TX	Bolling
25 Oct.	San Antonio TX	Bolling
25 Oct.	Texas City? TX	Bolling
1 Nov.	SF CA	Mays
2 Nov.	Sacramento CA	Mays
7 Nov.	El Centro CA	Mays
8 Nov.	Los Angeles CA	Mays
9 Nov.	Los Angeles CA	Mays
9 Nov.	Bakersfield CA	Mays
13 Nov.	SF CA	Mays
	LA CA	Mays
11 Oct.	Martinsburg PA	Fox
11 Oct.	Everett PA	Fox
12 Oct.	Saltillo PA	Fox
12 Oct.	Fayetteville PA	Fox
13 Oct.	New Castle PA	Fox
14 Oct.	McConnellsburg PA	Fox

1958

Date	City / State	Team
14 Oct.	New Castle PA	Fox & Groat
15 Oct.	Youngstown PA	Fox & Groat
16 Oct.	McConnellsburg PA	Fox & Groat

Date	City / State	Team
17 Oct.	off PA	Fox & Groat
18 Oct.	Newton-Hamilton PA	Fox & Groat
18 Oct.	Chambersburg PA	Fox & Groat
19 Oct.	Cumberland MD	Fox & Groat
18 Oct.	Lansing MI	Maxwell
18 Oct.	Battle Creek MI	Maxwell
19 Oct.	Grand Rapids MI	Maxwell
17 Oct.	Salisbury MD	Nieman
18 Oct.	Salisbury MD	Nieman
19 Oct.	Baltimore MD	Nieman

1959

Date	City / State	Team
11 Oct.	Richmond VA	Killebrew
12 Oct.	Newport News VA	Killebrew
13 Oct.	Winston-Salem NC	Killebrew
14 Oct.	Charlotte NC	Killebrew
15 Oct.	Macon GA	Killebrew
16 Oct.	Mobile AL	Killebrew
17 Oct.	Dallas TX	Killebrew
18 Oct.	Ft. Hood TX	Killebrew
19 Oct.	Waco TX	Killebrew
20 Oct.	Fork Worth TX	Killebrew
21 Oct.	Fredericksburg TX	Killebrew
23 Oct.	Eagle Pass TX	Killebrew
24 Oct.	Austin TX	Killebrew
25 Oct.	Harlingen TX	Killebrew
	Philadelphia PA	Gottlieb
	Syracuse NY	

1960

Date	City / State	Team
14 Oct.	Durham NC	Mays
	Greensboro NC	Mays
	Rocky Mount NC	Mays
	Charlotte NC	Mays
	Hickory NC	Mays
	Birmingham AL	Mays
5 Nov.	Shreveport LA	Mays
6 Nov.	Houston TX	Mays
7 Nov.	Houston TX	Mays

1961

Date	City / State	Team
15 Oct.	Wilson NC	
16 Oct.	Durham NC	
17 Oct.	Greensboro NC	

Date	City / State	Team
18 Oct.	Charlotte NC	
19 Oct.	Winston-Salem NC	

1962

Date	City / State	Team
15 Oct.	St. Joseph MO	Mays

Date	City / State	Team
16 Oct.	Bartlesville OK	Mays
17 Oct.	Lawton OK	Mays
18 Oct.	Monroe LA	Mays
19 Oct.	Little Rock AR	Mays

Appendix E:
Letter from
the Commissioner

Office of the Commissioner
30 Rockefeller Plaza
New York, N. Y.
August 22, 1961

Notice No. 25

Re: Barnstorming

To All Major League Players and Clubs

Gentlemen;

Major League Rules relating to barnstorming and exhibition games will be interpreted this year as follows;

1. Team barnstorming may start on Saturday, October 14, and MUST END on Monday, November 13, both dates inclusive.

2. Only three Major League players of any one club may appear on the same barnstorming team.

3. In any exhibition game, not more than three players out of the JOINT MEMBERSHIP of the two World Series' teams will be permitted.

4. To obtain approval for barnstorming, follow this procedure;

(a) Ask your own club for permission.

(b) If club grants permission, request your club to send this information to the Commissioner's Office.

(c) You must PERSONALLY petition the Commissioner for approval. You must make this request by letter and not through any agent who may be handling the schedule.

5. Every player MUST obtain permission from both his club and the Commissioner before he may do any barnstorming. Failure to obtain such permission will subject the player to a minimum penalty of $200.

6. Player conduct, on and off the field, in connection with such post-season exhibition games, shall be subject to the discipline of the Commissioner.

7. For 1961 barnstorming outside of the continental United States will not be permitted.

8. The director of any barnstorming team must file the schedule of games with the Commissioner's Office prior to commencement of the exhibition tour. Failure to comply with this requirement will subject the director and players to such penalties as the Commissioner may impose.

Bibliography

Alexander, Charles. *Breaking the Slump: Baseball in the Depression Era.* New York: Columbia University Press, 2002.

Ardolino, Frank. "Babe's Banyan Tree Grows in Hawaii." In *The National Pastime: A Review of Baseball History* 18. Cleveland: Society for American Baseball Research, 1998.

Bak, Richard. *Turkey Stearnes and the Detroit Stars.* Detroit: Wayne State University Press, 1994.

Barthel, Thomas. *The Fierce Fun of Ducky Medwick.* Lanham, MD: Scarecrow, 2003.

_____. *Pepper Martin: A Baseball Biography.* Jefferson, NC: McFarland, 2003.

_____. *Those Peerless Semipros.* (Forthcoming.)

"Base-Ball in San Francisco, 1887." *Harper's Weekly* 31, no. 1614 (November 26): 859.

Beirne, Rev. Gerry. "The Day Joe DiMaggio Wore a Red Sox Uniform." In *The National Pastime: A Review of Baseball History* 19. Cleveland: Society for American Baseball Research, 1999.

Bergen, Phil. "The Curse of Mickey Haefner." In *The National Pastime: A Review of Baseball History*, Number 17. Cleveland: Society for American Baseball Research, 1997.

Burk, Robert F. *Much More Than a Game: Players, Owners, and American Baseball since 1921.* Chapel Hill: University of North Carolina Press, 2001.

Casway, Jerrold. "A Monument for Harry Wright." *The National Pastime: A Review of Baseball History*, Number 17. Cleveland: Society for American Baseball Research, 1997.

Charlton, James, ed. *The Baseball Chronology.* New York: Macmillan, 1991.

Cole, Robert. "Ersatz Octobers: Baseball Barnstorming." *Baseball History* 4, 1992.

Cole, Robert C. "The End of the Sticks." *Elysian Fields* Q–XIII (Winter 1994): 17–25.

Creamer, Robert W. *Babe, The Legend Comes to Life.* New York: Simon and Schuster, 1974.

Crissey, Harrington E., Jr. "Baseball and the Armed Services" In *Total Baseball, New 1994 Edition.* CD-ROM. Creative Multimedia and Professional Ink, 1994.

Daniel, W. Harrison. *Jimmie Foxx: The Life and Times of a Baseball Hall of Famer, 1907–1967.* Jefferson, NC: McFarland, 1996.

Derby, Richard E., Jr., and Jim Coleman. "House of David Baseball." In *The National*

Pastime: A Review of Baseball History, Number 14. Cleveland: Society for American Baseball Research, 1994.

DeValeria, Dennis. *Honus Wagner: A Biography.* New York: H. Holt, 1996.

Dunbar, William H. "Baseball Salaries Thirty Years Ago." *Baseball Magazine,* no. 3 (July 1918): 291–292.

Einstein, Charles. *Willie's Time: A Memoir.* New York: Lippincott, 1979.

Elfers, James E. *The Tour to End All Tours: The Story of Major League Baseball's 1913–1914 World Tour.* Lincoln: University of Nebraska Press, 2003.

Falkner, David. *Great Time Coming: The Life of Jackie Robinson, from Baseball to Birmingham.* New York: Simon and Schuster, 1995.

Feldman, Jay. "Bluegrass Baseball: Barnstorming Band and Ball Club." In *Baseball Research Journal.* Cleveland: Society for American Baseball Research, 1984.

Feller, Bob, and Bill Gilbert. *Now Pitching, Bob Feller: A Baseball Memoir.* New York: Carol, 1990.

Figueredo, Jorge. "Winter in Cuba, 1992." In *The National Pastime: A Review of Baseball History.* Cleveland: Society for American Baseball Research.

Figueredo, Jorge S. "November 4, 1920: The Day Torriente Outclassed Ruth" In *Baseball Research Journal.* Cleveland: Society for American Baseball Research, 1982.

Fitzgerald, Ed. "Bob Feller, Incorporated." In *Twelve Sport Immortals.* New York: Bartholomew House, 1949.

Frazier, Robinson. *Catching Dreams.* Syracuse: Syracuse University Press, 1999.

Goewey, E.A. *Leslie's Illustrated Weekly* 110, no. 2835 (January 6, 1910).

Gough, David. "Home Run Derby." *The National Pastime: A Review of Baseball History,* Number 17. Cleveland: Society for American Baseball Research, 1997.

Green, Guy W. *Fun and Frolic with An Indian Ball Team.* Lincoln, NE: Woodruff-Collins, 1907.

Gregorich, Barbara. *Women at Play: The Story of Women in Baseball.* San Diego: Harcourt Brace, 1993.

Hageman, William. *Honus: The Life and Times of a Baseball Hero.* Champaign, IL: Sagamore, 1996.

Halper, Barry. "Titanic Relief Fund Program." In *The National Pastime: A Review of Baseball History* 4, no. 2 (Winter 1985). Cleveland: Society for American Baseball Research, 1985.

Hawkins, Joel H., and Terry Bertolino. "Pepper with House of David." *The National Pastime: A Review of Baseball History,* Number 20. Cleveland: Society for American Baseball Research, 2000.

Hoepf, Tom. "Remembering the Pheastival." *Holy Cow — Newsletter of the Halsey Hall Chapter of SABR,* January 1997. Article originally appeared in *Antique Week,* date unknown.

Holway, John. *The Complete Book of Baseball's Negro Leagues: The Other Half of Baseball History.* Fern Park, FL: Hastings House, 2001.

Holway, John B. *Black Diamonds: Life in the Negro Leagues from the Men Who Lived It.* Westport, CT: Meckler Books, 1989.

_____. "Head-to-Head, Black Teams Outplayed Whites." *USA Today Baseball Weekly,* November 1, 1995: 38.

_____. *Josh and Satch: The Life and Times of Josh Gibson and Satchel Paige.* Westport, CT: Meckler Books, 1991.

Kaplan, Jim. *Lefty Grove: American Original.* Cleveland: Society for American Baseball Research, 2000.

Keene, Kerry, Raymond Sinibaldi, and David Hickey. *The Babe in Red Stockings: An In-Depth Chronicle of Babe Ruth with the Boston Red Sox, 1914–1919.* Champaign, IL: Sagamore, 1997.

Keetz, Frank. "When 'The Big Train' Met 'The Red Ant.'" In *Baseball Research Journal* 20, Cleveland: Society for American Baseball Research, 1991.

Kelly, Brent. *"I Will Never Forget": Interviews With 39 Former Negro League Players.* Jefferson, NC: McFarland, 2003.

Kemp, David, and Phil Dixon. "The All Nations Vs. The Soos." *Minor League History Journal.* Cleveland: Society for American Baseball Research, 1993.

Kermisch, Al. "Cubs and Tigers Played Exhibition Game after 1908 Series." *Baseball Research Journal* 27. Cleveland: Society for American Baseball Research, 1998.

_____. "The Day Babe Ruth Conquered Redland Field." *Baseball Research Journal.* Cleveland: Society for American Baseball Research, 1990.

_____. "The Day Don Heffner Beat The Black Sox." *Baseball Research Journal* 9. Cleveland: Society for American Baseball Research, 1980.

_____. "First World Series Just Exhibitions." *The National Pastime: A Review of Baseball History* 2, Cleveland: Society for American Baseball Research, 1982.

_____. "Ruth and Koenig Tangled In Exhibition Game." *Baseball Research Journal* 27. Cleveland: Society for American Baseball Research, 1998.

_____. "When The Babe Came Home In 1919." *Baseball Research Journal* 13. Cleveland: Society for American Baseball Research, 1984.

Knight, Tom. "Tri-Cornered Game." *The National Pastime: A Review of Baseball History* 14. Cleveland: Society for American Baseball Research, 1994.

Kubiak, Ted. Letter to the author, March 16, 2005.

Laing, Jeff. "Lou Pierotti's Clowns." *The National Pastime: A Review of Baseball History* 19. Cleveland: Society for American Baseball Research, 1999.

Lansche, Jerry. *The Forgotten Championships: Postseason Baseball, 1882–1981.* Jefferson, NC: McFarland, 1989.

Levine, Peter. "Business, Missionary Motives behind World Tour." *The National Pastime: A Review of Baseball History* 4. Cleveland: Society for American Baseball Research, 1984.

Light, Johnathan Fraser. *The Cultural Encyclopedia of Baseball.* Jefferson, NC: McFarland, 1997.

Mays, Willie. *Willie Mays: My Life In and Out of Baseball, As Told To Charles Einstein.* New York: Dutton, 1966.

McBane, Richard. "When The Champs Were No-Hit." *Baseball In Pittsburgh.* Cleveland: Society for American Baseball Research, 1995.

McCarthy, Kevin M. *Baseball in Florida.* Sarasota, FL: Pineapple, 1996.

McGlynn, Frank. *Baseball Magazine*, no. 4 (August 1914): 59–68.

McNeil, William. *The California Winter League: America's First Integrated Professional Baseball League.* Jefferson, NC: McFarland, 2002.

Millikin, Mark R. *Jimmie Foxx: The Pride of Sudlersville.* Lanham, MD: Scarecrow, 1998.

Nemec, David. *Great Baseball Feats, Facts, and Firsts.* New York: New American Library, 1987.

Nicholson, William G. "Three Dimensional Baseball." In *Baseball Research Journal* 8. Cleveland: Society for American Baseball Research, 1979.

Overmyer, James. *Queen of the Negro Leagues: Effa Manley and the Newark Eagles.* Metuchen, NJ: Scarecrow, 1993.

Petersen, Keith. *Company Town: Potlatch, Idaho, and the Potlatch Lumber Company.* Pullman: Washington State University Press, 1987.

Peterson, Robert. *Only the Ball Was White.* Englewood Cliffs, NJ: Prentice-Hall, 1970.

Pietrusza, David. *Judge and Jury: The Life and Times of Judge Kenesaw Mountain Landis.* South Bend, IN: Diamond, 1998.

Rader, Benjamin G. *In Its Own Image.* New York: The Free Press, 1984.

Ribowsky, Mark. *Don't Look Back: Satchel Paige in the Shadows of Baseball.* New York: Simon and Schuster, 1994.

Ritter, Lawrence S. *The Glory of Their Times: The Story of the Early Days of Baseball Told by the Men Who Played It.* New York: Macmillan, 1966.

Robinson, Ray. *Iron Horse: Lou Gehrig In His Time.* New York: W.W. Norton, 1990.

_____. *Matty: An American Hero: Christy Mathewson of the New York Giants.* New York: Oxford University Press, 1993.

Rogosin, Donn. *Invisible Men: Life in Baseball's Negro Leagues.* New York: Atheneum, 1985.

Ryczek, William. *When Johnny Came Sliding Home.* Jefferson, NC: McFarland, 1998.

Schacht, Al. *My Own Particular Screwball: An Informal Autobiography.* Edited by Ed Keyes. Garden City, NY: Doubleday, 1955.

Schoor, Gene. *Bob Feller: Hall of Fame Strikeout Star.* Garden City, NY: Doubleday, 1962.

Selzer, Jack. "Baseball in the Nineteenth Century: An Overview." In *The National Pastime: A Review of Baseball History* 6. Cleveland: Society for American Baseball Research, 1986.

Seymour, Harold. *Baseball: The Golden Age.* New York: Oxford, 1971.

_____. *Baseball: The People's Game.* New York: Oxford, 1990.

_____. *The Early Years.* New York: Oxford, 1985.

Sickels, John. *Bob Feller: Ace of the Greatest Generation.* Washington, D.C.: Brassey's, 2004.

Smelser, Marshal. *The Life That Ruth Built: A Biography.* New York: Quadrangle, 1975.

Snyder, Brad. *Beyond the Shadow of the Senators: The Untold Story of the Homestead Grays and the Integration of Baseball.* Chicago: Contemporary Books, 2003.

Spalding's Official Base Ball Guide. New York: Spalding, 1903.

Speer, Ren. "Schuey's Big Day." *Baseball Research Journal* 17. Cleveland: Society for American Baseball Research, 1988.

Spink, J. G. Taylor. *Judge Landis and Twenty-Five Years Of Baseball.* New York: Crowell, 1947.

Staten, Vince. *Ol' Diz: A Biography of Dizzy Dean.* New York: Harper Collins, 1992.

Suehsdorf, A.D. "The Commissioners." *Total Baseball, New 1994 Edition.* CD-ROM. Creative Multimedia and Professional Ink, 1994.

Terry, James L. *Long Before the Dodgers: Baseball in Brooklyn, 1855–1884.* Jefferson, NC: McFarland, 2002.

Thomas, Henry W. *Walter Johnson: Baseball's Big Train.* Foreword by Shirley Povich. Lincoln: University of Nebraska Press, 1998.

Tygiel, Jules. "Black Ball." *Total Baseball, New 1994 Edition.* CD-ROM. Creative Multimedia and Professional Ink, 1994.

Voigt, David Q. "The History of Major League Baseball, Part 1." *Total Baseball, New 1994 Edition.* CD-ROM. Creative Multimedia and Professional Ink, 1994.

_____. "The History of Major League Baseball, Part 2." In *Total Baseball, New 1994 Edition.* CD-ROM. Creative Multimedia and Professional Ink, 1994.

Wagenheim, Kal. *Babe Ruth: His Life and Legend.* New York: Praeger, 1974.

Ward, Geoffrey, and Ken Burns. *Baseball: An Illustrated History Based on a Documentary Filmscript.* New York: Knopf, 1994.

Ward, Mike. "Throwbacks, 2000." In *The National Pastime: A Review of Baseball History* 20. Cleveland: Society for American Baseball Research, 2000.

Wayman, Joseph M. "The Editor's Grandstand Page." *Grandstand Baseball Annual, 1993.* Downey, CA: Wayman, 1993.

_____. "Interleague Championship Series Pitching Records, 1901–1920." *Grandstand Baseball Annual, 1989.* Downey, CA: Wayman, 1989.

Weigand, Jim. "The First All-Star Game." *Grandstand Baseball Annual 1992.* Downey, CA: Wayman, 1991.

Williams, Frank J. "Post-Season Interleague Series, 1901–1920." *Grandstand Baseball Annual, 1989*. Downey, CA: Wayman, 1988.

Wilson, Lyle K. "Mr. Foster Comes to Washington." *The National Pastime: A Review of Baseball History* 18. Cleveland: Society for American Baseball Research, 1998.

Wilson, Nick. *Voices from The Pastime: Oral Histories Of Surviving Major Leaguers, Negro Leaguers, Cuban Leaguers, And Writers, 1920–1934*. Jefferson, N.C.: McFarland, 2000.

Wood, Joe. "Not Far from Slumgullion Gulch." *Third Fireside Book of Baseball*. Edited by Charles Einstein. New York: Simon and Schuster, 1968.

Web sites

http://www.aafla.org/SportsLibrary/BBM/1914/bbm4i.pdf
http://www.baseball-almanac.com
http://www.berksweb.com/histsoc/articles/flu.html
http://www.cyberenet.net/~gsteiner/cchs/
http://eh.net/hmit/ppowerusd — buying power Money —
http://www.encarta.msn.com
http://marian.creighton.edu/~besser/baseball/second.html
http://www.fhwa.dot.gov/ohim/summary95/hm212.pdf
http://www.greatdepression.bravepages.com/
http://www.hbs.edu/bhr/archives/bookreviews/77/2003
springzimbalist.pdf#search='show%20his%20wife%20a%20private%20detective's%20report
http://www.jsonline.com/sports/brew/sat/base62098.stm
http://www.mediahistory.umn.edu/time/1920s.html
http://www.pbs.org/wgbh/amex/influenza/filmmore/transcript/index.html
http://www.pubdim.net/baseballlibrary
http://www.rcls.org/lawson/story2.htm
http://www.superstation.com/hankaaron/Aaron4A.html)
http://www.thebaseballpage.com/past/pp/bakerfrank
http://www.time.com/time/archive/preview/0,10987,711647,00.html

Newspapers

Ada, OK, *Evening News*
Altoona, PA, *Tribune*
Arkansas, AK, *Democrat*
Asheville, NC, *Citizen*
Atlanta, GA, *Constitution*
Atlanta, GA, *Constitution*
Auburn, NY, *Citizen-Advertiser*
Baltimore, MD, *Sun*
Beaver Falls, PA, *Daily Tribune*
Bethlehem, PA, *Daily Times*
Birmingham, AL, *News*
Bismarck, ND, *Tribune*
Bloomsburg, PA, *Morning Press*
Boise, ID, *Idaho Daily Statesman*
Boston, MA, *Globe*
Broken Bow, OK, *News*
Brooklyn, NY, *Daily Eagle*
Brooklyn, NY, *Eagle*
Buffalo, NY, *Courier Express*
Butler, PA, *Citizen*
Camden, NJ, *Post Telegram*
Carbondale, IL, *Free Press*
Charlotte, NC, *Observer*
Chester, PA, *Daily Times*
Chicago, IL, *Daily Tribune*
Chicago, IL, *Defender*
Chicago, IL, *Tribune*
Cincinnati, OH, *Enquirer*
Clinton, PA, *Republican*
Columbia, PA, *Spy*
Des Moines, IA, *Register*
Des Moines, IA, *Daily News*
Des Moines, IA, *Capital*
Devils Lake, ND, *Journal*
Durant, OK, *Daily Democrat*
Easton, PA, *Free Press*

Effingham, IL, *Record*
Elmira, NY, *Star Gazette*
Fargo, ND, *Forum*
Fremont, OH, *Daily Messenger*
Grand Forks, ND, *Herald*
Greensburg, PA, *Press*
Guthrie, OK, *Daily Leader*
Harrisburg, PA, *Evening News*
Hartford, CN, *Courant*
Hazleton, PA, *Standard-Sentinel*
Hudson, NJ, *Observer*
Hugo, OK, *Daily News*
Huron, SD, *The Evening Huronite*
Ironton, OH, *Irontonian*
Jacksonville, FL, *Times*
Jamestown, ND, *Sun*
Johnstown, PA, *Daily Tribune*
Kansas City, MO, *Journal-Post*
Kennebec, ME, *Journal*
Kingston, NY, *Daily Freeman*
La Salle, IL, *Daily News Tribune*
Lawton, OK, *Constitution*
Little Falls, NY, *Evening Times*
Los Angeles, CA, *Illustrated Daily News*
Los Angeles, CA, *Evening Herald*
Los Angeles, CA, *Times*
Louisville, KY, *Courier-Journal*
Lowville, NY, *Journal and Republican*
Marysville, CA, *Appeal-Democrat*
Memphis, TN, *Commercial Appeal*
Milwaukee, WI, *Sentinel*
Minneapolis, MN, *Tribune*
Moscow, ID, *Daily Star-Mirror*
Muskogee, OK, *Phoenix*
Nashville, TN, *Banner*
New Brunswick, NJ, *Daily Times*
New Orleans, LA, *Times-Picayune*
New York, NY, *Daily Tribune*
New York, NY, *Times*
Newark, NJ, *Star Ledger*
Norfolk, VA, *Sun*
Norwich, NY, *Sun*
Oklahoma City, OK, *Daily Oklahoman*
Omaha, NE, *World Herald*
Oneonta, NY, *Star*
Ottumwa, IA, *Daily Courier*
Paterson, NJ, *Daily Press*
Perry, IA, *Daily Chief*
Philadelphia, PA, *Evening Bulletin*

Philadelphia, PA, *Tribune*
Philadelphia, PA, *Inquirer*
Pittsburgh, PA, *Courier*
Pittsburgh, PA, *Sun*
Pittsburgh, PA, *Dispatch*
Pocatello, ID, *Tribune*
Ponca City, OK, *News*
Portland, ME, *Express-Herald*
Pottsville, PA, *Journal*
Pottsville, PA, *Miners*
Reading, PA, *Daily Times and Dispatch*
Reading, PA, *Times*
St. Joseph, MO, *Gazette*
St. Joseph, MO, *Daily Herald*
St. Louis, MO, *Globe-Democrat*
St. Louis, MO, *Argus*
San Diego, CA, *Union*
San Francisco, CA, *Examiner*
San Jose, CA, *News*
Santa Barbara, CA, *The Press*
Schenectady, NY, *Gazette*
Scranton, PA, *Times*
Seattle, WA, *Post Intelligencer*
Seminole, OK, *Producer*
Sharon, PA, *Herald*
Shoshone, ID, *Southern Idaho Democrat*
Sioux Falls, SD, *Daily Argus-Leader*
Sioux Falls, SD, *Daily Argus-Leader*
Springfield, MA, *Republican*
Stockton, CA, *Independent*
Sulphur, OK, *Times-Democrat*
Syracuse, NY, *Post-Standard*
Tacoma, WA, *News Tribune*
Tiffin, OH, *Daily Advertiser*
Trenton, NJ, *Evening Times*
Trenton, NJ, *Times*
Tulsa, OK, *World*
Twin Falls, ID, *Times-News*
Ventura, CA, *Free Press*
Washington, DC, *Post*
Wichita, KS, *Morning Eagle*
Wilkes-Barre, PA, *Record*
Williamsport, PA, *Sun*
Williamsport, PA, *Gazette & Bulletin*
Williamsport, PA, *Grit*
Woodward, OK, *County Republican*
York, PA, *Daily*
Zanesville, OH, *Daily Courier*

Sporting Life
The Sporting News

Index